ROTARY INTERNATIONAL AND THE SELLING OF AMERICAN CAPITALISM

ROTARY INTERNATIONAL AND THE SELLING OF AMERICAN CAPITALISM

Brendan Goff

HARVARD UNIVERSITY PRESS
Cambridge, Massachusetts
London, England
2021

Printed in the United States of America
First printing

LIBRARY OF CONGRESS CATALOGING-IN-PUBLICATION DATA

Names: Goff, Brendan, 1966– author.
Title: Rotary International and the selling of American capitalism / Brendan Goff.
Description: Cambridge, Massachusetts : Harvard University Press, 2021. | Includes index.
Identifiers: LCCN 2020045423 | ISBN 9780674989795 (cloth)
Subjects: LCSH: Rotary International. | Business networks. | Economics—Sociological aspects. | Capitalism. | Publicity. | Humanitarianism.
Classification: LCC HF5001.R79 G64 2021 | DDC 369.5/20973—dc23
LC record available at https://lccn.loc.gov/2020045423

For Joanne and Aunt Ann

CONTENTS

ROTARY INTERNATIONAL AND THE SELLING OF AMERICAN CAPITALISM

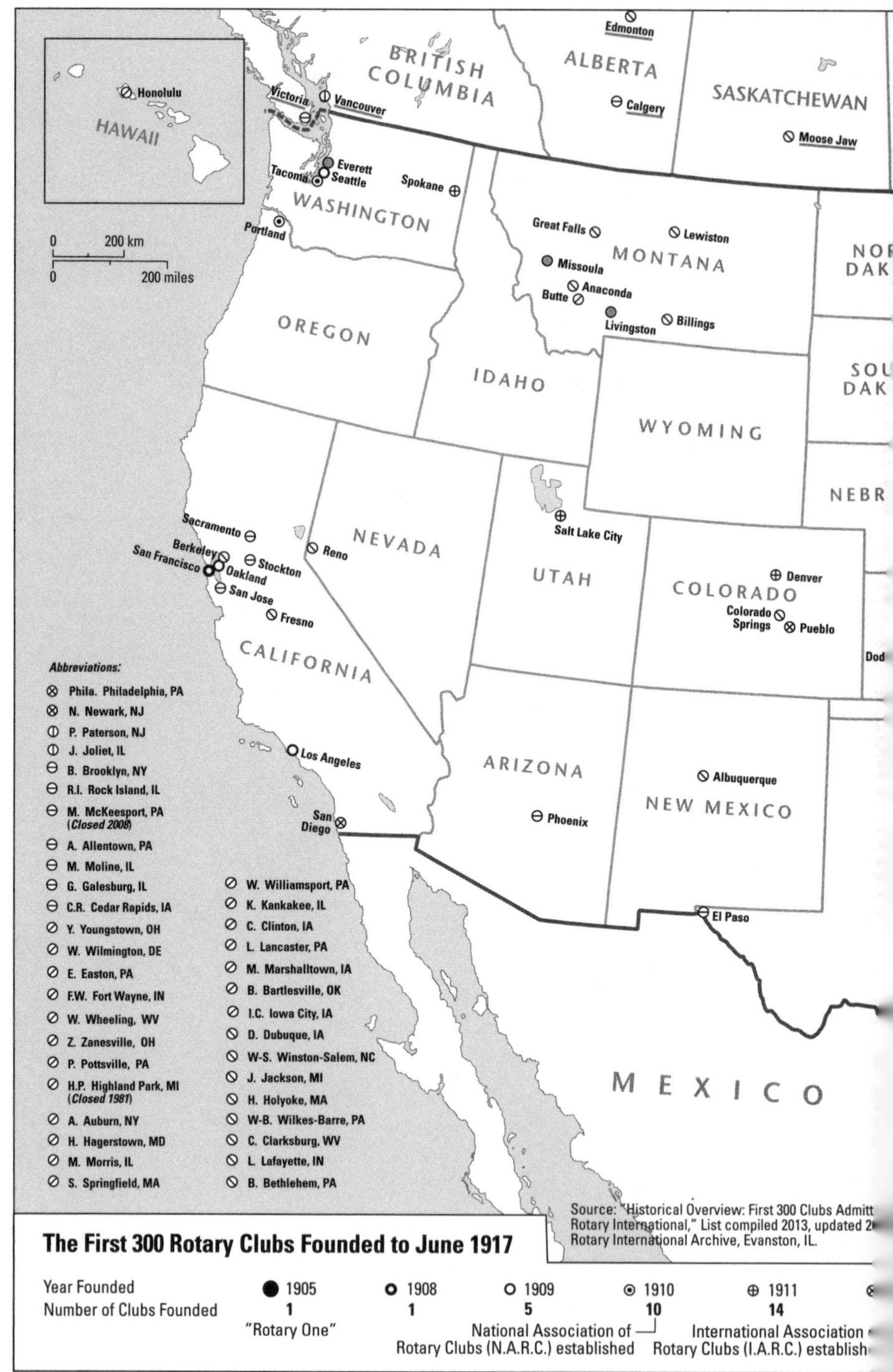

The First 300 Rotary Clubs Founded to June 1917

ONTARIO
QUEBEC
NEW BRUNSWICK
St John
MAINE
Halifax
NOVA SCOTIA
Augusta
Lewiston & Auburn
Portland
Montreal
Ottawa
Ogdensburg
Watertown
VERMONT
NEW HAMPSHIRE
Fort William and Port Arthur
MINNESOTA
Duluth
Superior
St Paul
Minneapolis
Marquette
MICHIGAN
WISCONSIN
Merril
Wausau
Green Bay
Stevens Point
Appleton
Oshkosh
Sheboygan
Madison
Milwaukee
Rockford
Grand Rapids
Muskegon
Kalamazoo
Battle Creek
Bay City
Flint
Sag.
Lansing
Detroit
H.P.
J.
A.A.
Toronto
Hamilton
London
Rochester
N.F.
Buffalo
Syracuse
Ithaca
Binghamton
Elmira
Utica
NY.
Troy (Closed 2011)
Albany
Kingston
Haverhill
Boston
Worchester
MA.
H.
S.
Hartford
CT.
Providence
RHODE ISLAND
J.C.
W.
P.
B.
O.
E.
N.
New York
Trenton
Camden
NEW JERSEY
Atlantic City
PA.
Scranton
W-B.
Sunbury
Reading
Harrisburg
Lancaster
L.
York
Phila.
New Castle
Pittsburgh
M.
G.
A.
Cleveland
Akron
Canton
Y.
Massillon
Toledo
Lima
Piqua
OH.
Springfield
Columbus
Dayton
Cincinnati
Z.
N.
Mason City
Waterloo
D.
Sioux City
IOWA
Council Bluffs
Des Moines
M.
C.R.
I.C.
Davenport
Burlington
Ottumwa
R.I.
C.
M.
K.
G.
Chicago
Ottawa
Peoria
Bloomington
Danville
Decatur
Springfield
Quincy
ILLINOIS
South Bend
M.C.
L.
H.
F.W.
INDIANA
Indianapolis
Terre Haute
Vincennes
Evansville
New Albany
Louisville
Owensboro
Paducah
Lexington
Ashland
Huntington
KENTUCKY
WEST VIRGINIA
Charlestown
C.
St Joseph
Kansas City
St Louis
East St Louis
MISSOURI
Parsons
Pittsburg
Joplin
Independence
B.
Tulsa
Muskogee
Oklahoma City
Shawnee
Rogers
ARKANSAS
Fort Smith
Little Rock
Helena
Hot Springs
Pine Bluff
Paris
Texarkana
Waxahachie
Palestine
Shreveport
LOUSIANA
Alexandria
Lake Charles
Beaumont
Houston
Galveston
Port Arthur
New Orleans
MISSISSIPPI
Meridian
Jackson
Memphis
Jackson
Nashville
TENNESSEE
Knoxville
Johnson City
Chattanooga
ALABAMA
Birmingham
Tuscaloosa
Selma
Montgomery
Mobile
Pensacola
GEORGIA
Rome
Atlanta
Augusta
Macon
Columbus
Albany
Savannah
SOUTH CAROLINA
Spartanburg
Greenville
Columbia
NORTH CAROLINA
Asheville
Charlotte
W-S.
G.
Durham
Raleigh
Wilson
Wilmington
VIRGINIA
Lynchburg
Roanoke
Richmond
Petersburg
Newport News
Norfolk
Baltimore
Washington
H.
MD.
D.C.
DELAWARE
W.
FLORIDA
Jacksonville
Tampa
Miami
Key West
Havana (Closed 1979)
CUBA
Scotland
Glasgow
Edinburgh
Belfast
Ireland
Dublin, UK (when chartered in May 1913)
UNITED KINGDOM
Manchester
Liverpool
Birmingham
England
London
Abbreviations continued:
O. Orange, NJ (Closed 2010)
A. Altoona, PA
J.C. Jersey City, NJ
G. Greensburg, PA
A.A. Ann Arbor, MI
M.C. Michigan City, IN
W. Waukegan, IL
N.F. Niagara Falls, NY
S. Shamokin, PA
N. Newark, OH
Sag. Saginaw, MI
C. Champagne, IL
G. Greensboro, NC
K. Kewanee, IL
A.C. Arkansas City, KS
E. Elizabeth, NJ
W. Waterbury, CT
A. Alliance, OH
H. Huntington, IN
1914
44
Kiwanis International established (Detroit)
1915
60
1916
71
Lions International established (Chicago)
1917
36 to 1 June
"Rotary Foundation first announced"
Clubs Founded
Denver Domestic
Belfast International

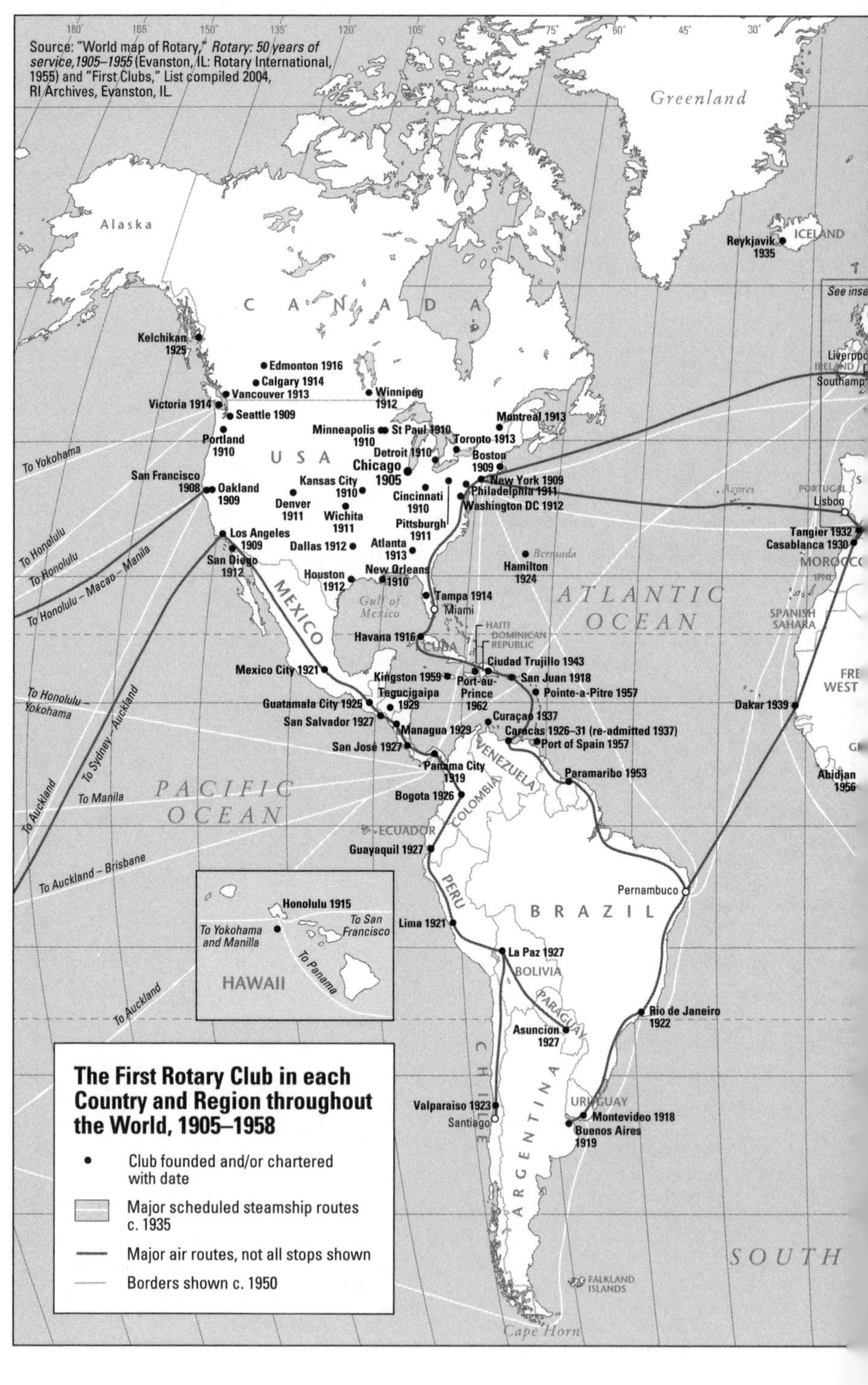

Source: "World map of Rotary," Rotary: 50 years of service, 1905–1955 (Evanston, IL: Rotary International, 1955) and "First Clubs," List compiled 2004, RI Archives, Evanston, IL.
Greenland
Alaska
C A N A D A
Reykjavik 1935
ICELAND
See inse
Liverpo
IRELAND
Southamp
Kelchikan 1925
Edmonton 1916
Calgary 1914
Vancouver 1913
Victoria 1914
Winnipeg 1912
Seattle 1909
Portland 1910
Minneapolis 1910
St Paul 1910
Montreal 1913
Toronto 1913
Detroit 1910
Boston 1909
U S A
Chicago 1905
To Yokohama
San Francisco 1908
Oakland 1909
Kansas City 1910
Denver 1911
Wichita 1911
Cincinnati 1910
New York 1909
Philadelphia 1911
Washington DC 1912
Pittsburgh 1911
Azores
PORTUGAL
Lisbon
Los Angeles 1909
Dallas 1912
Atlanta 1913
Tangier 1932
Casablanca 1930
MOROCCO
To Honolulu
San Diego 1912
Houston 1912
New Orleans 1910
Bermuda
Hamilton 1924
To Honolulu – Macao – Manila
MEXICO
Gulf of Mexico
Tampa 1914
Miami
ATLANTIC OCEAN
SPANISH SAHARA
HAITI
DOMINICAN REPUBLIC
Havana 1916
CUBA
Ciudad Trujillo 1943
Mexico City 1921
Kingston 1959
Port-au-Prince 1962
San Juan 1918
Tegucigaipa 1929
Pointe-a-Pitre 1957
FRE WEST
To Honolulu – Yokohama
Guatamala City 1925
San Salvador 1927
Curaçao 1937
Dakar 1939
Managua 1929
Caracas 1926–31 (re-admitted 1937)
Port of Spain 1957
To Sydney – Auckland
San José 1927
Panama City 1919
VENEZUELA
Paramaribo 1953
Abidjan 1956
To Auckland
To Manila
PACIFIC OCEAN
Bogota 1926
COLOMBIA
ECUADOR
Guayaquil 1927
To Auckland – Brisbane
Pernambuco
PERU
BRAZIL
Honolulu 1915
To Yokohama and Manilla
To San Francisco
To Panama
HAWAII
Lima 1921
La Paz 1927
BOLIVIA
PARAGUAY
To Auckland
Rio de Janeiro 1922
Asuncion 1927
C H I L E
The First Rotary Club in each Country and Region throughout the World, 1905–1958
Club founded and/or chartered with date
Major scheduled steamship routes c. 1935
Major air routes, not all stops shown
Borders shown c. 1950
A R G E N T I N A
URUGUAY
Valparaiso 1923
Santiago
Montevideo 1918
Buenos Aires 1919
SOUTH
FALKLAND ISLANDS
Cape Horn

UNION OF SOVIET
SOCIALIST REPUBLICS
FINLAND
Moscow
Omsk
Irkutsk
CURTAIN
MONGOLIA
Vladivostok
Seoul 1927–40
(re-admitted 1949)
NORTH KOREA
SOUTH KOREA
JAPAN
Tokyo 1920–40
(re-admitted 1949)
Yokohama
PEOPLE'S REPUBLIC
OF CHINA
TIBET
Shanghai 1919–43
(re-admitted 1946–51
then 2006)
Ankara 1955
TURKEY
Nicosia
1938
Damascus
1937
Beyrouth 1932
Tehran
1956–82
Baghdad 1956–59
Amman 1956
IRAN
Jerusalem 1929
Cairo
1929
EGYPT
SAUDI
ARABIA
AFGHANISTAN
PAKISTAN
Lahore 1927
Delhi
Kathmandu 1959
NEPAL
BHUTAN
INDIA
Dhaka 1938
Calcutta
1920
BURMA
Hong Kong
1931
Taipei 1941–43
(re-admitted 1948)
TAIWAN
Macao
1947
Arabian
Peninsula
OMAN
Bombay
Arabian
Sea
Bay of
Bengal
LAOS
VIETNAM
THAILAND
Rangoon 1929
Bangkok 1930
PHILIPPINE
ISLANDS
Manila
1919
Guam 1939
MARIANA
ISLANDS
Khartoum
1938
ANGLO-
EGYPTIAN
SUDAN
ERITREA
Asmara
1957
ADEN
PROTECTORATE
CAMBODIA
Phnom Penh
1957
Saigon
1953–79
FRENCH
SOMALILAND
BRITISH
SOMALILAND
Addis Ababa
1955
ETHIOPIA
SOMALIA
Colombo
1929
CEYLON
Penang
BRITISH
NORTH
BORNEO
Jesselton 1952
BRUNEI
Belait District 1954
SARAWAK
Kuching 1936
MALAYA
Kuala Lumpur 1929
Singapore 1930
PACIFIC
OCEAN
Bangui
1957
KENYA
Kampala 1957
Nairobi 1930
Bujumbura 1956
TANGANYIKA
Dar-el-Salaam
1948
INDIAN
OCEAN
INDONESIA
Djakarta 1927
NETHERLANDS
NEW GUINEA
NEW
GUINEA
PAPUA
Port Moresby
1957
Fiji
Suva
1936
PORTUGUESE
TIMOR
Ndola
1953
NYASALAND
NORTHERN
RHODESIA
Blantyrd 1955
SOUTHERN
RHODESIA
MADAGASCAR
MOZAMBIQUE
Tananarive
1958
Normanton
AUSTRALIA
Brisbane
Fremantle
Sydney
1921
Melbourne
1921
Hobart
Auckland 1921
NEW
ZEALAND
Wellington
1921
Bremersdrop
1956
Durban
Port Elizabeth
Belfast
1913
Glasgow
1913
Dublin
1913
UNITED
KINGDOM
IRELAND
London 1912
Oslo
1922
Stockholm
1926
Helsinki
1926
DENMARK
Copenhagen 1921
Amsterdam
1922
Hamburg 1927
WEST EAST
GERMANY
Warsaw 1931–40
(re-admitted 1989)
POLAND
Ostend 1923
Paris 1921
Vienna
1925
HUNGARY
AUST.
Zürich 1924
SWITZ.
FRANCE
Trieste 1924
ROMANIA
Milan
1923
YUGOSLAVIA
Monaco
1937
BULGARIA
Sofia
1933–41
ITALY
ALBANIA
SPAIN
PORTUGAL
Madrid
1921–40
(re-admitted
1977)
Lisbon
1926
GREECE
Athens 1929
TURKEY
1. Prague 1925–40 (re-admitted 1946–49 and from 1990)
2. Budapest 1926–42 (re-admitted 1989 to present)
3. Luxembourg 1929
4. Bucharest 1929–42 (re-admitted 1992)
5. Belgrade 1929–41 (re-admitted 1992)
6. Saarbrücken 1930
7. Tallinn 1930–40 (re-admitted 1991)
8. Riga 1933–40 (re-admitted 1990s)
9. Kaunas 1934–40 (re-admitted 1990s)

INTRODUCTION

The Civic Internationalism of Main Street

Everyone agreed the Rotary club of Granite City, Illinois, had the best display on "international service" for the 1929 conference of Rotary clubs in southern Illinois. The display "illustrated in a forceful way the interdependence of nations" by showing "the particular product of each of fifty-three nations, upon which the United States depends . . . with a world map as the background." The display was so popular, in fact, that it ran the circuit of local public schools. Thanks to their local Rotary club, the schoolchildren of Granite City could now learn about their place in the world—along with hundreds of Rotarians from surrounding towns and cities.[1]

The details of the display, however, reveal much more about how fifty Granite City Rotarians envisioned their place in the world. Laid out across a table were cards, one for each nation, printed with its name and flag, along with a small, physical representation of each nation's "particular product." A dark ribbon connected each nation's card to a stylized world map hovering in the background. Rather than serving to link each card with its place on the world map, however, the ribbons were connected to the teeth of a gear, inside which was written "Rotary International": the familiar symbol of all Rotary clubs worldwide, in 1929 and today. The "Rotary wheel" dominated the world map as it stood out in relief. For the Granite City Rotarians, the circuits of world trade went through Rotary International (RI), their international service club, rather than through nearby St. Louis or Chicago to the north, or for that matter the Midwest, the United States, or North America. Why would the Rotarians of Granite City, with a population of about twenty-five thousand, imagine their international service club as the hub of all world trade? Why would they choose an international nongovernmental organization (INGO) instead of physical or geographical centers of trade? What vision of international relations gave rise to this public exhibit, and how did it compare with—and compete with—other internationalisms of the interwar period? Though there are no simple answers to these questions, this book raises them because, until only recently, this kind of business and cultural internationalism has largely gone unrecognized by historians.[2]

The oversight is understandable. Easily lost in the disdainful tones of Sinclair Lewis's caricature of small-town Babbitry and the sweeping waves of global warfare and economic turmoil were several generations of Main Street's businessmen, denizens of both middle America and middle-class America, who saw themselves as participants in the rise of the United States as a world power during the first half of the twentieth century. And for so many of these businessmen, joining their local Rotary club often proved a useful way to realize those aspirations. Rotary clubs, found in the largest of cities and the smallest of towns throughout the United States and much of the world by the late 1920s, made their own unique contributions to the ascendance of US economic, political, and cultural power in surprisingly consistent and effective ways. What set the clubs apart from so many other forms of internationalism was their members' abiding faith in the redemptive character of American capitalism as a moral force in the world, their belief in the intrinsic ties between business dealings and civic responsibilities, and their trust in the professionalism of modern business as the bedrock of all cultural and economic exchange.

By way of example, let us return briefly to the Rotarians of Granite City. For their public exhibit on world affairs, the Rotarians had much more than just market relations in mind. To the left of the world map

FIG I.1: The Granite City Rotary club's public exhibit located the club's place in the world economy through its place in the world of Rotary. *Rotarian*, September 1929, 40. *Courtesy of Rotary International.*

and the Rotary wheel was a placard with a stylized image of an East Asian couple and to the right another placard representing what appear to be Indian men riding and guiding a decorated elephant. Forming a kind of triptych of both world commerce and world cultures, the three-paneled display made one simple point: "Under Rotary All the World is One—Through Service and Intertwined Interests" (figure I.1). For the Granite City Rotarians, no nation was too isolated, no culture too exotic, no civilization too distant, because "under Rotary" the world found unity "through service and intertwined interests." Cultural difference and economic "inter-dependence" merged into a harmony of interests anchored by these Rotarians' shared devotion to the civic ideals of co-operation, the presumed bedrock of American exceptionalism. Their small city formed only a part of the greater whole. Nowhere could one see the flag of the United States, as it was just one of many nations forming a large web of global trade—with Rotary International at the center.[3]

This book explores what I call the civic internationalism of the Granite City Rotarians and their tens of thousands of counterparts throughout the United States and around the world, with particular focus on the first forty years of Rotary's existence—1905 to 1945. In 1929, Rotary International had at least one club in forty-five independent nations and many more in US, British, and other European possessions and territories around the world. Though originally from and concentrated in the United States, Rotary clubs outside the United States constituted about one fourth of RI's 3,178 clubs in 1929.[4] This far-flung institutional footprint bore many revealing challenges for the international service club, as we shall see. But RI's international ideological roots emerged from the business progressivism and cultural internationalism of the United States during the first four decades of the twentieth century—from what I call Rotary's service ideology.[5] In this vein, RI sought to position itself as a kind of institutional Esperanto for an emerging transnational class of businessmen and professionals brought together by a common dedication to an alternative to political partisanship and quixotic nationalist agendas. Service to their respective communities, professions, and industries was the touchstone of Rotary's ideology, while participation in emerging webs of international trade drove RI's institutional growth. RI's civic internationalism thus claimed to rise above the political fray because it defined its members as responsible, professional marketplace actors and its organizational mission beyond the purview of the state—any state. Nonpartisanship was its North Star.

Positioned as a kind of middle ground between the United States and the international community, between the business and professional classes of multiple nations and empires, and between states and markets at all levels, Rotary International sought to mediate through its own brand of informal cultural diplomacy across political and territorial divisions.[6] More than just a function of the "awkward dominion" of US power after World War I, an iteration of the associational model of the New Era, a branch of Christian internationalism, or one of many "chosen instruments" of prewar US foreign policy, RI sought to operate whenever possible with a strategic distance from the state.[7] Though hardly unique to Rotary International, that institutional strategy increasingly became a fundamental feature of the ever-expanding number of nongovernmental organizations that have come to populate the global community over the course of the twentieth century. RI just happened to be an early innovator—with significant historical ramifications. In one sense, therefore, RI formed only one tributary in a growing current of INGOs designed to move within, around, and sometimes despite state agencies, national policies, and international institutions.[8] But in the case of RI, blurring boundaries evolved over time into a complex and revealing dance among nations and empires, races and cultures, cities and regions, professions and industries. In this manner, RI also emerged as a useful means of entry for both US corporate and state interests as their employees established, joined, and contributed to the success of their local Rotary clubs both inside and outside the United States, attended weekly luncheons, spoke at a variety of club and public events, and mingled with their families at intimate social events and charitable activities—all of which proved to be an effective formula for growth and influence throughout the commercial centers of the world. In 1919, it was certainly a stretch for John Poole, Rotary's incoming president, to proclaim that "the sun never sets on Rotarians."[9] Like many other aspects of US cultural, economic, and political influence, however, within a decade, the statement was a simple, glaring fact of modern life.

THE INTERNATIONALISMS OF THE INTERWAR PERIOD

In this historical context, RI's civic internationalism expressed one important yet overlooked conduit through which the business and professional classes of the United States journeyed abroad—both in person and in mind—after 1918. Just as US hegemony was in rapid ascent in the aftermath of "the Great War," the Western Hemisphere in particular began to experience even more decline in European colonial influence, providing yet more opportunity for US corporations and their managerial ranks to fan out from Canada to Chile.[10] Rather than view the interwar period as an interregnum between two violent paroxysms of global war and the United States as a hapless wanderer in international affairs after the rejection of the League of Nations, historians now appreciate just how many opportunities for growth the

United States—through its citizens, industries, and foreign policy—exploited during this period. Put another way, the interwar period was much more than a cautionary tale of how not to manage international relations. Consequently, the explosion of Rotary clubs throughout the Americas and across the Atlantic and Pacific during this period provides us with a deeper, more-textured understanding of American ascendancy during the first half of the twentieth century.

No nation "goes abroad" in monolithic fashion, to be sure. But countless everyday interactions and negotiations of power and resistance do form, in aggregate, distinct social movements and historical trends. As a result, historians have deployed analytical terms like "US empire," "liberal internationalism," "international progressivism," and "Wilsonianism" to describe and explain the many dimensions of rising US hegemony, especially between 1898 and 1945.[11] Meanwhile, anti-interventionist, antimilitarist, anti-imperialist, and antiglobalist trends of the same period often fall under terms like "protectionism," "neutrality," "isolationism," "nativism," and "economic nationalism." The oppositional nature of these terms—"imperialist" and "anti-imperialist," for example—can become even more entrenched when mapped onto traditional regional identities of the United States: the cosmopolitanism of urban centers on the coasts versus the provincialism of smaller cities and towns in the South, Midwest, the Plains, or simply the American "heartland." Such analytical terms, however, share a common focus on what Thomas Bender called "the national box": the methodological privileging of the state and its activities when examining international encounter and exchange.[12] From this perspective, the power and presence of the United States in the world arose primarily as a function of the actions, agents, and policies of the US government.

To counter this analytical stance, I have approached Rotary's civic internationalism as a balancing act between all domestic US commercial centers—including "the heartland" of small-town, middle America—and the world "abroad" comprised of international business networks and centers of trade. This approach captures the extraterritorial—even transnational—imaginary of Rotary and its primary self-identification as an international nongovernmental organization.[13] That Rotary clubs could be found both inside and outside the United States in such quantity before World War II is not an incidental fact. The constant entanglement, negotiation, and exchange that have comprised the social and business worlds of Rotary International since its founding in 1905 encapsulate in many ways the on-the-ground evolution of global capitalism.[14] Much like the exhibit in Granite City, this book seeks to represent these many links and layers of meaning-making that have spun out of Rotary International's earliest and most enduring goals: "The advancement of international understanding, goodwill, and peace through a world fellowship of business and professional persons in the ideal of service."[15]

The Granite City Rotary Club's exhibit of 1929 was just one example drawn from a constant stream of similar community activities supported by local Rotary clubs as well as many other religious and secular organizations. For example, concurrent with the Granite City exhibit was an initiative by the Beaumont Rotary club of California to bring both Mexican and US Rotarians together "in a concerted study of Mexican labor immigration and allied problems," while the Rotary club of Racine, Wisconsin "planned to federate the different sokols, vereins, clubs, and other overseas societies for the purpose of advancing international understanding." But RI's civic internationalism was hardly limited to the United States. For example, at the International Convention for the Exchange of Youth, hosted by the Rotary club of Copenhagen, "it was decided to ask Rotary clubs in Europe to form central committees to facilitate the exchange of youth between countries." At the same time, the *Rotarian* provided coverage on the role of women in the League of Nations, including the activities of Jane Addams and the history of the Women's International League for Peace and Freedom.[16] Taken as a whole, the vibrancy, creativity, and worldwide scope of these activities on the eve of the Great Depression is astonishing.

Although just one year later, in 1930, the US Congress passed the Smoot-Hawley Tariff Act, implementing the most protectionist tariff in US history, one year earlier, in 1928, the United States had also signed the Kellogg-Briand Pact, which formally renounced war "as an instrument of national policy." The Granite City exhibit—along with countless other local activities sponsored by organizations like Rotary both inside and outside the United States—should be seen in this light and not as an outlier in purpose, design, and popularity. Simply put, the

United States during the interwar period was hardly lost in a sea of isolationism. As this book seeks to demonstrate, Rotary clubs throughout the United States and the world offered up a steady stream of similar stunts, exhibits, activities, plans, lectures, pageants, and publications in celebration of "international peace and mutual understanding" from the earliest days of Rotary's expansion out of Chicago in 1908 until the present day. How and why did businessmen even in smaller places like Granite City come to see their place in the world in such an expansive and open-armed manner? How did their local Rotary club—and by extension, Rotary International—serve as a catalyst in the evolution of this expansive mix of US business and cultural internationalism long before the midcentury advent of US global hegemony? Finally, how did RI's civic internationalism unfold outside the United States? How might historians interpret and evaluate the vast contributions of non-US Rotarians to RI's entire project? In other words, how might we examine RI's civic internationalism "from the outside in"?[17]

THE TRANSNATIONAL TURN

Many historians have come to recognize the important contributions made by transnational networks, international corporations, and international nongovernmental organizations (INGOs) working across borders, regions, and continents both before and after the Great War.[18] The United States has been in and of the world—a "transnational nation"—because a wide range of individual citizens, religious groups, corporate executives, predatory investors, professional societies, and voluntary associations have been circulating new (and old) ideas, policy agendas, business practices, and cultural products since the foundation of the country.[19] This methodological approach, labeled the "transnational turn," has opened up much greater capacity for understanding how and why the United States adapted to its expanding global ties and interests.[20] At the same time, this approach helps inoculate the historian from framing the United States as an unstoppable, indivisible force expanding and penetrating "abroad" at will—from imagining "the world" as so much backdrop to the great story of the rise to global power. In short, examination of daily, face-to-face interactions, encounters, and negotiations outside the purview of the state and beyond the territorial confines of the United States has become a useful lens for identifying and accounting for the deep and enduring embeddedness of the United States in the world—and of the world in the United States.[21]

For these reasons, this book takes up this general call for a transnational approach to US history by exploring the rapid growth of Rotary International across the Atlantic, across the Pacific, and throughout the Americas before World War II, presenting us with a remarkable case study in the flow of ideas, norms, and practices within a transnational network of US and non-US businessmen and professionals forged at the height of the Progressive Era. Though episodic in growth and fraught with contradictions and failures, RI's international expansion after 1912 led to one out of three clubs being outside the United States by 1935.[22] However utopian RI's ideology and rhetoric may have been before World War II, its institutional reach was and still is undeniable. With more than 1.2 million members in more than thirty-five thousand clubs worldwide in 2020, it is clear that Rotary did indeed find a way to transform its internationalist aspirations born of the Progressive Era into an expansive INGO with active clubs established in nearly every corner of the globe a century later. Moreover, if one considers the three major US-based service clubs as a whole (Rotary, Lions, and Kiwanis), their aggregate membership in 2020 amounts to more than 2.8 million scattered throughout most towns and cities of the world. For the sake of comparison, active US military personnel worldwide in 2017 totaled about 1.3 million (with about 800,000 in reserves), while the US State Department employs about 24,000 in Foreign Service and Civil Service positions and Walmart has more than 2.2 million employees. Given their sheer size and scale of operations, these three service clubs have been responsible for countless community projects, education programs, philanthropies, and health initiatives.[23]

Finally, given Rotary's focus ever since its inception on linking commercial centers of trade, it also stood to reason that cities were identified as the real centers of change in a global economy. Virtually all clubs are named according to the city, town, or neighborhood they represent and almost never in national or regional terms. Though Rotary's headquarters briefly flirted with the possibility of national units shortly after World War I, the organization soon chose to credential only specific clubs in specific cities thereafter.[24] As nodal points of global and regional trade, urban centers have always occupied an important place in the transnational imaginary of Rotary.[25] Transnational and transregional business networks, sales routes, corporate territories, and industrial hinterlands, all anchored by urban nodal points, proved to be the main engine of growth for Rotary International from its very beginning.

CLUBS FOR GROWTH

RI's success at institutional reproduction both inside and outside the United States emerged from a series of adaptations during the Progressive Era that ran parallel to the development of women's organizations.[26] Established in the chaotic business world of Chicago in 1905, the first Rotary club combined the benefits of social networking among businessmen and professionals with the claims of social trusteeship through "community service."[27] Not bound by the genteel codes of older, more elite social clubs or by the secrecy and ritualism of fraternal lodges and Freemasonry, the Chicago club first began by rotating its regular lunch gatherings among its members in order to learn more about the business or profession of each member—resulting in the club's name.[28] Paul Harris, the original founder of the Chicago Rotary club and, by extension, Rotary International, envisioned a kind of weekly re-creation or re-enactment of small-town Main Street in a metropolitan setting. Why must one lose sight of one's moral compass, he wondered, to make one's way in the chaotic world of modern business? His answer came in the form of a new kind of businessmen's club that replicated the small-town feel of Main Street even as it embraced the rapid economic changes of corporate America.[29] This merger of nostalgia for nineteenth-century "island communities" with the twentieth-century urbanity of clubhouse retreats proved surprisingly effective.[30] After a few years of experimentation and debate within the original Chicago club, by 1910 the mix of social networking and moderate business progressivism had developed beyond a simple form of back-scratching among a small group of hard-scrabble Chicago businessmen into an institutional formula for greater civic cooperation among middle-class, urban professionals and businessmen in first-tier cities like San Francisco, Los Angeles, Kansas City, New York, Boston, and Philadelphia. It is crucial to note that, contrary to later stereotypes of Babbitry, the earliest wave of Rotary clubs represented an urban social movement of businessmen that was national in scope and just as rooted on the coasts as in the American heartland (see map on pp. x–xi). Regardless of exact location, each club thrived on a powerful mix of middle-class sentimentality and businesslike pragmatism.[31]

The formula also seemed to cross political borders with relative ease. The merger of the new "business conscience" in public discourse with growing demands for better regulation of national markets and professionalization of business practices had widespread national appeal by 1910.[32] As a result, the National Association of Rotary Clubs (NARC) formed that year and continued its radial pattern of expansion from the largest US cities into second-tier urban centers across the United States.[33] Within just two years, however, clubs were also popping up in Canada, Ireland, Northern Ireland, Scotland, and England without any formal direction from the original club in Chicago. Renamed the International Association of Rotary Clubs (IARC) in 1912, the organization was fast on its way to international growth despite no official plans for it. Moving from inside the city limits of Chicago to beyond the borders of the United States and across the Atlantic took only seven years—and into Latin America only ten years. The Rotary club, in other words, took form as both a local civic organization and an international nongovernmental organization running on high-octane boosterism from its earliest stages of growth.

WILSONIANISM WITHOUT THE STATE

Furthermore, the struggle to rationalize and standardize the institutional growth of the IARC—renamed Rotary International in 1922—became a

FIG I.2: Like so many other voluntary associations, the IARC responded with great patriotic fervor to Woodrow Wilson's call to make the world "safe for democracy." For Rotary, the call to arms was firmly embedded within the organization's growing internationalist aspirations. *Rotarian*, May 1917. *Courtesy of Rotary International.*

significant social, administrative, and intellectual challenge that resonated with contemporary debates on the roles and responsibilities of the United States in the world (figure I.2). As an emerging transnational social network of businessmen and professionals, the Rotary club became a vehicle for expressing and acting on competing visions of international engagement from the club level to the international. With the outbreak of war in Europe, however, the US clubs turned toward Cuba—

and soon most of Latin America—as even more opportunities for growth became manifest. The Great War turned out to be a boon for US voluntary associations in general, to be sure, but especially so for Rotary clubs and their newfangled imitators: the Lions and Kiwanis clubs.[34] The smell of opportunity hung in the air of many of these service club luncheons just as much as in the corporate headquarters of many US firms. With the eager support of hundreds of Rotary clubs spread throughout every part of the United States, the IARC was already moving forward with "international extension" well before Armistice Day.

As we shall see, Rotary clubs were particularly well positioned to take off internationally by 1919. Even more so than similar civic and fraternal clubs and comparable voluntary associations in the United States at the time, Rotary clubs were already well on their way to constructing their entire institutional vision around both service to the local community and international engagement with businessmen and professionals around the world.[35] In the moral universe of Rotary, these two fundamental impulses of the Progressive Era—service and internationalism—merged into a market-friendly form of humanitarian uplift that was distinctly business-class, fraternal, and local in nature. This combination distinguished any given Rotary club from the many missionary societies and religious groups active outside the United States well before the advent of war in Europe as well as large philanthropic foundations like the Rockefeller Foundation that began to emerge during the Progressive Era.[36] Rotary's rolling debates over and experimentation with international expansion evolved in this transnational context, where "service" was often depicted as an ideological common denominator for local civic activism the world over.

Yet Rotary's notion of "service" was riven with profound contradictions that reflected US nationalist fervor; free market ideologies; and hierarchies of gender, race, and class. In short, the Rotary club was very much a product of its time and place of origin. Despite those deep contradictions, however, this combination of community and international service into one ideological bundle was couched in universalist terms much like President Wilson's rhetoric in support of US involvement in European warfare after 1916 and his vision for a postwar international system for peace and self-determination after 1918.[37] When President Wilson left for Paris in late 1918, consequently, thousands of Rotarians throughout North America, Cuba, and Great Britain raised their voice in their support of Wilson's new world order.

Unlike the Wilsonian vision for a new international system, however, Rotary's civic internationalism turned on its formal status as a nonstate, nonprofit organization.[38] The adjective "civic" captures the diverse forms of "community service" carried out by local clubs in cooperation with kindred voluntary associations and without formal state control, while the term "internationalism" points up the transnational nature of Rotary's business progressivism, its appeal beyond US borders soon after its inception, and its faith in an international system that guaranteed peace and stability as an imagined endpoint shared by all members in all countries that hosted Rotary clubs. Though idealistic in its managerial approach to international relations, RI's internationalist vision was no more naive than the Kellogg-Briand Pact nor more ineffective than the League of Nations in preventing war. Moreover, unlike the ultimate failures of the League of Nations, first in the US Senate and then in international politics by the 1930s, Rotary clubs managed to achieve significant growth and evolution during the interwar years. Though Wilsonian in flavor, Rotary's civic internationalism blossomed in the interwar years largely as the result of its organizational strategies as a nonstate actor operating in a transnational setting and in the name of serving the local community. While Wilson's dreams unraveled and US foreign policy lacked coherence, Rotary clubs thrived throughout the United States and around the world. This was not a paradox. The international expansion of Rotary clubs was an alternative way for US businessmen and professionals to connect with their presumed counterparts, their fellow Rotarians, in the rest of the world—and for the world of business to respond in kind. A transnational perspective that encompasses the activities of an international voluntary association like RI removes this apparent disconnect between public and private modes of international engagement in the interwar period.

Rotary's expansion outside the United States during the interwar years, therefore, serves as an important counterfactual to the familiar narratives of Wilson's failures in US domestic politics, the presumed strength of isolationist and nativist sentiments in the smaller towns and cities of the American heartland, the disorganization of US economic and cultural interests abroad, and the central role of the nation-state in understanding the nature of international contact in general.[39] As a transnational history of a nonstate institution, the story of Rotary's international expansion offers unusual insight into the participation of the American heartland in the projection of US cultural, economic, and political power in the world and the impact of that same dynamic on the United States as well. The capacity of individual Rotarians, clubs, and the international organization itself to weave in and around state agencies, laws, and officials was hardly unlimited. But, driven by its civic internationalism, the organization's activities and aspirations, when seen in aggregate and from a transnational perspective, show how international engagement at the personal, social, and nonstate levels during the interwar period were far thicker and more enduring than previously understood—and far more than just US foreign policy done "on the cheap." Though a consensus has emerged on a transnational methodology, we still lack a coherent understanding of the interwar years as a key transitional period in US international relations. Examination of RI's vision of civic internationalism takes us one step further in this direction.

As a point of departure from the state-centered focus of Wilsonianism, I will examine Rotary International from three distinct yet related perspectives. The first centers on RI as a catalyst for global marketization and accelerant of US consumer culture—what Victoria de Grazia called the "market empire" of the United States. Deeply embedded in market relations and devoted to a consumerist ethos, Rotary clubs represented much more than a cultural expression of local economic power.[40] They were also expected to embody—quite literally—the business community at each week's luncheon and to spend their resources in support of the community at large. Second, Rotary did often operate in cooperation with and sometimes even in place of the US government before World War II, patriotically advancing the national interests of the United States abroad in numerous informal, unofficial, yet consequential ways. What Emily Rosenberg called "chosen instruments of the promotional state," it turns out, were far more complex and pervasive than ever imagined.[41] Third, as a voluntary association contributing to the growing transnational web of nonprofits and INGOs, RI participated in what Akira Iriye called the emergence of a "global community" in the twentieth century. But RI's civic internationalism represented particularly important ideological and institutional innovations at the nexus of the state, civil society, and the marketplace.[42] These three interlaced perspectives, I contend, should help us fill in the conceptual gaps in our historical understanding of international engagement between the United States and the world during the interwar period. From this three-pronged perspective, we can evaluate better the many layers and nuances of the Granite City Rotarians as they envisioned for their local community

> an expansive civil society that has continuously flourished beyond the territory and sovereignty of the United States, forming grids of action and interaction that both constituted the United States in a global space and entangled it in the history of globalization.[43]

Their own manner of participation in this entire project found expression first and foremost through the discourses and iconography of Rotary's sweeping mission of civic internationalism.

CENTRALITY OF CAPITALISM

The transnational networks that linked together Rotary clubs were much more intricate than a simple binary of US and non-US categories would allow, particularly during a period when the US State Department remained underfunded, understaffed, and overwhelmed.[44] The circulation of ideas, practices, and norms among Rotarians often complicated greatly the divide between US and non-US categories as "fellow Rotarian" became a trustworthy badge of intraclass and fraternal solidarity.[45] RI's civic internationalism, in fact, celebrated the cordial, face-to-face interaction of individual businessmen as well as the sharing of new ideas on best practices, professional standards, and effective means of civic improvement—no matter where those ideas were from. As a result, the dignified camaraderie that undergirded RI's civic internationalism did not presuppose nor require any necessary connection with the United States. Untethered from any formal ties with US nationalism, Rotarians only had to share allegiance to a capitalist way of life. Given the centrality of capitalism to what later became known as the "American way of life," however, that was no small price of admission.[46]

By 1930, for example, it was perfectly normal for Japanese Rotarians to visit Australian Rotarians in their factories, for Mexican Rotarians to wine and dine Italian Rotarians on business trips, for Polish Rotarians to attend conferences hosted by Cuban Rotarians, and so on—all without direct reference to or guidance from US Rotarians. In other words, participation in RI's civic internationalism by non-US clubs and members had already achieved global proportions by the advent of the Great Depression—the only period of sluggish growth in RI's history until the 1990s. In her examination of Rotary clubs in Germany before World War II, for example, Victoria de Grazia overlooks this fundamental reality, resulting in a narrative structured by a somewhat simplified dichotomy of US or middlebrow culture versus European or highbrow culture. The rapid spread of Rotary clubs in Cuba and Japan, as we will see, greatly underscored this point. In actual fact, RI's civic internationalism resonated throughout Asia, Africa, Latin America, and the Caribbean as much as across the North Atlantic. Furthermore, the US-European dichotomy, when reduced to Duluth, Minnesota, versus Dresden, Germany, ultimately flattens out the US side of the equation to the familiar caricature of small-town Midwestern provincialism while limiting the European side to the bourgeois anxieties of one cultural center of Weimar Germany. I am seeking to remove such dichotomies altogether by examining RI's international engagement unbounded by Eurocentrism, American exceptionalism, or any other prepackaged set of political and cultural categories of the transatlantic world.[47] In the end, global capitalism defies these terms, models, and frameworks in a variety of ways.

In similar fashion, Rotary's civic internationalism proved flexible enough to serve as an effective platform for such international engagement because membership in Rotary promised greater participation in an emerging global economy with a brighter, more democratic future than communism and fascism. The cultural and political relevance of this project to US policies—both foreign and domestic—were manifold. Even during the depths of the Great Depression, when capitalism itself was under such great scrutiny, Rotary's capacity to promote capitalism in the soft-glow terms of international inclusion and service to the community should be recognized for its contributions to the rebranding of capitalism as the best path to modernity, as the "American Way"—an important set of innovations identified by Wendy Wall as central to the rebirth of corporate capitalism during the cold war.[48] The emergence of transnational corporations and global transportation and communications networks entailed constant movement of personnel, commodities, investments, and ideas.[49] In practice, Rotary clubs thrived on such movement and flow, often partnering with specific corporations, professions, and industries in synergistic support. Consequently, participation in the global economy and in one's Rotary club were easily seen as symbiotic, but particularly so for clubs outside the United States. The embrace of cultural pluralism featured in "the family of Rotary"—symbolized, for example, by the East Asian couple and the Indian men riding the elephant in the Granite City club's triptych—was counterbalanced by strong emphasis on business and professional credentials among its members. To be a Rotarian, one had to represent one's given profession or business to the club and to the community. In the name of intraclass harmony and equality, the original Chicago club built up its membership by guaranteeing each member his own uncontested niche or "classification" within the club: one dentist per club, one patent lawyer per club, one real estate agent per club, and so on. The Chicago club's "classification principle" soon evolved into a central part of Rotary's internationalist vision by World War I, as equality of station across an entire spectrum of businesses, industries, and professions trumped, in theory, all cultural and racial differences. Engineers in China, Czechoslovakia, Malaysia, and Canada were all professional peers—regardless of their specific national identity, religion, language—by virtue of their shared professional status.

These equals in the world of business were what I call the exotic peers of Rotary International, joined together through a transnational subjectivity premised on an individual man's status within the marketplace, within a given profession, within the local community. In fact, the celebration of exotic peers in the world of Rotary hinged on this egalitarianism among international businessmen and drove the institution's inclusion of non-US membership into its "parliament of businessmen." Membership across cultural and national differences entailed transformation of local elites into exotic peers within RI's fold. When combined with a strong sense of fraternity—social equality of men among men—and social trusteeship of the local community, these cross-border class identities became a powerful source of social capital for local businessmen and professionals on the move. Whether inside or outside the United States, membership had its privileges.[50]

But I seek to challenge the category of "social capital" as the best way to approach this form of social interaction in a transnational context, replacing it with the more helpful approach of analyzing the history of capitalism and transnational capitalist subjectivity.[51] For all its claims to political neutrality, Rotary's civic internationalism expressed an idealized form of civil society emergent from and amenable to US political and market cultures of the Progressive Era.[52] By institutional design, Rotary clubs were free to engage in whatever local forms of civic activism each club deemed most useful—from construction of new playgrounds and highways to public health initiatives, from boys' camps to girls' scholarship funds. In a sense, local clubs were imagined to be as autonomous as individual actors in the marketplace and to be as representative and inclusive of the entire vocational spectrum of the marketplace as possible. Yet, given RI's rather strict parameters on class status across its membership rolls, the Rotary club in essence served as a gatekeeper for local commercial and professional elites by defining the boundaries of class status at the local level in very precise terms: Each member joined his respective home club under a specific "classification" within his profession or line of business. This credentialing process also required ultimate approval from RI's headquarters in Chicago, especially when new clubs were being established in cities outside the United States. In effect, the form of citizenship participation posited by RI's civic internationalism typically functioned as a subset of US marketplace identities and norms and therefore "as an instrument of social stratification."[53] Social networking during a Rotary luncheon or any club event, in other words, served as a focal point for economic and political privilege and power, demonstrating through private ritual and public spectacle the natural order of things.[54] Much more than the social glue necessary for civic engagement, social networking in Rotary clubs also provided local elites the opportunity to reinforce community norms, usually—though not always—in accord with any national or imperial power structures as well. Social networking in the local Rotary club, as a result, was both an act of economic privilege and a means of social control.

Although promised full participation in RI's "world parliament of businessmen," the exotic peers of Rotary always circulated within a web of social relations defined by economic privilege, racial hierarchy, and gender exclusion.[55] Consequently, Rotary clubs were never just innocent venues for fun social gatherings; rather, the clubs were expressions of political and economic power. Despite all claims of benevolent inclusion, RI's civic internationalism offered up models of both civil society and citizenship delimited by boundaries of class, race, and gender. Except in celebration of the power to incorporate distant lands and peoples within the gentle orbit of American trade and civilization, Rotary generally avoided overt reference to racial identities in its membership requirements after 1920. As a rule of thumb, the more vexing racial differences were in any given time and place, the more silent was Rotary. Indeed, RI's notion of citizenship was so entrenched in market relations that the exclusions of racial hierarchies usually functioned in subtler, more pernicious ways.[56] Just as the generation of racial differences was crucial to the construction of European empires, so the universal promise of inclusion was to the denial of empire in the United States. The dynamics of racial hierarchy and class distinction worked in tandem. The social capital forged in hundreds of Rotary clubs worldwide before World War II entailed much more than the camaraderie of a bowling league: it was the substance of an imperial system in all but name—a consummately American way of informal empire.

There are reasons why one cannot produce a map of the United States as an empire. There is no geo-body for an informal empire.[57] But hierarchies of sovereignty do not require territorial expression. RI's ability to collapse the distance between US and non-US cities served in the deterritorialization of US cultural and economic power by enabling "the replacement of European by American global power in the twentieth century . . . and a replacement of Old World territorial inheritances by the New World rule of moral and economic principle."[58] Henry Luce's "American century" scripted the United States as a nonspatial, atemporal nation able to press universal and moral claims of global leadership: the heart and soul of the denial of empire in the United States.[59] In parallel manner, RI's transnational network of private service clubs invited local business and professional elites into the fold without reference to any US political ambition. Informal networks of business and professional peers meeting on a theoretically level playing field of "free markets" were not exactly redolent of colonial administration and territorial control. RI's managerial worldview eschewed such formal hierarchies of imperial power as the "Old Diplomacy" of the "Old World" that had no place in the "New Diplomacy" of modern business. Yet the power to invite some also meant the power to exclude others. The power of the local Rotary club to credential some as "representative members of the business and professional community" meant that others did not make the cut. RI's civic internationalism promised a future of international peace through greater solidarity and civic-mindedness among the world's business and professional classes—the new managers of an emerging global economy. To unmask the egalitarian and humanitarian conceits of RI's civic internationalism, therefore, is to interrogate the American denial of empire during its formative moment of global ascendancy.

THE AMERICAN CENTURY BEFORE "THE AMERICAN CENTURY"

As a form of Wilsonianism without the state, therefore, RI helped reconfigure the national mission of the United States from reluctant world power to righteous world leader through its engagement with and inclusion of the clubs' counterparts outside the United States. RI's success both inside and outside the United States helped pave the way for a much more active role for the United States in the world after World War II. More than a holding pattern of private sector diplomacy until the emergence of the national security state and its concomitant policies and institutions in the early cold war, the international initiatives of Rotary and comparable INGOs between the wars developed important continuities in contact and exchange between the United States and the rest of the world that ultimately bridged the two world wars. But RI's own rootedness in international market relations, embrace of cultural internationalism, and global scale of operations distinguished it as an INGO. When Henry Luce, publisher of *Time*, *Life*, and *Fortune* magazines, announced "the American century" in 1941 by challenging his fellow Americans "to accept wholeheartedly our duty and our opportunity as the most powerful and vital nation in the world," his words would have sounded rather familiar to the Rotarians of Granite City, Illinois and their 140,000-plus fellow US Rotarians.[60] For them and for another more than 60,000 Rotarians throughout the world, Henry Luce was not a prophet. He was stating the obvious. But where Luce saw the power of the United States as both a nation and a government, Rotarians worldwide imagined a level playing field across markets.

Given the sprawling nature of Rotary's presence over both time and space, I have chosen to focus on revealing case studies rather than seek to provide one overarching narrative. There are already institutional histories of Rotary that serve such purposes, as well as a plethora of websites for almost every single club in the world at this point. Chapter 1 traces the evolution of the Rotary club from a social space for networking among Chicago businessmen in 1905 into a national organization simultaneously branching out into Canada, Europe, and Latin America after 1912. The emergence of Rotary's "service ideology" drove its own brand of business progressivism as the organization developed its gendered, managerial approach to community service. Rotary's strategic uses of its nonprofit, nonstate status found expression in many forms of community service both inside and outside the United States. But Rotary clubs consciously built their entire internationalist vision around a managerial worldview akin to Woodrow Wilson's model of collective security and international cooperation. Though religious in tone, Rotary's civic internationalism emerged as a secular businessman's version of a civilizing mission performed outside the state. Despite the absence of any strong diplomatic infrastructure or coherent US foreign policy during the interwar period, Rotary International sallied forth, establishing clubs wherever and whenever possible during the interwar period.[61] But in doing so, Rotary encountered many challenges as other nations, races, and cultural differences were considered for membership. What happened when Rotary's exotic peers moved from the abstract to the real, when business cultures in the US and in the Anglophone world clashed with rather distinct business cultures, when social gatherings entailed intimate personal contact with "fellow businessmen" and their spouses? What sort of protocols evolved out of these challenges? Chapter 2 considers these questions both in the abstract and concretely, revealing some key moments in the formation and defense of what many scholars have called "racial capitalism" during the interwar period.

Chapter 3 considers the Wichita Rotary club as a case study in boosterism at all levels, local to national to international. Placing the club in the midst of US business progressivism during 1910s, the chapter explores the club's many attempts to position Wichita prominently in national and international markets through promotions, publications, and community service activities. The transformation of Wichita's economy into a hub for military production in the aviation industry after 1938 had great impact on the Wichita Rotarians' conceptions of international cooperation and engagement, resulting in a vision of "armed primacy" for the United States in the postwar era.[62]

The history of the Tokyo club in Chapter 4 demonstrates that Japanese Rotarians could also be both deliberate and strategic about developing their business contacts with the rest of the world through their networking in the world of Rotary. Working in parallel fashion with the Wichita Rotarians, the Tokyo club promoted itself and its nation in the world of RI through its own brand of civic internationalism. Over time, the Tokyo Rotarians' high level of standing in Japanese industry and commerce meant close affiliation with Japanese imperial expansionism into East Asia and ultimately the closure of all clubs by 1940 as the US and Japan moved toward open conflict.

In tandem, Chapters 3 and 4 evidence as well the unintended consequences and unimaginable horrors of other forms of international engagement. RI's civic internationalism proved no more capable of preventing war than the League of Nations and the Kellogg-Briand Pact. In fact, RI helped build the institutional and ideological foundations for postwar US global hegemony by blending the denial of empire with the business of empire. Like the United States itself, RI's civic internationalism, in short, had its dark, violent side. In contrast to the heady optimism of the 1920s, Rotarians on both sides of the Pacific proved to be private businessmen desperately seeking economic growth and accommodation with their respective nations a decade later. First and foremost, they were citizens of their respective countries in times of peace as well as war. Yet, in the postwar era, the social networks forged through prewar Rotarianism proved fertile ground for business and cultural international exchange under the aegis of Rotary.

RI's institutional position as a nonstate, nonprofit organization opened doors for the US business and professional classes in cities throughout the world and then promised reciprocity. Chapters 4 and 5 examine these processes through the particular experiences of Japanese and Cuban Rotarians, tracing out two very different national trajectories before World War II that, nevertheless, arrived at similar endpoints: economic, political, cultural, and military subjugation by the United States in the early cold war. The Rotary clubs of Havana and Tokyo, followed by the many satellite city clubs, played out in microcosm the gradual encroachments of US power and influence in those very different cities and nations over the interwar years. Particularly in the case of Havana, the incorporation of business and professional elites into US ways of doing business, organizing civil society, and positioning themselves in a globalizing economy represented powerful forms of cultural and economic imperialism in all but name. Despite the promises of full participation through RI's civic internationalism, the Cuban Rotarians not surprisingly found themselves over time at the mercy of US corporate and national interests.

Chapter 6 investigates the same processes of adaptation and incorporation during the long journey of Jim and Lillian Dow Davidson through most of Asia from 1928 to 1931. How Jim Davidson, the "Marco Polo" of Rotary, managed to recruit Rotarians in cities, nations, regions, and empires far removed from the American heartland provides a picture of how RI's civic internationalism operated in practice over a large amount of space and a wide variety of contexts rather than in one place over a long period of time (Tokyo and Havana). Meanwhile, Lillian Davidson popularized their travels and Jim's successful establishment of

Rotary clubs through regular dispatches in RI's international monthly, the *Rotarian*. Her mediation of Jim's mission, laced with the exotica of world travel and in the standardized format of a serialized travelogue, made the world accessible for her mostly middlebrow readers. Together, the Davidsons forged deeper ties between the American heartland and the world abroad through Jim's selling of RI's civic internationalism to the business and professional elites of key Asian cities and through Lillian's recounting of the lands and peoples of Asia in her friendly, homespun tone of voice. The Davidsons' travels encapsulated all too well the bright optimism of RI's civic internationalism: it was a friendly world for America.

1

COOPERATION AMONG GENTLEMEN

Main Street Meets the World

In June 1918 in Kansas City, Arch Klumph addressed a convention hall crammed with several thousand fellow Rotarians regarding the Great War in Europe. As the outgoing president of the International Association of Rotary Clubs (IARC), Klumph, a successful businessman from Cleveland, Ohio, was in essence giving his valediction. Entitled "Rotary Throughout the World," Klumph's speech pondered what a postwar world would look like and what role Rotary might play in that new world order:

> There never was a time when the human race stood in greater need of "service" than the hour just ahead of us. Millions of people are being killed and billions of treasure are being spent; empires are tottering; governments are trembling in the balance, and the spirit of friendship and brotherhood among men as lived and taught by the lowly Nazarene, seem almost to have vanished from the earth. . . . Will this peace treaty be any different from the peace treaties of the past? How can all further danger of war be averted?[1]

Arch Klumph, a religious man as much as a businessman, answered his own query with the words of another president, Woodrow Wilson:

> The only cement that will hold this world together will be the cement of friendship. Mere agreements may not make peace secure. It will be absolutely necessary that a force be created as a guarantor of the permanency of the settlement. . . .
>
> The right state of mind, the right feeling between nations is as necessary for a lasting peace as is the just settlement of questions of territory, or of racial and national allegiance.
>
> The free, constant, unthreatened intercourse of nations is an essential part of the process of peace and of development.[2]

Mr. Klumph touted Wilson's vision of a peaceful postwar world that transcended the power politics of nation-state diplomacy and then linked Wilson's glowing model for world unity with the mission of his own organization:

> Therefore, I ask what agency greater than international treaties by governments, can assure the world of a permanent peace; can assure the weak and lowly nations that the great and mighty will not suddenly pounce upon them and crush out their life's ambitions?
>
> I can see but one answer. It is the establishment of a great international friendship—the worldwide inoculation of the virus [of war] by the principle of *Service, not Self.*[3]

Klumph translated Wilson's messianic call for a new and just world order into terms quite familiar to the conventioneers of Kansas City: "international friendship" and "service, not self."

But how deep and durable was this alliance of Wilsonian faith in collective security with the service club ideals of Rotary? How would Klumph's call to action find concrete expression in the weekly meetings and club activities of its members? Wilson believed that international peace and security were something beyond the capacities of any one nation, and Klumph seemed to be taking Wilson at his word by challenging his fellow club members to heed Wilson's call both as a local club and as *an international organization* driven by the highest ideals. With hundreds of Rotary clubs already scattered throughout North America, Great Britain, and the Caribbean at the time of the Kansas

City convention, Klumph understood well that the IARC was on the verge of something big—and that Wilson's postwar vision might be at the center of it all.

But such rapid growth brought significant challenges. Rotary clubs in 1918 were struggling to carve out their own institutional and ideological space within the multiple layers of government agencies, marketplace actors, and comparable voluntary associations and nonstate actors such as the American Red Cross, the YMCA, the Freemasons, the Boy Scouts of America, and a panoply of religious organizations. In fact, the annual convention in Kansas City—like so many others before and after 1918—featured "special assemblies" on "Rotary and the Chamber of Commerce" and "Work Among Boys" as well as a keynote address, "Rotary, a Builder of Business Men," by Rotarian C. E. Buchner, general secretary of the YMCA.[4] Though eager enough to serve the wartime needs of the Allied Nations through successive waves of Liberty Loan drives and War Encampments for Military Training, US Rotary clubs generally worked in an ad hoc manner with government, with industry, and with other voluntary and religious associations in developing their club activities and community service. For Arch Klumph, however, these wartime energies needed to be rechanneled into "a world force" active throughout "all commercial centers of the world" if Wilson's postwar vision had any chance of success.

But the challenges of rapid growth and the ambiguities of organizational status and mission were also a source of opportunity. Transcendence of international borders coupled with the blurring of the public-private divide proved to be a powerful engine for the spread of Rotary clubs both inside and outside the United States after World War I. More significantly, after 1918, Rotary's civic internationalism quickly evolved into an ideological project that (1) linked the "community service" of local clubs with a sweeping vision of international engagement during the interwar period and (2) drew from the Wilsonian conceit of the United States as a new kind of world power capable of inaugurating "a universal and permanent peace based on righteousness." At the core of this postwar vision lay a managerial worldview that was highly gendered in nature, resulting in a paternalism that imbued not only Rotary's understanding of community service but also international relations.

As this chapter will demonstrate, the civic internationalism of Rotary—functioning as a form of Wilsonianism without the state—was much more than just a helpful companion to Wilson's postwar vision of collective security. In significant ways, Klumph's call for Rotary to become a "mighty force" in the world succeeded where Wilson the statesman failed.[5] What constituted that successful formula? And what tested it the most?

"SERVICE IS THE BASIS OF ALL BUSINESS"

Understanding the origins of the first Rotary club in Chicago and its brand of business progressivism reveals the common ground between Wilsonianism and RI's civic internationalism. There was a reason why Klumph put so much faith in the "principle" of "Service, not Self" in his convention address. Early in 1905, a young lawyer named Paul Harris convinced three friends and business associates—an engineer, a tailor, and a coal dealer—to start a luncheon club that rotated among the members' places of business in Chicago's Loop, or downtown business district.[6] The purpose of the meetings was to overcome the sense of alienation the four men were experiencing in the sprawling industrial chaos of Chicago, to establish a network of contacts with whom they could do business, and to learn about one another's line of work. The Chicago Rotary club sought to distinguish itself from the broad range of competing fraternal organizations, women's charities, private social clubs, secret societies, and voluntary associations throughout Chicago by emphasizing the many social opportunities the Rotary club provided for making business contacts among its members. An early membership promotional circular trumpeted this distinction: "Other clubs frown down any effort on the part of members to use the club as a means for securing business. . . . What is done sub-rosa in other clubs is here done openly—a part and parcel of the club's work."[7] Harris's club showed little patience for the niceties of business decorum of the day. Instead, if economic success depended on greater sales, and sales upon conflating one's social and business circles, then what purpose was there in soft-pedaling the matter? For two years, the Chicago club grew to include more than a hundred members as the result of "a hunger on the part of isolated business and professional men for the friendships and warm personal contacts so largely denied to them in the work-a-day world in which they lived, and a desire to promote their own businesses and professions by exchanging orders, contracts, and patronage among themselves."[8] Harris's simple formula worked: "Many members who, in joining, have been animated largely by a desire to be helped, have, on the maturing of acquaintance, found their chief pleasure in helping." Out of this celebration of business reciprocity through fraternal sociability emerged a vibrant luncheon club in the heart of Chicago's business district.[9] The first Rotary club was very much a child of its hometown, the "Windy City."

A critical turn came in 1907, when the club brought together representatives from numerous civic, religious, social, and business organizations to meet with key city and public health officials in order to create public comfort stations in Chicago. Given the lack of public restrooms in the chaotic streets of downtown Chicago, city residents and visitors had to resort to entering private establishments such as department stores and saloons. As a matter of public safety, the latter option was of particular concern to women and those men who saw themselves as protecting women from such dens of iniquity. At the same time, the corruption of the Chicago police department and malfeasance of the city government on the matter further provoked the original Rotarians into their first organized civic action on behalf of their city.[10] The success of the club's drive for comfort stations only strengthened the growing awareness of the value of blending business networking with activities and discourses on "public improvement." As a result, in addition to the "promotion of the business interests of its members," a new objective appeared in the Chicago club's constitution in 1907: "The advancement of the best interests of Chicago and the spreading of the spirit of civic pride and loyalty among its citizens."[11] Although adoption of this civic-minded purpose was hardly cutting-edge in Progressive Era Chicago nor was there any "intention the club [be] a factor in politics," the Chicago Rotary club, in orchestrating this public forum, played host to a wide range of reformist leaders and organizations—though women speakers were conspicuously absent. In short, the club was not just evolving with its new focus "on questions of public benefit," but also entering into a new phase of growth in its club life.[12]

That a concern for the safety of women in the business and retail districts of downtown Chicago triggered a public forum at which the input of women was precluded revealed much about the Chicago Rotarians' paternalist conceptions of the public sphere, scientific expertise, managerial practices, and professionalism. The "advancement of the best interests of Chicago" was a matter for the city fathers—those men with the economic and technical wherewithal to improve (and gain from) urban infrastructure and the moral rectitude to fight corruption in city hall. In other words, the need for public comfort stations was a commercial problem in need of a technical solution by professionals and managers from both the public and private sectors. Shorn of overt sentimental dimensions of uplift, the club's activities in the name of community service and public improvement, as a result, did not seem to require formal membership of women in Rotary. Professionals, managers, technicians, and public officials were and ought to be men—indeed, men of a certain class. Yet, given the moral as well as civic dimensions of such public projects, the increasing emphasis on community service and philanthropic activities called for a stricter policing of the gender barriers between the public worlds of business and the private worlds of domesticity.[13] But segregation by gender was hardly an easy line to draw and defend, especially when it came to the vibrancy of reformist politics in Chicago at the height of the Progressive Era. Even when the Chicago club hosted its first national convention of Rotary clubs in 1910, there were some Rotarians pushing for official recognition of "women's auxiliaries." Despite the convention's emphatic rejection of any formal role for women in the organization in its very first convention, the issue caused a stir even outside the world of Rotary.[14] In short, the encroachment of professional and business men into the supposedly feminine domain of charitable activities came at a price—the barring of women altogether from club activities (and membership), except as domestic partners attending special social events.[15] The Chicago Rotarians' subsequent entrance into progressive political agendas demonstrated that businessmen could, in fact, "care" about their city and their homes as well as their own business interests.[16] Businessmen could "serve" their community without gendered anxiety because the marginalization of the status of women within the club guaranteed the manly qualities of the men's newfound "social trusteeship."[17] Put another way, the Chicago Rotary club's service to the community was their answer—as businessmen—to the "municipal housekeeping" of women's organizations.

Within a few years, the core of Rotary's formal set of institutional objectives developed into the overarching theme of "service"—to the club, to the community, to one's own vocation, and to international peace. Although the original club in Chicago made no secret of its focus on profiting from networking with fellow club members, the club's rapid evolution into the National Association of Rotary Clubs in 1910 (NARC) and then the International Association of Rotary Clubs (IARC) in 1912 reflected broad national trends in the growth and development of the new middle classes of urban America and the emergence of a national, corporate culture.[18] At the first convention of Rotary clubs in Chicago in 1910, the first general secretary, Chesley Perry of Chicago, made clear where he and his fellow Rotarians stood in the political economy of the United States and where he envisioned them in the near future:

> We are here in all the vigor of our manhood ready to do our part of the world's work, anxious to have a share in the great civic uplift of our day and desirous of establishing and maintaining the highest business standards. . . . Already there are sixteen clubs represented in this National Association with a total membership of nearly three thousand and with a combined capitalization of the business interests represented of upwards of $300,000,000, but there are in the United States exactly fifty cities with a population of 100,000 or more.[19]

Perry merged the "manhood" of the clubs' members with the "capitalization of the business interests" they represented and their involvement in civic reforms. For Perry, progressive politics was a function of individual masculine initiative, private wealth, and corporate power. But most revealing was his vision of what that combination meant on a national scale and how Rotary could tap into it as a new organization. Perry sensed that neither the secrecy and ritual of the fraternal lodges nor the sobriety and decorum of the elite social clubs would fit with the assertive middle-class camaraderie of his fellow Rotarians and their turn toward both professionalism and community service.

Nor would partnership with women in club life. Since Rotary was no longer just one club based in Chicago, the tensions over gendered limits on club membership in 1910 were only just the beginning. The "manhood" Perry spoke of required constant definition and reinscription. For example, undeterred by the Chicago convention's rejection of female membership, all-women Rotary clubs set down roots in Minneapolis and Duluth, Minnesota, resulting in one member of the Duluth club making the case for permitting women to formally join Rotary at the 1912 convention in Duluth—but to no avail. When the newly formed Belfast Rotary club considered the admission of women into the fold about the same time, the same results ensued. Even as "Rotary Anns" became more of a fixture at club social affairs, conferences, and especially conventions after 1914, the highest levels of the IARC continued to discuss and reject the possibility of women attaining formal membership in Rotary while showing minimal tolerance for women's auxiliaries to Rotary clubs. Regardless of their formal status, however, women in Rotary were constantly defined in terms of their relationship to the men in Rotary—as wives, daughters, mothers, and sisters rather than as business partners, social peers, and potential mentors. Many clubs only complicated matters by occasionally bestowing "honorary" membership to women, usually public figures like noted opera singer Florence MacBeth.[20] As such, from the earliest days of Rotary's expansion out of Chicago to San Francisco and the West Coast (Oakland, Seattle, Los Angeles, San Diego, and Tacoma) and to the East Coast (Boston, New York City, Philadelphia, and Washington D.C.), women were formally absent but always present—both figuratively and physically. (We shall return to this point later in this chapter.)

Amid ongoing debates over defending the fraternalism of the Rotary club, for Perry and the earliest Rotarians, the organization's combination of manly duty, managerial skill, and civic uplift translated into a significant opportunity for a national presence. At the same Chicago convention, Daniel Cady, a New York attorney, announced that "the

Rotary idea includes all that is meant by the new business conscience and progressive business methods. It brings together people who desire to deal honestly. . . . It is cooperation among gentlemen. It believes, with Robert Owen, that if a transaction does not show a profit to both parties, it is immoral."[21] Another conventioneer suggested that "a certificate of membership bearing the official seal of the National Rotary Club be issued to members in good standing as a traveling passport from one city to another, whereby the member may be recognized." Another Rotarian then amplified the point: "It would mean much to those of us who are manufacturers or jobbers to feel that there was somebody in each of the various centers who was really vouched for in the way that a Rotary Club man is. It means a great deal, and I can't help feeling that this is the beginning of an era of business . . . and we can all understand among ourselves that good service means good standing."[22] In need of greater legitimacy and public trust at the height of the Progressive Era, businessmen from coast to coast were turning to the respectability of a professional identity combined with a formal dedication to public service as a personal badge of honor.[23] The fifteen Rotary clubs represented at the first convention in 1910 were a crystallization of this process, incorporating the encouragement "of civic pride and loyalty" and the promotion of "progressive and honorable business methods" into their first formal constitution.[24] Many managers, salesmen, and professionals of the new middle classes were highly mobile and in great need of portable credentialing as they moved from town to town. Proof of membership in a Rotary club could meet such a need.

The service ideology of Rotary and the rise of the new middle classes were all of a piece, with the rehabilitation of the public image of corporate capitalism as the point of contact. The forging of a "business conscience" in popular culture, political discourse, and the world of business itself was as much a central component in the stabilization and rationalization of market relations during the Progressive Era as it was in the evolution of Rotary's service ideology.[25] Glenn C. Mead, the first president of the International Association of Rotary Clubs in 1912–1913, put the moment into historical perspective for all those attending that year's convention in Buffalo:

> Commodore Vanderbilt expressed the autocratic attitude of business years ago by the blunt and defiant phrase, "The public be damned." A less truculent but equally insulting observation revealed the business philosophy and practice of Barnum when he exclaimed "The people like to be humbugged." It is a far cry from the days when those ideas characterized business methods to our own era that has accepted the doctrine of social service and made all business, great or small, realize that its real function is serving mankind. The tables have been turned . . . and the public may no longer be damned or humbugged by corporations, captains of industry, or small dealers.[26]

For Mead, any chance at reviving the respectability of business in public opinion depended on creating a sense of rupture between the charlatans and "Bourbon methods of business" of the prior century and the modern, scientific, and socially responsible business practices of the new order: "If righteousness exalteth a nation, surely this bloodless revolution in business that has taught it the wholesome lesson of social service and that morality and business *must* mix, is an epoch in history."[27] The aura of religious virtue mixed with the patina of modern science brought stability to these new class structures. For good reasons, the managers of corporate capitalism were here to stay.

What drove Mead's Rotarians into the arms of public service was a preemptive move at avoiding impending state regulation of business practices and gaining ground at the expense of "big business." Citing the San Antonio club's suggestion that "business men should establish a code of ethics just as the professions have done," Mead intoned against the "evil practices that . . . bring disrepute and public scorn upon the whole body of business men" and warned that "they should not wait for compulsion from outside their ranks."[28] Given the turn of political fortunes in the national elections of 1912, Mead's advice made sense. Becoming professional in one's business methods and serving the public represented both a necessity and an opportunity.

As with many other organizations and initiatives that emerged during the same period, Rotary clubs became useful vehicles in legitimizing the managerial-masculine authority of the new middle-class professionals and businessmen in state, economic, and local affairs. The Rotary club's membership was increasingly imagined as an assembly of all the "representative men of the community" who bore some mark of character and success in the marketplace. The impetus for growth in the original Chicago club was to maximize the degree of harmony (and potential clients) among club members by opening membership to "all worthy and dignified vocations," but then only allowing one representative from each "distinct line of business" or profession within the club. Each member of each Rotary club, theoretically at least, represented his own specific line of business or profession before the club since, once a given "classification" was occupied, no one else in that line of work could enter the club. If a man sold bricks in Chicago and no one held that "classification" in the club, for example, he would be a possible candidate to join the club under that specific classification. If the club already had a member who sold bricks at least 60 percent of the time, then there was no possibility of membership until the specific classification was vacated or another club opened up. The Chicago Rotarians, in fact, actually maintained statistics on how much business was gained by whom and from whom from 1908 to 1911 as they tried to demonstrate the profitability of such an arrangement.[29]

As a result, for the most common professions and businesses in a large city like Chicago, membership in a Rotary club could be a particularly profitable piece of social and economic real estate—in the pecuniary sense and in the social sense as well. Moreover, an expanding economy entailed a growing number of possible "classifications." And with so many cities without a Rotary club across the United States, the potential for growth within clubs as well as nationally was self-evident to mobile, enterprising businessmen in need of instant business credentials. The portability and interconnectedness of Rotarians' professional and business lives soon translated into the demand for Chicago's service club model in other cities. As noted earlier, preexisting business and social networks, sometimes defined by a common industry, profession, or line of business and sometimes by more informal social, religious, educational, and cultural affinities, proved to be fertile ground for growth from the local to the regional to the national level—and, as we shall see, at the international level as well.[30]

When the National Association of Rotary Clubs met in 1911 for its second convention in Portland, Oregon, however, the "back-scratching" model of limited membership and maximum profits was already not in tune with the times. Purely acquisitive individualism in the marketplace being at a relative nadir in US political and popular culture, the "classification principle" of membership quickly evolved into a much grander purpose: "The Rotary Club demands fair dealing, honest methods, and high standards of business. No obligation, actual or implied, to influence business exists in Rotary. . . . Membership in the Rotary Club is a privilege and an opportunity and its responsibility demands honest, and efficient service and thoughtfulness for one's fellows. Service is the basis of all business."[31] More precisely, business was the basis of all "service." The service ideology was deeply embedded in the market and professional status of its members. The chance to engage in community service through one's local Rotary club was defined as a function of masculine character, an expression of old-fashioned republican virtue, and a demonstration of the spirit of civic cooperation. The institution, though, only recognized each member through his own economic standing within the marketplace.

This conception of an economic citizenship was often invoked in justifying limits on membership to white men of a certain class status for decades to come. Because public service came only through private means, the headquarters of Rotary in Chicago had already begun to work out increasingly elaborate systems of classification for specific lines of business and professions by 1912–1913. The strategy soon developed into a detailed way of documenting the credentials of each potential member's social and economic status, a kind of "scientized" vetting process of the ranks of the new middle classes, often as they first made their appearance. Eventually, the credentialing of new members became a core practice of Rotary clubs, evolving into an intricate set of institutional and cultural practices for membership certification well before World War I.[32] By 1921, Rotary arrived at a formal definition of membership requirements that each club's committee on membership and classification had to follow: "Any adult male person of good character and good business reputation, engaged as proprietor, partner, corporation officer, or manager, of any worthy and recognized business."[33] Beyond these parameters, each club had some degree of autonomy in assigning a formal classification—orthodontist, cardiologist, shoemaker, civil engineer—to any of its members. But a classification had to be assigned for membership to be granted. Indeed, one's very reason and purpose for being in the club hinged upon the confirmation of that status through a club's membership committee. As we shall see, this credential process did not always translate well outside the United States. (See Chapter 6.)

Glenn Mead himself understood well the benefits to be had from the professionalization of business at both the local and national level, for it was his life story. Though a product of the "common schools" of Pennsylvania, he managed to enter Phillips Academy in Exeter, New Hampshire, and to attend Harvard, where he graduated in 1891. While teaching the classics at the Episcopal Academy in Philadelphia, Mead studied law and became a member of the bar in 1900. He entered local politics under the tutelage of Judge James Gay Gordon, "a leading lawyer and public man" of Philadelphia, and Mead opened up his own practice in 1908. As an independent Republican, he agitated for urban reforms, achieving success in the 1911 elections in Philadelphia and becoming assistant city solicitor. In 1910, he organized and then became president of the Philadelphia Rotary club. During his two years as club president, Mead raised the profile of Rotary in Philadelphia to a level comparable to the "older business organizations" of the city.[34] In terms of education, mobility, and opportunity, Mead's entire career reflected the burgeoning opportunities of the new middle classes of the period, culminating in his personal challenge to Rotarians to develop and propagate a "professional code of ethics" for all businessmen. There were many more like Mead and many more who followed in his footsteps.

Finally, the credentialing of new club members often provided a quick entrée for highly mobile businessmen into new cities and new sales territories—so long as they met the formal requirements for membership and there was an opening for that classification in the prospective club. Over time, this mobility helped many clubs shift from a regional provincialism to a more cosmopolitan outlook. For instance, the Atlanta Rotary club, formed in 1913, was established after the attendance of three members of the Atlanta chapter of the American Association of Advertising Clubs at their annual convention in Baltimore. The new club drew its membership from many in the business community who were not from Atlanta or even Georgia. As a result, by 1938, only forty members, or 15 percent of the Atlanta Rotary club, were native to that city, only three of its first twenty-six club presidents had been from Atlanta, while more than thirty-two states and four countries (Canada, England, Scotland, and Belgium) were represented.[35] Restrictions on club membership, in effect, could actually entail professional opportunities for those setting up shop in new venues who managed to classify their business in distinct terms. For others, like Rotary's president, Mead, "the limitation of membership establish[ed] a high standard of business discussion at club meetings. A heavy responsibility rests upon a man . . . to show a mastery and knowledge of his business in presenting it to his fellow-members. He cannot afford to offer an inexpert or slovenly exposition of that business in which he is accredited with leadership." The weekly club meeting, in its loftiest form, was in essence a series of "business talks," which were "as valuable and scientific as lectures at a university . . . and very appropriately named a post-graduate course in business."[36] Since there were only so many formal business schools in existence in 1913, the weekly meetings of the "parliament of businessmen" provided an important measure of stability and authority among the ranks of the new managers and professionals of corporate America as they began to appear among the older professions and more established small businessmen of any given US city. A vibrant club life offered up the chance for both personal and professional edification and advancement that could not easily be found elsewhere. Additionally, the classification principle centered on creating a club "representative" of its community, a practice that also helped prevent clubs from being taken over by one industry, profession, or corporation. Most important, according to Ivan Allen, one of the Atlanta club's founders and father to Atlanta's fifty-second mayor, Ivan Allen, Jr., this lyceum of businessmen helped the Atlanta club graduate from the somewhat crass boosterism of admen in 1913 to a world-class, cosmopolitan hub by 1939: "It is a far cry from these original and perhaps local objectives mainly commercial in their aspects, to the present aims and objectives of world-wide fellowship among business and professional men of all races and creeds."[37] As we shall see later, Allen's celebration of Rotary's civic internationalism ignored the glaring contradictions of Jim Crow not only within the city of Atlanta and the state of Georgia in 1939, but also among Rotary clubs worldwide. To be sure, the club's large membership was wide-ranging in terms of business classifications and professional fields by 1939, but the cosmopolitanism of the Atlanta club was much more bounded by race than Allen would or could admit. The Atlanta Rotary club, in fact, had helped see to that two decades earlier.

SERVICE TO THE COMMUNITY

In contrast to the specificity of vocational roles within clubs, the various charitable projects and community activities taken on by local clubs typically did not have any particular plan or coherence within the United States until the mid-1920s. Given the relatively large degree of autonomy on the part of the local clubs, this lack of coordination was no surprise. Because of the broad range of projects and activities taken up by clubs both inside and outside the United States, in fact, there was a push by World War I to distinguish acceptable community service activities from uncoordinated, ad hoc club activities done in the name of the public good.[38]

Despite the experimental nature of community projects in the first decades of Rotary's existence, most club activities done on behalf of the community generally fell within three broad categories.[39] The first centered on charity and philanthropy. Clubs often involved themselves in fundraising for the community chest, "crippled children," building new playgrounds and parks or else supporting and mentoring through the Boy Scouts of America, student loan funds, and organizations like the 4-H clubs and the YMCA. In fact, working with the Boy Scouts and on "Boys Work" in general had become one of the most common projects of Rotary clubs in the United States during the interwar period. The Boys Work Committee of the Rotary club of West Point, Mississippi, for example, hosted the annual Boy Scout Jamboree for six local counties in the summer of 1928. More than two hundred Scouts, Scoutmasters, and executives joined more than forty Rotarians for a barbecue as medals were given to many of the Scouts.[40] Such club events played out in the thousands every year and in almost every country where both Rotary clubs and Scouting or similar organizations existed. Such strong interest working with the Boy Scouts of America stemmed from many Rotarians' understanding that such activities offered tutelage in the ways of citizenship for future generations of men.[41] Clubs were supposed to forge this kind of interlocking relationship with other community organizations, both public and private, and to meet social needs unfulfilled by any other local group, organization, or agency. The teeth on the outside of the gear of Rotary's emblem are said to symbolize the efficient interlocking of the club with other community organizations.

The second category of community activities tended to focus on economic and civic improvements—in a word, infrastructure. Better traffic regulation, fire protection, communication lines, new sidewalks, new hospitals, and zoning laws were typical aims, as well as support for public works and the creation of chambers of commerce where none existed. Though not quite as common as charitable endeavors like fresh air camps and aid to underprivileged children, this type of community outreach emphasized a streamlined municipal government, more efficient management of public resources, improvement of public health facilities, and development of transportation and communications infrastructure; activities directed toward these goals often were carried out in collaboration with the local chamber of commerce.[42] Born of the Progressive Era in both form and rhetoric, Rotary's countless local campaigns for the building up of community infrastructure became so common that companies like Ketchum, Inc., which specialized in fundraising on behalf of "colleges, hospitals, churches, and fraternal organizations," regularly advertised its success stories in the *Rotarian*. But RI's reform efforts in particular tended to focus on face-to-face charity projects and especially on helping boys become good adult male citizens, while the construction of roads, parks, hospitals, swimming pools, and playgrounds were generally seen as secondary but also significant priorities. Given the constant mixture of sociability, boosterism, and religious themes in almost all clubs' weekly meetings and publications and the high priority placed on the maintenance of harmony among the Rotarians' ranks, Rotary clubs tended to gravitate toward meeting social needs that were personal, local, and charitable in nature rather than overtly political and systemic. Community service projects, in other words, tended to reflect the individualist ethos of classic liberalism as well as the traditional dichotomy of the deserving versus the undeserving poor as Rotary's reformist agenda was always understood to be gradualist and conservative in nature.

The third type of club activity devoted to community service tended toward the reinforcement of civic values, the celebration of patriotic causes, and the raising of awareness of issues of national and international import. For example, three boys from the United States who had won an essay contest sponsored by the *American Boy,* a national magazine, were guests of the Tokyo Rotary Club in 1933. Each boy delivered a short speech on what interested him most about Japan.[43] The hosting of essay contests and letter-writing campaigns in local schools was a common service club activity at the time, not just for Rotary. But the exchange of national flags and club emblems also played out during countless Rotarian luncheons and conference settings—a feature somewhat unique to Rotary clubs compared with other local civic clubs before World War II. For example, when Rotarians from Guatemala City visited the New York Rotary Club in 1928 and received a flag of the United States as a gift, the Guatemalans responded with a gift of their own: "a stuffed quetzal—a bird whose beautiful plumage was once reserved for the adornment of the Maya chieftains."[44] This specialized form of public gift-giving among clubs remains a mainstay in Rotary's brand of informal cultural diplomacy. More important, in the midst of the Neutrality Acts and the appearance of the America First Committee in 1940, US Rotary clubs were hosting almost two hundred "Institutes of International Understanding" throughout the United States—many of them in smaller towns and cities outside of the major metropolitan areas—as part of this kind of community service activity. Typically held at local high schools, public halls, and libraries, each institute combined school assemblies with evening forums that featured guest speakers and noted experts on US foreign policy, world trade, and international cultural exchange. These efforts reached, in aggregate, an audience of more than a million during this period. Though often blurred in label as both "international service" and "community service," these didactic activities, meetings, conferences, institutes, rituals, and exchanges constituted a significant and consistent wave of community engagement across the United States and, indeed, throughout the world of Rotary. Even after the elimination of scores of Rotary clubs in Germany, Italy, and Japan as a result of the rise of fascism and the closure of many others because of the outbreak of warfare in Spain, China, and continental Europe, there still remained more than seven hundred Rotary clubs in the British Empire and several hundred more in Latin America, Asia, and Africa carrying on with all manner of community service activities.[45]

But for all the moral connotations of service, only rarely did any type of community service activity by Rotarians directly challenge political or social inequalities in any significant way—by tacit design. As with many other measures put forth by Progressives, the real objectives of reform were about the defense of what were seen as traditional middle-class, republican values in the midst of rapid social and economic change. Again, stabilization of the social order drove the cooperative model of club sociability among business and professional equals who privileged intraclass harmony among their peers of white businessmen over all else. As a result, community service was almost exclusively conceived in apolitical terms. Moral uplift, individual charity, and civic improvement pervaded club projects and rhetoric without direct reference to the inequitable social and economic relationships and inequalities that were behind the need for such charities. The middle-class philanthropy of Rotary, bleached of overt partisan or political dimensions since the Chicago club's first foray into municipal politics in 1907, tended to reinforce rather than challenge power relations at any level of governance—as club harmony required.

Much like Woodrow Wilson's own postwar vision of international peace and definition of "self-determination," Rotary's use of the term "service" was loaded with contradictions from the start. The origins and evolution of the service ideology reveal RI's primary purpose of grafting the profit motive of managerial capitalism onto the rhetoric of democratic engagement, social equality, and civic cooperation. That the service club made the latter dependent on the former, however, did not merit consideration any more than the equation of democracy with capitalism did in the rhetoric of liberal internationalism and US foreign policy. Long before the advent of the Great Depression, there were constant debates within Rotary clubs and within Rotary's official publications over the responsibilities of the employer to the employee, of management to its workers, of capital to labor, resulting in a constant stream of pamphlets out of Chicago for national and international consumption. Club activities slowly evolved in response to those rolling debates, sometimes developing into an international discourse as Rotary clubs appeared throughout the world after 1918. As a result, by the mid-1930s, RI's two basic mottos—"He profits most who serves best" and "Service above self"—had been translated into scores of languages, invoked by thousands of ambassadors and corporate dignitaries, and expounded on countless times in club meetings, conferences, and conventions held "in all the commercial centers of the world."

The management of Rotary's community service activities paralleled the Wilsonian approach to international affairs: moralistic, top-down, middle-class, managerial, and highly amenable to corporate capitalism. The gendered language of community service contradicted its own claims to transparency, expertise, and social trusteeship of the community just as the international system imagined by Wilson never survived the political intrigues of Versailles or the US Senate. For both RI's civic internationalism and Wilsonianism, "international friendship" was not, in fact, for everyone. As we shall see, high moral sentiments aside, management of the community, like management of world affairs, always came from a position of power.

THE PIONEERS OF BOOSTERISM

How did the boosterism of the earliest Rotary clubs evolve into the service ideology of RI's civic internationalism by the end of World War I? After the inaugural convention in Chicago in 1910, demands began to emerge in the ranks of all sixteen original clubs for an administrative headquarters in Chicago run by professional administrative staff, a national convention every year in a different city where major institutional decisions were adopted, and publication of a monthly magazine that contained all the latest news and views of fellow Rotarians across the country. These three developments formed the institutional and administrative core of Rotary as a social movement among businessmen from its start. Through an odd mixture of unplanned organizing and concerted development of specific business contacts, the earliest non-US clubs mushroomed in Winnipeg, London, Dublin, Belfast, Manchester, and Glasgow, making the embrace of the "international" in many ways a fait accompli—even if it was limited at first to the "Anglo-Saxon" world of North Atlantic trade circuits.[46] As a result, the organization's monthly publication, the *Rotarian*, advertised itself in the opening pages of its first publications in the unmitigated language of boosterism: "Trade Expansion: Here is the opportunity for you to make a trade expansion excursion into sixty leadings cities of the United States, Canada, and Great Britain. Advertise in *The Rotarian* and you will be introduced to six thousand active up-to-date business and professional men."[47] That same year, the *Rotarian* began devoting its monthly editions to cities where Rotary clubs were already flourishing. These editions quickly became tabloids of boosterism as many Rotarians often joined or helped establish their local chambers of commerce as part of their eagerness to promote their home base of operations.[48] Though more informative than a standard chamber of commerce pamphlet and not limited to Rotary's own organizational concerns, the early editions were not quite up to the standards of *Printer's Ink* and similar established trade publications. The content was predictable and consistent in blurring the line between advertisements from featured local merchants and gushing articles on the city in promotion. The June 1912 edition, for example, trumpeted that "Pittsburgh promotes progress and the energy of her industry rotates throughout the world," while Boston, Philadelphia, Cleveland, New York and other major industrial centers also got their own editions with similar thematic thrust.[49] Other cities were soon able to make their own case for being the next metropolis of their particular state, region, or province, as the organization fanned out across the United States.[50]

In fact, the pattern of growth across the United States foreshadowed the hub-and-spoke pattern of expansion in other nations after 1919 (map 1).

After a rapid start in the largest cities of the West Coast and East Coast, Rotary clubs began to sprout up in the South, the Plains, Midwest, Canada, and the United Kingdom as well such that, by 1914, with the hundredth club receiving its charter in Phoenix, Arizona, the geographical distribution of clubs had leveled off at approximately three clubs in the Midwest for every two in the South, two in the Northeast, and one on the Pacific coast.[51] The fourteen clubs in Canada and the United Kingdom demonstrated just how quickly Rotary clubs leaped across the US-Canadian border and across the Atlantic from Chicago well before reaching much closer cities like Milwaukee or Indianapolis. Nor did regional distribution change significantly with the next one hundred cities to charter a Rotary club in the United States before World War I. What did change was the size of the new host cities, as regional and national centers of trade became saturated, leaving secondary and tertiary urban centers open to expansion.[52] After an initial burst of club growth on the East and West Coasts from 1908 to 1912, in other words, Rotary clubs eventually began to fan out into the hinterlands of the larger urban centers through known networks of business interests, social contacts, trade routes, and sales territories. In short, while most of the first one hundred clubs were in large cities embedded within national and international circuits of trade, the overall distribution of clubs began appearing in the more familiar small-town environs of popular lore throughout the Midwest, the Plains, the South, and rural America in general by the end of World War I. The point cannot be emphasized enough: well before the publication of Sinclair Lewis's *Main Street* in 1920 and *Babbitt* in 1922 and the Lynds' *Middletown* series, based on Muncie, Indiana, in 1929 and 1937, Rotary clubs had been actively engaging with the world through the largest cities of North America, the British Isles, and even Latin America and East Asia.[53]

Woven into the enthusiasm for the emerging industrial prowess of so many cities in the early editions of the *Rotarian*, however, one finds a glorification of the cultural and historical roots of the "island communities" of midwestern Protestantism. The radial spread of Rotary clubs from cities like Chicago, Kansas City, and St. Louis reflected the cultural geography of middle America's idealism as the Midwest in particular achieved a kind of regional self-awareness as well as national appeal.

Urban growth, ethnic and religious diversity, and the spread of large corporations challenged the cultural authority of the mostly Protestant middle classes of the region as its leadership class came to include Catholics, corporate managers, urban professionals, and small producers in large cities from recent immigrant stock. This new and expanded leadership group articulated a patriotic symbolism that drew a mythic arc from the original settlers and pioneers as idealized patriots to the character and virtues of the new middle classes of an urbanizing America. Patriots and pioneers became the basis for much public commemoration and a dominant model for citizen behavior. John Bodnar, in *Remaking America,* describes well the cultural seedbed of the midwestern worldview and the challenges it faced as the Progressive Era hit its full stride:

> The nationalization of mid-western culture, which had already begun in the nineteenth century, was intensified after the 1890s. This could be seen most clearly in the rising influence of the patriot symbol. During the nineteenth century, the region's culture had been dominated by a native, Protestant middle class that celebrated self-reliant, small-scale capitalists as model citizens. This cultural construction reflected the belief of middle-class leaders that they had been responsible for the region's growth and an attempt by them to reform the behavior of thousands of immigrants whom they felt did not share their commitment to self-improvement and progress. These leaders and the communities in which they lived were certainly proud of the patriotism of their ancestors, but they saw all that they had built grounded ultimately in the rugged individualism which they believed they and their pioneer ancestors had exhibited.[54]

Within the pages of the *Rotarian* appear countless examples of this Pioneer patriotism: Rotary clubs organizing and leading parades, celebrations, and anniversaries in the name of civic pride and respect for local tradition, and very often as a means of fundraising for local charities. During the war years, the same impulse found expression in Preparedness Parades and countless voluntary drives for the war effort, particularly for Liberty Loan drives.[55]

Grafting the dynamism of a rapidly industrializing economy onto the rugged stalks of citizen-pioneers demanded some creative interpretations, and Rotary was up to the task. For instance, Chesley Perry, the indefatigable general secretary of Rotary and editor of the *Rotarian* (1911–1928), introduced his readers to the French voyagers, priests, and settlers of what later became Peoria, Illinois, as

> intrepid men with a mission to perform. Dangers, hardships and sufferings did not prevent them from doing their duty. The traders that followed them into the wilderness were equally as brave and the pioneers, who came later and established settlements in the wilderness, likewise were rugged men, who believed in the spirit of fair play and possessed a respect for the rights of others. Peoria's ancestry is one of which any city might be proud. The early inhabitants would make good Rotarians today. It is from such an ancestry that Peoria has inherited her progressive spirit and many of her high ideals.[56]

The boosterism of a Rotary club could be played out well beyond the local level, as the Chicago headquarters sought to position itself as a clearinghouse for many other "Peorias" in the United States.[57] It was an effective marketing campaign on the part of Perry, as he came to know his readership well through the constant stream of communications to and from Rotary's headquarters in downtown Chicago and through regular face-to-face meetings at district conferences and annual conventions.

Attracting new advertising dollars at the *Rotarian* involved weaving together the local patriotic traditions of individual clubs with a national as well as international narrative of economic progress through the business practices of modern corporations. In the case of Kansas City, Rotary's version of a frontier thesis soared in rhetoric:

> A century ago, herds of buffalo grazed where colossal skyscrapers now stand. At the junction of two great rivers . . . , the painted braves of the Kanzas tribe fished, hunted and scalped.

> Palefaces appeared on the Santa Fe trail, westward highway of progress on which the prairie schooners of the traders rumbled in journeys of commercial conquest. Blood was spilled. Tepees vanished. Cabins were built. Grain was sowed and crops harvested. Traders voyaged and returned with wealth from the Spanish southwest.[58]

To be sure, rewriting the construction of an inland empire continental in scale and genocidal in practice into a tale of "commercial conquest" and vanishing tepees has been a common trope of all popular forms of US history. But the eagerness to deploy such a narrative in the context of a magazine devoted to boosterism stretched over an international canvas demonstrates the mutually constitutive nature of developing a national corporate and consumer culture and an image of the United States as an emerging and benevolent world power. It was not settler colonialism, violent extraction of natural resources, and bloody land grabs that "won the west" for the United States. Rather, it was the unfolding of trade over time and "the progressive spirit" and "high ideals" that thrived in the present. A glossy, stylized version of Frederick Jackson Turner's frontier thesis left little room for talk of empire, either at home or abroad. The republican virtues and frontier ruggedness exemplified in the glorious transformation of former prairie towns like Peoria and Kansas City into modern cities with "colossal skyscrapers" were safe and sound in the first decades of the twentieth century. Such virtues were alive and well, still animating the pioneering spirit of Rotarians as they were now casting their nets abroad for new opportunities of growth.

It is in this light that the extensive small-town nostalgia of Rotarian literature and rhetoric needs to be understood. For understandable reasons, Paul P. Harris, the founder of the original Rotary club of Chicago, was seeking to replicate the face-to-face familiarity of the small community he experienced during his boyhood living with his grandparents in Wallingford, Vermont. Through the camaraderie of his newfangled social-turned-civic club in the heart of Chicago's bustling business districts, Harris and his fellow club members had created a social space redolent of nineteenth-century Americana, where artisanry, economic independence, and rootedness in the community were fused with modern business practices and middle-class, urban masculinity.[59] In a sense, Rotary clubs in the United States were designed from the start to serve as microcosms of the "island communities" of an earlier period of American history, even as Rotary the organization was increasingly advancing and normalizing the business relations of modern corporate and consumer relations. The *Rotarian,* for example, regularly published articles and editorials on the virtues of small-town America written in the folksy, plain-speech tradition of an earlier era on one page and then articles—and advertisements—on modern business practices, new office technologies, the upside of chain stores, and the latest techniques for managing advertising and employer-employee relations on the next page. Similar thematic juxtapositions can be found throughout the programs, speeches, and presentations at Rotary's luncheons, district conferences, and annual conventions. The Rotary club was not only the place for bonding among business and professional peers, but also an institution for bridging the American past with corporate America.[60]

Yet, like the industrial age into which he was born in 1868, Paul Harris was also about motion—surprisingly so. Though he spent his youth in a small town in Vermont, Harris left for Princeton University in 1887 and then to study law at the University of Iowa. Stopping in Chicago along the way, Harris was, like many others, overwhelmed by the industrial scale of the city and its sheer social complexity. After completing his studies in 1891, Harris decided to travel before establishing his law practice. But his wanderlust was exceptional, taking him west to San Francisco, as a reporter; to Los Angeles, as a teacher in the Los Angeles Business College; to Denver, also as a reporter, and as an actual cowboy; and to Jacksonville, Florida, where he was a hotel clerk and then a salesman traveling throughout the Jim Crow South. But Harris wanted more travel, so he signed up as a cattleman on a cargo ship bound for Liverpool to embark on the first of his many travels abroad. Harris then did a repeat Atlantic crossing, this time to London. When Harris returned to Chicago in 1893, he briefly attended the Columbian Exposition before heading out one last time to work as a "vagabond" in the orange groves of the Louisiana bayou and then as a salesman of marble and granite in Jacksonville; this time his travels for his job took him to Cuba, the Bahamas, Scotland, Ireland, Belgium, and Italy, and for his own sake he also traveled throughout central and western Europe. By 1896, Harris was finally ready to establish his new law career. He chose to do so in Chicago, the city that had so awed him years before.[61]

Harris's personal and professional trajectory was, in many ways, prologue to Rotary's. Harris had experienced the two great extremes of the era: a childhood in an idyllic small town in Vermont, where he was raised by grandparents from the earliest days of the republic, and a decade of education and travel throughout most of the North Atlantic working as a common laborer, a reporter, and a traveling salesman before hanging out his shingle as a lawyer in Chicago. "The story of a life out of the ordinary," reads the preface for one of RI's biographies of Harris; "that of the Founder of Rotary, a social movement which in the span of a few brief years has girdled the world and served as an inspiration to many other organizations different in name but similar in purpose now following the trail blazed by Rotary."[62] The wide-ranging travels of Paul Harris were ideologically just as useful for Rotary as his youth in Vermont. He was living proof that the modern, global economy was not so foreign after all—nor were other nations, races, and religions. As a result, amid the paeans to industrial progress, pioneer patriotism, and business civilization in the American heartland in the earliest editions of the *Rotarian* was also an emphatic welcome of the new Canadian, British, and Irish clubs. The cover of the September 1912 edition, in particular, announced the establishment of the International Association of Rotary Clubs with an image of the English lion and the American eagle spinning the symbolic wheel of Rotary in unison. Within the year, three more editions appeared touting US, British, and Canadian cooperation, followed by Edinburgh's own special edition in April 1914. The inclusion of British and Canadian clubs into Rotary's flagship publication reflected a key institutional as well as editorial choice: the Rotary club could not be limited to the celebration of the pioneer-citizens of the modern, industrial order in the United States. If Rotary's mission really did extend beyond the borders of the United States, then the "usable pasts" and origin myths of other nations would also need to be deployed—or at least recognized.

The year 1915 proved a critical turning point. Until the outbreak of war in Europe, there was no consensus on whether the IARC should focus on expanding from Great Britain into continental Europe or south into Latin America. Both views had strong internal support. But the decision to hold the annual convention of 1915 in San Francisco during the Panama-Pacific International Exposition tipped the balance in favor of Latin American expansion. It also helped that the Panama Canal had just opened for business and that Rotary clubs all over the nation actively lobbied their congressmen on behalf of the San Francisco club and its members' desire to bring the Exposition to the Bay Area.[63] Peppered throughout the *Rotarian* from 1913 until 1915 were advertisements for the International Exposition, sometimes paid for by San Francisco Rotarians themselves.[64] Calling the Exposition "a remarkable opportunity for us," the IARC's board of directors spent the week calling on "the representative men from South America . . . at the exhibits of their respective republics." By the fall of 1915, a special committee had formed dedicated to "extension work in non-English speaking countries and particularly in Latin America," and by April 1916 the first Rotary club in Latin America came together in Havana, Cuba. Within three years, Havana Rotarians sponsored new clubs in Santiago de Cuba (1918), Matanzas (1918), and Cienfuegos (1919), resulting in the establishment of a Rotary club in practically every Cuban city by the early 1930s. (Chapter 5 provides much greater detail about this history.)

By the time the United States entered the war in April 1917, Rotary had already been fostering its own brand of Anglo-American relations for five years, leaving only one possible ally in the war in the minds of many US Rotarians. The cover of the August 1917 edition of the *Rotarian,* for example, could easily have been produced by George Creel's Committee on Public Information. Designed by the Toronto Rotary club, the cover featured two soldiers towering over North America: a US and a Canadian soldier both in defensive posture with fixed bayonet staring across the Atlantic toward Europe with steely resolve. With a caption that read "Comrades in arms," the image left no doubt where the IARC stood on the war. By the war's conclusion, Rotary clubs had proven themselves to be solid contributors to the war effort, particularly adept at taking the lead on the Liberty Loan Drives in the United States, Cuba, and Canada. Moreover, the clubs' weekly luncheons were ideal venues for noted guest speakers from the US government and military and for the indefatigable "four minute men" of George Creel's Committee on Public Information.[65]

FIG 1.1: Creating the civic soul of a new service club through the alchemy of civil religion, the idealism of public service, and the celebration of a consumerist ethos. *Rotarian,* February 1915. *Courtesy of Rotary International.*

The advent of peace in Europe showed just as clearly in the *Rotarian*—now subtitled "The Magazine of Service." The hawkish theme of the Toronto club's cover from the previous year gave way in December 1918 to the appearance on the cover of the symbol of the International Red Cross and a warning to readers that "Reconstruction Problems Bring Greater Responsibilities." Though these views were not necessarily shared by all the rank and file, within the pages of Rotary's monthly publication one can easily follow the trajectory from the eager boosterism of "sturdy pioneers" and "Pittsburgh promotes progress" before 1917 to full-scale war mobilization, to the humanitarian internationalism of the Red Cross, and to a nation's call to rebuild a European continent ravaged by industrialized warfare. Already committed to international growth by 1912, the IARC had become fully enveloped not only in the war effort but in the emerging world of international nongovernmental organizations as well. Both boosterism, drenched in the mythical waters of rugged frontiersmen, and war mobilization, underscored by prewar economic and social ties with Canada and Great Britain as well as the power of US government propaganda, contributed significantly to the evolution and content of Rotary's civic internationalism during its formative years between 1910 and 1920. But along with the Red Cross symbol gracing the magazine's cover in late 1918 came a revealing reminder for readers: "JOIN: A Christmas duty to help mankind." With Armistice Day having been celebrated just weeks earlier, Rotary's flagship publication was already calling attention to the humanitarian dimensions of its burgeoning form of civic internationalism. Just as Rotarians had answered President Wilson's call to "make the world safe for democracy" in a time of war, so they were now being urged to join the "humanitarian awakening" in a time of peace.[66]

CREATING A CIVIC SOUL: SALESMANSHIP, SPIRITUALITY, AND CIVIL RELIGION

In addition to Rotary's embrace of Wilson's call to action and to the establishment of Rotary clubs beyond the Anglophone world during the war, there also emerged a complex mix of salesmanship and spirituality, of profits and prophets, in the iconography and rhetoric of Rotarians before 1918 that, in aggregate, began to function as its own brand of civil religion. Perhaps the most poignant expression of Rotary's new syncretism appeared on the cover of the *Rotarian* in February 1915 (figure 1.1).[67] In contrast to the overt boosterism of earlier editions of the *Rotarian*, this edition featured a striking and revealing front cover. Under the slogan "Rotary's Faith: International Peace & Goodwill" stand Jesus to the left, Abraham Lincoln to the right, and Florence Nightingale in the middle. Below these three figures one finds Rotary's first official motto: "He Profits Most Who Serves Best." First coined by

Arthur F. Sheldon, an early marketing and salesmanship "expert" from Chicago and later cofounder of the London Rotary club, the slogan was meant to sell the public on Rotary's authenticity as a "force for good" in the community and in the world. According to the motto, serving others—the community, the church, the nation—trumps the profit motive. Though Sheldon's "psychology of commerce" was hardly original to him, his particular brand of "scientized" selling mimicked the cadence and vocabulary of Newtonian physics to almost absurd lengths.[68] Why were Sheldon's views—and his motto—featured so prominently at Rotary conferences and conventions and official publications like the tenth-anniversary number of the *Rotarian*? What impact did Sheldon's popularity have on the crafting of RI's civic internationalism during Rotary's formative years?

As many historians have already pointed out, on the eve of the twentieth century, traveling salesmen, national advertisers, and public relations firms were anxious to distance themselves from the sordid reputations of hawkers, charlatans, and confidence men of the nineteenth century.[69] By the 1910s, businessmen of the new middle classes—many if not most Rotarians among them—were also struggling with the same problem. As we have already seen, there was a significant overlap in membership, rhetoric, and early growth of the American Association of Advertising Clubs and Rotary clubs.[70] In a similar vein, the very first Rotary clubs outside of Chicago appeared in San Francisco, Oakland, Los Angeles, and Seattle in 1908–1910 in large measure as a result of the interests and activities of highly mobile professionals in the emerging service economy. Revealingly, the second Rotary club in the world was founded in San Francisco in 1908 through the efforts of Manuel Muñoz, a lawyer and personal friend of Paul Harris in Chicago, who was then sent to the West Coast by his firm, and Homer Wood, another lawyer already based in San Francisco. Homer Wood and Arthur Holman, another founding member of the San Francisco club, then conspired to establish the third Rotary club in Oakland. But Rotary spilled out of the Bay Area thanks to Holman's trip to Seattle to attend the Alaska-Yukon-Pacific Exposition in 1909. As a general agent for the Travelers Insurance Company, Holman traveled between cities quite often. Upon arrival in Seattle for the exposition, Holman then proceeded to establish the fourth Rotary club in Seattle through his colleague at Travelers, Roy Denny, who then became the founder and first president of the Seattle club. The earliest Rotarians not only were seeking to legitimate their new, white-collar professions in the midst of rapid social and economic change through a new kind of civic club, but were also doing so through emerging sales routes, corporate links, and trade networks. In other words, the earliest Rotarians often lived, worked, and thought in terms of cities, not just their own city—a crucial development for Rotary and for that age.[71]

But Rotarians of this period went one step further than their contemporaries in the emerging fields of advertising, marketing, and public relations. Well before Sheldon's motto swept Rotary's second annual convention in Portland in 1911, there was a growing emphasis on "The Golden Rule of Business" as a way to temper criticism of Rotary clubs as merely vehicles for crass profiteering through business networking.[72] The Seattle club in particular pushed for the first detailed platform to which all original sixteen clubs of the National Association of Rotary clubs could point as a transcendent purpose for each city's Rotary club. By 1914, the motto "He profits most who serves best" had evolved into "The Holy Doctrine of Service," exceeding even the exemplary standards of customer service claimed at the time by AT&T and Wanamaker's.[73] Later that same summer at the annual convention in Houston, Russell Greiner of Kansas City, Rotary's incoming president, announced his vision for the coming year as if from a pulpit:

> A real Rotarian is a safe man for anyone to do business with. . . . Rotary is making men, it is a melting-pot and a cleansing crucible. Rotary is the Golden Rule of business. Its principles are those of the church. Its work is to lead men out of themselves into the noblest channels of existence. I know it is the truth, for through Rotary I have been instructed, encouraged and uplifted. . . . It takes no great flight of fancy to picture its effectiveness in the building of civic righteousness and the betterment of business.[74]

Greiner's sermon drew from a deep well of religious tropes and biblical allusions with no hint of apology, mixing a market-based scenario—

doing business with strangers—with the moralistic language of "civic righteousness" and the "Golden Rule of Business" to form a seamless narrative. The Rotary club's capacity to blur the lines between the private interests of its members and the public interest of each community had its counterpart in the rhetorical merger of economic citizenship and manly Christian virtue. The presence of Jesus on the cover of *Rotarian* in 1915 served just this purpose: Christian ethics and modern business were all of a piece.

But such imagery required text as well. If modern business practices were not anathema to Christianity—indeed, if capitalism itself were fundamentally the product of a Christian civilization—then there had to be a code to live by. In 1913, Glenn Mead challenged Rotary to develop its own professional code for businessmen, and in 1915 the 167 Rotary clubs of the IARC adopted their first official code of ethics at the San Francisco convention. However, despite the prevalence of lofty religious sentiment throughout Rotary literature at the time and the prayerful invocations given at countless weekly luncheons, there were no overt religious references in the code. Instead, the official code placed better business practices in a progressive, secular, and humanitarian language and in the form of a personal oath:

> My business standards shall have in them a note of sympathy for our common humanity. My business dealings, ambitions and relations shall always cause me to take into consideration my highest duties as a member of society . . . so when I have ended each of them I shall have lifted the level of human ideals and achievements a little higher than I found it.[75]

The official creed of the professional and reputable businessman, it turned out, did not require any explicit religious framework. With a code "founded on love" and neutral on "the present dispute in society between the Conservative and the Liberal," Rotary was beginning to develop a form of civil religion that was tentatively pluralist and tolerant in nature—at least in theory.[76]

And any civil religion comes with its attendant rituals: the pledge of allegiance, parades on national holidays, the commemoration of historical anniversaries, the building of public monuments, and so on. For all its claims of avoiding "partisan politics," Rotary clubs had already begun to signal their willingness to align with the national state well before the "war to end all wars." Rotarians were called to be not only good businessmen but also good patriots, especially in times of war. It would be hard to overstate the importance of Rotary's brand of civil religion not only during the 1910s, but ever since. For example, when President-elect Woodrow Wilson spoke on the meaning and purpose of "service" in 1913, the IARC was quick to point out the resonance of Wilson's words with the organization's own objectives:

> This is the solemnity that comes upon a man when he knows that he is about to be clothed with the responsibilities of a great example which America shall set to the world itself. The word that stands at the center of what has to be done is "service." The one thing that the businessmen of the United States are now discovering is . . . that they must render a service or get nothing; and that in the regulations of business the government . . . must determine whether what they are doing is a service or is not a service, and that everything in business and politics is going to be reduced to this standard. . . .
>
> I want to proclaim for my fellow citizens this gospel for the future, that the men who serve will be the men who profit.[77]

The editors at the *Rotarian* left no doubt as to why they wanted to feature Wilson's speech: "And Mr. Wilson might well have added the Rotary motto and said in conclusion, 'He Profits Most Who Serves Best.'" Though the relationship between Rotary, a private voluntary association, and the state could at times be ambiguous and contested, at other times the service club was more than happy to work hand in glove with government. Celebrating the words of President-elect Wilson in 1913 as if he were one of their own was mere prologue to the involvement of so many Rotary clubs in the Preparedness Movement and then especially in the war effort four years later. Given Rotary's rootedness in the nationalist fervor of the 1910s and the establishment of its own form of civil religion, the placement of Abraham Lincoln on the right side of the cover of the *Rotarian* in 1915 had its purpose as well.[78] Though nonpartisan in its original conception, the Rotary club left plenty of room for variations on patriotism and national pride.

Moreover, that Abraham Lincoln, such a divisive political figure from the nineteenth century, could be invoked in the early twentieth century as a symbol of national unity for almost 200 Rotary clubs spread throughout the United States was revealing enough. But given that more than 40 of those clubs—1 out of 5 clubs in the United States—were established in cities like Birmingham, Montgomery, Jackson, Atlanta, Richmond, Nashville, New Orleans, Dallas, and Houston, it was clear that the most important urban centers of the "New South" already had a significant presence in the IARC by 1916. The regional reconciliation of the North and the South in the Jim Crow era, forged out of the Compromise of 1877, affirmed by the Supreme Court in *Plessy v. Ferguson* (1896), and then sealed in the bloody jingoism of war with Spain in 1898, found expression as well in this new national network of Rotary clubs. As we shall see, the racial caste system of the United States informed the content of Rotary's civic internationalism much more than any Rotarian of the period would care to admit—or even imagine.

As a result, the religious and patriotic elements of Rotary's service ideology helped reconfigure the national mission of the United States at the dawn of the twentieth century from a rising world power to a righteous world leader. Much like the missionary impulse driving the internationalisms of the YMCA, the Women's Christian Temperance Union, the Salvation Army, and similar religious organizations, the civic internationalism of the Rotary club was built on the belief that its code of ethics was not only normative but also transformative for those who accepted it.[79] Only in Rotary's "world fellowship," conversion and redemption came through acceptance of professional codes and higher business standards. The "muscular Christianity" of Protestant evangelicalism had its counterpart in the modern, upright businessman and his code of ethics. Once Rotary clubs began to appear in China after 1919, however, RI took great pains to distinguish itself from missionary societies, given their stigma in the minds of many Chinese as well as international businessmen. When James Davidson, member of Rotary's extension committee and former consular agent in China before coming to Rotary (see Chapter 6), wrote to his fellow members of the committee in 1923 regarding the possibility of establishing a new club in Peking, he left no doubt about his primary concerns:

> No one, who has not lived in the Orient, can appreciate the intense hostility that there is towards the missionary; in fact he is more disliked by the white business community than he is by the Chinese. . . . At the same time, [Julean Arnold, commercial attache in Shanghai] understands the importance of keeping the Club there out of the hands of the missionary element. I admit that owing to the fact that missionaries are doing an outstanding work in higher education in Peking, and that the foreign trade community there are a higher type of men than the average resident of the treaty ports, still this feeling will exist even in Peking to the extent that would be bad for Rotary.[80]

For Davidson, maintaining a strategic distance from US-based missionary societies with a long history in China was just as important to Rotary's successful growth in China as avoiding any appearance that Rotary was merely an extension of the United States government and its propaganda—a point of concern in the founding of the Tokyo Rotary club some three years earlier.[81]

But the 1915 code of ethics was only the beginning. Guy Gundaker, a successful Philadelphia restaurateur, laid out the straight and narrow path of modern business practices in his presidential address to Rotary's annual convention in Toronto in 1924.[82] Opening with a quotation of Abraham Lincoln praying for divine guidance, he then explained:

> A world fellowship, while necessarily contingent on the extent and successful establishment of Rotary in all the nations of the world, is likewise contingent on the correctness of the standards of business practice of the men privileged to enter that fellowship.
>
> Until men meet on the common ground of correct business methods, there can be no world fellowship of business men. . . . The major Rotary activity for the immediate future will be an

increasing and unceasing activity for better business methods and their standardization in codes of ethics.[83]

To become a true professional and honest businessman through personal adoption of "correct and ethical standards of business" was the only way to enter Rotary's "world fellowship." For potential Rotarians outside the United States, however, participation in that fellowship was presented as an ethical choice, not an imperial imposition; an economic opportunity, not a colonial proposition; a civic duty, not a coercive act.

The idealism of Rotary's internationalist vision placed the growing influence of the United States in the world within a framework of humanitarian outreach, business civilization, and civic uplift. The expansion of the United States into markets the world over emerged over time as a moral imperative, since standardization of ethical codes and improvement of business methods on a global scale were merely commonsense goals and inevitable steps in the march of progress and civilization. After its first formulation in San Francisco in 1915, Rotary's Code of Ethics received great attention at the following year's convention in Cincinnati, resulting in a formal resolution from the business methods committee that each Rotarian strive for the establishment of updated standards of practice for their respective trades and crafts. By the early 1920s, the code had developed into a central theme of Rotary's weekly luncheon speeches through each club's "business methods committee" and the organization's constant stream of publications on the topic.

Guy Gundaker, the restaurateur from Philadelphia, led an in-house, exhaustive study of all existing professional and trade association codes with the goal of sifting out the best elements and incorporating them into an official and detailed code for all of its members—a kind of encyclopedia of "best practices" for the everyday businessman and professional and his local Rotary club. RI's pamphlet, *Codes of Standards of Correct Practice,* emerged from the process in 1924–1925 and became a template not only for many trade associations in the United States through the influence of Rotary's individual members in each association, but also for those in many non-US cities through translations of the codes.[84] Gundaker's vision of the associative state, anchored by professional codes of ethics, greatly informed international dialogue on this topic within the world of Rotary for much of the interwar period as Rotary International sought to carve out its brand of civic internationalism between the Christian internationalisms of missionary societies and the diplomatic missions and foreign policy of the US government.

In this light, Florence Nightingale's central role in the tenth-anniversary cover of the *Rotarian* takes on fuller meaning. In fact, as the central and dominant figure standing between Jesus and Abraham Lincoln, she completes the tableau in two important ways. First, her image suggests the many mission-oriented and humanitarian international organizations like the Red Cross, the YMCA, and the Boy Scouts of America that came before and worked side by side with Rotary, especially during and after World War I. Second, her character amplifies the sympathetic and sentimental dimensions of Rotary's civic internationalism in ways only a woman of her historic stature could. In particular, her presence softens the presumed hard-edged, no-nonsense masculinity of the marketplace much as Rotary's service ideology did. One Pittsburgh Rotarian took the sentiment to a whole new level:

> A new child of God has been born on Earth. Industry is his father, Justice his mother. By the holy bonds of love and a vow to be of mutual service were they united. And to them was born the child Rotary—dedicated to spread among men the divine qualities of Industry, Justice, and Unselfish Service, that humanity might gather the fruitful profits thereof.[85]

Hyperbole aside, the gendered figures of industry and justice brought together in a companionate model of marriage expressed the sense of new possibilities for social and community activism among businessmen now unburdened by traditional models of an aloof and distant father figure. The offspring of that union, naturally, was a boy.

A poignant example of this developing trend in the gendered imaginary of Rotarians appeared in a cartoon, "The New Road," in the *Rotarian* in 1923 (figure 1.2).[86] At a crossroads stands a woman dressed in a flowing gown that reads "Rotary Ethics." Before her stands a befuddled "Business Man," hat in hand and in clear need of direction on which way to go. The road sign offers only two options: "Service Above Self,"

FIG 1.2: The gendered dimensions of Rotary's service ideology were essential in establishing the legitimacy of modern business practices. *Rotarian,* May 1923, 266. *Courtesy of Rotary International.*

which leads down the sunlit path to the "Golden Rule: Fair Profit," or "Anything to Make Money," which leads past a "Closed" sign to a precarious bridge across a deep chasm. Lest there be any doubt as to the wickedness of the latter choice, the bridge is labeled in multiple ways: dishonesty, jealousy, selfishness, and greed. Though the woman is pointing the way to righteousness, it is the man who is in the position to decide what kind of marketplace relations to pursue as a future course and to act on that decision. Meanwhile, she remains fixed in place and above the fray. Women, no matter how much they were formally barred from membership in any Rotary club, were a key ideological component in the reimagining of RI's service ideology as a masculine way to perform in the marketplace as well as the home and the community.

Constructing manly forms of pity, charity, and sentimentality in the stern, unforgiving world of business depended on the incorporation of the feminine under the social trusteeship of "the representative businessmen of the community." The service ideology embedded within RI's civic internationalism opened up a complex reworking of gender identities in ways that updated and stabilized the relationship between masculinity, business, and community service while marginalizing the role of women as leaders in the community.

This new formulation of manly action on behalf of the community opened up an array of new possibilities for Rotary clubs after 1918. But probably the most common application of this new man-of-loving-action were club committees dedicated to "Boys' Work" and club activities celebrating Boys' Week. During the interwar period, these club activities came to dominate club programs, conference assemblies, and official publications in Rotary clubs all over the world. As common as it was for a Rotary club to collaborate with established organizations like the YMCA, the Red Cross, the chamber of commerce, and local schools and libraries, the Boy Scouts of America during the interwar years tended to receive the most attention—and likely the most dollars.[87] The immense popularity of Boys Work and Boys' Week across all parts of the Rotarian world by the 1920s revealed just how central—and transnational—this gendered conception of manly responsibilities toward the community had become. The responsibility of rearing of young boys into men was the social glue for much of Rotary's cross-cultural fraternalism.

Though Rotary's fraternalism led to new opportunities for the involvement of businessmen serving their community, it also came with a high price of admission: no women allowed. As noted earlier, since the first convention in 1910, women were kept formally absent despite their pervasive presence in the social world of Rotary. When the wives of top Chicago Rotarians proposed the formation of "Women's Auxiliary Units of Rotary Clubs" in 1921, for example, the board responded in a manner consistent with earlier rejections of similar proposals: "If we should permit the name 'Rotary' to be used by this organization there would undoubtedly follow a rapid spread of the idea. This might develop problems and complications that would prove very serious to Rotary."[88] Proprietary concerns over use of the term "Rotary" papered over deeper concerns over the defense of Rotary's fraternalism and its prerogatives. That same year, the bar to admission was formalized at Rotary's twelfth annual convention in Edinburgh, Scotland—the first of many annual conventions held outside the United States—through the adoption of a standard club constitution and bylaws. In article III, section 3 of the now-standard club constitution stipulated that "any adult male of good character and good business reputation, engaged as proprietor, partner, corporate officer or manager of any worthy and recognized business . . . may be eligible to membership." Gone were any ambiguities over the possibilities of women becoming members of any Rotary club in the world. Embedded within Rotary's service ideology was a gendered division of labor that barred women from club membership even as their contributions and presence remained in high demand. Revealingly, the same standard constitution that formally asserted male-only membership also removed any direct reference to racial requirements. Just as "white" was removed from membership requirements in the standard constitution in 1921—a particular cause for concern in all new clubs in the Jim Crow South—"male" became the most fundamental requirement for membership. Many wives and daughters of Rotarians were thus drafted into club life through auxiliary organizations, often functioning under the informal label of "Rotary Anns" or more formal organizations like Women of Rotary (based in Chicago). Though limited in their membership only to women who had a direct relationship with a Chicago Rotarian and kept within the organizational structure of the Chicago Rotary club, Women of Rotary nevertheless carved out an impressive record in philanthropic activities for decades to come, serving as a template for similar women's auxiliaries throughout the country.[89] But for all their charitable causes and philanthropic initiatives, Women of Rotary remained an adjunct to Rotary One. In contrast, women affiliated with British Rotary took a different path, culminating in the formation of The Inner Wheel in Great Britain in 1924. Born out of wartime necessity and founded by a professional nurse, Margarette Oliver (née Owen), The Inner Wheel charted its own institutional trajectory, evolving into something much more than an auxiliary organization within British Rotary. As a result, The Inner

Wheel has evolved into a large and growing international service club in its own right.[90]

Though the constitution required gendered discrimination after 1921, that discrimination clearly went much deeper than whether women were formally recognized or not by Rotary's constitution and bylaws. Put simply, as the cartoon from the *Rotarian* demonstrates, women were not permitted formal membership status in Rotary—either as individuals or as independent clubs—because their equality of station in the world of business was not imaginable. A key component of RI's crystallization of its rules and regulations in the wake of World War I was the delineation and enforcement of this gendered imaginary in ways that proved appealing and, indeed, essential to RI's civic internationalism. Men joining with men from around the world had its international appeal as RI's service ideology allowed them to forge a common commitment to a managerial and professional approach to charitable endeavors and community service from the local to the international.[91]

As an ideological triptych, the frontispiece of the tenth-anniversary edition of the *Rotarian* turns out to be far greater than the sum of its parts. Taken as a whole, the image provides a moral and narrative framework in which not only Rotary clubs but the United States as a nation appear as an unfolding force for good. American civic and religious virtues were ready for presentation to an international audience. The juxtaposition of Jesus Christ, Abraham Lincoln, and Florence Nightingale reinforced the preferred narrative of the United States as a moral, civic, and humanitarian presence in the world even as Rotary clubs enabled the expansion of US corporate interests into foreign markets. To paraphrase one of the best cultural historians of corporate capitalism, the tenth-anniversary magazine cover—like Rotary's entire service ideology—created a civic soul.[92] The benevolent inclusion of non-US business and professional elites into the fold would only serve to confirm the world historical mission of "the commercial square deal" that was the calling of the United States in the aftermath of the Great War. A more Wilsonian view of international engagement would have been hard to find.

Or could it? The year before Arch Klumph's rousing speech at the Kansas City convention in 1918, when he called for "the establishment of a great international friendship—the worldwide inoculation of the virus [of war] by the principle of service, not self," Klumph delivered his inaugural speech to the thousands of conventioneers in Atlanta in June 1917. Amid the patriotic parades and rhetorical flourishes of wartime solidarity on the part of Rotarians and most citizens of Atlanta, Klumph announced something rather unwarlike: the formation of "a future endowment fund for Rotary." Given Rotary's commitment to community service, he argued, Rotary should:

> accept endowments for the purpose of doing good in the world, in charitable, educational or other avenues of community progress; or such funds could be well used for extension work. I know of no more commendable use for the vast millions possessed by men in this country than that certain sums might be endowed to Rotary for the purpose of establishing Rotary clubs in all the nations of the world.[93]

Initially lost in the wartime fervor and summer heat of Atlanta, Klumph's call for the creation of a Rotary endowment began to take shape with the creation of the Rotary Foundation in 1928, leading to donations to the International Society for Crippled Children and the creation of the Institutes for International Understanding during the 1930s. As a result of a change in tax laws for personal donations in 1945; the passing of Paul Harris, Rotary's founder, in 1947; and the creation of Paul Harris Fellowships in 1957, the Rotary Foundation began to amass significant funds in the postwar era, making possible the establishment of its Ambassadorial Scholarship program in 1947, Group Study Exchanges in 1965, the 3-H (Health, Hunger, and Humanity) grant programs in 1978, the PolioPlus vaccination program in 1985, the Global Polio Eradication Initiative in 1988, the Rotary Peace Centers in 1999, partnership with the Bill & Melinda Gates Foundation in 2007, the International H2O Collaboration with USAID in 2009, and too many other ongoing initiatives to name here. The PolioPlus program alone raised almost $247 million between 1985 and 1988 while more than thirty thousand students participated in the Foundation's Scholarship program for more than half a century (this author included).[94] And this was only the Rotary

Foundation's growth and achievements. Meanwhile, Rotary International itself continued to grow over the twentieth century, and sometime in the 1970s a majority of its 1.2 million members began to be drawn from outside the United States. With 35,000-plus clubs in more than two hundred countries in 2020, RI has managed to carry out its Progressive-era vision of civic internationalism to a surprising degree.[95]

For the past century, it has been all too easy for historians to dismiss Wilsonianism as a failed vision for securing and maintaining international peace. And for good reason. Like virtually all statesmen of his day, Wilson saw the world through the eyes of white supremacy. As many postcolonial elites worldwide came to discover, "self-determination" was highly contingent upon racial categories of fitness for self-government. As we will see in the next chapter, Rotary struggled with white supremacy as well, both at home and abroad. Moreover, much like Rotary at the time, Wilson's managerial worldview was unabashedly paternalistic. Finally, with the meteoric rise and fall of the League of Nations in US domestic politics and eventually in the international arena with the outbreak of yet another global war, Wilsonianism evolved into one of several cautionary tales that formed the ideological core of cold war internationalism. Serious consideration of the evolution and contributions of INGOs like Rotary International in aggregate, however, as examples of Wilsonianism without the state, frees historians from the myopia of postwar historical revisionism on the interwar period and state-centered historical narratives of the twentieth century. Rotary's civic internationalism was—and still remains—one of many alternative internationalisms that emerged out of the early twentieth century and are still thriving today.

2

NO FOREIGNERS ALLOWED

The World Meets Main Street

In the midst of the Great Depression, Rotary International chose to hold its twenty-sixth annual convention in Mexico City in late June 1935. Though it was the fifth convention that RI had held outside the United States since 1910, it was the first RI convention that could be reached by both train and automobile, resulting in more than 5,300 registrants. Hosting so many visitors was an enormous undertaking on the part of the Mexico City Rotary club and the thirty-four Rotary clubs of Mexico, requiring the orchestration of twenty-seven special trains to and from the nation's capital, which became known as "Pullman City."[1] Though Lions International, Rotary's main competitor outside the United States, also hosted its annual convention in Mexico City that same year and even managed to have Amelia Earhart, an honorary Lions member, fly in for a guest appearance, the Lions' presence had nowhere near the impact that the Rotary convention had.[2]

Two of the most astounding spectacles of the convention centered on the women of Mexico. The first was a "Fería Ranchera" for "more than a thousand of the visiting ladies" who were "guests of the ladies of the Rotary Club of Mexico City" being entertained by "some three score señoritas in their fiesta costumes." But the second spectacle went to a whole other level, offering up an "historical pageant . . . with three thousand people in costumes of the different epochs in Mexico's history." As guests of the nation of Mexico, the visiting Rotarians and their spouses occupied the front rows of the stadium where the pageant was held, while the rest of the stadium filled up with about twenty-five thousand Mexicans there to see "groups from different parts of the country [who] were brought to the capital to portray the historical scenes of their native region."[3] This event operated on multiple levels of meaning and exchange, of production and consumption of spectacle: thousands of Rotarians from outside Mexico "taking in" this "foreign land" and its peoples and customs, Mexican Rotarians looking to establish their city and their country's reputation in the minds of so many international businessmen and their wives, Mexican citizens participating in the pageantry of their own nation-making moment, the Mexican state seeking to define itself over and above its regional diversity, and Mexican women in native costume entertaining the wives and daughters of visiting Rotarians. And all of this was taking place because Rotary International had come to town.

Much like the modern Olympiad, the pageantry of this kind of international event had evolved into a whole new level of sophistication during the interwar period. And year after year, Rotary International was on the vanguard of this trend. But what distinguished Rotary's pageants and conventions from so many comparable international events and organizations of the period, I argue, was RI's particular reliance on an imagined transnational community of businessmen whose equality stemmed from their individual success in the marketplace, their adoption of a professional ethos, their dedication to the uplift of their community, and their elite status within their local business community. Bounded by their shared class status, their clubs' fraternalism, and their embrace of their own national identities, few Rotarians were true cosmopolitans—however well-traveled and worldly they might have been. But within the "world fellowship" of Rotary International, they performed in the role of exotic peers: businessmen and professionals from all over the world with a common devotion to some form of global capitalism as well as some form of open society. For them, both nation-states and international markets constituted the natural order of things. Put simply, these men were adherents of Rotary's civic internationalism.

One notable adherent, Armando de Arruda Pereira of São Paulo, Brazil, spoke on the third day of the convention at the International Service Round Table, which was attended by hundreds of Rotarians from around the world. Much like the other members leading the roundtable discussion, Pereira was a rising star in Rotary because he was already a rising star in his native country. In fact, Brazil's ambassador to Mexico was seated next to Pereira when he stood to speak about his country, with its five thousand miles of coastline and "an area larger than the United States without Alaska." After reciting the history of Rotary in Brazil—the first club was established in Rio de Janeiro in 1922, and the organization's presence had grown to thirty-two clubs by 1935—and citing the importance of "friendship, good ethics in business . . . and good will between people of different professions, religions, and races," Pereira pointed out that "before the advent of Rotary in [his] country, the general rule of admitting a person in a club was that he should be of the same political creed." From Pereira's perspective, "the foundation of Rotary clubs in several localities made it possible for foreign residents . . . to collaborate with the nationals," resulting in "several benefits for the people, for the towns and for the country, and specially from the international point of view, for universal peace."[4] Educated in Italy, England, and the United States, Pereira also served as a member of several Brazilian trade associations, as mayor of São Paulo, and as vice president of a tile manufacturer. Pereira thus embodied the fullest possibilities of international travel, education, and business during the interwar period. His membership and leadership of the São Paulo Rotary club (and of all Brazilian clubs by 1935) only added to his internationalist credentials in the eyes of his fellow Brazilians as well as fellow Rotarians. There were many compelling reasons for Pereira to speak on Rotary's civic internationalism at this roundtable in Mexico City.

Though Pereira presented a strong case for the power of Rotary "to gather men of different religious and political creeds . . . to bring about benefits to the locality, the state, and the country where they lived," how accurate was his depiction of Rotary's "world fellowship"? In what ways did the "global color line" undermine and complicate Pereira's rosy picture of international comity? What did Rotary's expansion worldwide reveal about the relationship between global capitalism and racism?

Although Pereira was able to straddle the world of Brazilian politics and international business in his own career, how did Rotary International manage to walk the line between states and markets—especially in a time of Great Depression, trade blocs, protectionism, and open warfare? Or was that even possible under those conditions? This chapter considers these questions in light of the most basic unit of Rotary's civic internationalism—the "world fellowship of businessmen" committed to international peace and understanding—and its primary constituent, the exotic peers of international club life.

AT THE CORNER OF STATE AND MAIN

There was a dual legitimation process unfolding within Rotary clubs in the United States before the 1920s that reflected broader national and economic challenges: business struggled to redefine itself in professional, progressive, and humanitarian terms while the nation sought to reinvent its own identity and purpose before a new array of international pressures and colonial possessions. The standardization and codification of business practices at local, state, and national levels not only accelerated integration of US national markets and a deeper sense of middle-class identity across state lines but also introduced strains of Wilsonian rhetoric of uplift and moral purpose to the modernization of business well before the elections of 1912. With the growing demand for regulation of market excesses, especially after the Panic of 1907, came increasing disenchantment with the businessman as an independent and self-interested actor struggling to survive among cutthroat competitors. As a result, Rotary's sense of mission in service to the world, though wedded to familiar notions of limited state oversight, carried as well quasi-religious commitments to civic improvement, philanthropic duty, and material progress that, in sum, promised to counterbalance the human cost of rapid changes and deep inequities endemic to unregulated market competition. The rehabilitation of the US businessman as a middle-class champion of a more progressive and abundant tomorrow paralleled and contributed to the construction of the United States as a benevolent, civilizing force abroad during the Progressive Era. Insofar as the chaotic streets and shockingly inhumane business practices in American cities like Chicago were "cleaned up" in the name of greater efficiency and social responsibility, the claim that the United States had something of substance to offer the world in the way of a modern business civilization became more compelling. Put another way, economic expansion of the United States beyond its borders increasingly required a more compelling moral narrative than "caveat emptor," the cruelties of social Darwinism, or the condemnation of "the other half" living in terrible poverty. As a result, Rotary's "national movement" of business and professional men committed to the improvement of their cities and communities proved a valuable contributor to the construction of that new moral narrative. But the borderlines between Rotary—a private, voluntary association and nonprofit organization—and both the state and the marketplace were a work in progress from the organization's inception. And where those lines were drawn had great import on the evolution of Rotary's civic internationalism.

Though membership in a Rotary club hinged upon one's business reputation in the marketplace, Rotary's expansion outside the United States was, from the start, much more than a secondary effect of US corporate penetration of new markets abroad. Rotary's ideological and institutional adaptations to the pervasive distrust of business activities at the dawn of the twentieth century—distrust of monopolies and big business, on the one hand, and of the slipperiness of salesmen and the shoddy work of nonprofessionals, on the other—centered on the establishment of Rotary's nonprofit status, the development of its language of civic engagement and community service, and the cultivation of its reputation of true professionalism and nonpartisanship. In short, the moral heft of Rotary's service ideology hinged on its organizational status as both a nonstate and nonmarket actor as well as its balancing act between the Bourbon and Barnumesque extremes of American business.

And so, by extension, did Rotary's civic internationalism. One of the most crucial innovations of Rotary as it rapidly evolved into an international movement after 1910 was learning how to position itself with a strategic distance from the US government as well as from any one US corporation or industry. If Rotary was to have any success in establishing clubs outside the United States, and especially outside the

Anglophone world, then it absolutely had to define itself and its members as independent from both US national interests and US commercial interests. For a service club built on the celebration of its members' success in the marketplace, this was not an easy task. Probably the earliest test for Rotary as an international organization arose when the newly formed London Rotary club was considering whether to affiliate formally with the US clubs in 1911 or assert its own independence. When the club wrote the newly formed headquarters of the National Association of Rotary Clubs in Chicago asking why the club should affiliate, the initial response focused on the economic advantages from developing "inter-city trade" and the irrelevance of the club's origins in the United States: "Just forget the word 'National' is in the name . . . If Winnipeg and London and Manchester and a few more cities outside of the States come into the Association, it will simply have to change its name to the Inter-national Association."[5] In the minds of the Chicago Rotarians, becoming "international" was a rather pragmatic, almost ad hoc matter. But in the minds of the Londoners, this was a serious concern.

The new headquarters for the National Association of Rotary Clubs downplayed the national origins of its organization from its inception in 1910 and chose, instead, to highlight the benefits of deepening intercity trade relations and to deploy these as a template for international relations: "From a recent visit to Omaha and Lincoln, Nebraska we learned that these two cities have been drawn closer together in friendship since the establishment of Rotary Clubs of these cities. May it not be so with our two great nations?"[6] Contrary to the popular imagery of the period, the common ground between the Chicago and London Rotary clubs was not couched in the language of shared Anglo-Saxon racial identity. The clubs' vision was not one of Uncle Sam and John Bull joining hands in global rule. To be sure, bonds between US, Canadian, and British Rotarians were easier to imagine and establish than with other nations because of imagined Anglo-Saxon solidarities; however, concerns on both sides of the Atlantic were more mundane—and more ambitious—than the deepening of racial kinship. Rather, the focus lay in the inexorable logic of thickening trade relations built on cooperation and a managerial, professional competence that transcended political and national identities. The rational growth and guidance of the markets should trump all other differences—at least in theory. Though separated by distinct national identities and the North Atlantic, still, the Chicago and London clubs were ultimately just two cities—like Omaha and Lincoln—developing closer trade links and greater understanding "in friendship" through ever-thickening business and social networks. Rotary simply meant to smooth the way, to rationalize the process. In the end, the basic unit of Rotary was understood to be the city first, not the nation.[7] The focus on inter-city trade relations enabled the denial of empire.

Yet the marketplace had its pitfalls and dangers. The London club was not entirely convinced by the Chicago office's reasons for joining. Founded through the particular efforts of Arthur Sheldon, the self-styled purveyor of the science of salesmanship from the United States mentioned earlier, the London club wanted evidence that "the National Association [was] not a money making institution"—that the London club would, in fact, be engaging in a burgeoning international movement among businessmen and professionals with goals genuinely loftier than the mere collection of dues from members and application of the slick bromides of new sales techniques imported from America. The response from the founder of the original Rotary club in Chicago, Paul Harris, was direct: "The National Association is not at all a money making concern, it is incorporated under our laws relating to 'Corporations not for pecuniary profit,' nor is it in any indirect manner, an institution of profit." Harris, a lawyer by trade, touted the nonprofit status of the organization as being incorporated according to "our laws" in the state of Illinois and as absolute proof that Rotary stood for something greater than mere "money making."[8] Their fears assuaged, the London Rotarians voted unanimously to affiliate with the soon-to-be international association of Rotary clubs and follow the lead of its headquarters in Chicago by defining their new club as "the Rotary Club FOR London and not OF London."[9] The following year, one of the London club's delegates to the convention in Duluth announced: "We come as students to this great country of the United States, to learn something about Rotary, and it is up to you, my friends and brethren, to see that we go back live, red-hot missionaries."[10] As London went in 1911–1912, so thousands of cities and towns throughout the world have gone ever since. Rotary's marketing pitch about being a nonprofit for reticent Londoners proved a useful means of recruitment in subsequent international expansion, while the disavowal of profit-seeking enhanced the legitimacy of American-style capitalism.

But the nonprofit status of Rotary went only so far and meant only so much. When it came to developing a coherent plan of expansion into Latin America after 1915, the organization first relied on enterprising US members traveling abroad on business to seek out opportunities for new clubs and report back their successes and failures in their efforts to "spread Rotary among the native peoples of other countries more than among our American brethren who happen to be in other countries."[11] The approach, however, was ad hoc until 1915, when the first concerted effort at "extension" of Rotary clubs began with the Pan-Pacific Exposition in San Francisco in 1915. The IARC planned to work through "representative men of South America" who were expected to attend. The international convention for Rotary, in fact, was held in San Francisco that year to take advantage of international contacts at the Exposition.[12]

Rotary's activities at the Pan-Pacific Exposition led to the creation of the Committee on Extension of Rotary in Latin America in 1916, which began working with and through the foreign departments of specific corporations already looking to expand their Latin American operations, including National City Bank, Singer Sewing, the Waterman Pen Co., National Cash Register, Metropolitan Life, Underwood Typewriter, and Wurlitzer of Cincinnati.[13] When one US corporate agent in Buenos Aires informed the Extension Committee that Argentina, Brazil, and Uruguay were not ready for new clubs despite his efforts to "instill the Rotary spirit," the first-ever chairman of Rotary's extension committee, John Turner, was undaunted, announcing to the thousands attending Rotary's annual convention in Atlanta in 1917 that "the greatest opportunity for Rotary is at the present time in South America. . . . We have got to find a man who is in sympathy and has the viewpoint of Latin America."[14] The United States had only just declared war on Germany some nine weeks before. Amid the patriotic ebullience at the Atlanta convention was the recognition of a business opportunity. Rotary's top administrators, like those of Rotary's corporate allies, knew an emerging market when they saw one. The only real questions focused on identifying the most effective means to establishing new clubs in Latin America and how to pay for that expansion. Building up a nonprofit organization's international branches challenged Rotary's administrative capacities and cost money. Fortunately, the good offices of many US corporations were more than available.

National Cash Register (NCR) was particularly eager to help. After initially experiencing a cold indifference to the establishment of a Rotary club in Caracas, Venezuela, in 1917, several US businessmen visited John H. Patterson, NCR's president, "with the idea of having Rotary taught to his foreign representatives as they visited Dayton." Patterson, who had played a major role at the prior year's convention in Cincinnati and had his own particular version of morally responsible capitalism, was glad to help out. A special committee of the Dayton Rotary Club took up the training of "these National Cash Register men in Rotary" in order to "form a splendid nucleus for work in Latin America."[15] Though the actual results from NCR's pairing up with Rotary in its expansion into Latin America was never well documented, the alliance of specific US corporations with the growth of Rotary had already found its precedent before the entrance of the United States into World War I. And more alliances were to come as city after city in Latin America found itself with its own Rotary club over the coming decades. By and large, the greater the presence of US corporations in Latin America, the more likely the growth and success of a city's Rotary club. Despite the fundamental differences between a private, transnational corporation like NCR and an international nonprofit like the International Association of Rotary Clubs (IARC, until 1922), the synergy for both was undeniable.

Years before the turn to the foreign departments of corporations for help in international growth, the IARC also looked to the federal government as a possible ally in their national aspirations. The question was what kind of relationship Rotary would develop with the state over time. And the answer was not at all clear in 1912, when one of the most critical national debates on banking and currency reforms took place, ultimately leading to the creation of the Federal Reserve System. Given the central importance of the debate, Rotary's convention in Duluth in 1912 featured Robert Bonynge of Denver, former US congressman, member of the national monetary commission, and representative of the National Citizens League, as a keynote speaker. After schooling the conventioneers on the nature of banking as an industry in the United States, how all other industries depended on the soundness and efficiency of banking, how the old system was open to the whims of speculation on Wall Street, how the "scattered units" of the banking system led to a reliance on foreign banks for stability in times of crisis, and how the "inelasticity" of the credit system undermined the US dollar in general, Bonynge concluded: "We need some institution clothed with proper powers to discharge those duties. They cannot be performed by any local banking institution for profit. Those duties are national in character and the institution to perform them must likewise be of a national character."[16] Working through the National Citizens League, Bonynge was given access to as many Rotary clubs as he could attend to deliver his message that only the federal government of the United States, not the speculators on Wall Street, could guarantee structure and stability for the US banking industry and, by extension, all other industries both at home and abroad.

Bonynge found a receptive audience among the Rotarians in 1912 because their conception of a private, voluntary association did not preclude selective uses of the state like those proposed by Bonynge. To be sure, discussion of any entity that could provide stability in the national banking system in 1912 was welcome at a weekly Rotary club luncheon. In many ways, Rotary clubs were already beginning to do something similar themselves at the state, local, and municipal levels as Rotary's Committee on Public Affairs reported the pressing need to support legislation on the National Highway System and National Water Ways.[17] Regulation by the state—and debates over how and when regulation might be employed—was hardly taboo for even the earliest wave of Rotary clubs. When it was a question of better management of macroeconomic structures and improvement of transportation and communications systems, the state had its place and the Rotary club—from local to national in scale—would gladly consider how the state might best act and lend Rotarians' support. Whether one supported Theodore Roosevelt's New Nationalism or Woodrow Wilson's New Freedom in the 1912 election, the building up of America's business civilization required the support of a responsible state free of corruption and capable of reining in the trusts; that much was clear. This strategic approach to both the state and to marketplace actors, already adopted at Rotary's first international convention in 1912, set the stage for successive generations. From the perspective of the earliest Rotary clubs, therefore, state-enabled economic and infrastructure development were never seen as a political—that is, "partisan"—matter. For the world of business, as for Rotary, the state had its uses—but preferably from a distance.

Though in constant evolution over the course of the entire history of Rotary International, the administrative structure of the organization has generally reflected this same strategy of keeping the state at arm's length. Starting with "Rotary One" in 1905, the basic unit of Rotary has always been the individual member of a Rotary club that represents a specific city or portion / neighborhood of a city. Even in 2020, the governance of each club still hinges on the annual rotation of the club president and vice-president, thus guaranteeing a constant churn within each club's administrative ranks and the opportunity for each club's members to ascend within the club's ranks over time should they choose to do so. Particularly before World War II, the day-to-day administrative duties would usually fall to the club secretary, who would remain in that position sometimes for many years or even decades, thus providing crucial "institutional memory" and administrative continuity for each club over time.[18] Before the 1930s, continuity was invaluable as clubs tended to form a wide range of committees tasked with a variety of goals ranging from "promotions" and "publications" committees unabashedly devoted to boosterism, to "Boys Work," "Girls Work," and many other charitable community endeavors. Consequently, when attending any annual convention, Rotarians were identified primarily by their individual classification, club, and city; secondarily, by any roles or positions they held within their club; and then by membership in the organization as a whole.

But another organizational layer emerged during the 1910s that still remains just as important to the administrative infrastructure in 2020 as it did one hundred years ago: the Rotary district. Usually comprising about twenty to fifty clubs and administered by a "district governor" elected on a regular basis like the club president, the district and its annual conferences became an essential connective tissue within the structure and evolution of Rotary, linking each local club with Rotary as a regional and worldwide movement. Most relevant for this discussion is that, in contrast to probably most voluntary associations of the period and even today, the district emerged out of the model of "sales territories" during the 1910s rather than as a replication of preexisting state and national structures. For an organization centered on the market-based identities of its members and clubs, moving in this direction was a logical choice. However, by the 1920s, as Rotary clubs began appearing throughout the world, national, imperial, and international borders loomed large. Before the 1922 annual convention, however, it was still possible for Rotary clubs to form their own national or "territorial" units within Rotary, a familiar organizational model for nonprofits based on membership. The only national unit that formed during this period under these terms, however, was Rotary International in Great Britain and Ireland (RIBI). Though in nations like Japan, Cuba, Australia, and Italy, Rotary districts eventually formed that were isomorphic with national borders, after 1922, Rotary International's organizational development stayed true to its original emphasis on the individual Rotarian, club, and district as the organization's primary building block.[19] For higher levels of organization, RI instead began forming advisory committees such as the Canadian or European Advisory Committees or regional units of cooperation while building out RI's own committee structures—such as the extension committee and business methods committee—responsible for streamlining, stabilizing, and standardizing club activities, bylaws, procedures, membership credentials, and so on. Just as each club had its rotation of president and vice presidents as well as an evolving structure of various committees, so did Rotary International—a form of governance sometimes state-like in organization but emphatically not beholden to nor rooted in any one city, state, or national unit. The neutrality of RI's civic internationalism evolved around this core identity and has remained faithful to it ever since.[20]

But maintaining a distance from the state during a time of war proved surprisingly difficult. The period of greatest overlap between the state and US Rotary clubs came, not surprisingly, during the Great War. As with many voluntary organizations, Rotary clubs fell under the power of patriotic fervor unleashed by the war effort. By July 1917, Rotary had pledged to work with the Red Cross through support "in the educating, the giving, the organizing, the soliciting"; to help the Boy Scout movement, since so many scoutmasters were enlisting; to "provide business capability, influence and money for the Y.M.C.A., the Y.W.C.A., and the corresponding Hebrew societies"; and to guarantee that the US Army would have "the finest moral tone in the history of armies" by providing "wholesome recreation" in government training camps and to keep "vice from preying" upon soldiers in training.[21] But it fell to A. M. Briggs, established member of the Chicago Rotary club and president of the A. M. Briggs Co., which specialized in poster advertising, to merge the national network of Rotary clubs with wartime censorship by the US government, taking Rotary's wartime support to an unprecedented degree. While on a business trip in New York City, Briggs "became imbued with the idea that Rotary could play a part in protecting our government from insidious propaganda and damage and loss of life" through German espionage. Briggs then contacted Chesley Perry, general secretary of the IARC in Chicago and fellow Chicago club member, and sold him on the idea. With Perry's consent, Briggs went to Washington, D.C., and spoke with Attorney General Thomas Gregory and eventually President Woodrow Wilson. With their support, Briggs "wired Perry that the idea had been sanctioned and asked Perry to gather a small group of Chicago Rotarians to put his ideas into action."[22]

The American Protective League (APL) emerged as a private, national organization for the quashing of political dissent and labor "unrest" in a time of war. Led by Chicago Rotarians, the IARC became an active supporter of the US government's propaganda and surveillance apparatus.[23] About a dozen Chicago Rotarians, guided by Hinton G. Clabaugh, division superintendent of the Department of Justice's bureau of investigation in Chicago, wasted no time. Meeting on a Sunday at the Clark Street office of Bill Kier, another Chicago Rotarian, the group wired "Rotary clubs throughout the United States explaining the idea, and within 36 hours there were more than 200 organizations in the field. Many Chicago Rotarians acted as officers and privates in the Chicago branch of the American Protective League."[24]

While the APL specialized in "slacker raids" against idle men in public suspected of being draft dodgers, the organization and its 250,000 auxiliaries also joined in the persecution of labor organizations during the war, but particularly the Industrial Workers of the World (IWW).[25] The squelching of wartime dissent served the state as well as business interests, united in common cause by Chicago Rotarians who understood well the power of networking and propaganda and the advantages of blurring the public-private divide: "its ultimate success as an element in the elimination and apprehension of dangerous characters, insidious propaganda, and destruction of property and life was due largely to the manner in which it was organized and the energy and speed with which it was carried on."[26] Given the ambiguous legal status of the APL, the wartime alliance between the IARC and the US government did not last beyond 1919. But the Rotary club's notion of "community service," it turned out, could serve as a powerful weapon in the US government's battle against the IWW and labor internationalism more generally. Though Rotary's commitment to the defense and growth of a capitalist society was never in question from its inception, Rotary International showed its greatest willingness to accommodate and even learn from socialism and communism as competing economic and political systems, not surprisingly, during the Great Depression.[27]

The ambiguous boundaries between the state and the markets served many strategic purposes abroad as well. At times, the inevitability of increasing market ties across borders and oceans proved the most compelling argument for Rotary's growing presence outside the United States. The presumed mutuality of economic growth and rationality of corporate capitalism took on an air of managerial authority without reference to any one nation or national agenda. This was a crucial facet of Rotary's international expansion. Harry Wheeler—first president of the US Chamber of Commerce (established 1912) and an old friend of Paul Harris, founder of the original Chicago Rotary club in 1905 and Wheeler's colleague at the Chicago Association of Commerce—predicted that Rotary would "benefit not only this country of ours in a business way, but, as you extended your own influence to foreign shores, that like benefits would come to those countries where you might extend your principles."[28] Rotary's extension was a matter of business principles, not nationalist aspirations; of efficient management techniques, not mere partisanship. In this vein, Rotary could position itself as mediator between Chicago and London, Tampa and Havana, Dayton and Caracas, New York City and Montevideo.[29] "Take a strong Rotary club, say in Germany, and take a strong Rotary organization in England. Those Rotarian clubs combine the best moral and intellectual men of their respective cities and countries. Do you think that, if they would alike put out their splendid strength, you are going to have millions a year wasted in useless armaments?" queried a British Rotarian in 1913.[30] The question, of course, went from rhetorical to tragically ironic within a year.

At other times, the nonstate and nonmarket status of the organization enabled RI to present itself—and, by extension, its local clubs and members—as above the market fray. Service to the community was not a mere business opportunity; it was a higher calling for an enlightened leadership and an act of love on behalf of the community. Founded in 1912, the same year as the Better Business Bureau and the US Chamber of Commerce, the International Association of Rotary Clubs was ideologically more akin to the former but functionally more akin to the latter. After all, from its earliest iterations, Rotary clubs were often expected to overlap in membership with the local chambers of commerce. But Rotary was carving out a middle ground that over time became institutionally stable thanks to the nonprofit status of the organization and ideologically flexible because of its remoralization of business in professional, nonpartisan, and paternalist terms. In multiple ways, the organization welcomed better regulation of emerging national and international markets, conformity to the interests of corporate capitalism, and the demands of patriotic fervor—a combination with little tolerance for revolutionary movements of any kind, but especially for labor activism, "bolshevism," and social unrest. As a result, on both the domestic and international fronts, there was little ideological daylight between the Wilsonian administration and the IARC: the managerial worldview of liberal internationalism was their moral compass. On the question of race, however, would both Wilson and Rotary also speak the same language?

NO FOREIGNERS ALLOWED?

In 1921, the Chicago Office of the IARC renamed the Foreign Extension Committee simply the Extension Committee. Over protests from British

Rotarians, the US committee members believed the adjective "foreign" was inconsistent with Rotary's international mission. According to the logic of the US side, there were no "foreigners" per se, only business and professional counterparts in portions of the world that still happened to fall outside the purview of Rotary's "world fellowship"; it was only a matter of time before they received their own personal invitations to the new dispensation.[31] Meanwhile, all those who were already within the purview of the "world fellowship" were, by definition, colleagues and peers—regardless of race, creed, or nationality. In pursuing its idealized counterparts, the international service club was actively working out administrative routines through its Extension Committee for surveying new towns, cities, countries, and even entire regions of the world for potential new clubs by the early 1920s. When the committee agreed upon its basic principles for international expansion in 1925, it summarized its approach:

> In extending Rotary, Rotarians may be likened to salesmen selling an idea or missionaries preaching a gospel; and a good salesman does not give up because at first his prospective customer will not buy his merchandise; nor does a good missionary quit because the heathen are slow to accept his gospel.[32]

The merger of salesmanship and the missionary impulse was much more than a metaphor: it was the logic of transformation through contact with and involvement in the modern world of international business and progressive government administration (figure 2.1).

But contact and transformation were clearly not as universal in practice as RI's rhetoric. The strategies of inclusion and exclusion that actually developed within the "parliament of businessmen" imagined by Rotary's civic internationalism belied the welcoming of all worthy and distant strangers into the fold. Put simply, the closer to home in the United States, the more likely prevailing categories of racial hierarchy took effect in the conferring of membership and in the establishment of new clubs. But doing more and more business abroad, particularly after World War I, forced the issue in new and destabilizing ways. Expansion of US firms into other countries, and vice versa, could only force RI's

FIG 2.1: The globalism behind Rotary's transnational vision of "international friendship" was already well established only a few years after the US Senate's rejection of the League of Nations. *Rotarian,* February 1923, 64. *Courtesy of Rotary International.*

hand in that direction as the opening of international branches worked as a kind of centrifugal force against the hierarchies of race as an organizing principle of both US domestic politics and business practices. In 1926, for example, Latin American Rotarians complained to Tom Sutton, one of the top officers of RI at the time, about the prevalence of "American slang and negro stories" in RI's own monthly, the *Rotarian.*[33] Sutton, a native of Michigan who made his money during the oil rush in Tampico, Mexico during and after World War I, had already become an important mediator between Mexican and US Rotarians by the early 1920s and later was named RI's first Catholic president in 1929. Sutton had RI's publications committee look into the matter, and its conclusion was instructive: "The articles in *The Rotarian* all in all were written in good English, at least the kind that is in general use in the United States, but that it would be preferable not to have anymore so-called negro stories in *The Rotarian.*"[34] "Preferable" was a diplomatic way to put it. Although such stories were less and less common in RI's monthly by the mid-1920s, they did continue to appear in various forms in individual club bulletins, speeches, songbooks, and "stunts" well into the Postwar era.

Despite RI's official silence on the matter at the international level, practices of racial exclusion in affirmation of white supremacy found constant expression at the club level in the United States, Canada, and Great Britain in many ways. The minstrel show was a particular favorite of these Rotary clubs in the interwar years as a means of fundraising as well as source of camaraderie among fellow "white" men. RI actively supported the club activity as a "great promoter of good fellowship in Rotary itself, the spread of a better public understanding of Rotary ideals, and the development of Rotary spirit throughout the community wherever the Rotary minstrel idea has been tried out."[35] A feature article of the *Rotarian,* in fact, offered details on how to put together a successful "Rotary Minstrel," down to the best ways to purchase "clean, snappy material" and "excellent negro wigs" at "modest prices." Advice also included the involvement of "the ladies": "Mixed minstrels, as they are called, have come into great popularity. Many clubs are putting on shows of this style with considerable success." The clearest point of the article, however, was just how popular and widespread the Rotary minstrel shows had become as the writer reviewed the success of shows in Prescott, Arizona (resulting in $1,112 for a playground donated to the city); Harriman, Tennessee; Portland, Oregon; Hillsdale, Michigan; Dodge City, Kansas; and Calgary and Edmonton in Canada—where "the minstrel show flourisheth transplanted far from Dixie soil." Each city's Rotary club raised up to $3,000 in some cases for local charities; the shows became highly anticipated annual community events. Eager to push the Rotary minstrel show both as a good source of fun among club members and as a means of fundraising for community service projects, the author claimed that "space does not permit even listing the numerous other successful minstrel shows that have been given by Rotary clubs in the United States and Canada during the last year or two." But, as photos from various shows demonstrate, they were all-out social events involving the rental of a local theater and large stage productions. Given the prevalence of minstrel shows as a club activity in the United States, it seemed hardly necessary to stipulate formal racial boundaries of club membership throughout the United States and Canada, let alone in the Jim Crow South. When it came to marking off boundaries of race during public events held in the name of community service and sponsored by countless local Rotary clubs, actions spoke louder than words.[36] To be sure, racial lines of demarcation among white and Black business communities found reinforcement in myriad ways long before there were service clubs in America. But through the regular singing of minstrel songs and the performance of minstrel shows, those racial lines were reinscribed in a most pernicious way.

In this manner, minstrel shows and imagery served as an effective way to forge solidarity among the white members of the new middle classes without overt reference to racial exclusions. Purging "negro stories" from its most visible publication in accordance with the Latin American Rotarians' demands was only one small measure RI could undertake with a minimum of resistance from its US clubs. But when it came to any formal position on race, what each club did on the matter was its own business, so long as that club formally adopted RI's standardized club constitution of 1922, which removed any direct reference to racial qualifications of its membership. Before 1922, membership was typically codified in individual cities' club constitutions as restricted to "any adult white male of good moral character" while club constitutions after 1922 formally became silent on matters of race and membership—a silence borne out of a tacit agreement among white men, from both North and South, to enforce their local restrictive covenants on race and club life without having any formal policy in place. As a result, by the late 1920s, RI's official organs, publications, conferences, and conventions became largely free of any overt forms of racial exclusion; (white) gentlemen did not talk that way in public.[37] Membership was solely a function of one's socioeconomic status in the community and masculinity—at least officially speaking. As a result, Rotary clubs were able to police the tacit boundaries of whiteness through social and economic class identities well into the postwar period.[38] Since membership required a certain economic status, a membership committee could turn a blind eye to members of the Black business community by invoking insufficient economic status as the cause of denial of access to club life and membership. Class identity and marketplace status functioned in place of older forms of overt racism. It was Jim Crow in all but name.[39]

Meanwhile, the use of minstrel shows in raising money specifically for Boys' Work campaigns worked in two dimensions at once. First, businessmen, through their Rotary club, claimed special tutelage of "the boy as a nation's greatest asset," thereby instilling in him the ways of good citizenship. Deemed unworthy of such efforts, children from the Black community were typically excluded from this citizenship training. Second, promoting and participating in a minstrel show inherently mocked and marginalized nonwhite elements of the community.[40] Through public theater and performance, the manipulation of racial markers and gendered boundaries helped solidify the authority of white, male business and professional leaders—all in the name of service to and development of the nation's youth.

After World War I, however, increasing international engagement began challenging and destabilizing the unspoken whiteness of RI's civic internationalism. As we shall see, the rapid growth of RI in Latin America and the ascendance of Latin Americans into the highest ranks of RI's administration presented an increasing source of resistance to RI's entire framework of civic internationalism, with Haiti, Jamaica, and the rest of the West Indies at the forefront.[41] As international travel and trade among smaller industrial and population centers developed throughout the United States and the Americas in general, it was inevitable that cities like Port-au-Prince and Kingston would come under consideration, just as all other major cities and capitals had in Central and South America. But the shared transnational status of business and professional peers imagined by RI's civic internationalism, it turned out, entailed deference among equals that could cut both ways: greater prestige through participation in RI's "world fellowship," as well as greater risk of who might be coming to lunch or dinner. With respect to its initial expansion into Europe, Asia, and Latin America, Rotary International managed to adapt—so long as those peers remained at a safe distance in its global imaginary. As we shall also see, the collapsing geography of global capitalism drove some adaptations in race thinking in some of the largest Rotary clubs of the most cosmopolitan cities of the United States and in Rotary's headquarters in Chicago. But, as an increasing number of non-US Rotarians entered RI's ranks and as clubs began forming in the smallest of towns and cities after 1918, the entrenched hierarchies of US race relations became increasingly tested. Rotary's international recruits triggered some veiled—and not so veiled—resistance to those adaptations at the local club level in the United States. Put another way, after 1918, Rotary clubs continued to appear in smaller and smaller cities and towns throughout the United States (as well as Canada, Australia, South Africa, and many other "neo-Europes" of the colonized world) while, at the same time, appearing more and more in the largest and most cosmopolitan centers of trade in the world: Shanghai, Tokyo, Manila, Bombay, Buenos Aires, Cairo, Hong Kong, and Singapore, to name a few. Moreover, during the interwar years, Rotary clubs also began to form like spokes from these capital cities into their respective hinterlands. Over time, something had to give. The racial center of civic whiteness could not hold.

Much like the Japanese government's demand for a formal statement on racial equality in the covenant of the League of Nations in 1919, the possibility of a Rotary club in Haiti and Jamaica directly tested the limits of Rotary's claims to racial pluralism and cultural internationalism within its institutional borders. First suggested to RI's Extension Committee as a potential host city in 1924 by one of its own residents, Kingston, Jamaica, was to be surveyed by the president of the Hamilton, Bermuda, club on behalf of the committee.[42] Yet the club did not materialize until 1959. The delay, according to Chesley Perry, RI's general secretary, resulted from "a feeling of American Rotarians generally, and particularly of those in the southeastern part of the United States, . . . not to organize Rotary clubs in North America or in the vicinity of North America with members of Negro blood." Though Perry recognized well enough there was, "of course, no justification for this policy in view of the many speeches that are made on the basis that Rotary knows no creedal or racial distinctions," he demurred to the wishes of some of the largest and most important clubs in Rotary by arguing that the racial policies of RI's board of directors were nevertheless constitutional.[43] Nor was Perry alone in his frustration over the matter. Paul King, the chair of the International Service Committee (the new name for the Extension Committee after 1927), reported in confidence to Chesley Perry that

> it [was] painful to have an illusion shattered. I lost one myself this year when the Board vetoed the proposition of organizing Rotary clubs in Haiti. Up to that time I supposed we really meant

> what we said about the Brotherhood of Man, but fortunately . . . Rotary I imagine will go on just the same despite the loss of an illusion now and then.[44]

Although for Paul King rejection of Port-au-Prince on grounds of white supremacy belied RI's claims of racial tolerance as part of its civic internationalism, the move was seen as a regrettable but necessary compromise for the sake of white racial solidarity among North America's Rotary clubs. The exotic peers of RI's civic internationalism had to remain within certain racial categories as well as meet certain class standards. The two went hand in hand.

THE RACE QUESTION(S)

Drawing and defending the global "color line" proved far more challenging and complicated than first imagined as real-world, on-the-ground applications for club membership began pouring in from unexpected places in the wake of World War I. And no one could see and appreciate the import of these administrative challenges more clearly than John Barrett, chairman of the IARC's Foreign Extension Committee during the crucial period 1918–1921. It was clear to all that this newly formed committee called for an experienced professional with credentials in the world of diplomacy and with a reputation in the international business community. And the IARC found their man in John Barrett, through the Rotary club of Washington, D.C.

What did Barrett bring to the world of Rotary? A lifetime of experience in boosterism, diplomacy, and international expertise. In short, he was the ideal candidate for the job. After graduating from Dartmouth, Barrett headed west in 1890 and soon became a commercial publicist writing on behalf of Oregon and Washington businessmen. In effect, Barrett's first career was as the mouthpiece for Northwest boosters looking to expand trade into Asia and Latin America. Barrett's regional trade promotion was so effective it got him appointed as minister to Siam in 1894 and then to other posts in Southeast Asia. But being linked with the Democratic Party came at a price for Barrett, who was recalled from

Asia in 1898 just as the United States was establishing its colonial occupation of the Philippines. Among the first eyewitnesses to send to the United States dispatches of Admiral Dewey's victory in Manila in 1898, Barrett put to good use his marketing skills on behalf of his country. Barrett then served as US minister to several Latin American countries between 1904 and 1906, before taking up the reins of the International Bureau of American Republics in 1907, which soon after became the Pan American Union. According to Barrett's biographer, under Barrett's guidance, the Pan American Union adopted a multi-lateralist approach in inter-American affairs, sought a resolution to the Mexican Revolution, attempted a redefinition of the Monroe Doctrine from a pan-American perspective, promoted science and trade, drummed up pan-American solidarity in support of the war effort, and pushed unsuccessfully for the transformation of the Pan American Union into the Pan American League, a regional alliance system in direct support of Wilson's League of Nations, in 1919.[45] When the officers of Rotary chose John Barrett, general director of the Pan American Union and lifelong booster of American trade in Asia and Latin America, to head up their newly formed Foreign Extension Committee in the fall of 1918, they were in effect choosing an internationalist vision that shifted US trade relations away from the transatlantic, welcomed international institutions dedicated to regional and collective security, and celebrated greater transparency and professionalism among the ranks of businessmen and civil servants. In substantive ways, the IARC's Foreign Extension Committee ran parallel to Wilson's own postwar vision. And John Barrett was their new, in-house expert: their man in D.C.

At war's end, however, the vast majority of Rotary clubs were still located in the United States, with fewer than twenty-five clubs in Canada, Cuba, Ireland, and Great Britain outnumbered by well over three hundred clubs peppered throughout the United States. In short, the Foreign Extension Committee had its work cut out for it. Between 1918 and 1920, while these existing clubs abroad served as springboards for growth within their own countries, the real work of the committee focused on establishing new clubs in entirely new regions and nations. Quite literally, the entire world had been flung open, with new markets, industries, and networks now available for development.[46] But given John Barrett's personal history and fields of expertise, the committee had chosen to emphasize growth across the Pacific and especially into Latin America. As you can see from the maps in the front of the book, the decade between the Treaty of Versailles and the onset of the Great Depression proved a crucial period of institutional growth for the IARC—so much so that the organization was renamed Rotary International (RI) in 1922. Between 1915 and 1920, membership jumped from 20,000 to 56,000 among 750 clubs mostly spread throughout North America and Great Britain, but membership almost tripled to 153,000 by 1930 among 3,300 clubs scattered throughout the Americas, Asia, and Europe.[47] Growth hinged on the establishment of clubs in strategic cities, especially those understood as important "trading centers," capital cities, or both. Following the hub-and-spoke model of growth already well established throughout the United States, Canada, and the British Isles, these gateway clubs in key cities would often spin off Rotary clubs throughout their respective hinterlands and satellite towns and cities. In the case of Cuba, for example, the Rotary clubs of Tampa and Jacksonville played a central role in establishing the Havana club in 1916, which in turn led to new clubs in Matanzas and Cienfuegos and ultimately throughout all of Cuba. (See Chapter 5 on Rotary in Cuba.) In similar fashion, the Rotary club in Montevideo, Uruguay (formed in 1918), led directly to the new club in Buenos Aires a year later as the hub-and-spoke model of growth played out again in these urban hinterlands.

But Rotarians from Tampa and Havana also worked together to establish clubs in Madrid and Barcelona. These transnational leaps—so to speak—often entailed a complex set of strategies and negotiations tailored according to the unique conditions of each new city, each new business culture, each new social network, and each new nation and region. For example, the Extension Committee was initially cautioned against setting up a new club in Barcelona that was seen as too partial toward Catalan independence and against planting new clubs in southern Italy. The new club in Buenos Aires, meanwhile, was formed through a committee headed up Jorge Mitre, a newspaperman based in Montevideo, along with another committee that met in the offices of the First National Bank of Boston.[48] But local committees did not always work hand in glove with one another, nor did the Foreign Extension Committee always have free rein in its decisions and activities. Tensions arose, for example, when the first vice president of the IARC argued against opening up a club in Tokyo in late 1919: "Japan is a non-Christian country and the very tenets of Rotary being based on the principles of Christianity I opposed the immediate organization of Rotary Clubs in Japan."[49] Yet within the year, Dyer's veto over setting up a club in Tokyo, and by extension all of Japan, had been overturned, as the Dallas Rotary club made the case for their club member, Rotarian Fukushima, to be empowered to do just that. The Dallas club's argument on Fukushima's behalf was revealing: (1) Fukushima was president of Southern Products Co., a subsidiary of Mitsui & Co., "the largest mercantile institution in Japan"; (2) he had been an upstanding member of the Dallas Rotary club for two years; (3) he was a Christian and "has enjoyed the society of American people"; (4) his children were born in Dallas; and (5) "during the war, he was among the largest contributors to all war activities" as he raised more money for the Liberty Bonds than anyone else in the Dallas club.[50] From the point of view of the Dallas Rotarians, it was only natural that Fukushima's return to Tokyo should result in the transplanting of the Dallas Rotary club along with him. It also helped that Fukushima held such a key position in the cotton and textile trades for both cities. By 1920, the Tokyo Rotary club was chartered through the good offices of Rotarian Fukushima, along with Walter Johnstone of the Pacific Mail Steamship Company and especially Umekichi Yoneyama, director of the Mitsui Bank. (See Chapter 4 on Rotary in Japan.)

Through these increasingly flexible strategies of club expansion, Rotary International entered the 1930s with clubs established throughout most of the world. One of the central tenets for international growth hinged on Rotary's goal of building its clubs out of the local business and professional elites—regardless of their national citizenship. In the case of the Buenos Aires club, for example, Chesley Perry, Rotary's general secretary and member ex officio of the Foreign Extension Committee from its inception, made clear how Rotary imagined each club:

> Let me emphasize one part of our program which is to organize clubs in the foreign countries with the membership largely composed of leading representative business and professional

> natives of those countries. Of course we expect that there will be a few Americans and Britishers to give the club guidance and understanding of the things which make up Rotary; but in Toronto we have a club of Canadians, in Dublin a club of Irishmen, in Havana a club of Cubans, and in Buenos Aires we want a club of Argentinos.[51]

The same formulation was used in Shanghai, Tokyo, Mexico City, Paris, Manila, and virtually every other city where the Extension Committee authorized clubs. In many ways, this formulation became the centerpiece of Rotary's civic internationalism and a key legacy of the Foreign Extension Committee's earliest work in the aftermath of the war. But exactly how were "leading representative business and professional natives" defined? And who defined them? It was one thing to imagine the exotic peers of RI's civic internationalism in the abstract, but quite another to establish and enforce membership requirements for individual candidates in real cities around the world on a rolling basis.

Let us return to the stories of Japan and Haiti, as their differences are quite instructive. While debating the possibility of establishing clubs in Japan in the fall of 1919, the Foreign Extension Committee also received an application for authorization of a Rotary club that had just been formed in Port-au-Prince by that city's business community. Although the Extension Committee had been constituted in order to bring some managerial control over the establishment of clubs outside the United States, what happened in Port-au-Prince was a fairly common story both inside and outside the United States: a local merchant, traveling businessman, corporate manager, military officer, member of a chamber of commerce, or US consular agent would rush ahead and establish a club and then petition for a club charter. The club was often seen as a fait accompli, as the club's organization could serve as a badge of honor for the local community—a rite of passage for any town or city with big dreams. But in the case of Port-au-Prince, as with Tokyo, questions were raised by some of Rotary's board of directors. Since the board oversaw the Foreign Extension Committee and controlled its funding and access to publications, each director's opinion carried much weight. In the case of Mr. Dyer's veto of Tokyo, however, the board outvoted him and the

Dallas Rotary Club outmaneuvered him. In short, Dyer's stand-in for racial discrimination—Japan's non-Christian culture—did not hold. Japan was already a key trading partner with the United States, and the Dallas club's arguments drove that home. But the potential Rotarians of Port-au-Prince had no such club to make their case behind the scenes. In fact, it turned out they had the opposite.

At first, however, it looked promising for the Haitians. Chesley Perry responded to one of the first letters asking for formal membership in a positive light: "I am hoping that the decision of the committee will be that there is no reason why we should not go ahead with organization work there." There seemed to be some confusion as to the source of the request, as Perry referred to the West Indies Trading Company but was responding to an officer of Oliver Brothers, Inc., a company based in New York City. That same day Perry wrote Barrett asking for advice on the matter.[52] Three weeks later, Perry received notice from W. E. Bleo, vice president of the Electric Company, of the club's charter membership, listing C. Edgar Elliott, president of the Haitian American Sugar Co. (HASCO) and US citizen, as the club president; Louis Roy, minister of public works and a Haitian citizen, as club vice president; and Louis Bourgeois, superintendent of education and also a US citizen, as the club secretary. The proposed members, in fact, easily met Rotary's professional and business credentials. They were, in short, "the right kind of men." The seventeen proposed members included eight US nationals, ranging from dentist to banker to electrical engineer; six Haitians, ranging from coffee broker to financial broker; and one man each from Britain, France, and Switzerland. Again, according to Rotary's standards for membership, they were all professionals and businessmen with a strong reputation in their local business community.[53]

As was often the case, the Foreign Extension Committee still needed to confirm the reputations of each proposed member. In this case, Perry wrote Barrett, asking him to inquire within diplomatic circles about the proposed members because "we want to satisfy ourselves as to the character and business standing of the charter members." Barrett saw no reason for concern: "looking over the list of names . . . I cannot help reaching the conclusion that a very good selection has been made."[54] He advised granting the charter, especially after receiving confirmation from his diplomatic contacts at the Haiti Legation in Washington, D.C., that "they are all respectable men" who "belong to respectable families and are among the best representatives of the Haitian society."[55] The case for the new club strengthened when L. J. Bourgeois, superintendent of public instruction in Haiti, reported to Chesley Perry in Chicago that "a committee of very prominent American men of affairs, under the leadership of Mr. Childs, Administrator of the Haitian American Sugar Company [HASCO], met some ago and conceived the necessity of such a society" based on his experience with the Rotary Club in San Juan, Puerto Rico. His letter came with a list of fifty proposed charter members.[56] With outside corroboration through diplomatic channels and with the backing of HASCO, the case for the new club seemed to be solid. In the midst of scores of similar requests for club charters coming in at the same time from all over the world, the decision process on Port-au-Prince was otherwise fairly routine.

But the following month, the "race question" finally reared its head in poignant manner. When C. Edgar Elliott, president of the Haitian American Sugar Co., responded to Perry in Chicago regarding the situation, Elliott tried to allay certain fears: "In answer to your question as to whether or not any of the members have negro blood, beg to advise that quite a number of them have." But Elliott wished to put the question of race within its Caribbean context: "The situation in Haiti is quite different from that in the States. Such Haitians as belong to the Club in Port au Prince cannot be judged by the class of negroes that we are in the habit of meeting in the States." As Haiti had been occupied by the US military since 1915, Elliott further distinguished his club's unique circumstances: "We Americans who live here believe that we are doing a very great service to the Treaty officials by the organization of this club. . . . We also feel that we are bringing the relationship between our country and the Republic of Haiti closer together." After arguing within the same vein as Rotary's own vision of civic internationalism—of a "world parliament of businessmen" united in the ideals of service to the common good—Mr. Elliott finally ended his case for Port-au-Prince by showing his own understanding of US racial sensibilities built on the edifice of Jim Crow:

> Having resided all my life in the United States I of course can recognize the situation which might arise from some of the membership in the South Eastern part of the United States, but I am quite sure that if the Clubs in that section understood the situation here, there would be no objection to the Haitian members. We have quite a few American members of this Club who come from that particular section and they in no way object to the Haitian members.[57]

Although the club's proposed membership had passed the initial vetting process in terms of class identity, the issue of race—of white supremacy in the United States—blocked any further advance. For Elliott, this would be an unfortunate application of Jim Crow to a city outside the United States: "It would be a matter of serious regret to us Americans here if by any chance the Port au Prince club will not be granted a charter."[58] As with the proposed clubs in Japan, the rapid expansion of Rotary into the Caribbean had forced the IARC's Foreign Extension Committee to grapple head-on with the inevitable question of race.

But the internal debates of Rotary's Extension Committee on Haiti had deep roots in the history of race in the Americas. After Haiti's independence in 1804, the nation embodied the greatest of threats to the political unity of the United States to the north: a successful revolt of enslaved peoples that had managed to stave off the French military and establish its own black, independent republic. In conjunction with other European powers, the United States refused recognition of Haiti until after the Civil War precisely for this reason. In many ways, the independence of Haiti was simply inconceivable in the minds of Thomas Jefferson, who first refused diplomatic recognition, and those who followed him. What the Foreign Extension Committee was struggling with was much more complex and treacherous than its members had first realized. Perry put it bluntly before the committee: "Following the unauthorized organization of a Rotary Club at Port au Prince, we have visions of a Rotary Club of black men. You know in the United States Haiti is looked upon as a country of black men."[59] In the meantime, the Extension Committee went forward with approval of clubs in Japan, Mexico,

Colombia, and many other nations, even in South Africa, where no clear initiative had emerged on its own. Sadly, the contradictory and selective nature of Rotary's civic internationalism in 1920—open-armed toward many parts of the world yet closed to many others—recapitulated the racial fissures within the American experience.

But it would not be fair for the historian to lay this at the feet of the Foreign Extension Committee and move on. As in the case of Japan, Perry was voicing the concerns of some members of the board of directors to the committee while Barrett and his colleagues argued against the decision. The primary objection seemed to come from the president of the IARC for 1919–1920, Bert Adams, former president of the Atlanta Rotary Club, as he called the Port-au-Prince club's application "one of the most serious questions that has come before us" and then suggested that the decision be taken to the floor of the annual convention held in Atlantic City in June.[60] For Barrett, making such a decision public and allowing for a floor debate on "the race question," with all the world to see and record, carried great risk: "We must do all we can to prevent . . . questions that would awaken sectional feeling. It would be impossible, moreover, to avoid publicity which would go all over the world and might hurt Rotary seriously."[61] Arch Klumph, president of IARC in 1916–1917, took this precedent to its logical ends: "As I understand this matter, Bert Adams and Jim Finlay [another member of the board of directors] disapprove of the extension of Rotary at this place, based entirely on the fact that some members coming in might possess a certain percentage of negro blood in their veins." For Klumph, the application of Jim Crow rules of social engagement and racial hierarchy outside the United States was untenable and potentially disastrous: "Where is this going to lead us to entirely throughout the Latin American Countries of the South? We will discover the same condition in all parts of South America."[62] In 1920, just as with the United States, so with the Foreign Extension Committee of Rotary: racial hierarchies trumped civic ideals.

Klumph put his finger on the real issue: Rotary's vision of civic internationalism, of creating "a world fellowship of business and professional men united in the ideal of service," could not afford to teeter long on the racial binary of the Jim Crow South. A decision had to be made not only by Rotary's Foreign Extension Committee, but also by its board of directors and, implicitly, by the organization as a whole. But this too was inevitable. Again, Barrett understood the stakes much better than his colleagues: "I am quite sure that the tendency throughout Latin American, in most of the European countries, and in Great Britain would be to sympathize with the Haitian side. . . . With this very race question in different parts of the world . . . there may be real dynamite hidden in it; and the explosion, if any, should take place in the Board of Directors or in an executive session."[63] And John Barrett, Arch Klumph, and Chesley Perry were hardly the only ones to recognize this problem within the back channels of the IARC. When Herbert Coates, a founding member of the Montevideo club, heard about the issue, he wrote Barrett in frustration and with his own perspective on race nuanced by his many years in South America:

> It would simply be impossible for any man I know to explain such a discussion in many of the foreign fields to the South, where a colored man has no more of the African negro than either of us. If Peru, Ecuador, and certain sections of Brasil are to be classed as outside the Rotary pale because their citizens do not have the same complexion that Swedes or Britons have, you had best determine not to extend Rotary in South America. If the organizing Haytian [sic] Rotarians admit Haytian citizens as of their own class, why in the name of reason should we in the USA wish to pass on their eligibility? Let us trust the fellow-countrymen in that port to have the same judgment that he would be credited with possessing if domiciled in Iowa or Texas![64]

Just as the Japanese Empire's Racial Equality Proposal at the Paris Peace Conference in 1919 was met with incredulity, so was the possibility of a Rotary club in Haiti. The latter was a microcosm of the former.

In late June of 1920, the Foreign Extension Committee met in Atlantic City to hold a formal vote on approval of clubs in multiple countries. There were so many new countries entering the fold so rapidly that Barrett had to pencil in the names of new countries, as the list had grown just in the time between the printing of the report and the meeting itself. Among those nations approved were both Japan and Haiti. Concurring with Chesley Perry and John Barrett were Rotarians from Washington, D.C.; Havana; Montreal; Cleveland; and Toledo. As the committee reasoned, "These other clubs outside the United States were organized almost spontaneously and without adherence to any fixt [sic] program of preparation or definite rules of procedure. Foreign extension, in other words, has gone so far that there can be no turning back."[65]

But the board of directors had the final say—and they were willing to use it. As a result, Port-au-Prince did not get a Rotary club until 1962. In fact, shutting down the possibility of a Rotary club in Haiti served as a template for handling "the race question" in the Caribbean for several decades to come. Though Rotary clubs continued to appear throughout the Caribbean, in Latin America, and even in Africa during the interwar period, the racial hierarchies of Jim Crow applied in the case of Port-au-Prince held firm. For example, when F. W. Teele asked for permission to establish a Rotary club in Port of Spain, Trinidad, in 1926, he promised the extension committee that, since he "personally know[s] practically every business and professional man in the city of Port of Spain," he would proceed only "if [he] can avoid the 'Color Question,' and [he] shall be positive of this."[66] Teele was only following "the usual precautions" set up by the extension committee in 1923 regarding new clubs in Bermuda; the Bahamas; the Leeward and Windward Islands; Jamaica; Barbados; Trinidad; and British, Dutch, and French Guiana.[67] Once the board of directors vetoed the recommendation of Barrett's committee on Haiti in 1920, the precedent had been set for expansion of Rotary clubs not only into the Caribbean, but throughout the world. Indeed, not until a decade after World War II would there be any African American members in any Rotary club within the United States, with documentation of the earliest examples of African American members of Rotary clubs difficult to come by.[68] Nor would there be any members of African heritage hailing from outside the United States either until after World War II. While tolerance of racial differences became the norm for new members in Japan, India, Southeast Asia, and many other places around the world, the precedent set in the case of

Port-au-Prince in 1920 became a deadweight on Rotary's international expansion, belying its greatest aspirations toward international peace and cooperation.

Dubbed "the Wilsonian moment" by Erez Manela, the year 1919 is often seen to encapsulate the triumphant tones of Wilson's Fourteen Points, Wilson's celebrated visit to Europe, the great compromises and many flaws woven into the Treaty of Versailles, Wilson's failure to win congressional approval of the League of Nations, the subsequent demise of Wilsonian aspirations for collective security through international institutions, and the supposed onset of isolationism during the interwar period. But Wilsonianism—in all its contradictions—also played itself out in other ways. The confluence of business internationalism, pan-Americanism, and institutional racism created a firestorm within the back rooms of Rotary as it struggled to manage its sudden expansion outside the United States after 1918. While nations throughout East Asia, Latin America, and Europe saw Rotary clubs established at a brisk pace after 1919, Haiti represented for Rotary what it has always represented for the United States: a fundamental challenge to political solidarity forged through white supremacy. Rejection of the Haitian club's application demonstrated the primacy of racial limits set by white supremacy over the soaring rhetoric of pan-Americanism and Wilsonianism. In the case of Port-au-Prince, racial identity trumped class status, revealing the central role of "civic whiteness" in Rotary's self-construction. Just as debates over race, civilization, and progress at Versailles in 1919 revealed the deep limits of Wilson's postwar vision of international peace, so the highest officers of Rotary allowed "the race question" to dictate the terms and limits of their brand of Wilsonianism. Rotary's administrative erasure of the Port-au-Prince application and its subsequent silence on the matter until well into the postwar era paralleled the historical erasure of Haiti in the historical record of the Americas. Like the nation of Haiti itself, treating independent black citizens as social and economic peers within the circle of Rotary was simply inconceivable.[69] But given RI's open-ended definition of membership based on all business and professional vocations, the exclusion of black leaders in cities like Kingston and Port-au-Prince was not only untenable, but also costly. No one could invoke a lack of business reputation, professional status, or amount of property to justify the barring of membership, as was so often the case in the United States. In the end, the exclusion was about race—pure and simple.

But the color line within Rotary also hinged on gender norms and the intimacies of informal social contact in the inner sanctums of white privilege. Long after the rejection of a club in Port-au-Prince, Perry found himself explaining the contradictions of race and Rotary to Edwin Rushmore, secretary of the New York City Rotary club, in the familiar terms of club sociability:

> If they are admitted to the club some day one of them will come up to the Atlanta Club, or to the Chicago Club, or to the New York club, or to the Toronto club, and he will naturally expect to attend the meeting, and if there is a ladies auxiliary, his wife will have to be invited to attend that meeting. Now this is all as it should be, but you and I know what would be liable to happen in any one of these cities from Atlanta to Toronto.[70]

Perry pointed out that, unlike a chamber of commerce, merchants' association, or professional society, "which might permit a mixed racial membership," the Rotary club was too close and socially intimate to accommodate the demands of white supremacy. Wives and daughters were involved. More than business was at stake. The formal invisibility of Rotarians' domestic partners in their weekly meetings and activities suddenly became crucial when race and gender relations worked in combination at social events. The Rotarians' luncheon club often met in very close quarters, while the luncheon (or dinner) itself often took place in segregated hotels—social spaces exclusive according to race as well as class. The complications such intimate social contact would bring to RI's social relations and events both public and private were simply not manageable since equality across certain racial boundaries and gendered contact was simply too transgressive.

But the logistics of social interaction aside, the issue was also a question of defending the privileges of whiteness in the United States and whiteness's perceived overlap with managerial authority and social trusteeship:

> Someone may say that there are already Rotarians that have Negro blood, but if so they claim to be white and not Negro. It would be different when we go into cities where business and professional men are Negroes and do not claim to be anything else, and the bigger and the more important men they are in their local communities, the more likely it would be that they would expect to be received on an equality throughout Rotary, and they would be right in expecting it, because having admitted them to fellowship, we should manifest no discrimination against them.[71]

When passing as whites, light-skinned members of Rotary clubs apparently were tolerated, so long as they wore the mantle of honorary whiteness. In short, the racial prerogatives of white businessmen in the United States and Canada were as nonnegotiable as their gender and class privilege.

With respect to Port-au-Prince and Kingston, RI's solution was to avoid almost all of the Caribbean Basin and West Indies well into the postwar era or else "the entire membership of the Atlanta Club would resign."[72] RI's civic internationalism, when considered in the abstract, affirmed a benevolent expansion of US power and influence in Latin America and the Caribbean. But when challenged on matters of racial tolerance within the close-knit intimacies of their own luncheon clubs and social gatherings, US Rotarians during the interwar years often responded in close alignment with national patterns of race relations. That RI's racial policies had direct manifestations in the regional patterns of its international expansion reveals not only just how crucial the nexus of race, gender, and class identity was to RI's civic internationalism, but also how central white supremacy and patriarchy were to US power in moments when it seemed least visible and most polite and inviting (figure 2.2). Like the Wilsonian vision of international peace and self-determination, the contradictions of race and gender lay at the core of

FIG 2.2: Rotary's civic internationalism hinged on the idealized businessman and the decision-making powers of the corporate world. *Rotarian*, February 1923, 62. *Courtesy of Rotary International.*

RI's expansive rhetoric of international engagement because racism was endemic to global capitalism.[73]

"OUR AMBITIONS BEING FULFILLED"

In sharp contrast to the experience of Rotary on matters of race in the Caribbean, the language of economic and social status of transnational peers in RI's civic internationalism did open up the possibility of overcoming some important racial and national barriers for many in Rotary. East Asia proved the most fertile ground for RI's incorporation of exotic peers into its fold.

The first Rotary club in Asia is a good example. When Roger Pinneo, former president of the Seattle Rotary club, set sail for Manila on behalf of his employer, the Pacific Steamship Company, in November 1918, he was also traveling as a representative of the IARC. Pinneo, an experienced Rotarian from one of the oldest clubs in the organization, proved to be an effective organizer by identifying his primary recruit as Leon Lambert, president of the Lambert Sales Company. Having chaired the most recent Liberty Loan drive, Lambert was "a good live wire." He was also Belgian by birth. After showing Lambert letters from Rotary's President Poole (of Washington, D.C.) and Rotary's home office in Chicago, Pinneo tasked Lambert with getting "five or six live wires together" so that they could carve out a charter membership of about twenty men that would grow to "a club of 50 to 75 within the year." When Pinneo left for Shanghai to carry on his duties as traffic manager for the Pacific Steamship Co., not only Manila but all of Asia had its first official Rotary club, with Lambert as president, Alfonzo Sy Cip as vice president, and three directors, including G. Nieva. While Lambert was Belgian, Cip and Nieva were Filipino.[74]

Like many clubs throughout the world, the Rotary club of Manila began to focus on the Boy Scout movement in the Philippines by 1922 as well as fundraising for organizations like the American School, the Society for the Prevention of Cruelty to Animals, the Red Cross, and the Manila Beautiful Movement, as well as for aid to Russian refugees, the Japanese Relief Fund (for the 1923 Kantō earthquake), and the Bureau of Public Works. But the club's guest speakers in its first decade revealed the high status of the Manila Rotary club and its crucial role in mediating US-Filipino as well as US-East Asian relations. High-level guests of the club included many of the top statesmen and military leaders of that era, including Governor-General Harrison; Manuel Quezon, first president of the Senate of the Philippines and later president of the Philippines; Robert Dollar, shipping magnate; Dean C. Worcester, zoologist and former member of the Philippine Commission; Edwin Denby, US secretary of the navy; Governor-General Leonard Wood; Brigadier General William Mitchell; Henry Morgenthau, former US ambassador to the Ottoman Empire; Henry L. Stimson, governor-general of the Philippines, US Secretary of state, and US secretary of war; Dr. C. T. Wang, premier of China and fellow Rotarian; Prince Purachatra of Siam; and Major General Douglas MacArthur. Out of this club and its involvement with the Boy Scouts emerged Carlos Romulo, who ascended to the top ranks of Rotary International as third vice president in the late 1930s before becoming brigadier general of the Philippines, top aide-de-camp to General MacArthur during World War II, and then president of the UN General Assembly in 1949. But Romulo's international career also included leadership at the Asian-African Conference at Bandung in 1955 and serving as ambassador to the United States from 1955 to 1962 and as minister of foreign affairs for the Philippines from 1968 to 1984. Out of a business trip by Roger Pinneo, traffic manager for the Pacific Steamship Company and Seattle Rotarian, to East Asia just days after the armistice of 11 November 1918 in Europe emerged a social and civic club that became a nexus for US political and military power on one hand and a springboard for international engagement and notoriety on the other.[75]

Encouraged by his success in Manila, Pinneo set out to achieve the same in his next port of call on behalf of the Pacific Steamship Company: Shanghai. Though a central port city for transpacific shipping lines like Manila, Shanghai was a very different city. In the end, Pinneo recruited Dr. Julian Petit to become the first president of the Shanghai Rotary club in 1919. Petit had great hopes: "I have often said that I came to China as a medical missionary, and not being able to accomplish the work I had in view I entered private practice, however, if I am able to put the Rotary Club over in Shanghai, I will feel that I have accomplished equally as important a task."[76] If Petit failed in bringing salvation to the "heathen" Chinese, at least he was providing something comparable in the form of spreading civic virtues. Nor was Petit alone in his great expectations. John Barrett, chairman of Rotary's Foreign Extension Committee at the time, saw the establishment of the Shanghai club from a much larger perspective:

> Shanghai is in many respects the key city of the whole Asiatic coast. Everybody who goes to the Orient must pass through it or visit there. There is, moreover, a wonderful opportunity for achievement in working out the ideals of Rotary. The Club may have a profound influence in that way upon the future of China and the development of that kind of civilization for which Rotary stands.[77]

The civic internationalism of RI allowed Petit to explain his long medical career in Shanghai in personal and secular rather than religious terms, culminating in his instrumental role in establishing the Shanghai club.[78] It also enabled John Barrett to describe the swelling of US business and political interests in Shanghai, China, and all of East Asia in neutral terms like "ideals of Rotary" and "that kind of civilization for which Rotary stands." Insofar as the Shanghai Rotary club showed no favoritism in its club membership, Rotary clubs in China presented no threat to Chinese sovereignty while Rotary clubs in East Asia maintained their strategic distance from all governments (European as well as the US). Moreover, Rotary International itself helped sell the growing presence of US corporate interests in China as a beneficent project both at home and abroad even as the Rotarians' endeavors stood in support of the United States' Open Door Policy toward China established two decades earlier by John Hay, secretary of state under Presidents McKinley and Roosevelt. In effect, both US foreign policy and US corporate interests in China had found a new friend in Dr. Petit, the former medical missionary; a new place to socialize on a regular basis at the tiffins of the Rotary club of Shanghai; and a new partner with the appearance of a new nonstate actor in the region—Rotary International. Neutrality took many forms during the interwar period.

But not all shared the hopes and ambitions of Petit and Barrett. In fulfillment of Petit's own dreams for the club, the Shanghai Rotarians' Charities Committee established the "Rotary Mobile Clinic" upon the outbreak of war in 1937.[79] Two years later, Alex Potter traveled through the region as RI's representative to investigate how the thirty-five Rotary clubs of China were managing in the midst of open conflict with Japan. Potter, the former head of RI's European Secretariat from 1925 to 1933, reported on the mobile clinic, managed by Dr. H. C. Hou of the Lester Institute of Medical Research and one of thirty-eight Chinese Rotarians in the Shanghai club (out of 127 total members). The clinic, set up to "administer to poor unfortunates in the Refugee Camps," was run by volunteer doctors and nurses who were themselves refugees in their own land. From late 1937 to early 1939, the clinic provided forty-two thousand treatments, "regularly visiting a total refugee population of 8,000 people housed in thirteen refugee camps."[80] Potter saw the clinic as confirmation of RI's civic internationalism at its best: provision of a vital community service developed through the leadership of Chinese professionals working with their local Rotary club and in conjunction with other international voluntary associations.[81]

Yet, when Richard Currie, one of RI's top international officials, visited Shanghai and Hong Kong a few months later, he saw a different picture:

> During the last few days I have been asking myself whether Rotary is meant for the Orient, except perhaps in isolated cities where there is a substantial English speaking population. . . . Extension must come naturally and slowly; if it grows too fast there will be a tendency for it to develop into a Rotary-Japan or maybe Rotary-Asia. . . .
>
> Dr. C. T. Wang has repeatedly said that the time will come when there would be 2,000 or 3,000 Rotary clubs in China. I wonder whether we should think of such a possibility for a long time to come. This visit has made me wonder whether we are not sailing in a fool's paradise, with dreams, ideals and visions of Rotary as a world-wide organization when there is not much hope of our ambitions being fulfilled in our life-time.[82]

A massive fault line ran between the success of the Rotary Mobile Clinic and the "fool's paradise" of Rotary as a "world-wide organization" that paralleled deeper tensions within the United States as its power and presence continued to grow.

Like so many other Rotary clubs outside the United States by the 1930s, the Shanghai club was much more than a cultural and political island for US citizens living and working abroad. Rather, for a noteworthy Chinese Rotarian like C. T. Wang and a Canadian Rotarian like Alex Potter, the dozens of Rotary clubs in China in 1937 represented great hope for the future of China, as was true for Petit and Barrett in 1919. C. T. Wang made his own views clear while traveling in the United States in 1936: "We have now eighty different countries or regions in which Rotary is represented. . . . Fellow Rotarians, let us go in, therefore, and multiply ourselves that the influence, the ideals, what we stand for in Rotary, will be a force for real world peace and world fellowship."[83]

For C. T. Wang, a member of the Chinese delegation to Paris in 1919 who had seen the loss of the Shantung Peninsula to the Japanese firsthand, such confidence in the promises of RI's civic internationalism required a leap of faith. But for an English Rotarian like Currie, the heavy inclusion of Chinese in so many of their own Rotary clubs was a source of consternation and an open invitation for RI to dissolve into a "Rotary-Japan or maybe Rotary-Asia"—an unthinkable outcome for Rotary's "world fellowship." Both in the halls of power as well as on Main Street, the question turned on what Currie meant by "our ambitions being fulfilled." Whose ambitions? At whose expense?

Chinese members, however, were beginning to predominate in clubs outside of Shanghai by the mid-1930s. Fong Sec, the Shanghai club's vice president, estimated that about one in five members were Chinese, the same proportion British, and the rest Americans in 1925.[84] Though Fong Sec then pointed to the city's "ever changing population" and "English language limits" as structural caps on the Shanghai club's ability to conjoin Chinese and non-Chinese businessmen and professionals, RI went on to establish well over thirty Rotary clubs throughout China by July 1937.[85] In some of those clubs, English was not the primary language, as Chinese members began to outnumber non-Chinese members and Chinese nationals began recruiting heavily among themselves.[86]

In many ways, RI's expansion into China between 1919 and 1937 reflected RI's international growth in general during the interwar period. On the eve of the outbreak of war in East Asia, RI had managed to burrow itself into practically all major cities of the region, from Hong Kong to Harbin, from Tokyo to Chungking, and most commercial centers in between.[87] Also, Japanese and Chinese Rotary clubs experienced similar patterns of growth and levels of success. But the nature of RI's presence was not comparable. Whereas the earliest Chinese clubs in Shanghai, Beijing, Tientsin, and Nanking began with a core of US and European members from transnational corporations, INGOs, and government agencies and then grew by accretion, the Japanese clubs were almost completely Japanese from the establishment of the first Rotary club in Tokyo in 1920. RI's successful recruitment of non-US Rotarians in the Americas, Europe, and Australasia was significant as well.[88]

In the midst of the Neutrality Acts of the US Congress and the toothless pronouncements of President Franklin D. Roosevelt's famous "Quarantine Speech" in 1937, RI continued with its forays into other countries until laws or open warfare shut down their clubs.[89] Well before the opening shots of World War II, the institutional reach of RI was not only transnational in scope, but also increasingly cross-cultural and selectively interracial in practice.

In many ways, RI appeared to be as color-blind as Wilson's rhetoric of self-determination. But RI's mission to the world meant opportunity for nations like China and Japan and total erasure for others like Haiti and Jamaica. As we have seen already, RI carefully chose the exotic peers who could enter its world fellowship. Inclusion for some came with exclusion for others. The dividing line, however, did not exactly follow the older political, racial, and cultural patterns of European colonialism because, theoretically, there was no "foreign" in Rotary's extension. Rather, it was the identity of the male actor in the marketplace, honorable and professional, virtuous and sympathetic, civic-minded and successful, that defined the ideal economic citizen for Rotary worldwide.

Yet inclusion did not guarantee full status. The Extension Committee captured this tension in its formal policy for the organization of the Mexico City Rotary club in 1921. Since most of the original thirty members of the Mexico City Rotary club that first year were US or British in origin, Rotary's leadership stipulated in a special agreement with the first Mexican club that:

> 1. In the selection of new and additional members, all things being equal, preference is to be given to the native Mexican, and it is further understood that a number of native Mexicans will be immediately added to the club roster.
>
> 2. It is understood that the Spanish language shall not be excluded, but shall be used when practicable and that at such meetings as may be presided over by a native Mexican, that he be encouraged to use the language of the nation, Spanish.
>
> 3. It was definitely understood that the Rotary Club of the City of Mexico must not be an American or British Colony Club—that it must not be used for the exploitation of American and British commerce, but that it is to be a Mexican Rotary Club for the benefit of the community and nation of Mexico.[90]

RI's civic internationalism demanded this kind of local representation for all of its clubs. The legitimacy of the entire project rested upon it. But could a growing representation of "native Mexicans" in the club ensure any meaningful "benefit" to the "community and nation of Mexico"? Though the Mexico City club's constitution provided for the preferential inclusion of local, native Mexican businessmen and professionals over any non-Mexicans of the same classification, that same club constitution also demanded complete "avoidance of politics" in all club meetings and activities.[91] It was one thing to welcome the business and professional elites of Mexico City into the "world fellowship," quite another to allow the club to serve as a venue for political debate and to enable Mexican sovereignty over and against US corporate and national interests. In short, a politically active and assertive Mexico Rotary club was as inconceivable as Mr. Currie's "Rotary-Japan or maybe Rotary-Asia." Like Wilsonian foreign policy, the mission of RI's civic internationalism drew a guarded line between the high moral tones of self-determination and any political aspirations not conducive to US economic and political interests.

At Rotary's annual convention in Denver, Colorado, in June 1941, Armando de Arruda Pereira of Brazil, the outgoing president of Rotary International for 1940–1941, gave a talk entitled "The Rotarian Amid World Conflict." The presidency had been a crowning achievement for him, not just as an ideal Rotarian, but as an international businessman and noted political leader from Brazil. In contrast to his speech at the International Service Round Table in Mexico City in 1935, Pereira's presidential address portrayed a world under siege: open warfare was already in its fourth year in East Asia and nearly its second in Europe. Since 1936, almost three hundred Rotary clubs in fifteen nations had either been banished by their national governments or terminated by Rotary while at least one hundred other clubs were continuing among their city's ruins (in Coventry, England), in air raid shelters (as in Chongqing), or in disguise as "day-of-the-week" clubs (throughout Japan after the prohibition of Rotary in September 1940). Though spoken in the crisp, sunny air of the Rocky Mountains, Pereira's words could not deny that the times were bleak. Nor could his audience. But Pereira wished to point out that not all was lost, reminding the thousands of Rotarians that there were still more than two hundred thousand Rotarians meeting every week in "5,000 cities, towns, and villages" throughout the world while the Rotary Relief Fund, established at the Havana convention the year prior, was delivering thirty packages of food each month to Rotarians in European prison camps.[92]

Pereira and his fellow Rotarians had good reason to see beyond the storm clouds of global war. Though hampered by two separate outbreaks of global warfare, the advent of the Great Depression, and the rise of economic nationalism and militarism by the late 1930s, the international expansion of Rotary clubs after 1912 represented a significant movement toward the institutionalization and stabilization of international engagement between the American heartland and urban centers and emerging markets worldwide. In the name of inculcating civic cooperation in familiar, small-town terms and developing cross-border business progressivism, RI defined itself as a mediator across national boundaries and cultural differences, an institutional bridge among "fellow" businessmen and professionals of specific cities and distinct nations not beholden to any one government, any one corporation, any one part of the world. As a result, RI's internationalist formula thrived during two postwar eras—the 1920s and the 1950s–1960s—and survived two great midcentury paroxysms—the Great Depression and World War II.

What was that formula? Rotary International presented itself as a kind of Esperanto for an emerging transnational class of businessmen and professionals and its civic internationalism as an apolitical, uplifting alternative to the vicissitudes of local partisanship, mere profit-making, and nationalist agendas. Service to the community—from the local to the national to the international—was the touchstone of RI's ideology, and participation in international circuits of trade the source of its institutional growth. As such, RI's civic internationalism claimed to rise above the political fray because it defined its members primarily as responsible marketplace actors and its organizational mission as beyond the purview of the state—any state. Rotary International sought to operate with a strategic distance from both states and markets as only an international nongovernmental organization could do. The strategy became a fundamental feature of the ever-expanding number of nongovernmental organizations that have come to populate the global community over the course of the twentieth century. In that sense, RI formed only one part of a growing trend of NGOs moving in, around, through, and despite state structures and policies over the same period. But clearly not all NGOs have the same relationships to states and markets. The boundaries are rarely discrete and always shifting with circumstances. In the case of RI, however, blurring boundaries between states and markets ultimately developed into a complex weaving and dodging among empires and imperialisms, races and cultures, nations and industries as Rotary clubs "girdled the globe" during the interwar period. In this manner, Rotary also became a useful means of entry for US corporate and state interests as their employees and agents joined their local Rotary clubs both inside and outside the United States, attended weekly luncheons, spoke at club and public events, and mingled with their families at intimate social events and charitable activities.

As an informal, nonstate, philanthropic form of cultural diplomacy among business and professional elites, RI's civic internationalism helped build the institutional and ideological foundations for postwar US global hegemony in its most conducive terms: the denial of empire woven into the daily business of empire. While the tenets of American exceptionalism and the market-hungry expansion of US corporate capitalism were in tension long before the Great War as well as long after, it was during the interwar years that a workable synergy developed between the two. Though Wilson's vision of collective security never materialized during that period, Rotary's vision of international engagement unfolded largely according to plan.

3

THE ELIMINATION OF DIFFERENCES

Main Street Meets Tokyo

When Umekichi Yoneyama took the stage at Rotary International's annual convention in Dallas in May 1929, it was like a homecoming for him. As the godfather of all Rotary clubs in Japan since 1920 and as a top industrial and financial leader from Tokyo, Yoneyama embodied the exotic peer imagined by RI's civic internationalism. He addressed the gathering of his fellow Rotarians as "this great parliament of business and professional men of the world" and then recounted how Dallas was "where I saw . . . the light of truth in Rotary some nine years ago."[1] Another Rotarian, Herbert Harris, an English professor from Whittier College, California, spoke moments before Yoneyama on the same theme. As vice chairman of RI's International Service Committee in 1928–1929, Harris was responsible for putting the rhetoric of RI's civic internationalism into practice. After describing how they were all "living in a new world . . . a small world of close neighborhood," Harris told his audience of a fellow Rotarian from a club located "two thousand miles from an international border" who had asked him, "What can my little club possibly do to better international relations?"[2]

The pairing of Yoneyama and Harris as speakers brought together the two extremes of RI's civic internationalism: the heartland and the world abroad, small-town America and a massive commercial hub of East Asia. Harris's answer to the small-town Rotarian was simple: "By a program of education that begins at home, . . . not by entering into politics but by cultivating the spirit of friendship and understanding in its members, . . . and then sending them out to spread that spirit among other people."[3] Were it not for the remarkable success of Yoneyama's Rotary clubs in Japan and RI's presence in dozens of other nations around the world, Harris's advice might have rung hollow. But at the time of the convention in Dallas in 1929, RI's civic internationalism was at its height—and the world was ripe for the Rotarians to conquer.

Within a dozen years, the United States and the Japanese Empire clashed violently over the future of the Pacific Ocean, East Asia, and Southeast Asia. By 1940, all forty-four Japanese Rotary clubs were disbanded and, by 1945, practically all of Japan's urban centers and industrial base had been devastated by total warfare. Meanwhile, US Rotarians girded up for the war effort much as they had in the prior war to end all wars only to find themselves forming part of an emerging permanent war economy in the United States in the postwar era.[4] The "spirit of friendship and understanding" among Rotarians like Harris and Yoneyama—such a compelling vision for international peace in Dallas in 1929—eventually melted in the heat of imperial collisions. What had been a high-water mark for RI's civic internationalism was transformed within just two decades by global depression, global warfare, and the rise of US global hegemony in unimaginable ways. The internationalist moment of Dallas 1929, of Rotarians Yoneyama and Harris, would be lost with time, reshaped by postwar realities and cold war alliances.

This chapter and Chapter 4 explore the fundamental paradox in how the United States has projected itself in the world through both violence and benevolence. The interwar experiences and parallels between the Rotary clubs of Wichita and Tokyo in particular serve as case studies in the nature of this paradox. Just as key businessmen, contractors, and corporate leaders of both cities were trying to construct institutional mechanisms of international exchange and deliberation long before Pearl Harbor, so also were these men actively involved by 1940 in each nation's preparation for and prosecution of total war. After World War I, there was a time when "conquering" was metaphorical in meaning for the business classes in cities like Wichita. Similarly, there was a time when Tokyo's industrial leaders could see themselves in friendly alignment with the interests and growth of the United States in the Pacific.[5]

These two chapters map out some of the contours of this transformation by examining what these cities' Rotary clubs did and said, what they hoped for and expected from each other as part of RI's "world fellowship," and how and why they imagined their worlds to be moving in such easy convergence during what turned out to be "the interwar period." The civic internationalism of Rotarians like Harris and Yoneyama was an attempt to smooth over the "imperialist logic of difference" at the core of the East-West binary by replacing it with the more palatable "logic of affiliation" that became such a predominant theme in postwar US foreign policy. In that sense, the worldwide expansion of Rotary clubs during the interwar years foreshadowed—indeed, helped lay the foundation for—the middlebrow turn toward the international in the postwar era.[6] But in other ways, RI's civic internationalism of the interwar period represents one of many internationalisms sacrificed on the altar of cold war historical revisionism and the severity of the cold war binary.

Rotary's civic internationalism furthered the myth of the United States as an inherently benevolent presence in the world and contributed to the "ideology of global interdependence."[7] Long-standing sentimental notions of uniquely American voluntarism and community service and Progressive Era notions of modern business standards and practices lay at the core of Rotary's sense of mission to the world. This ideological blend of Main Street's business culture with corporate capitalism on a global scale lies at the core of what is often called US "soft power." But that soft power is deeply imbricated in very real projections of economic, military, and political "hard power." The hard and the soft cannot be disentangled so easily.[8] Understanding better how the United States operated as a global hegemon in the postwar era requires a better grasp of the internal logic of this paradox of violence and benevolence—indeed, the unraveling of that paradox. A closer look at the civic internationalism of the Wichita Rotary club and its evolution during the interwar period is a useful step in that direction.

THE "WICHITA PLAN"

When Harry W. Stanley, a thirty-one-year-old native of Wichita, Kansas, and representative of the Equitable Life Insurance Company of Iowa, went to Chicago in the summer of 1911 to attend his company's convention, he heard about a new kind of club for businessmen, called "Rotary," from a fellow insurance agent and conventioneer from Des Moines. After meeting with the club's founder, Paul Harris, on the same trip to Chicago, Stanley returned to Wichita eager to start his very own Rotary club. It was just the ticket for a prairie town full of upstart businessmen and entrepreneurs seeking legitimacy from a great metropolis like Chicago—the paragon of intercontinental commerce and rapid urban expansion.[9] Would Wichita become "the next Chicago"?

So Harry—who was the son of Kansas governor William E. Stanley (1899–1903)—set about galvanizing support among his friends and peers. Within the month, more than seventy of them had signed on to the new club and its primary goal: "that the important men of all nations should know about Wichita, Kansas, U.S.A., and the products we raise, mill, and manufacture."[10] Harry Stanley and company meant to put Wichita on the map—as part of not just the national US economy but the international economy as well. The idea was not a stretch of the imagination for Stanley. After four years at Columbia University and a few more traveling through Europe, Harry had already journeyed far beyond the long, flat horizons of his native Wichita by 1905.

But just as Harry's own experience did not stop at Wichita's city limits, neither did his commitment to his new Rotary club. His drive to bring the first club to the state of Kansas in 1911 was clearly part of a greater mission to forge a metropolitan center out of the wheat fields, cattle ranches, and oil wells of south central Kansas. A businessmen's service club networking with similar clubs in North America was one way to move things along. So not only did Stanley found and serve as first president of the thirtieth club to join the National Association of Rotary Clubs, but he also became vice president of the National Association of Rotary Clubs in 1912–1913, when it more than doubled in size and became the *International* Association of Rotary Clubs, thanks to the creation of Rotary clubs in Canada and the United Kingdom that same year. Though Stanley did not, as vice president, have a direct hand in the creation of any of those clubs outside the United States, he was well aware of the international context in which his own city and its new service club found itself and how he might use this new businessmen's club to his beloved city's advantage. Wichita was a city to be reckoned with—a city on the move. Like Chicago, New York, San Francisco, Boston, Seattle, and many other major US cities, Wichita now had a Rotary club. With the Canadians and British mixed in, it was a fast-growing international club. The opportunities were endless.

On the local level, meanwhile, the newly minted Wichita Rotarians figured that "before the Club could serve the public, the Club had to become familiar with its members and their businesses." Stanley understood that developing trust among the civic leaders of Wichita came before developing the city of Wichita. To that end, the first year's biweekly dinners focused on members speaking on their particular line of business or profession. In accord with one of the key institutional goals of all other Rotary clubs, the Wichita Rotarians were learning the methods, standards, and procedures of their fellow members' businesses and professions. What exactly did a real estate agent do and why? How were farm loans given out? What was the latest in adding machines, dentistry, automobiles, aviation, and wholesale electric wares? There were more than seventy distinct professions and types of business within the club to learn about and to learn from while new members from other distinct "classifications" of industry and commerce were regularly joining the growing club as well. Each Rotarian's expertise in his own specific trade or profession became a given meeting's topic of discussion. Every member had his chance in the limelight to enlighten his fellow members on the importance and dynamism of his own particular line of work. Having each member speak before the club on his own specialty also gave him the chance to hone his skills at public speaking while serving on club committees that became a laboratory for developing organizational and managerial skills. As with Rotary clubs in other cities, however, "scientizing acquaintances" among the city's leading business and professional classes had other practical benefits: getting to know fellow Rotarians meant getting to know potential clients and business allies. Friendship in business meant networking, which translated into personal and commercial success.[11]

By 1914, developing that sense of friendship and fraternity moved to a whole new level under Gifford Booth Sr., manager of the Grit Printing Company and the club's second president. Members were divided into groups of ten and then given various wholesale businesses to visit and report on to the entire club. The club repeated the process months later, only with a focus on manufacturing companies.[12] Like many other clubs during this period, the Wichita club sought to function as a kind of right arm to the city's chamber of commerce by serving as a common ground for social interaction among those who would also be typical members of the chamber.[13] Learning about other members' industries and professions went well beyond the social space of the club's meetings in swank downtown hotels; all members were required to visit Wichita's factories, shops, and stores and report on their findings. Generating a sense of solidarity, civic identity, and common purpose among the Wichita Rotarians in the club's early years also had a practical purpose: to convince Rotary's headquarters in Chicago that the Wichita club could and should host one of the upcoming annual international conventions. Hosting a gathering of thousands of fellow Rotarian businessmen and professionals and many of their wives from cities throughout the United States and Canada would have been a booster's paradise—a consummate opportunity to show off Wichita's entrepreneurial prowess and make a lot of money while doing so.

As a result, when five trains filled with Rotarians were passing through Wichita on their way to their convention in Houston in June 1914, Gifford Booth seized the opportunity. As the trains arrived in Wichita in the early morning hours, the hundreds of traveling Rotarians were met with about two hundred Wichitans in their cars, given a tour of the city, and then provided breakfast at the Scottish Rite Temple by the women of the Ivy Leaf Chapter Order of Eastern Star. Rotarians like Giff Booth had social connections well beyond the chamber of commerce and knew how to use them to great effect. In this case, Giff Booth was just the man to pull off "one of [Wichita's] greatest advertising stunts."[14] As an active leader in the Masons, president of the Board of Education, director of the Wichita chamber of commerce for sixteen years, active member of the Salvation Army Board for more than thirty years, fundraiser for his Central Christian Church, member of the legislation committee of the National Red Cross, and chairman of the Sedgwick County War Funds Association and the State Jewish-American campaign during World War I, Giff Booth Sr. embodied the multifaceted nature of civic involvement that the Rotary club idealized. More than a mere booster, Booth was an active civic leader his whole life.

Nor were Stanley and Booth alone in this regard. The Wichita Rotarians' boosterism and civic activities were all of a piece. When Henry J. Allen, owner of the *Wichita Beacon,* began pushing hard for a commission-manager form of municipal government in early 1916, he turned to the Rotary club as a potential ally in the effort. It was a smart move. The club set up a committee to investigate the issue. With that committee's endorsement, the club began moving ahead. There were two obstacles to overcome in order to bring the city manager form of government to Wichita: an enabling act by the Kansas State Legislature and then approval by Wichita residents through a special election. Recognizing that they would need support from other cities for their initiative in the legislature, the Wichita Rotarians called a meeting of fellow Rotarians from Topeka, Hutchinson, and Parsons while they were all attending Rotary's annual convention in Cincinnati in 1916.

On their return home to Kansas, the Wichita members also met with J. M. Switzer, executive for the National Cash Register Company (NCR) in Dayton, Ohio, and also its city commissioner, and convinced him to speak at all the Kansas Rotary clubs on the virtues of that form of city government. Switzer, armed with "stereopticon views" provided by NCR, was already a regular speaker on the topic throughout the country. He was more than happy to oblige, since relations between NCR and Rotary clubs were already both national and international in scope. With both the *Wichita Eagle* and the *Wichita Beacon* publishing favorable articles on the topic, the club then garnered support from Robert Stone, a former legislator from Topeka and district governor for all Rotary clubs in Kansas; Lieutenant Governor W. T. Morgan; and R. L. Holmes, an attorney and active Rotarian. Meanwhile, the club continued to beat the drum in support of the change in city government. Wichita's club president at the time, Dr. Ernest Seydell, eagerly pointed out that: "opposition was supplied in abundance by the city hall crowd and the old time politicians." Dr. D. F. Garland joined in the rhetoric against the vices of city hall when he spoke at the club in December 1916, and promised a "harmonization of democracy and efficiency" through a city manager system of municipal government. In the end, the enabling law finally passed as the Nightswonger Bill. The Wichita Rotarians' visit to the Cincinnati convention and active recruiting of other Kansas clubs in support of their legislative goal had paid off. For men like Stanley and Booth, Wichita was halfway to bringing its city government in line with modern business practices and progressive reform movements since the business community's control of local and state government was the natural order of things. For a city with national and international aspirations, there was no other option.[15]

Getting the Rotarians' fellow Wichita citizens to pass the measure in an election was another matter, requiring different measures. Reflecting national trends toward the use of the referendum, recall, and initiative in local and state politics, the Wichita Rotarians canvassed house to house to get signatures for their petition for a special election on the matter. Club members turned to their wives and to the General Federation of Women's Clubs for help in the canvassing and managed to capture the five thousand signatures needed to bring about the special election. The club also deployed speakers throughout Wichita, such as club member Dr. Walter Scott Priest, pastor of Central Church of Christ, who promised "a marked decrease in crime" and "the elevation of the moral tone of the city." Meanwhile, several key Rotarians took over the Law and Order League and transformed it into the Greater Wichita Civic League, which then endorsed seven of the seventeen candidates for city commissioner, canvassed the city's precincts, and worked on get-out-the-vote activities on election day, 3 April 1917. Five new city commissioners were voted into office that day; two of them were already Rotarians, and the other three joined the club by midsummer 1917, along with Louis R. Ash, Wichita's first city manager. By all accounts, including Ash's, the Wichita Rotarians were the primary agents in bringing about the city manager–commission form of government.[16]

That the whole process was typical of municipal politics in the Progressive Era is precisely the point. How the service club overcame political and legislative obstacles helps us locate the organization within the national context of progressive politics and business progressivism after 1910. But how the club managed the process and why it supported the commission-manager form of government also reveals the club's move toward a supposed apolitical stance toward civic responsibility as the corporate ethos of managerial liberalism deepened its roots in American society during that period. Just as the new middle classes asserted their reform agendas on the local and national level during the Progressive Era, so the city elders of the Wichita Rotary club blended the language of managerial efficiency, professional expertise, and modern business practices in the name of a new, more responsible form of city government. As with so many other cities in the United States before and after, the detached nature of the expert and the professionalism of the manager became the modern alternative to the decadence of city hall's political chicanery.

Reform agendas imbued with modern business practices, therefore, enabled certain types of political involvement even as they enhanced the pretense of nonpartisanship and dispassionate community leadership and development. In September 1916, the first issue of the Wichita club's monthly newspaper trumpeted the belief that politics "does not enter into Rotary" and pledged to ban political discussion from its pages. Overt partisanship would be below the Rotarians.[17] The Wichita Rotarians' boosterism, as such, dovetailed well with both its apolitical posturing and its civic projects. The same recipe also applied to other major club activities in the club's early years, such as the Liberty Loan Drives, the City Beautiful Movement, and the creation of playgrounds. Civic leadership of a disinterested and altruistic nature was at the core of Rotary's legitimacy in Wichita and in hundreds and later thousands of clubs worldwide. It was also the key to their political agenda—claims to nonpartisanship notwithstanding.

By 1925, the Wichita club had long since moved beyond the building of playgrounds, fundraising for the war effort, and improving municipal governance, just as Rotary itself had blossomed into a rapidly growing international institution with clubs in about twenty-eight countries and commonwealths around the world. From the perspective of Stanley and Booth, there appeared to be no reason state and national boundaries should limit Wichita's ambitious forays into the emerging world of international business. Whether it was oil, cattle, wheat, or airplanes, by the mid-1920s, Wichita's business community had a great deal to offer the world.

To that end, the club sent a form letter to all other Rotary clubs in the United States—about 1,600 in total—inviting them to support what soon became known as the "Wichita Plan." Much as the club had established a program a decade earlier for educating Wichita Rotarians on one another's lines of business and Wichita's own industrial base, the Wichita club had divided its membership of more than two hundred Rotarians into twenty groups of about ten members in order to study "some one foreign country along peace lines." The Wichita Plan's immediate goal was to examine most of the countries where Rotary clubs had already been established as part of a "movement for World Peace, launched by Business and Professional men, who through their affiliation with Commerce and Science represent the great majority . . . free of sectarian or political complexities."[18] Each member "was assigned an aspect of the life" of a given country, and each group, after several months of study, was to report its overall findings on its assigned country to the club as a whole during one of the club's weekly meetings, "either through pageantry, speeches, papers, or the spoken word of a native of the country where possible."[19] The long-term goal of the Wichita Plan, however, was the club's old desire to convince RI's headquarters in Chicago and its convention committee, comprised of Rotarians from various countries by 1925, that the Wichita club could and should host an international convention—a goal held by scores of other clubs both inside and outside the United States.

The boosters' dream of a Wichita packed with thousands of fellow tradesmen from all over the world had only intensified since Giff Booth's 1914 breakfast for several trainloads of Rotarians en route to Houston. With these ends in mind, the club drafted a resolution for the 1925 convention in Cleveland that RI "inaugurate . . . a campaign of Education for the definite study of International Peace" so that "Rotary may be of service to mankind in doing its part to bring about World Peace."[20] RI sought to tap into and build upon the growing interconnectivity and contact among businessmen and professionals by serving as an institutional link, a common thread, between such disparate cities as Tokyo and Wichita. The Wichita Rotarians understood this as well and tried to take full advantage of RI's offices.

But the Wichitans never won their convention. Ultimately, the Wichita club withdrew its resolution at the Cleveland convention in 1925 in favor of a broader resolution that included ethical business practices, Boys' Work in the community, and worldwide expansion of Rotary. RI's Extension Committee and its board of directors, however, both claimed total support for the "sentiment" and goals of the Wichita Plan and then proved it when RI highlighted the Wichita Plan for approximately one hundred thousand readers in RI's monthly magazine, the *Rotarian*.[21] Everything about the Wichita Plan was emblematic of RI's internationalist goals. As artful boosters, the Wichita Rotarians designed it that way.

The Wichita Rotarians, however, were not alone in pushing for something like a Wichita Plan. In 1926, the Whittier, California, Rotary club managed to get unanimous support from the delegates representing all 130 clubs in its district (mostly the state of California) on a proposed resolution that "provides for a committee to suggest the programs and the methods of education in international understanding for which so many clubs are asking." Recognizing that "other forces are working among women and children to improve international relations," the Whittier club argued that "Rotary speaks directly to the only power which can stop war and maintain peace, BUSINESS. Every week in all the principal cities of the United States and in many of those in thirty-four other nations, Rotary mobilizes leading business and professional men."[22] The Whittier Club saw its peace proposal as part of a general trend toward "bettering international relations," but more important was the club's belief that the solidarity within its expanding international network of business and professional peers was the key to world peace. The principal driver behind the Whitter club's activities was Herbert Harris. As an English professor at a college established by Quakers in 1887, Harris was familiar with international peace initiatives from a religious perspective. Within two years, Harris was a top official on RI's International Service Committee and shaking hands with Umekichi Yoneyama in Dallas.

In the world of Rotary International, it seemed only natural to project RI's voluntaristic, associational model of governance and economic citizenship in the United States beyond its borders. The logic was simple: just as the competition of nations brought only war, so the marketplace of free trade and commerce could alone transcend national rivalry and provide enduring peace. Trade links and business standards trumped the pettiness of political disputes and the meddling of state regulators. Whether replacing a corrupt city hall with a professional city manager or the secretive diplomacy of the Old World with open negotiations, modern business—be it local or international in scope—was an apolitical, transparent, dispassionate force for good. The boys in cities as far apart as Tokyo and Wichita could both agree: the virtues of an international marketplace, not the vicissitudes of nation-states, were the hope of future stability and cooperation in the world. Though the term "globalization" was yet to come into fashion, the foundations were already there. And the world of Main Street was making its own contributions.

CIVIC INTERNATIONALISM—WICHITA STYLE

Why would more than two hundred Rotarians in Wichita, Kansas, in 1925 be so committed to learning about all other countries where Rotary clubs existed? More important, how and why did these Rotarians expect to welcome many more countries into their fellowship in the coming years? Though boosterism clearly played a key role, the answer is much more complex and more revealing. The imagined connections between Wichita and the twenty-eight countries where RI had a presence in 1925 reflected emerging networks of communication, transportation, and commerce at all levels on a global scale throughout the twentieth century. In one sense, each individual story was rather mundane: Harry Stanley of Kansas heard of Rotary while at a convention of insurance salesmen in Chicago and decided to start his own club in his hometown. But in pursuing the logic of RI's civic internationalism, the activities of businessmen like Stanley and his many brethren in chambers of commerce across the country demonstrated their support for expansion of US interests abroad—both economic and cultural.

Though Rotarians' understanding of international cooperation and peace was fraught with contradictions, their contributions along those lines were significant. For instance, how was it possible for the Whittier club in 1926 to convince well over one hundred fellow Rotary clubs of the importance of "bettering international relations" through stronger business contacts outside the United States when, at the same time, the state of California was brimming with anti-immigrant and especially anti-Asian sentiment? On the other hand, when Tokyo Rotarians like Yoneyama visited the United States, they were supposed to be treated well during their business trips because they represented something new and important to their fellow Rotarians in the United States. RI's "parliament of businessmen" promised a world of international business exchange on a level playing field among like-minded business and professionals who saw no contradictions between profit-making, corporate capitalism, and private philanthropy—so long as reasonable men maintained reasonable control over the direction of their economic development. But this managerial view of international business relations, of harmony and cooperation among the business and professional ranks of the world's commercial centers, required some fleshing out. While RI's "parliament of businessmen" had its contradictions, it also had genuine appeal for non-US members.

In the case of the Tokyo and Wichita clubs, how did they converge and then collide during the interwar period? In terms of convergence, RI's civic internationalism emphasized standardization of business practices; the establishment of codes of ethics in professional and trade associations; the "classification principle" for control of access to membership according to business and professional identities; and the capacities of a transnational class of businessmen to place all philanthropic endeavors above the interests of any given person, corporation, or nation. But RI's civic internationalism went further by combining these components with the boosterism and civic activism of men like Stanley, Booth, and their Japanese counterparts—both real and imagined.

RI's "ideal of service" provided the moral framework for its civic internationalism as it melded the worlds of business internationalism with local boosterism, some forms of progressive political activism with civic development, and philanthropic cooperation with individual effort—all in the name of service to the community. Crucially, "community" was a multifaceted term open to a variety of interpretations. The term could refer to a club's local environs, to a member's business and professional peers, to a town's regional interests and pride, to a national and even patriotic agenda, and to the international community loosely defined. RI developed and then harnessed its service ideology through particular institutional innovations after 1910 with real success. Like the Wilsonian tendencies of US foreign policy, RI's civic internationalism has proven durable because Wilsonianism and RI's civic internationalism shared a deep abiding faith in the moral imperatives of US international engagement; in the messianic sense of mission through uplift and compassion; in the disinterested nature of American involvement abroad; and in the universal nature of American social, political, and economic institutions. Businessmen in the United States could grasp and build upon such principles and sell them to their counterparts around the world.

In this vein, the Wichita Rotary club helps expose the exceptionalist pretensions of the United States as a "reluctant" empire. RI consistently saw its growth worldwide not only as one of its chief organizational objectives and crowning achievements, but as a measure of the associational "genius" of American civil society all wrapped up in one organizational package and ready for export as a gift from the United States to the world.[23] As such, the organization serves as a natural experiment—a concerted effort to send America's best into the world of international business before World War II. Similarly, the Tokyo Club had its own interpretations and uses of RI's civic internationalism. How and why did cities like Wichita and Tokyo imagine the possibilities of a common ground through their affiliated Rotary clubs and then go about making that happen?

THE SCIENCE OF BOOSTERISM—WICHITA STYLE

The Wichita Rotarians copied more than just the city manager form of government from their Dayton counterparts. Like Dayton, Wichita played a vital role in the rise of the aviation industry in the United States. But in the case of Wichita, the aviation industry eventually became the city's core identity as the "Air Capital of the world." An important first step in the city's self-transformation from a fading prairie town on the Chisholm Trail to a center of innovation in flight was an air meet at Walnut Grove in northwest Wichita in May 1911.[24] The meet, well advertised beforehand, featured four professional Curtiss aviators and attracted some eighteen thousand spectators. Unlike other air shows of the period, however, the event was more than just entertainment. Under the sponsorship of local businessman Orville A. Boyle, the air meet succeeded in demonstrating the practicality of "aeroplanes" as a means of transportation.

The large, flat, open prairies of Kansas and the constant flow of south winds into the region were an ideal setting for early aviators. And for a city still reeling from the economic shocks of the 1890s, such conditions might translate into a significant business opportunity. Even in 1911, the *Wichita Eagle* was already boosting aviation as Wichita's destiny: "The aeroplane is unreal to Wichita . . . until we see it soar over our own local habitat. Then by such a first-event, the aeroplane is ours, and we are of the aeroplane age."[25] The summer of 1911 brought Wichita its first real taste of aviation as its industrial future thanks in large part to Boyle. Just a few months later, Harry Stanley returned from Chicago convinced of Wichita's pressing need for a Rotary club. Orville A. Boyle eventually joined Stanley's new service club and became its president in 1925–1926, when he pushed hard for RI's adoption of the Wichita Plan for all Rotary clubs in the world. Whether selling Wichitans on the future of aviation or RI's board of directors on Wichita as a convention city, Orville Boyle knew how to promote a good business idea and make it a reality.[26]

But it took more than just promotional skills to get the aviation industry firmly rooted in Wichita. Developing the technical and entrepreneurial skills of early Kansas aviators like A. K. Longren and Clyde Cessna and the nascent technologies of the 1910s into an industrial sector by the 1920s and 1930s required available capital. Both Longren and Cessna understood this necessity when they sought military contracts in the opening phases of World War I—to no avail.[27] Fortunately, the El Dorado oil boom had hit the region, reaching maximum oil production just as the United States entered and fought the Great War in Europe. Skyrocketing demand for oil in a time of war resulted in a surplus of local capital.[28] One of the greatest beneficiaries of the boom was "Jake" Moellendick, who became a passionate investor in aviation in May 1919 after being flown in a plane to one of his wells by a young lieutenant and West Point graduate named Julius Earl Schaefer (future president of Boeing Wichita and director of its massive Plant 2 during World War II).

Within a few weeks, Wichita saw the birth of several airplane companies and, within a few years, the establishment of a whole new industry brimming with promise. The Wichita Aircraft Company, chartered only two months after Moellendick's first flight with Schaefer, received financing from Moellendick and several other Wichita businessmen, including George Siedhoff, president of his own concrete construction firm and longtime active member of the Wichita Rotary club. The aircraft company, after starting over in partnership with Emil "Matty" Laird of Chicago, eventually became the incubator for private aviation in Wichita, producing the likes of Walter Beech and Lloyd Stearman and their respective aircraft companies.[29] In the end, aviation in Wichita missed the stimulus of war production until orders for military aircraft began in the late 1930s in anticipation of another war. Instead, for the business community of Wichita during the interwar years, the growth of aviation was to be a mostly private and peaceful affair. For the Rotary club of Wichita and RI's civic internationalism, that was as it should be. Like its philanthropic endeavors, Wichita's future was supposed to emerge from private sector initiatives and from harmonious trade relations with the world.

Along with plenty of local money looking for investment, the war years also meant a surfeit of trained military pilots in the United States and cross-fertilization of aviation technology across the Atlantic. And there was plenty of local interest in attracting those pilots and that technology to Wichita and its competing cities. As a result, when the aviation committee of the Wichita chamber of commerce bought farmland just outside the city limits for a new landing field in 1919, the chamber publicized the event with the Victory Liberty Loan Flying Circus. Using techniques from war propaganda and showcasing ace pilots and their warplanes, the Flying Circus featured mock aerial engagements and "bombing" of the city of Wichita with twenty thousand copies of the *Wichita Eagle* newspaper so that "the people of this city will be able to get something of the feeling of the way actual battle conditions were carried out."[30] At least twenty-five thousand spectators came out to the new airfield to see the "bombings" and aerial combat while the rest of the city was treated to much the same spectacle, like it or not. Though the Great War in Europe had not directly spurred growth in the field of aviation for Wichita, in the wake of the war prosperity did return to the city and the region. By 1919, major breakthroughs in flight made during the war were becoming a source of entertainment as much as a business opportunity for the new era. There was no reason the two could not be combined.

The *Wichita Eagle,* in fact, had more of a part in the day's activities than merely serving as material for "bombs." Marcellus Murdock, part of the family that had been publishing the newspaper since the 1890s and soon to become its head of publishing, was the chair of the hundred-member aviation committee set up by Wichita's chamber of commerce and responsible for the day's events.[31] He was also an active member of the Wichita Rotary club, even to the point of establishing clubs in other Kansas cities.[32] Like so many of his fellow Rotarians, Murdock also belonged to other social and booster clubs.[33] Though the Wichita Rotary club had a particular devotion to making a success out of aviation, other organizations contributed as well. The Kiwanis club of El Dorado, Kansas, for instance, sponsored an air show in 1923 that attracted about five thousand people, while the Wichita Kiwanis club sponsored a competition for a logo in 1928 that best suited Wichita's self-proclaimed title as the "Air Capital."[34]

But the signature event came when more than two hundred businessmen managed to raise over $20,000 to attract the National Air Congress in 1924. Though the massive weekend show awed the audience of well over twenty-five thousand people with classic air show stunts and scores of various military and civilian aircraft, the real purpose lay in the attraction of national attention and investment in Wichita as a national hub for aviation production and distribution.[35] It was in this hotbed of boosterism and municipal development that the Wichita Rotary club hatched a plan to convince the Chicago headquarters to hold its annual international convention in Wichita sometime before 1930. Winning the right to host such a large, international convention attended by thousands of businessmen from around the world would be the ideal way to publicize Wichita's goal of becoming a hub for aircraft production and transportation—the new Detroit for airplanes. By the 1920s, businessmen like Orville Boyle, Marcellus Murdock, and Harry Stanley (tasked by the club with bringing RI's convention to Wichita in 1924) were already skilled at similar civic projects and promotions. Their involvement in Rotary, however, was the best means of fulfilling their goals and executing their projects. Boosterism, like aviation, was fast becoming a science. In Wichita, it was turning empty prairie lands just outside the city limits into concrete landing strips paved with civic pride and aimed toward a future of private gain through public support.

FLIGHTS OF FANCY

Like so many other local booster projects, the push to host RI's international convention lasted through the 1920s and constantly played up Wichita's post–World War I identity as a burgeoning center of aviation.[36] Developed as a way to learn about all other countries in the growing circle of Rotary and to present Wichita as an internationally minded city, the club's Wichita Plan was nevertheless rejected by RI as a model club activity on international affairs for all other clubs. Yet the Wichitans remained undaunted—so long as the possibility of getting that convention was in sight. Under the club presidencies of William Coleman, founder of Coleman Lamp and Stove Company, in 1926–1927 and Earle W. Evans, senior law partner and board member for Santa Fe Railroad, Mid-Plains Oil Company, and First National Bank, in 1927–1928, the club developed a new promotional strategy: mass circulation of the club's promotional literature among all Rotarians. In other words, if the businessmen of Wichita were not able to lure RI's members to their city through hosting the international convention, then the Wichita Rotarians would have to meet and greet their counterparts in Rotary in their own cities and in familiar terms.

Harry Stanley, the resourceful insurance salesman and founder of Wichita Rotary, was at the center of it all. So was his old friend, Giff Booth Sr., president of Grit Printery. Stanley formed a committee within the club devoted to highlighting RI's "Sixth Object": "The advancement of understanding, good will, and international peace through a world fellowship of business and professional men devoted to the Rotary ideal of service." The committee—a microcosm of the Wichita business community—centered on the publication and distribution of a booklet on the subject that offered up the Wichita Rotarians' own views on the future of international relations.[37] The Wichita club's publication, *The Five Ships and Cargoes*, was designed to sell the city of Wichita as a major player in an increasingly interconnected world economy and the local business and professional leaders as men dedicated to peaceful and mutually beneficial ties among nations and national economies. The Wichita club printed up thousands of copies and sent them to every Rotary club in the world and to the leaders of all national governments for good measure.[38] Essentially, the booklet served as Wichita's very own business card to the world. The publication also provides a revealing glimpse into the highest ideals of RI's civic internationalism—ideals that were revised and reversed by the cold war era (figure 3.1).

The booklet revealed in colorful detail and flowery prose just how the Wichita Rotarians—as a club—imagined themselves, their city, and their country in the emerging world of international business and social relations. The booklet is a remarkable testament to their confidence in the progressive inevitabilities of international trade and the intrinsic benevolence of the United States in the world. As such, the booklet documents an important cultural moment not only in the world of Rotary International but also in the hopes and dreams of Main Street's most active citizens in the interwar years.

The booklet's cover says it all. It is dominated by five airplanes flying in a V formation among clouds and yet somehow passing over the earth at the same time. With the Western Hemisphere in full view, the outlines of the Americas, Europe, Africa, and central Asia are well contoured. Noticeably absent are any political boundaries. Also, only a small dot marks the location of Wichita. For a book designed to put

FIG 3.1: Taking its cue from the world of professional advertising and public relations, the business community of Wichita sought to position the city in a global context through promotional materials. The Wichita club was one of thousands seeking to "boost" their cities' business prospects through Rotary's networks worldwide. *Reproduced from a copy of the pamphlet "Five Ships and Cargoes," in the Wichita Club Historical Files of the Rotary Club of Wichita, Kansas.*

Wichita on the mental maps of commercial leaders around the world, this is an unexpected subtlety. The image drives home the point: the world is much bigger than the city limits of Wichita, the state of Kansas, and for that matter the United States of America. In the foreword, the Wichita Rotarians explain that, in a recent meeting on RI's "Sixth Object" of international peace and cooperation, they had "felt the thrill of fellowship with all the world" and that in "seeking a means of communication and interchange of thought, the idea developed of sending a fleet of ships that we might know each other better."[39] The "ships" are the five airplanes flying in V formation above the earth, and they are introduced in order as Craftsmanship, Acquaintanceship, Sportsmanship, Friendship, and Kinship. Each "ship," in turn, gets its own short chapter with a detailed explanation of its components. Taken as a whole, the five ships represent the basic categories of understanding, so to speak, of the Wichita Rotarians' world outlook and their city's relation to it. The businessmen of Wichita, the "Air Capital," had their own original take on RI's civic internationalism—and they wished to express it through their promotional circular to their business peers around the world.

Each "ship" appears in its respective chapter first as a close-up of an airplane flying over the city of Wichita, with only the thematic names on the planes changed with each chapter. Below each airplane, zooming through billowing clouds, is the newly built Wichita Municipal Airport with the other four airplanes parked in front. Most revealing, however, is the large number of oil derricks off in the distance and the roads with trucks and cars connecting the airport to the oil fields. Moreover, between the airport and the oil wells is a recently harvested field of wheat. The productivity of the land comes in two measures: agriculture and natural resources. Both are in harvest and both are in easy transport to markets far and wide, thanks to the ribbons of new roads and the miracles of flight. The point is simple enough: Wichita is no mere prairie town trapped in the heartland of North America by the continental scales of distance to other markets and nations. Armed with its five "ships," Wichita had a lot of good—and goods—to offer the world.

The airplane called "Craftmanship" comes first because "labor is foremost in the scheme of life designed for men." The marketplace provides the foundation of all social relations because "the results of constructive labor constantly widen the scope of contacts with others." "Contact," as in trade with others. Consistent with the portrayal of Wichita below each airplane, the chapter argues for the "indispensability of materials" (such as oil, wheat, and airplanes) because it is "recognized that the fate of nations may depend upon the method of distributing the natural and artificial products of the world. True civilization is not only the satisfaction of individual or national ambitions to possess materials; but equally it is the manner in which possession is accomplished." The just distribution of "materials" and "products" in the international marketplace lies at the core of "true civilization." And the guarantor of that just distribution is "honest craftsmanship," which is "not a legal definition but the proved ability to surpass in quality of product. To oppress or restrict those who have shown this ability is a denial of the common brotherhood and a confession of inferiority. The enforced distress of one race is the dishonor of another." Moreover, fair and open trade and equality of access to all other markets had its corollary in the marketplace of ideas since "the advance of the Human Race is in direct relationship to the improvement of facilities for the exchange and interchange of facts, information, knowledge, truth."[40] Adam Smith would be proud.

Reflecting the giddy hopefulness of the business internationalism of the period, Harry Stanley's committee was hitting the keynotes of a market-based ideology that was as basic to the Open Door Note of Secretary of State John Hay a generation earlier as it is to the World Economic Forum of today. The Rotarians' own twist comes in how they infuse their notions of free trade with such lofty moral purpose:

> The present generation has witnessed the greatest advance of all time in communication and transportation. What significance does this vital truth hold? . . . Shall it be said that this generation used these marvelous forces of nature with their terrific power only to gain selfish advantage in the competitive struggle for existence, or shall we see to it that these forces are employed for the high purpose of bringing the nations into that close relationship where we realize that no part of mankind can sustain injury without the whole suffering thereby.[41]

The global sweep of the Wichita club's vision matched the imagery of the club's booklet. That vision also recapitulated the basic tenets of RI's civic internationalism in the most progressive and all-encompassing terms of modernity. Within only a few years such an optimistic view of international trade and foreign relations would come to seem a remote dream at best, lost in the competing economic nationalisms of the 1930s followed by global warfare; but for the Wichita Rotarians in 1928, the scientific wonders of a rapidly shrinking modern world posed a profound moral challenge for an entire generation of humanity. In reaching out to their fellow Rotarians, the Wichita businessmen believed themselves to be living up to that challenge.

The airplane called "Acquaintanceship" follows suit. Here a different kind of contact is in mind. Unlike the "products of labor," the second theme covers the intangibles of international exchange by introducing an imaginary man who takes off "on his first trade expedition" and meets up with another from a different land. The moment of "acquaintanceship" arrives: "Encouraged by these first steps and lured on by ever-extending vistas of the world beyond, he makes more and more acquaintances and develops contacts with the men of all races and all nations until the whole world is of him and he of the whole world." Affiliation and fellowship overcome difference through the establishment of a new "bond of sympathy and mutual interests" such that "even those who differ radically in their ideas and view may, if generous, meet and discuss their differences with pleasure and delight." The transformative power of face-to-face contact has no limits, so long as those coming together do so in mutual respect and in a reasonable way. The simple "grasp of the hand" becomes something that "links and binds the races of men in the bonds of moral fraternity."

The sociability of the local Rotary club, in this light, becomes a microcosm of the constantly multiplying conventions, conferences, and assemblies held by clubs in various cities and regions around the world that, in aggregate, help bring forth the foundation for international peace and prosperity. So the theory goes:

> Acquaintanceship will lead him on into the broader fields of life. It will teach him respect for the views, manners, customs, and peculiarities of others. And as it turns him into the paths of fellowship and friendship he will learn the lesson, which the world most needs today, that his enemy is not that hateful being he was so apt to paint him and that "the man he hated was the man he did not know."[42]

The business internationalism of Wichita's boosters, in fact, was also imbued with a great deal of cultural internationalism—if only in rhetoric. The imagined intimacies with distant lands needed only the collapsing of distance and the fair exchange of views to overcome hatred and distrust among the nations.

However lofty the notions, the language was revealing. The world described in *The Five Ships and Cargoes* committed the Wichita club to a level of tolerance for difference—religious, ethnic, cultural, and in some ways racial—that was somewhat surprising. Though the club members could imagine their counterparts in business only as other men, the Wichita Rotarians imagined themselves as part of an unfolding international arena where there were "many men of many nations getting together on the ground of associated interests—interests athletic, scientific, political, diplomatic, religious, or, as in Rotary, in business and professional—but all starting from items of agreement and common acceptance and *culminating in the elimination of differences*" (emphasis added).[43] The club's paean to modernity and progress centered on the welcoming of an exotic peer not only within the "perfect democracy" of the Rotarians' own international organization but also in the world at large.

The final three parts of the booklet develop these themes even more as the three remaining airplanes leave the hangar and take off from Wichita's Municipal Airport, laden with the three final cargoes of international peace and understanding: "Sportsmanship," "Friendship," and "Kinship." The first term is shorthand for "a spirit of tolerance" combined with "team-work and cooperation" and serves as a metaphor for the international marketplace as a fair and level field where "a game [can be] played cleanly and manfully." "Friendship," on the other hand, soars much higher in sentiment:

> The destiny of a nation is to serve its people in the highest sense by the development of human resources. The world is gradually becoming more civilized and tolerant. In such a development upward national progress is not dependent upon the sword and the bayonet. These are no longer the insignia of power, but in this more civilized world they are becoming the insignia of

> decay. They represent waste and misery and paralysis of the works of commerce and art which are leading man ever upward.[44]

The progress of civilization entails the rejection of war. Businessmen and professionals who understand this reality of the modern condition, like those of the Wichita Rotary club, are ready to receive their shipment of "Kinship," the cargo for the final airplane to leave the hangar and go aloft. The stakes cannot be higher as "men must finally realize their community of interest and destiny or perish." It is here that the United States enters furtively as the modular nation: "In this country we have a cosmopolitan race; we are the world in miniature. Here all peoples of the earth have descendants who share the pride of ancestry that animates the Old World. All strains of blood are as old as man, and all children of the dust are brothers despite themselves." The universal nation, it turns out, has a cosmopolitan pedigree. As a result, the uniquely cooperative nature of Americans finds its most sublime expression in the everyday working out of competing interests and races in the imagined harmonious pluralism of the marketplace:

> We have had to be practical. Races rich in variety must find a common road to peace. In commerce, addicted to bargaining, we are used to finding a common ground of agreement. The conciliatory point of view thus forced upon us has made competition and conflicting interests a source of enlightenment, profit, and friendly association. And why not? Doesn't trade offer more opportunities for friendship than enmity?[45]

What makes the American nation so exemplary is its success at forging a pluralistic harmony out of the cacophony of free market relations. For a reputable businessman or professional looking to deepen international ties with like-minded peers around the world, this is a national identity that makes sense at home and sounds good abroad—a kind of boosters' mission statement for world peace. The booklet then closed with an open invitation: "Thus together, do we woo the friendship of the world, and lowly listen for the returning wings of these evangels of peace."[46] When

Wichita's boosters considered the international, they presented the United States as a great place to do business and as a harbinger of future prosperity for the entire world. For a committee chaired by a man like Harry Stanley, could it have been any other way?

DALLAS, 1929

RI's international convention in Dallas in 1929 was simply a must for Umekichi Yoneyama. Dallas was the city where his friend, "Bill" Fukushima, first introduced him to Rotary in 1920. Yoneyama had to be there. Making the long trip on an ocean liner across the Pacific would take a lot of time, however, from Yoneyama's very busy schedule. Serving as president of the Mitsui Trust Company had its many obligations. But so did serving as the district governor for the Seventieth District and its seven clubs in Japan and five in China. The top echelons of RI had their own reasons for wanting Yoneyama to attend that particular convention. For the first time in the organization's history, during the previous year, more clubs entered into the organization from outside than from within the United States.[47] Also, with the addition of clubs in Nicaragua and Honduras, "every republic on the western hemisphere [was] now in the Rotary family."[48] This was patently untrue, actually, as RI continued to avoid Haiti, Jamaica, and the rest of the West Indies assiduously from the early 1920s to the late 1950s, as detailed in Chapter 2. Nevertheless, with many clubs fast appearing in Asia and Southeast Asia, from Palestine to India to Thailand to the Malay States and the Dutch East Indies, there was a sense that a crucial tipping point in the organization's worldwide growth was at hand.[49] As a result, the featured plenary session of the entire convention was titled "What Rotary Means to Rotary Clubs and Rotarians around the World." Yoneyama was the first of many district governors from around the world to speak to the massive audience on the topic.

Having become one of the earliest and most successful exports of Rotary outside the English-speaking world, the Tokyo club and its founder, Yoneyama, had celebrity status by 1929. He and his club embodied what it meant to "extend Rotary" to far-off places and cultures, to reach and transform the exotic peers of Rotary's "world fellowship." As such, when the roll call of nations sounded out alphabetically before the entire assembly, the Japanese delegation was passed over for dramatic effect: members of the delegation were asked to stand up at the end of the roll call to receive their own ovation from the assembled throng.[50]

On many levels, Yoneyama saw the long trip from Tokyo to Dallas as a personal pilgrimage—and so did his counterparts among the leadership of RI. For more than twelve thousand attendees and visitors crammed into the Texas State Fair Park over five days in late May, the overall theme was inescapable: international service. As Yoneyama spoke before thousands on the meaning of "international service" using "the platform of this great parliament of business and professional men of the world," he recounted his first time in Dallas and the subsequent establishment of Japan's first Rotary club in Tokyo. He told the audience he had come to a simple conclusion that same year: "Fellow Rotarians, this is an age of international organization. Many kinds of seed have been transplanted into Japan of late. But some varieties have not entirely agreed with the soil there. . . . Rotary is one variety that is steadily growing, and is firmly rooted." Nine clubs, with almost five hundred members, the vast majority of whom were Japanese, guaranteed the roots were deep,

> because Rotary holds the best worked out principle and fittest application of a code as to the practice of a golden rule always wanted by humanity, but particularly needed by the present age after the World War which was fought, we know not why. An organization like ours, with a high moral standard, composed of representative men of business and the professions. . . . must succeed in what all the other practices and theories have failed in doing—bringing satisfaction for the well being of humanity.[51]

Yoneyama's interpretation of RI's presence and influence in Japan reflected how Japanese Rotarians tended to approach the teachings of Rotary—in a quasi-mystical way, bordering on a kind of syncretism of Japanese Buddhism and modern, business internationalism. (His translation of the autobiography of RI's founder, Paul Harris, into Japanese was seen as the personal contribution of a disciple.)[52] More revealing was Rotarian Shun Mizushima's translation of Japanese characters over an altar at a Buddhist temple in Kyoto for RI's president, Tom Sutton, during his visit there in 1928: "It would do for a Rotary Motto, as it says 'If you look upon the world through eyes of kindliness and mercy, it will come back to you in oceans of happiness.'"[53] Yoneyama's words to the Dallas audience, therefore, were not mere mimicry of Rotarian jargon. When he turned proudly to the president of the Dallas Rotary club and official host of the entire convention and presented a flag of the Japanese Empire with "the sincerest greeting of the Tokyo Rotary Club," he did so as a proud, independent, and very high-level Japanese businessman. Yoneyama was direct: "I love my own country; therefore I can sympathize with other people who love their own. I am glad that I am a Rotarian, privileged to join with you in the common interest." The Dallas Rotarian matched the sentiment, saying that the Japanese flag "typifies the flag of your friendship, which we shall always hold dear." Thousands stood and roared with applause.[54]

Yoneyama echoed fundamental debates coursing through RI as its international expansion began to take off in the late 1920s. These debates dominated the Dallas convention as well from beginning to end. In his welcoming address at the opening ceremony at Fair Park Stadium, the mayor of Dallas (along with the governor of Texas) offered the city residents as "your servants" and the city's swimming pools as "free to you." Had there been Black Rotarians from Haiti and Jamaica at the convention, this would have been an insurmountable problem for the Jim Crow city—an impossible invitation. Whether from Asia, Latin America, or Europe, however, the exotic peers of Rotary and their families did not threaten the social and economic structures of white supremacy.

Instead, it was a night of international harmony and pageantry as the stadium, stuffed with thousands of conventioneers, became center stage for the "Procession of Flags": hundreds of Dallas high school girls, dressed in the costumes of the fifty-one nations "composing the great family of Rotary," escorted into the stadium the flags of each of those nations in the order in which they "were welcomed to their places in the Rotary world." The procession reenacted "the progress of each country . . .

toward one goal, that of the ideal of service and friendship as typified by Rotary. When the realization of true worth of such an ideal was reached, each country gave its treasured possession—its flag—to seal the pact." While the submersion of the national to the international was mostly symbolic, the stagecraft was Olympic in scale: "a mammoth castle of service with Rotary flags waving from its top" and "a veritable Grecian palace from which long staircases led to a beautiful garden wherein lay a huge Rotary wheel on a revolving base." Amid bright lights, a drum roll, and the blare of trumpets, on each side of the great Rotary wheel RI's two mottoes appeared—"He profits most who serves best" and "Service above self"—so that "the message destined to reach all corners of the earth was visible to all." The flag of the United States, however, entered last, "followed by the Spirit of the South, known as 'Dixie.'" Meanwhile, the speeches, fireworks, applause, and national airs of each nation played during "this great spectacle of patriotism and international accord" were captured as well by a KRLD radio broadcast for thousands more in their homes.[55] The "procession of the flags" played out the imperial trappings of an American business empire in the sights and sounds of international peace and progress. The theatrical blurring of nationalist and internationalist themes came together in a pastiche of transnational business class triumphalism. There were no spatial limits to Rotary's growth but "the far corners of the earth." Like the United States itself, RI's expansion was only a question of time, its goal of benevolent assimilation self-evident.

But pageantry and spectacle aside, there was genuine concern among both US and non-US Rotarians that RI's "international service" was really just so much Americanization. During the smaller "international service assemblies" at the Dallas convention, club members and conventioneers at times showed greater sophistication than the stage managers of the "procession of flags." Rotarian Joe Porter of Lexington, Kentucky, was one of the most articulate:

> If we want to take them simply the ideals of Rotary and let them adapt these ideals to their particular needs, we are going to accomplish a great deal more than if we try to take the ideals and put upon them the western interpretation. . . . I happen to be

> connected with the missionary society that is having some discussion along this line. When we attempt to impose upon those people the interpretations of a western civilization of certain ideals . . . , we are getting into a pitfall. . . . If we will take to them the ideals of service and let them take those ideals and work them out in terms of their own civilization, Rotary is going to have a much more successful career in its extension work than otherwise.[56]

Toledo's Frank Mulholland, "past president" of the IARC in 1914–1915, was more concise: "We Rotarians of the United States must learn that we cannot Americanize the world through Rotary. Neither can we Anglo-Saxonize American Rotary throughout the world. It is international."[57] Another gathered assembly on the same topic heard from delegates from Pittsburgh and Washington, D.C., who had the consuls and ambassadors of various nations to their weekly meetings as guest speakers and then considered what clubs in cities without such dignitaries might do for "international service activities." A Rotarian from New Orleans suggested having members of the club speak on other countries: "I think I know the psychology of the eastern countries, such as India, Persia, Egypt, and Palestine. I could speak to the club on that subject because I am familiar with it. . . . I was born in America but I have been in Persia and southern Russia, too." Countless businessmen with similar travel experience held the same view. Yet "Americanization" also had economic as well as cultural dimensions—a point made clear by a Rotarian from Tulsa, "the metropolis of the oil world," where every year the club hosted the International Petroleum Exposition and its "large group of petroleum-producing fellows . . . from the different petroleum-producing countries." In Tulsa, club life and the oil industry fell under the heading "international service."[58]

A modern business traveler's view of the world would suffice in many clubs as a voice of authority on "other races and nations" and "international differences": some familiarity with another country was better than none. But a Rotarian from Peoria, Illinois cautioned against being content with seeing the world from a hotel window and offered an alternative source of expertise on things international:

> I conducted a study class (nearly all the churches today have study classes) . . . on a book that related to the South American republics. . . . The books that are written today for the church are written intelligently and attractively, and you will find them of great interest. I suggest that in the small towns, especially, they turn to some of these books that you find the women of our churches reading. The women probably know more about these countries than the men do today.[59]

As with the "procession of flags," women of all ages were often used in display mode for "international service" activities, but rarely in the capacity of experts on the subject, as suggested by the man from Peoria.[60] Tensions between older forms of missionary internationalism and newer, secular forms of business internationalism were evident in such exchanges as RI continued trying to hold together a civil religion premised on older religious injunctions as well as modern, professional business practices. Meanwhile, tensions over gender roles and the authority of experts were also manifest as the claims of white, established businessmen to social trusteeship of the community were growing more dependent on their internationalist credentials. Appearing ignorant of the world outside the United States risked the loss of face locally—especially when men were standing next to their better-informed wives, sisters, and daughters.

Some small towns were already finding ways to demonstrate their connections with people abroad—at least in theory. The central question posed by RI's International Service Committee to all twelve separate assemblies held on the meaning of "international service" was a mouthful: "By what kind of international service programs can a Rotary club promote knowledge; first, of other races and nations; second, of economic and racial problems that may cause international strife; and third, of arbitration and other plans for adjusting international differences?"[61] A big question for a small-town Rotary club. But some responses were revealing. A Rotarian from tiny Uvalde, Texas, population six thousand, explained, when Mexican Rotarians complained that "we wouldn't let Mexicans eat in our town. We had International Service right there." The Texan explained further that, in conjunction with forty-five other clubs in their district in Texas, the Rotarians decided to "get well-informed on the districts of the world. So they named my little town Finland. . . . In getting information concerning Finland I found that the presiding officer of the League of Nations was from there, that Finland took second honors in the Olympic games, etc."[62] In Mission, Texas, each of the town's more than forty Rotarians was given a card with the name of the first president of the first Rotary club in a given country and then asked to imagine himself as that man and to speak on the details of the club's founding as provided on the back of the cards. The "great international conference" of Mission, Texas, was, in effect, a modified, small-town version of the Wichita Plan.[63]

Meanwhile, another Rotarian from Rexburg, Idaho, said the "procession of flags" had given him an idea to "place a small flag of all the countries with a Rotary club before the club members during an 'international service program' and have that member get up and announce the flag, tell when that nation came into Rotary, and try to find out something about the meaning of that flag. . . . For instance, take the Austrian flag. It is red, white and red. That flag has a meaning the same as our flag."[64] The visual and material nature of RI's civic internationalism would often manifest in such practical ways in daily club life.

The Idahoan's assertion that its "meaning [was] the same as our flag" bordered on a kind of small-town internationalism voiced by another Rotarian from South Hill, Virginia: "Don't judge the citizen of another country, take for instance China, by the boy or the man in the laundry, or in some other phase of commercial activity in your town. Don't judge the nation by the individual, and be lenient in your understanding of what these people have to say."[65] While more substantial programs of student exchange, visitations, and correspondence developed in larger cities and towns with greater resources and breadth of contact, we find that, even in the smallest of clubs and in the most attenuated of forms, tolerance of "international differences" and engagement with an imaginary world of exotic peers had its cachet—and Rotary had the capacity to tap into and cultivate that engagement.

Finally, what was the value of RI's internationalist ambitions without the content of its civic activities—the core of what Rotary was imparting to the world? Only a half hour before Yoneyama led off the crucial plenary session titled "The International Service Program," another key plenary, "Community Service," took place. After further talks including "Student Loan Funds," "Rural-Urban Acquaintance," and "Boys' Work," the final speaker stood up to detail how his home club of Toledo, Ohio, had brought about the creation of the Ohio Society for Crippled Children and the International Society for Crippled Children. The accomplishments of Ed Kelsey and his fellow Toledo Rotarians over the prior eight years were significant:

> May I say to you that we have thirty states and provinces of Canada that are today holding out the opportunity of life for these crippled children, these five hundred thousand children in this country alone who never had a thing done for them until Rotary pointed the way, and today the Elks, the Shriners, The American Legion, have all fallen in and now we are working on the finest thing in our program.[66]

The Toledo club's project stemmed from the realization that no other organization in their city was even aware of the children's presence and numbers, let alone doing anything to rectify it. Filling in such a gap in community service and bringing in other organizations to help solve the problem was considered the ideal way for a Rotary club to operate. It was American voluntarism at its best: efficient, philanthropic, cooperative, and private. And there was nothing like sentiment to motivate the volunteers:

> Can you imagine what comes into a child's face the first time he throws away his crutches and is able to walk, stand erect and hold his own before men? . . . I have seen tears come unashamed down the cheeks of every man because they have looked into the faces of these crippled children and known they have had a part in the making of a man.[67]

Sentiment aside, the story of the Toledo Rotary club's first forays into coping with the ravages of polio in children in the 1920s soon became a common community service activity for Rotary clubs even after the advent of Jonas Salk's polio vaccine in 1955. In fact, these consistent club efforts, in aggregate, eventually blossomed into one of the most significant public health initiatives of the postwar era as the Rotary Foundation, which began significant growth soon after World War II, partnered with the UN's World Health Organization in 1985 with the common goal of eradicating polio through oral inoculations by 2005—Rotary International's centennial. Except for a few outbreaks in a small number of countries, the goal has been nearly met.[68] In all its aspects, the civic internationalism of RI was nearing its early phase of maturation just as the storm clouds of the Great Depression, trade protectionism, European and Asian fascism, and global warfare were gathering on the horizon.

FROM THE "AIR CAPITAL OF THE WORLD" TO BOEING PLANT 2

For the Wichita Rotarians, the Dallas convention was not so much a personal pilgrimage as a sales opportunity. Not only was the distance between Wichita and Dallas nothing like what Yoneyama had to traverse, the Wichitans were able to travel much faster than Yoneyama on his Pacific steamship. As yet another publicity stunt, the Wichita Rotarians flew to the convention in one large fleet of private aircraft. Naturally, Harry Stanley was behind the stunt. His committee's booklet, *The Five Ships,* had made such a splash in the world of RI the year before that everyone had expected him and his fellow Wichitans to arrive in Minneapolis, the convention city for 1928, in airplanes. In preparing for the next convention in early 1929, Harry Stanley, with Merle Bennett, general manager of the J.O. Adams Music Co., and Earl Hutton, of A.M. Hutton & Son, casualty insurance, hatched a plan to exceed all expectations. About twenty-five Rotarians and their spouses formed the "Wichita Armada" of five Travel Air monoplanes, a Phillips Petroleum plane, three Stearman biplanes, and another six aircraft all "designed, built, tested, and flown by and from the air-minded city" and flew to Love Field in Dallas on a "mission of peace and prosperity." Even though the original plan involved convincing Charles Lindbergh and Walter Beech to lead the "flying squadron" of some thirty planes, the Wichita Armada, half that size and without celebrities, still drew a large crowd and made headlines and the newsreels. In preparation for the stunt, the Wichita club held one of their weekly meetings at the Travel Air factory, where half of the three hundred Rotarians and their spouses got to fly in one of Travel Air's "big cabin" planes.[69]

But Harry Stanley's promotion did not stop there. During the massive opening dinner of the convention, paper airplanes shot across the tables while the Wichita Rotarians handed out tickets for free airplane rides. In the end, the Wichita Rotarians pitched their city as the "Air Capital of the World" to an estimated five hundred or so conventioneers as they rode the bus to and from the airport for their free rides. The entire affair was considered a major promotional success for Wichita, searing the city's image as "wide-awake, up-to-date, and air-conscious" into everyone's mind at the convention.[70]

This image was also in the minds of investors on Wall Street. Of the four most important aircraft manufacturers in Wichita in the 1920s (Swallow, Travel Air, Stearman, and Cessna), only Cessna made it out of the decade still a locally owned and independent corporation. In the case of Stearman, what started as a $60,000 investment by Marcellus Murdock and other local investors in 1920 became a part of the United Aircraft and Transport Corporation only three months after the Wichita Armada made its trek to Love Field. Put together thanks to City Bank of New York, the new conglomerate had $80 million in capitalization and $250 million in total assets, including Stearman of Wichita, Boeing of Seattle, and several other aircraft manufacturers. Though Stearman was debt-free and turning a modest $65,000 in annual profit in 1929, it was too small to compete on its own and too big to avoid the attention of investors at the national level. The newly formed United Air Lines began investing money into its experimental works in Burbank, run by John K. Northrop. Wichita got some investment as well, resulting in the construction of a new $400,000 factory that later became known as Boeing Plant 1. The wide-open space around the new plant would become a major selling point for greatly expanding Stearman's production capacities a decade later to accommodate mass production of B-29 bombers designed to fly thousands of miles across the Pacific. That second plant would become known simply as Plant 2 and Stearman as

FIG 3.2: The culmination of decades of evolution within the business community of the city, Boeing's Wichita Division, led by Rotarian J. Earl Schaefer, became the defining corporate model for rapid economic growth in a time of war. *Reproduction courtesy of Kansas Aviation Museum, Wichita, Kansas.*

Boeing Wichita, with Rotarian J. Earl Schaefer managing its production and labor (figure 3.2).[71]

Wichita was fortunate, in fact, that Schaefer was in charge during the worst years of the Depression. With Cessna and Travel Air shutting down operations in 1931 and 1932, respectively, and the First National Bank—a local bank with Rotarian Earle Evans on its board—calling in its loan on Stearman, Schaefer made his own trek to the headquarters of United Air Lines to try to save Stearman's operations in Wichita. He succeeded in two ways: he negotiated a loan through the Fourth National Bank, and he won Stearman its first military contracts. By 1933, Stearman managed to design and build the Kaydet biplane. Using outdated technology, the desperate aircraft company nevertheless had come up with a workhorse airplane that was perfect for training new pilots because of its no-nonsense design and ability to take a beating from newcomers to flight. The airplane became the salvation of Stearman as it went through repeated versions through the 1930s until the last days of the war in 1945. The success of the Kaydet translated into Stearman's—and later Boeing Wichita's—specialization in the production and delivery of military aircraft, while Boeing Seattle focused on the production of commercial, passenger airliners. An estimated sixty thousand cadets learned to fly for the Army Air Corps in the cockpit of a Kaydet by the end of World War II.[72]

Rotarian Schaefer's company may not have been at the forefront of aviation technology throughout the 1930s, but it was at the forefront of political and economic developments and in a solid position by 1940 to receive one of the largest and most daunting orders for military aircraft in the history of aerial warfare. Boeing's Plant 2 had exceeded the demanding production schedules for the B-29 first set out in 1943. By early 1945, Plant 2 had reached its peak production, producing four bombers per day and serving as the model for B-29 production in Georgia, Nebraska, and Washington. By war's end, Wichita alone had built 44 percent of the entire fleet of 3,895 B-29 bombers.[73] From the first raids on Japan's steel center in Yawata in June 1944 to the firebombing of Tokyo in March 1945 to the annihilation of Hiroshima and Nagasaki later that summer, the impact of the B-29 bomber on the nature and outcome of the war in the Pacific would be hard to overestimate. For the city of Wichita, the US Army Air Corps, and the Boeing Corporation, the venture was a profitable one all around. In fact, massive demand for war production transformed the political imagination of Wichita's business community, much as it did the United States as a whole.[74]

But the war also transformed J. Earl Schaefer and his fellow Rotarians of Wichita into dedicated cold war warriors. In his address, "Facts on Air Power," to the Wichita Rotary club on Army Day, 7 April 1947, Schaefer—a West Point graduate and early devotee of the use of aviation in the army—reminded his audience that "in 1939, as the war clouds began to gather, the aircraft industry ranked 44th in value among all industries." Stated another way, "aircraft was sandwiched in between the sausage and candy industries." The lesson was clear: the rise of Wichita's industrial base effectively began after 1939. After reviewing the rapid expansion of B-29 production, the promising future of the B-52 bomber, and President Truman's Air Coordinating Committee, Schaefer pointed out the common theme: "Peace is still not assured." Though "aviation is global in its aspects," Schaefer explained that Boeing "cannot realize the full potential market for Stratocruisers in a war torn world. We must have peace to organize and exploit this market properly." In sharp contrast to the "Wichita armada" in Dallas 1929, Schaefer saw a very different world and a very different future for Wichita's industry: "We want peace, but we also want to be realistic in our approach toward peace. It is not here and at the moment it is not imminent." To that end, Schaefer ended his talk with a five-year program to develop US aviation industries to meet the pressing needs of the cold war. As a first lieutenant in the Aviation Section of the Army Signal Corps from 1917 to 1919, Schaefer experienced firsthand the effects of the sudden withdrawal of federal defense spending on aviation during the 1920s, and he was determined not to allow that to happen again. In 1949, Schaefer attended a Joint Orientation Conference by invitation from the secretary of defense, which allowed Schaefer—along with some eighty other business executives from defense industries—to observe demonstrations of current military technology. In recounting this experience to the Kiwanis club of El Dorado, Kansas a year later (11 May 1950), Schaefer made clear that only "when other means than Air Power can assure our security and ultimate Peace, my company is ready and willing to confine its efforts and energies to Peacetime pursuits and designs." But only six weeks later, North Korea unleashed its invasion into South Korea, driving home Schaefer's drumbeat for wartime preparation all too well. When it came to selecting a national candidate for the Republican Party for the next election, Schaefer had no interest in supporting the early front-runner and longtime noninterventionist, Senator Robert Taft. "Isolationism" in 1952 was not an option for Schaefer, who had been vice president of Boeing Wichita since 1938. Instead, he became one of the earliest proponents for drafting his fellow West Point graduate from Kansas, Dwight D. Eisenhower.[75]

Wichita's full incorporation into the postwar world of international business, however, came at a price: a faded, circumscribed vision of cultural exchange with business peers abroad and economic and political reliance on US military spending priorities at home. Success in B-29 bomber production at Boeing Wichita under Schaefer during World War II led to further important contracts for production of the B-47 and B-52 after the war and well into the cold war era and to the location and development of McConnell Air Force Base—a crucial base for long distance operations for the US Air Force to this day.[76] But becoming a key player in a permanent war economy was far from the minds of the adoring crowds at Love Field when the Wichita Armada was touching down in Dallas in 1929. For the Wichita Rotarians in 1929, the term "armada" was part of a promotional stunt, a metaphor for private sector, industrial ambitions. By 1945, however, the term was anything but a metaphor—particularly for millions of Japanese citizens in urban centers.

Though social networking among businessmen brought it together, the Wichita Rotary club represented something more than bridging and bonding among the city's economic leaders. The club's constant boosterism on the city's behalf contributed greatly to the rise of the aviation industry long before the advent of World War II. In short, the city of Wichita—the "Air Capital of the World"—knew its airplanes. When the Wichita club sent out its booklet *The Five Ships and Cargoes* to all the Rotary clubs and national leaders of the world in 1928, the Wichita Rotarians were sending out their own take on RI's civic internationalism. Their belief in the power of aviation technology to annihilate distances and therefore differences between nations and peoples paralleled their faith in RI as international institution capable of bringing the business classes of the world together in collective harmony.

The airplane, however, could be used to annihilate cities as well as distances. Because of the city's long commitment to developing aviation as its core industry, the War Department decided to invest more than $60 million in Wichita by the summer of 1940. The decision, however, was more complex and revealing. First, war planners in 1940 saw the location of key production centers in the interior of North America as a strategic benefit. Unlike the coasts, the heartland was safe from attacks from abroad. Second, locating defense production in a region that had never escaped the clutches of the Great Depression meant regionally targeted economic growth outside the urban centers of the Northeast and

Midwest. The construction of Boeing's gargantuan Plant 2 with massive contracts from the Army Air Corps for delivery of thousands of B-29 bombers marked one of the first significant steps toward the postwar fiscal policy of military Keynesianism. Third, an abundance of native-born farmworkers familiar with machinery and an industrial base already built on private aviation and open-shop traditions meant a cheap labor pool ready to transition to the mass production of warplanes with limited labor strife and minimal security concerns.[77] Fourth, Wichita's chamber of commerce lobbied Congress and the War Department to boost Wichita as the ideal investment spot while the city council approved funding for a new runway and infrastructure at the city's municipal airport.[78] The streamlined civic machinery put in place a generation earlier by Wichita Rotarians was paying off handsomely in effective lobbying at the War Department. Like many of his fellow Wichitans, Rotarian Schaefer, the president of Boeing-Stearman, relished federal and local investments and the coming economic boom.

Yet Wichita's close alliance with the US military after 1940 had its consequences in Japan as well. When General Curtis LeMay took over the XXI Bomber Command and began to change the B-29 missions over Japan from high-altitude, inaccurate bombing to low-altitude, incendiary bombing, the tactical change proved devastating for both Japanese citizens and their industrial base. The first of many ghastly applications of this new bombing strategy occurred on March 9 and 10, 1945, over Tokyo, resulting in at least seventy-eight thousand deaths that night alone.[79] Like so many other newspapers in the United States, the *Wichita Eagle* ran the story from the Associated Press the following day, describing how "a sea of flame" fifteen square miles in area could be seen forty miles away. General LeMay explained that "hundreds of small business establishments directly concerned with the war industry . . . in the area [were] now wiped out."[80]

LeMay's euphemisms of war aside, it fell upon the longtime editor in chief of the *Wichita Eagle*, Victor Murdock, younger brother to Wichita Rotary's Marcellus Murdock, to interpret the meaning of Tokyo's firebombings for the readers of the Wichita daily. Murdock emphasized the fundamental change in the meaning of Wichita's geography. Global warfare meant that the "crops to be gathered in the Southwest this year" and the "oil resources of the prairies" could all be "as easily dispatched from Wichita east to Russia and France as west to the Philippines and Burma"—thanks to the "most modern of arms, the airplanes."[81]

For Murdock, the lesson of the firebombings was the geographical reconception of Wichita from a prairie town in the American heartland to a key point from which the United States could project its industrial, political, and military will east toward Europe and west toward the Pacific—simultaneously. "Thus despite the liability a location in the deep interior may have been for Wichita and cities like it in the past, it is today and will be tomorrow an asset."[82] Geographically, America's heartland now played a central part in the nation's emerging global role. The people of Wichita, Murdock argued, should embrace this new reality. Militarily and politically speaking, the Far East was now the Near West.

Victor Murdock's interpretation of General LeMay's firebombing of Tokyo as a moment of civic pride, though heartless, was not unfounded: "Wichita is indeed proud to have so important a part in one of the more impressive phases of the conflict to put down tyranny and make men free again. This community can feel that it is doing as much as any city, and more than most, in the urgent task of shortening the war and removing the menace to the lives of our youth."[83] Through its contributions to military aviation in general and to the production of the B-29 bomber in particular, the city of Wichita was maturing as an industrial center of national and international import just as the Wichita Rotarians had imagined in their *Five Ships* booklet almost two decades earlier.[84] Wichita experienced almost a ninefold increase in the number of new factory workers from 1939 to 1944, leading the way among new "defense cities" during that period.[85] The scale and means by which Wichita was fulfilling its long-held industrial ambitions, however, were inconceivable for the Wichita Rotarians in 1928. The city was not only a happy witness to the marriage of war and economic growth but also the postwar beneficiary of that marriage.

The daily political cartoon opposite Murdock's editorial drove home what everyone in Wichita already understood: war meant lots of business. In the cartoon, a diminutive female angel called "Peace" stands before a massive, bearded Roman soldier named "War." Though both are holding a magician's hat, the brawny soldier also holds up by the ears a

FIG 3.3: After so many years of struggle during the Great Depression, this political cartoon left no doubt about what proved to be the salvation of Wichita's business community. *Reproduced from the* Wichita Eagle, *12 March 1945*.

rabbit bearing the sign "Full Employment." Through a menacing grin, the soldier exclaims, "See! Perfectly simple!" while the angel stares in surprise at his empty hat, saying, "It looks easy when you do it" (figure 3.3). Titled "It's a good trick if you can do it," the cartoon reflected the social and economic transformation of Wichita and many other "defense cities" during World War II.[86]

But the real trick was Wichita's embrace of its new role in projecting US military and political power the world over. So long as the gruesome destruction of hundreds of thousands of civilians in the distant cities of Tokyo, Nagoya, Osaka, Kobe, and many others in the coming weeks and months remained an acceptable price to pay for bringing a rapid end to the war, the citizens of Wichita were free to go about their business with full confidence in their nation's continuing republican heritage. Murdock's conclusion was most telling: "The B-29's are winged harbingers of the closing in of conquering hosts."[87] The contradictions of Wichita's new status in the world did not seem to matter to Murdock. Business was booming in the heartland, and victory was imminent abroad.

The wartime transformation of Wichita outpaced the ideals of RI's civic internationalism. The faith shared by Rotarians Harris, Yoneyama, and the Wichita Rotarians in "cultivating the spirit of friendship and understanding in its members, . . . and then sending them out to spread that spirit among other people" held no ground before the emergence of total warfare and the advent of US global hegemony. Informal cultural diplomacy among businessmen from many nations, like private philanthropic efforts by voluntary associations more generally, had to work out new institutional roles in a postwar world dominated by professional diplomats working through state agencies and by economic systems increasingly centered on state regulation and global military commitments.

4

THROUGH EARTHQUAKE AND FIRE

Tokyo Meets Main Street

In 1919, the Japanese government sent Umekichi Yoneyama, then director of the Mitsui Trust Bank, on a "financial mission" with the Baron Megata to the United States. On his return trip, Yoneyama spent New Year's Day 1920 in Dallas, Texas, where he met and stayed with Kisoji Fukushima, assistant manager of the Mitsui Bussan Kaisha. Fukushima, who was living and working in Dallas as a wool exporter to Japan, used the opportunity to tell Yoneyama of his experience as a member of the Dallas Rotary Club. Known simply as "Bill" rather than "Kisoji" by his fellow Dallas Rotarians, Fukushima and his club made quite an impression on the commercial banker, as "he thought the principles of Rotary exactly coincided with his philosophy." Yoneyama returned to Tokyo and immediately set about organizing Tokyo's very own club. After months of discouraging results, Rotary's headquarters in Chicago appointed Walter L. Johnstone, agent for the Pacific Mail Steamship Company in Yokohama, to assist Yoneyama in creating one of the first Rotary clubs in East Asia.[1]

Johnstone was a good choice. Already instrumental in establishing the Shanghai Rotary club in 1919, Johnstone knew how to form a Rotary club in such environs.[2] With Johnstone's guidance, Yoneyama invited "several of his intimate friends to a dinner at the Bankers' Club," where he finally met with success. "Every one present was thoroughly convinced of the noble purpose of the Rotary club, as expounded by Mr. Yoneyama."[3] By November 1920, Yoneyama's Rotary club had seventeen charter members, all of whom were partners, presidents, managing directors, or owners of corporations in all variety of Japanese industry and business.[4] In short, Yoneyama's friends were highest echelons of Tokyo industrialists, bankers, retailers, and media—except "Bill" Fukushima, recently returned from Dallas, who was still a mere assistant manager in wool importing from Texas. With some help from Dallas and Chicago and from Fukushima and Johnstone, Yoneyama had managed to bring back to Tokyo a very unusual souvenir from his "financial mission" to the United States. How could two cities from America's heartland and a handful of private businessmen contribute so much to the establishment of an outpost of American business culture in Tokyo in 1920? What attracted so many top Japanese businessmen to join so quickly? What relationship did the organization have with the Japanese government, and how did that relationship evolve over time?

The nature of Rotary's institutional transference to Tokyo emerged from networks of global trade and transportation. At the Tokyo club's sixth meeting in June 1921, Zenjuro Horikoshi, senior partner of Horikoshi & Co., described his most recent business trip to the United States in some detail. As a silk exporter with branch offices in New York, London, Paris, and Sydney, Horikoshi had crossed the Pacific Ocean a remarkable fifty-two times, making him an all-star globetrotter. This particular journey, he explained to his fellow Rotarians in Tokyo, was quite different for him:

> I have been to the United States many times, but this was the first trip I made as a member of a Rotary Club. I was treated very kindly by fellow Rotarians everywhere. When I arrived at Chicago, for example, they met me at the station with an automobile and took me to a Hotel. They did everything I wanted, in fact, they treated me as though I was their long-time friend. I attended the New York Club meeting several times. There were present at every meeting something like 500 members, consisting of various trades and professions. . . . The members are

> very friendly to each other and *perfect democracy* exists among them.[5] (emphasis added)

Horikoshi's experience is instructive. The friendship, hospitality, and deference shown to him in Chicago and New York City contrasted sharply with the nativism that drove the Emergency Quota Act through the US Congress only a month earlier and, three years later, the Johnson-Reed Act of 1924, which formally blocked all Japanese immigration to the United States. The growing anti-Japanese racism behind the Gentlemen's Agreement of 1907 and California's Alien Land Law of 1913 was baring its teeth by the time of Horikoshi's triumphant welcome into the inner sanctum of the Chicago and New York Rotary clubs. But Horikoshi was hardly moving in a social world of isolationists, nativists, and provincials. His rosy description of the Rotary clubs of New York and Chicago as a "perfect democracy" of trades, professions, and businesses was not entirely fanciful, just limited to his own experience with one type of Rotary club in one type of American city—large, industrial, and international. While more elite clubs existed in cities like Chicago and New York City, those cities' Rotary clubs were willing to accept Horikoshi as a full member from afar rather than as a dignified guest for the day. For someone like Horikoshi and his fellow Rotarians in Tokyo, this was a business opportunity that paralleled new diplomatic openings between the United States and Japan in the wake of World War I.[6]

What Horikoshi meant by "perfect democracy" is a key concept. The world of international business and its currency of transnational class identity made possible the transplanting of a Rotary club from the cotton belt of America to the imperial capital of Japan. Driven by his belief that the "principles of Rotary so coincided" with his own Japanese philosophy, Yoneyama became the godfather of more than forty Japanese Rotary clubs by 1940. Meanwhile, the royal treatment of Japanese businessmen like Horikoshi while visiting the United States in a period of heightened nativism expressed two countervailing trends in US culture during the interwar years. The experiences of Horikoshi in Chicago and New York and the activities of Yoneyama, Fukushima, and Johnstone in Dallas and Tokyo were not historical anomalies, mere blips on the screen of supposed American isolationism after the rejection of the

League of Nations and the adoption of landmark anti-immigrant legislation. Rather, the activities of these men and their organization were a sign of things to come. Not only did Rotary clubs thrive in East Asia and the Pacific Basin long before the outbreak of war between China and Japan in 1937, but clubs were also cropping up in smaller and smaller cities and towns within the United States, Canada, Great Britain, and in many European, Latin American, and Asian countries as well. As we have already seen, Rotary International's civic internationalism found expression in a variety of imperial, national, regional, and local settings.

But the particular success of Rotary clubs in Japan during the interwar period presents a special case. The activities, goals, and evolution of the Tokyo Rotary club in response to massive change during the Taishō Democracy and early Shōwa period reveal some important divergences as well as continuities in US-Japan relations before and after World War II.[7] In a sense, this history helps explain how postwar Japanese industry and civil society could adapt so well to the postwar US military occupation of Japan (1945 to 1952) and postwar US hegemony in the Pacific in general. The transition seemed relatively smooth because it was well on its way long before the formal surrender of Japan on the USS *Missouri*.[8]

Like the cultural influence of American baseball, the diplomatic contacts of the Institute of Pacific Relations, the cosmopolitan exchange through the U.S.-Japan Societies, and the presence of organizations like the YMCA and the Boy Scouts, RI's expansion into Japan during the interwar years fit within a greater pattern of international engagement. Within this context, Rotary made its own contributions. As a well-funded nonprofit, RI had a specific institutional focus driving its presence and growth—unlike baseball.[9] As a nonstate actor, RI was not formally beholden to state sponsorship or any particular corporate foundations—unlike the Japan Council of the Institute of Pacific Relations.[10] As an international service club, RI was not limited to US-Japan relations—unlike the U.S.-Japan Societies.[11] And as a businessmen's luncheon club, RI drew upon the upper echelons of Japanese economic and cultural elites for its membership—unlike the YMCA and similar organizations.[12] Most important, however, the singular success of Rotary clubs in Japan before 1941 allowed one of the most familiar elements of Main Street to enter the everyday world of Japan's urban, industrial elites and offer itself as a normative model for social and business relations within the Japanese context. What did Horikoshi, his fellow Japanese Rotarians, and their counterparts in the United States and all around the world, believe RI's "perfect democracy" to mean? What were the consequences of that belief?

Just as the Wichita Rotarians were finally fulfilling their dreams of economic growth by turning to military spending by the US government in a time of total war, their fellow Rotarians of Japan were experiencing the nightmares of that warfare as the industrial output of US cities like Wichita laid waste to Japanese cities in what John Dower has called a "war without mercy." Yet amid the frenzied racism driving the attempted eradication of the Japanese enemy lay an undercurrent of international engagement and imagined co-destinies within RI's "perfect democracy." Hidden during wartime as Japanese "day-of-the-week" clubs that dodged the surveillance of the Japanese government, this undercurrent sprang back to life as reborn Rotary clubs under the encouraging eye of General MacArthur and with the eager support of veteran Japanese Rotarians and sympathetic Japanese political leadership after 1948. The palimpsest of racial relations between the United States and Japan had many layers—some not so bloody as others. How RI's civic internationalism took root and developed in Japan during the interwar period demonstrates in microcosm some of the complexities of these relations and how they spilled over the parameters of US-Japan relations into East Asia in general.

CIVIC INTERNATIONALISM—TOKYO STYLE

The summer of 1928 was a busy time for the Tokyo Rotary Club. In late July, both the Marquis Tokugawa Iyesato, longtime speaker of the House of Peers, and Mr. Ariyoshi, the mayor of Yokohama, entertained the eighty members in attendance at that week's luncheon. As always, the club meeting was held in English. The marquis first pointed out the club's growing reputation in Tokyo and throughout Japan and then joked about the need for such regimented time management in the House of Peers, since every speaker before the club was strictly limited to five minutes by a large clock. The Tokyo Rotarians' strict sense of time and efficiency during their luncheons was notorious.

Mayor Ariyoshi's comments, however, went much further. Quite the regular attendee at the Yokohama club's meetings, he was more than familiar with the practices, beliefs, and goals of the international service club. He argued that "what churches had done for the advancement of the moral standard in the 19th century, Rotary [was] doing in the 20th century."[13] Ariyoshi saw RI not only as the vanguard of modern, international business standards but also as a moral force for good in the world at large. But the globality of his vision for Rotary's secular calling in the emerging world of international business was imbued with a strong sense of Japanese identity as well, since "that patriotism which brought about the restoration of the Imperial Government at the beginning of the Meiji era was the same as this spirit of Rotary. The idea of Rotary existed in Japan even then; but now it has become the prime factor in business morality, advocated by the influential business and professional men of the world."[14]

As such, Ariyoshi argued, it was imperative that the Yokohama and Tokyo Rotary clubs deepen their ties and cooperation in the future. Since Yokohama and Tokyo shared the same harbor, doing so was only a matter of time anyway. But Ariyoshi's belief that the two city's Rotary clubs could serve as an informal meeting ground for the commercial elites of each city and as conduits for forging international business ties for those elites is revealing. For many key Japanese politicians and businessmen (many in attendance at such club events as guests, if not members), the Rotary club was a neutral platform, a means of building bridges between distinct groups of urban elites within Japan.[15]

In recognition of this fact, only one week before the visit by Ariyoshi and the marquis, Japan's six clubs were granted formal district status within RI by the headquarters in Chicago. In the organizational structure of RI during this period, the district represented the most significant organizational layer between an individual club, RI's headquarters in Chicago, and all other clubs in the world. A "district," in short, was the closest administrative layer to state structures. In effect, the move confirmed the transformation of the Tokyo club from outpost to regional hub within a few short years and reflected the emerging status of Japan itself as a central player not only in RI but in the world of international business and world politics as well. RI's president Everett W. Hill in 1924–1925, in fact, had already promised as much a few years earlier:

> Your club is an important integral unit in Rotary International and you play an important part in your community life . . . I want you to feel that your International Officers and Directors, as well as the International Office in Chicago, are at your service . . . that we may all be brought into closer contact with one another. For we are all working for the same purpose, striving for the same objectives, hoping to attain that goal toward which we are looking—the goal of International Peace and fellowship.[16]

Hill, an ice manufacturer from Oklahoma City, knew the business language of "service" well. Written in the pleasant tone of a customer service representative to a valued client, Hill's letter reinforced how the Tokyo Rotarians already saw themselves and foreshadowed RI's own administrative adaptations to the Tokyo club's influence in East Asia. As rooted in the world of public relations and customer service as the civic activism of Progressive Era politics, RI's civic internationalism proved a useful instrument in developing a new language of diplomatic relations among key elements of Japanese and US businessmen built on the common grammar of market relations, salesmanship, and corporate capitalism.

The newly formed seventieth international district, as a result, encompassed clubs not only in Tokyo, Osaka, Nagoya, Kobe, Kyoto, and Yokohama but also in Shanghai, Peking, Tientsin, and Nanking as well as three up and coming clubs in Manchuria (Mukden, Harbin, and Dairen) and one in Seoul (or Chosên, according to the Japanese).[17] That the seventieth district did not exactly replicate either national boundaries or political structures was deliberate. The internationality of the seventieth district was designed to demonstrate RI's commitment to creating an international organization in its fullest sense.[18] The governor of the new district was none other than Yoneyama, now president of the Mitsui

Trust Bank as well as a member of RI's international board of directors in 1926–1927. In only six years, the "father of Japanese Rotary" had ascended to the highest possible level of RI's international organization, apart from being its international president. Respect and honor for Rotary in Japan followed a similar arc of success.

In every way possible, RI embraced the growth of Rotary clubs in Japan and endorsed the local autonomy of those clubs as part of a broader strategy of expansion into the Pacific Basin as a whole. Consequently, Tokyo's hosting of the Second Pacific Rotary Conference in early October 1928 would, in effect, be its coming-out party as scores of delegates and VIPs from China, Korea, Australia, New Zealand, the Philippines, Hawaii, and the mainland United States were to attend.[19] Joining RI's own VIPs and new international president, Tom Sutton of Tampico, Mexico, were the highest possible ranks of Japanese government and industry. In anticipation of the conference, classes in English, western dance, and community singing began in earnest just one week after the announcement of the conference. The Japanese businessmen and their wives and children needed to learn very un-Japanese ways of social interaction in order to play host to so many Rotarian visitors from so many different countries and cultures.[20] Ariyoshi's syncretism of the Meiji Restoration with RI's civic internationalism could only meld so much together at a time. In the world of business, one could not afford to be too exotic.

But the emphasis on philanthropic and civic activities was very real. Before the marquis and the mayor spoke to the Tokyo Rotarians, that day's meeting began with a small but revealing transaction. The club's board of directors had sent a "message of sympathy" to the Lima Rotary club because of the recent "disastrous earthquake" in Chachapoyas, Peru. The club had just sent a donation of $250 to the relief fund, to "loud applause." Though it might seem like so much back-patting and self-congratulation, there was good reason. On the first of September 1923, Tokyo experienced a massive earthquake resulting in tens of thousands of casualties known as the Great Kantō Earthquake. With fifty members, the relatively young and untested service club became a nexus point for receiving relief funds from fellow clubs in the Americas, Europe, and the Antipodes. In the end, more than 73,000 yen were donated from 374 individual clubs in the US and Canada and another 92 clubs mostly in Great Britain and Mexico. The Chicago office of RI also wired $25,000 in support within days of the catastrophe.[21]

RI's actions formed only one part of a broader relief effort as the US fleet entered Yokohama with emergency provisions within the week. Yoneyama saw RI's support as part of a greater international effort as he recounted how "the American government sent General McCoy with a Red Cross corps. Ship after ship came in from the States loaded with food, clothing, and building materials. When both General McCoy and Ambassador Wood were leaving Japan, old and young were seen lined up at the station to express their heartfelt thanks for the kindness of the American Government."[22]

In the midst of Tokyo's near destruction, the benevolent power of the United States became manifest in a two-pronged humanitarian outreach through its military and through private relief agencies, making available naval logistics and disaster relief. The Tokyo Rotarians understood their club's collection of $250 for relief efforts in Chachapoyas, Peru, within this greater context of international cooperation in times of crisis.

The grateful sentiments of the Japanese bidding farewell to McCoy and Wood paralleled those held by Yoneyama and his fellow club members. Yoneyama understood the value of sentiment and symbol well, as he

> showed the members [of the Tokyo club] a Rotary badge which was given to him by an American friend. It had been dug out of the ashes of his office and miraculously found to retain its original shape and color. In showing it he said, "Like this little badge, the Rotary spirit lives and shines through earthquake and fire." He then urged the members to be more active and to show their appreciation of what the Rotarians have done for Japan in this time of great disaster.[23]

Their sense of appreciation toward the international community and civic obligation toward their own citizens became manifest in the rebuilding of 188 schools throughout Japan, along with the donation of maps and blackboards to resupply them over a period of several years. The remainder of funds, meanwhile, went toward a charity hospital and an orphan asylum. The club was very careful to account for all expenses before the Rotarian brethren as proof of fulfillment of the club officers' fiduciary roles.[24] The transparency of the club's actions and spending was crucial to forging its reputation within the "world fellowship of business and professional men." The Tokyo Rotary club's first real step into philanthropic activity was quite literally a baptism by fire.

There was another first for the club in the midst of that conflagration. The Tokyo club's first and only "alien" member at the time, Edward D. Berton, used his automobile nonstop as an ambulance for days afterward, resulting in "high recognition both from his own Government and from ours."[25] "Ed" Berton, a representative of U.S. Steel in Japan, joined the Tokyo club in March 1922 and was classified officially on the club register as working in "Steel-Distributing." In fact, his first speech to the club was on the history of U.S. Steel and its management practices. Berton also had the respect of the club as he "spared no pains in helping the needy and visiting the sick," leading to the creation of the club's Visiting Committee. Having introduced the club to community singing as well as charity work and modern corporate governance, Ed Berton was seen by his fellow Japanese Rotarians as the paradigmatic Rotarian—and he was their creation, their first "Japan-made Rotarian from America!"[26]

It was a sad day in late July 1928, therefore, as Berton prepared for his return to the States because of a promotion within U.S. Steel. The club's sense of loss upon Ed's departure was sincere and meaningful. The shared intimacy between Berton and his fellow Tokyo Rotarians over a six-year period was not to be found in any factory, boardroom, hotel lobby, or conference hall. Could Rotary's "perfect democracy" transcend the profit margins of U.S. Steel and the Mitsui Bank and hold out the promise of bridging the many cultural and political differences between the two Pacific powers through such close, personal ties? It was possible. Ed Berton—Tokyo's first homegrown non-Japanese Rotarian—embodied that hope.

Nor was the sentiment unprecedented or unrequited. Berton's heroics in the aftermath of the 1923 earthquake were matched by one of his own fellow Rotarians of Tokyo. When Rotarian E. L. Irvine of Kalamazoo,

Michigan, visited a few years after Berton's departure, he recounted how Watari "Kitty" Kitashima, stockbroker and partner of Kitashima & Co., received a telegraph from the Kalamazoo club inquiring about the fate of their very own Mr. Williams and his wife, who had been in Yokohama at the time of the devastating earthquake struck. Kitashima

> actually walked the approximately eighteen miles to Yokohama and, after great difficulty, ascertained that both Mr. and Mrs. Williams had met death in the great disaster. This service of "Kitty" which was so unselfishly rendered at a great sacrifice to himself, has created a deep feeling of affection in the hearts of all the members of the Rotary Club of Kalamazoo for Kitashima, and has bound the Rotary Club of Kalamazoo to the Rotary Club of Tokyo in an enduring manner.[27]

It is not often that these two cities appear in the same sentence, let alone in such an intimate, personal way. The institutional link was an international service club and the ideological framework of RI's civic internationalism.

And international links were Kitashima's specialty. By 1930, Kitty had become a veritable celebrity among the 153,000 Rotarians in 3,300 clubs spread throughout most of the Americas, Europe, East Asia, and the Antipodes—but not because of his service to Kalamazoo. Rather, as the club's stalwart secretary, Kitty took it upon himself in 1923 to begin writing up in English and then distributing the club's weekly bulletins to all the clubs of the world. The practice continued well into the 1930s and had a long-lasting effect on the thousands of clubs receiving Kitty's weekly bulletins. As a result, club president Noboru Ohtani reported that, while attending the 1928 annual international convention in Minneapolis as Japan's representative, he

> had the opportunity of talking with very many of the American delegates and I found them without exception keenly interested in Rotary in Japan and very sympathetic with our work. I listened to many complimentary and commendatory remarks about our Tokyo bulletin, and also about the special book "Japan" which we published last year.[28]

Like the Wichita Rotarians and their booklet, "Kitty" Kitashima and the Tokyo Rotarians understood well the promotional value of RI's vibrant and international print culture. Meanwhile, Ohtani himself added to the prestige of the Japanese Rotarians during his visit as guest speaker on Chicago's WMAQ radio station the evenings of 16 and 17 June 1928, along with Dr. Eduardo Moore of Santiago, Chile; Kenneth Young of Cape Town, South Africa; and Dr. Edouard Willems of Brussels, Belgium.[29] RI's civic internationalism had its moments, as cultural links were made and boundaries traversed in the name of greater international peace and cooperation. But Tokyo's brand of civic internationalism had developed quite an audience throughout the world thanks to the club's generous distribution of publications as well as through the cultural diplomacy of the club's members traveling abroad, hospitality toward visitors at home, and hosting of regional conferences.

There was a weekly audience in every Rotary club of Japan and East Asia as well. Just as Wall Street was undergoing its worst nightmares in late October 1929, the Tokyo Rotary club was playing host, as always, to a dozen or more international visitors at its weekly meeting. But the combination of visitors that week was unusually revealing—as were their comments. Rotarian Wong, of the Peking Rotary club, was the first to speak, drawing parallels between the annual district conference of Rotary clubs in Japan and China being held in Kyoto the same week the World Engineering Congress and the World Power Congress were going on in Tokyo: "We are having meetings like those of the Rotarians, for there is no racial or diplomatic boundary in science, and each and all are exchanging ideas for the advancement of civilization of the world; and [I feel] so happy to attend such a meeting as an engineer and as a Rotarian." Since the Tokyo club did not often have visitors from Peking, Rotarian Wong's presence and assertions were eagerly received. The next speaker, H. H. Dow, from "the state of Henry Ford," told of his earlier visit to Tokyo before the 1923 earthquake and his particular interest in Japanese gardening. In fact, on his prior trip back to the United States on a steamer, he met a Japanese landscape architect, Takuma Tono, who ended up assisting him "in laying out a park in his home town after the Japanese style, which is now the pride of the town." Tono first became a member of Dow's Rotary club in Michigan and then, upon returning to

Tokyo, Tono became a Rotarian in his native city. Rotarians Dow and Tono, in other words, had known each other for years and were quite familiar with each other's hometowns.[30]

But it fell to Rotarian Senda of Calcutta to capture best the complexities of RI's civic internationalism that day, portraying the ten-year-old Rotary club of Calcutta as:

> struggling against unimaginable difficulties and prejudices of race, religion, and caste distinction. The club, however, has made a steady growth and now has nearly 100 members, embracing Mohammedans, Hindoos, Englishmen, Americans, French and other nationalities. It is really the "League of Nations" in itself, and they are all united under the banner of the Rotary precepts.[31]

Senda's vision of religious and cultural pluralism swirled together in a melting pot of business internationalism was a tough act to follow for Rotarian Hunt of Moline, Illinois. Instead, he stood up, gave "extended hearty greetings from his home club, saying he would be delighted to tell his home people about the interesting meeting he had attended in Tokyo," and then returned to his seat so that the club's featured speaker that week, Mr. Bouter, the commercial attaché of the British Embassy, might begin his speech.[32] The mix of professions, businesses, nationalities, and races in the Tokyo club offered itself up as an ideal showcase for RI's civic internationalism. For Rotarian Hunt of Moline, and tens of thousands like him back in the United States reading about the Japanese Rotarians in RI's many publications, it probably was a very "interesting meeting." But the Tokyo club was not limited to RI's interpretations of its purpose, growth, and activities. The club was finding its own voice and beginning to use it.

WELCOME TO *JAPAN*

Watari Kitashima's weekly "Tokyo bulletin" sent to more than 350 Rotary clubs outside Japan was only one of two principal reasons for the growing curiosity on the part of Main Street's best known denizens in the success of Rotary in far-off Japan.[33] The other was a book simply named *Japan,* published by the Tokyo club in 1927, that took the boosterism of Tokyo's Rotarians to a whole new level of sophistication. In response to interest expressed by US clubs in learning more about Japan, RI's Chicago office wrote the Tokyo club asking for a "pamphlet" that could be used by all clubs in the United States and Canada for preparing "20 to 30 minute presentations" on Japan in their meetings. Instead of a short pamphlet, the Tokyo club produced a gem that far exceeded RI's prosaic expectations.[34]

Replete with photos, printed in gorgeous text and colors, and distributed to thousands of Rotary clubs worldwide, all at the Tokyo club's expense, *Japan* was the Tokyo Rotarians' attempt to introduce and explain both Japanese industry and culture to all their Rotarian brethren. The book was the perfect marriage of business information and cultural representation. The beautiful, nuanced, ancient culture of Japan also happened to be a wise, stable place for investment and an emerging industrial power eager to build bridges of commerce with the United States and the world. Though the imagery throughout was decidedly exotic—a Japan far away and emphatically non-Western in culture, history, language, religion, art, and architecture—the book spoke the language of modern international business. Not only was the text written in a smooth English vernacular, but the whole approach—the very manner in which the Japanese clubs packaged and represented themselves, their cities, and their country—was couched in the idiom of RI's civic internationalism. Kitty's fans in Kalamazoo, to be sure, loved *Japan.* The Tokyo club's own publication and international distribution of the book, therefore, stands out as a focal point of international engagement between Japan and every Rotary club outside Japan and as a kind of protonationalist document asserting Japan's claim as an emerging industrial power in the Pacific.[35]

After presenting the music and lyrics of the Japanese national anthem and giving a brief explanation of the meaning of the Japanese flag, the book launches into a series of chapters that explain how Japan moved from a secretive, "hermit" country before 1854, to the Meiji Restoration of 1868, to a constitutional form of government in 1889 with a bicameral Parliament, to the industrial powerhouse of Asia in the early twentieth century. In effect, the book itself was a kind of national anthem, since the story of Japan's unfolding national destiny was clear: "Because of the onward sweep of democracy, particularly since the world war [i.e., World War I], the House of Representatives is growing in power, and no cabinet is now able to function smoothly without the support of the political party or parties that command the majority in the House." The promises of a modern political form of government were paying off, since the "practice of party cabinet being established, the politics of Japan will gradually come to resemble that of Great Britain, with two parties in the House to take turns in organizing cabinets." But, like the Western powers, democracy had its limits, as the colonies of Japan would also "resemble more or less the crown colonies of the British Empire with appointed Governor-generals and no elected assemblies."[36] As with the British, why should modernizing Japan's industrial base and expanding its commercial ties worldwide preclude Japanese colonialism? Just as the Europeans and Americans schooled their colonies in the ways of modern industry and representative democracy, so would the Japanese. In time, the lesser nations and possessions would achieve a modicum of independence—all in good time.

In fact, from the table of contents and the list of contributors, one can readily see the outline of the six Japanese clubs' strategies for marketing their country before the world's Rotary clubs (table 4.1). The Japanese Rotarians knew their worldwide Rotarian audience well.

The Tokyo club's message was clear: the Japanese Empire was a friendly empire, and its expansion into mainland Asia both benign and inevitable. In particular, the final two chapters on Korea and the Sakhalin Islands present those Japanese colonial possessions using the simplest logic of empire: "[Korea's] easy access to the most promising markets in the world, China, Manchuria, and Siberia is in itself a great economic asset. . . . Its proximity to Japan will be of even greater significance now that fate has combined the two."[37] Katsusaburo Watanabe, president of the Oriental Development Company and classified in the club as "Colonization Service," further explained that Korea's "healthy, industrious and willing native population provides a plentiful supply of labour," which left "little room to doubt the great economic possibilities of the country."[38] Proximity, cheap labor, and regional economic growth were

Table 4.1. Japan Table of Contents

Chapter Title	Author	Occupation / Corporation
History and Present Type of Government	Yusuke Tsurumi	"Municipal Administrator"
Geography and Topography of Japan	Chuji Inomata, F.R.G.S.	General Manager, Japan Tourist Bureau
Natural Resources and Foreign Commerce	Takashi Isaka	President, Yokohama Fire and Marine Insurance Co.
Mercantile Marine of Japan	Noboru Ohtani	Director, Nippon Yusen Kaisha
Industry	Junichiro Imaoka	President, Uraga Dock Co.
Present Foreign Wireless Communication Systems	Baron Yasushi Togo	Managing Director, Japan Wireless Telegraph Company
Journalism in Japan	Kotaro Sugimura	Chief, Intelligence Dept., Asahi Shinbun
Education and Religion	Rt. Rev. Bishop Charles S. Reifsnider	President, St. Paul's College, Tokyo
Customs and Traditions	Daniel H. Blake	Vice-President, Frazar Trust Company
Development of Dramatic Art in Japan	Kyuzaburo Yamamoto	Managing Director, Imperial Theatre
Chosen (Korea)	Katsusaburo Watanabe	President, The Oriental Development Company
Karafuto (Saghalien)	Reisuke Danno	Managing Director, Nichiro Fishing Co.
Historical and Commercial Reviews of Cities, where Rotary is established	By each club	Tokyo, Osaka, Nagoya, Kobe, Kyoto, Yokohama

Source: Japan (Tokyo: Tokyo Rotary Club, 1927).

Watanabe's selling points to his Rotarian counterparts. For every Rotary club in the United States, the conclusion was simple: Korea [Chōsen] ought to be a satellite of Japan. This was not a foreign concept. The Tokyo businessmen had their country's own version of the Monroe Doctrine. Apparently, no one in the United States voiced concern or raised a question. Though Watanabe remained in the club for less than three years, his presence there and his contribution to the Tokyo club's book demonstrated the intertwining nature of empire and market penetration, of expansion and resource extraction, even at the height of peaceful US-Japan relations during the interwar period.

Watanabe's translation of Japanese imperial aspirations into the soft, pragmatic tones of modern business English, however, found even smoother, subtler expression in Noboru Ohtani's review of Japanese shipping. Serving as the Tokyo club president in 1927–1928 and Japan's main representative at RI's annual convention held in Minneapolis in 1928, Ohtani presented a narrative of Japan's move from a "hermit country" to "her position as an island country, which, in relation with the continent of Asia, closely resembles that of the British Isles in the latter's relation with the Continent of Europe."[39] Ohtani's narrative was in accord with the book's overall theme. Though the "serious depression in shipping" Japan experienced from 1920 to the time of Ohtani's writing in 1927 resulted in a "severe test," Ohtani put much faith in his own company's recent absorption of the Toyo Kisen Kaisha's Pacific services: "By this important consummation, the Nippon Yusen Kaisha has become a more powerful concern than ever, now ranking third among the world's ship-owners." Ohtani eagerly pointed out the building of three new passenger liners "more than 16,500 tons each" to run between San Francisco and "the Orient"—two at the Mitsubishi Shipbuilding and Engine Works of Nagasaki and one at the Kawasaki Dockyards in Kobe. Business was looking up. The world was shrinking as commerce applied new technologies in transportation to annihilate distance and overcome difference. Japan and the United States were partners in developing the Pacific Basin. With great confidence, Ohtani concluded that upon the "restoration of the peaceful industries and commerce to a normal condition, with the consequent recovery of the world's purchasing power, the Japanese Mercantile Marine will continue to have its due share in contributing to the peaceful needs, and so enhancing the prosperity and happiness of mankind at large."[40] No Rotarian from the United States could have put it better.[41] And there was good reason why the Tokyo Rotarians knew so well how to package their country's expansion into Asia for consumption in the United States. Though the Tokyo club opened each weekly meeting by singing their national anthem in Japanese before their Japanese flag, the members almost always spoke

English during their weekly luncheons. With so many non-Japanese visitors at the Bankers' Club each week, doing so even became a point of pride.[42]

Rotary's language of civic internationalism served other purposes for the Tokyo club and its political allies in Japan as well. In 1924, when Baron Matsui spoke at the Tokyo club's celebration of the nineteenth anniversary of Rotary's founding in Chicago, he saw no reason to hold back: "There is no East and there is no West today. . . . Men everywhere have come to realize the wisdom of a policy of international cooperation rather than one of rivalry," adding that "the wise nation, like the wise business man, has come to see that its best interests run in the same channel as its best instincts. It is, happily, a new era upon which we are launched."[43] For the Tokyo Rotarians, these words had become a veritable mission statement.

Serving as the minister for foreign affairs at the time, Baron Matsui reflected "the politics of good intentions" of the 1920s.[44] Despite the passage of the Johnson-Reed Act of 1924 in the United States and the limitations placed on Japan's "Asian Monroeism" by the treaties of the Washington Naval Conference of 1922, there remained much hope during the period in successful collaboration with the United States in particular and with the League of Nations in general. The Tokyo Rotarians were in full accord. The following year, at the Tokyo club's celebration of the anniversary of Rotary's founding in Chicago in 1905, Japan's Prime Minister Kato gave his own interpretation of Rotary's "Sixth Object" on international friendship and peace: "But the world has learned its lesson—bitter for those of evil intent, comforting and fortifying for those of sound ideals. We are entering an era in which the pursuit of national interests is accompanied by the perception that the welfare of one depends on the welfare of all others."[45] Speaking just after the prime minister, Baron Shidehara, the new minister for foreign affairs, linked RI's civic internationalism directly with Japan's foreign policy goals, proclaiming that "the settled desire of Japan is to avoid as she has ever avoided, all aggression on others, and to see all her sister nations, great and small, putting forth their utmost efforts . . . for the common good of mankind." Shidehara's well-known policy of international cooperation had an eager ally with the Japanese Rotary clubs and their many counterparts abroad:

> No work can be better worth doing, and few organizations are so well qualified to undertake it. Governments cannot do it. They are not sociable institutions. . . . Religions cannot do it. They are too diverse. Formal Peace Societies cannot do it. . . . They are too specialized. Real good fellowship between the nations must rest on a foundation of real personal intimacy and good feeling. That good fellowship is the very object and kernel of the Rotary conception. If . . . you can turn it into the channel of international relations, you will be fulfilling one of the most urgent needs of mankind.[46]

The Tokyo Rotarians promised to do just that. The spirit of Wilsonianism pervaded the Japanese Rotarians' civic internationalism.

The club was already useful as an instrument for cultural diplomacy and was becoming more so. A year before Shidehara and Kato gave their ringing endorsement of Rotary International's goals, the club took in two new members: Yukichi Iwanaga, listed euphemistically as a journalist, and Yusuke Tsurumi, classified under "railway service." Just as the Tokyo club and Shidehara asserted their common foreign policy goals at the club's celebration of the twentieth anniversary of RI's founding, so the induction of Iwanaga and Tsurumi into the Tokyo Rotary club in February 1924 marked an important confluence of public and private interests. The two men were old friends before becoming fellow Rotarians. After he founded the *Uiruson kurabu*—the Wilson Club—in 1915, Tsurumi had Iwanaga as one of several guest speakers at the debating club.[47] Their interests in Rotary's civic internationalism, in short, had common roots in their earlier interests in a Wilsonian vision of international peace.

While the Wilson Club's name revealed Tsurumi's own devotion to Wilsonianism, the club itself proved to be a breeding ground for a small circle of national elites devoted to service to the Japanese state and the promotion of its interests abroad. Having Iwanaga speak at the Wilson Club was an obvious move for Tsurumi. While working for the South Manchurian Railway from 1911 to 1917, Iwanaga saw how foreign news agencies—Reuters in particular—determined how Japan's actions were interpreted by the rest of the world mainly because there was no comparable news agency in Japan itself. Iwanaga sought to remedy the situation by creating his own news agency in 1920—hence his classification as "journalist" in Rotary. But there was much more to him:

> Iwanaga's idea of a national news press agency was . . . more to do with his sense of duty to the state / empire as a member of the national elite and a post-League internationalist. His duty was to present a correct picture of Japan and ensure that the Japanese view was understood correctly in the world.[48]

As if establishing his own news agency weren't enough, Iwanaga lobbied for a national news agency as well, resulting in the creation of Rengo in 1926.[49] Though Iwanaga did not contribute directly to the Tokyo Rotary club's publication of *Japan*, he was certainly a supporter of the book's overall purpose for many reasons beyond his status within the Rotary club. Iwanaga was already doing his fair share of boosterism for Japan. Boundaries between state- and nonstate-sponsored forms of international boosterism during this period were quite blurred.

Iwanaga's old friend, Yusuke Tsurumi, did contribute directly to the Tokyo Rotarians' efforts at boosterism, however. As the author of the opening chapter on Japan's "History and Present Type of Government," it fell to Tsurumi to introduce Japan—or at least their version of "Japan"—in its entirety. The Tokyo Rotarians not only knew their audience of fellow Rotarians well but also knew who could reach them best. Only six months after Tsurumi's induction into Rotary and in full anticipation of Japan's involvement in the Institute of Pacific Relations after 1926, he traveled to North America for a year and a half, lecturing at universities, conferences, and institutions such as the Foreign Policy Association. He was an excellent and tireless promoter of Japan as a "liberal" nation on the move away from militarism and toward full partnership in the burgeoning post–World War I international system.[50] Tsurumi's point was the same, no matter where he spoke: "For over two and a half centuries Japan had no wars both internally and externally. Peace as a practical phase of national life is not new with us." When summarizing his long lecture tour in North America for the Tokyo Rotary club, Tsurumi also observed: "I think the guests of this evening have found out many things common between Japan and America. You must have been made home-sick by the sight of so many Ford automobiles parked at the curb. And the streets of Tokyo as in Boston are so crooked that you will meet yourselves coming back."[51] Over time, driving the same mass-produced Fords on the winding streets of Tokyo and Boston could only serve to bring the two nations together.

Just as Rotarian visitors from the United States often preceded their formal greetings to the Tokyo Rotary club after 1924 with disclaimers and caveats on the National Origins Act and its ugly nativism, so Japanese Rotarians often found themselves explaining away Japanese expansionism in Asia and the Pacific to their international visitors while traveling abroad.[52] The apologetics of nationalist and nativist agendas came from both sides of the Pacific. But armed with a shared faith in the unifying powers of international cooperation, business, and exchange, Rotarians on all continents in the 1920s believed strongly in their ultimate capacity to move beyond the obstacles of national, regional, and local rivalries and differences.[53] Time and progress were on their side.

FRAMING THE EXOTIC PEER

Tsurumi's message dovetailed so well with Rotary's vision of world fellowship that RI's international monthly magazine, the *Rotarian,* featured him twice in 1926. While the second article was a reprint of the speech he gave at the Tokyo Rotary club after returning from his long lecture tour in the United States, Tsurumi's first appearance, though much shorter, revealed much more in its context. Presented as one of four "Rotarians in the Public Eye" and listed as a "municipal administrator" in Tokyo, Tsurumi was credited for being the effective advocate of Japanese culture and business in the United States that he was. What stands out, however, is the company Tsurumi kept: George F. Johnson, president of the Endicott-Johnson Shoe Company in Binghamton, New York; Hugh E. Van de Walker, life insurance salesman in Ypsilanti, Michigan; and Roger Miller, head of the National School for Commercial Organization Executives, from Asheville, North Carolina. Each of the four had their own reasons for receiving such attention: Johnson's company offered profit-sharing to its employees—a model of welfare capitalism; Van de Walker sold life insurance at record rates; and Miller held national prominence as a leader of chamber of commerce executives. Surrounded by a benevolent corporate executive, a highly successful insurance salesman, and an outstanding executive for the chamber of commerce, Yusuke Tsurumi seemed safe and normal—an exemplary Rotarian who was more than welcome at any local club's luncheon. The effect was deliberate. Like many other articles, portraits, and interviews before and after, the editors of the *Rotarian* often slipped non-US Rotarians into the pages of their monthly magazine in ways that normalized their presence in the everyday world of RI's readership. Dressed in a modern business suit just like his fellow Rotarians, the administrator from far off Tokyo exuded respectability and approachability (figure 4.1). Yusuke Tsurumi was a modern, trustworthy professional with whom anyone could do business.

The Tokyo club returned the favor in 1927 by featuring two US members of their own club as contributors to its glossy publication *Japan*. Oddly enough, Bishop Charles S. Reifsnider, president of St. Paul's College in Tokyo, and Daniel Blake, vice president of Frazar Trust Company, wrote on the topics of "education and religion" and "customs and traditions" of Japan respectively, while Japanese members wrote on the financial, industrial, and political dimensions of their country.[54] The predominance of Japanese contributors to the publication pointed up the relative constitution of the Tokyo club between Japanese and non-Japanese members during the interwar years. Out of 375 members listed over the twenty-year period of 1920–1940, only twenty-four were of non-Japanese origin, with most being from the United States and representing mostly private corporate interests ranging from lamp manufacturing to news bureaus to "road-making machinery."[55] Ed Berton of U.S. Steel, in other words, was not a complete rarity, but the Tokyo club always held its meet-

24 *THE ROTARIAN* *March, 1926*

GEORGE F. JOHNSON, Binghamton, N. Y.

YUSUKE TSURUMI, Tokyo, Japan.

HUGH E. VAN DE WALKER, Ypsilanti, Mich.

ROGER MILLER, Asheville, N. C.

ROTARIANS IN THE PUBLIC EYE

FIG 4.1: During most of the 1920s, the *Rotarian* magazine featured a section titled "Rotarians in the Public Eye," with one purpose: to demonstrate Rotary's capacity to incorporate businessmen and professionals from all parts of the world into their "world fellowship of businessmen." *Rotarian*, March 1926, 24. *© Rotary International. All Rights Reserved.*

ings in English out of choice, not necessity. Still, non-Japanese representation in other Japanese clubs tended to be even less than Tokyo's.[56] When it came to Rotary's expansion into Japan from 1920 to 1940, there was little difficulty in generating "native" participation and membership growth. With more than forty Rotary clubs meeting every week in the late summer of 1940, Japan was as much a thriving part of the "perfect democracy" of Rotary as any other country—if not more so.

TOKYO MEETS AUGUSTA, KANSAS

Let us return once again to the Tokyo club in 1928. Attending the club's mournful farewell to Ed Berton that same day in late July was Jesse C. Fisher of Augusta, Kansas, seated with his two nephews. Though it is unclear whether Fisher and Berton actually spoke with each other during or after the meeting, they would have addressed each other as "Jesse" and "Ed"—and in no other way—since within the confines of club sociability, equality was the rule. The representative of U.S. Steel in Japan and some of the most important businessmen of all Japan were Jesse Fisher's business and professional peers during that luncheon, fellow members of the "parliament of businessmen" brought together by the world of Rotary. Before introducing Fisher and the other visitors from Yokohama and Seoul, however, the club first welcomed its newest member, Masakazu Takata, managing director of the Tokyo Gomu Kogyo K.K. Like all other new members since the club's inception, Mr. Takata had exactly five minutes to speak on his particular business classification, "rubber goods manufacturing." He described the future prospects of the rubber industry as very bright "even if only in the making of auto tires, for the number of cars is being increased at a tremendous rate nowadays."[57] Takata's reference to an increasing number of automobiles in Japan would undoubtedly have interested Jesse Fisher; his own town of Augusta was labeled as an "Oil Center" in Rotary's own club reports and located near the oil boomtown of El Dorado, Kansas, which got its own Rotary club in 1919, a year after Augusta. El Dorado, moreover, was where Jake Moellendick got his first plane ride to one of his many oil wells with a young pilot named J. Earl Schaefer.

But Jesse Fisher's reason for traveling with his nephews from little Augusta, population four thousand, to Tokyo, population five million, had nothing to do with tires, automobiles, petroleum, or commerce in any form. After his introduction and greetings to the Tokyo Rotarians on behalf of his fellow Augusta Rotarians, he remarked that, after only three days into his first visit to Japan, he "felt quite at home attending the Rotary meeting—just the same sort of meeting as they have in America—and after mentioning many things which seemed so familiar to his eyes, he said they did not have an automatic clock in his home club, but thought it was a fine thing and was thinking of taking one back with him."[58] Oddly enough, Jessie Fisher admired the same clock and strict time management as the Marquis Tokugawa.

Fisher then turned to his nephews and explained that "he thought traveling and seeing the different countries the best education for everybody, and the first step in the realization of the Sixth Object."[59] For Fisher to attend the Tokyo Rotary club's luncheon and explain his presence in terms of Rotary's "Sixth Object" on international peace and cooperation reflected quite a cosmopolitan view for a man from a decidedly provincial town in south central Kansas. That Fisher was in the Tokyo Rotarians' weekly lunch spot at the Bankers' Club, let alone describing the place as a home away from home, was welcome assurance of who all Rotarians were and where they were going—together.

All members and visitors of the Tokyo club would have understood exactly what Fisher meant by RI's "Sixth Object." But the meaning and value of RI's sixth object depended greatly on its audience and location. Formally adopted at Rotary's annual international convention in Edinburgh, Scotland in 1921, the "Sixth Object" was Rotary's particular commitment to the international expansion of the service club into all the "commercial centers of the world." Augusta, Kansas, was hardly a "commercial center of the world"—not even of Kansas. Nonetheless, Jesse Fisher was welcomed as one of Rotary's own. In theory, he was. In theory, Augusta, Kansas, and Tokyo, Japan, were just different parts of an integrating, globalizing whole. But Umekichi Yoneyama had come to know better:

> In America, there seems to be more private business and professional men in the Rotary clubs than the executive officers of the leading firms and companies. In the small towns especially, grocers, shoemakers, etc. are found among the members. There, he said, is the Rotary spirit—the recognition of all useful occupations, and the dignifying by each Rotarian of his occupation as an opportunity to serve society. . . . All seemed to have fully absorbed the true meaning of Rotary. America being such a

> large country, however, in some of the smaller places he feared that they do not fully grasp the magnitude of the international nature of Rotary.[60]

In the language of Sinclair Lewis, Yoneyama's observations would easily be understood as a description of Main Street's Babbitts, small-town boosters and provincials with little understanding or interest in anything outside their own city limits: rubes in suspenders and seersucker suits. Augusta, Kansas, in particular serves as an important marker of Rotary's trend toward smaller and smaller locales and lower and lower levels of the managerial, business, and professional classes, since it was one of the earliest "cities" anywhere with a population less than five thousand to have a Rotary club.[61]

Fisher's fascination with the Tokyo club's strict adherence to time limits and meeting agendas contrasted sharply with the biweekly club meetings in Augusta, which in the 1920s and 1930s often rolled lackadaisically from dinnertime into the late evening. One visitor, in fact, described the Augusta meetings as "very much of a social affair as well as a Rotary club."[62] Fisher's and Tokugawa's shared interest in the club's time management techniques reflected the two very different worlds in which they moved: a small service club in a small town nestled among the oil wells and wheat fields of the Kansas prairie versus Japan's House of Peers. Yet both sat together and ate the same lunch at the Tokyo Rotary club in the summer of 1928. Though most of the Augusta Rotarians were members of the local chamber of commerce and some members served as mayor and even in the Kansas legislature, they were hardly movers and shakers like their Japanese counterparts. Some of the time zones RI straddled were cultural and economic rather than temporal. How long could RI manage to encompass the middle-class world of small-town Kansas with the urban elites of Japanese industry?

This relative class difference spoke volumes as well about the fundamental contradictions behind Rotary's sixth object. The Tokyo club met for most of the 1920s in the very prestigious Bankers' Club. Given the high status of Yoneyama and other club members in Japanese banking, this was never questioned. Augusta, on the other hand, had hardly any hotels to accommodate the gatherings, resulting in club meals being served by local "ladies' organizations." Though the Tokyo Rotarians leaned heavily on their wives and daughters to make a success of their hosting the Second Pacific Rotary Conference in Tokyo in early October 1928, the Tokyo Rotarians did not count on their spouses to provide the club's meals as in Augusta (figure 4.2).[63] Rather than serving the food at the club meetings, the Japanese wives and daughters served as the embodiment of Japanese culture and dignity at important social events outside the club. At the Third Rotary Pacific Conference in Sydney in March 1930, in fact, the wives of all the gathered Rotarians made such an impact that Tokyo's club president, Tahara, "hoped that, in the future, Rotarians would all take their wives along with them when they visit foreign countries. They will then be received more warmly by Rotarians everywhere. It is impossible to enter into intimate and friendly relations without the help of our Rotary Anns."[64] Clear differences in how a given Rotary club used its time and where it ate its meals belied the classless ideal of RI's "perfect democracy." But it was in the appearance and comportment of their wives that the true test of dignity and social class took place.[65]

Yoneyama was right in his assessment in 1928. His fellow Rotarians in towns like Augusta, Kansas, were hardly living and breathing in anything like the regal, cosmopolitan airs of the Bankers' Club. Whereas the first major club project for Tokyo Rotarians centered on rebuilding practically the entire city in the wake of the 1923 earthquake with significant international aid, for example, the Augusta Rotarians' first significant project was their small contribution to the Fourth Liberty Loan drive of southern Butler county in the summer of 1918. Years later, in a club report from 1931 that asked how the Augusta club's "international service committee" was faring and whether the club was promoting RI's "Sixth Object" within the community, the response was unadorned: "We have made but little use of it. Our community is practically 100% white American so that our problem is one of education regarding other peoples." What was meant exactly by "other peoples" was unclear, except to say not white and very far away—at least in mind.[66] One must wonder how the club would have received a visit from a fellow Rotarian from Japan. Would it have been anything remotely like Horikoshi's experience in Chicago and New York City? The Augusta club was not even

2ND PACIFIC ROTARY CONFERENCE

TOKYO, OCTOBER 1 *to* 3, 1928

ROTARIANS... Your fellow members in Japan invite you to visit them during this memorable meeting. They recommend for your voyage the "Conference Ship" the luxurious "TAIYO MARU," the largest and most comfortable of any steamer in regular service between America and the Orient touching Honolulu. It will sail from San Francisco September 12, arriving in Yokohama September 28, three days before the Conference opens.

To visit Japan on a NYK liner is the delightful and logical way to go. Once across the gangplank you feel you are already in Japan. This pre-Nippon atmosphere—enjoyed for two weeks under congenial circumstances—will greatly add to your understanding of the people to whose country you are going. On ships of the NYK line you will find pleasant and interesting fellow passengers. You will take keen enjoyment in the unsurpassed NYK table and cabin service, so smartly American in standard, yet so promptly, courteously and smilingly Japanese in accomplishment.

And added joy—the journey from and to San Francisco is broken with a sightseeing day at Honolulu.

Rotarian Motto—*"Service Above Self"*
NYK Motto—*"Service Above Silver"*

LOW FARES

Plan now to go to Japan—and go by NYK. *Frequent sailings from Los Angeles, San Francisco, and Seattle.* NYK *rates across the Pacific are as low as $195 for 1st class fare from Seattle: from San Francisco 1st class $230 and $300. Its around-the-world fares are from $875 up, 1st class, in either direction. Also various attractive all-expense tours.*

Specimen Combination Tour
Japan-China-Manchuria-Korea

and return including 2nd Pacific Rotary Conference October 1 to 3 and Imperial Coronation Ceremonies November 6 to 10. Rotarians, take advantage of this truly wonderful combination tour. To Japan for the Conference, thence to Hong Kong, Shanghai, Peking, Manchuria, and Korea, and back again in Japan for the magnificent festivities preceding the formal Enthronement of His Imperial Japanese Majesty Emperor Hirohito in Kyoto November 10.

Tour sails from San Francisco on Taiyo Maru September 12 and returns to San Francisco December 7. Price includes first class accommodations on steamers and in hotels, motors and rickshas for sightseeing and ordinary travel expenses. Inclusive cost of complete tour only $1995.00. For further information write any NYK office about Tour RO.

Early application
will insure choice of accommodation

Full information from any authorized tourist or ticket agent. For descriptive literature and free copy of the travel magazine JAPAN write

THE NYK LINE

NEW YORK
Maritime Building
8-10 Bridge Street

CHICAGO
Monroe Building
100 West Monroe Street

SEATTLE
801 First Avenue

SAN FRANCISCO
551 Market Street

LOS ANGELES
19 Biltmore Hotel Arcade

HONOLULU
63 Merchant Street

FIG 4.2: The Tokyo Rotary club hosted the Second Pacific Rotary Conference in October 1928, attended by hundreds of high-level Rotarians and their wives from Australia, New Zealand, China, India, the United States, and elsewhere. *Rotarian,* April 1928, 1. © *Rotary International. All Rights Reserved.*

attempting to correspond with Rotarians in other countries, which most other clubs managed to do even in the heart of the Depression and the height of economic nationalism. Instead, the club's passion during the interwar years generally revolved around helping the Boy Scouts of America and the 4-H clubs.[67] One could almost write off Augusta, Kansas, as the perfect counterpoint to the cosmopolitanism of the Tokyo Rotarians.

And yet there was Jesse Fisher with his two nephews citing RI's "Sixth Object" in the middle of the Bankers' Club of Tokyo. His presence, in fact, was not a complete anomaly. Augusta got its very own club thanks to ten Rotarians from Wichita, Kansas. Among those ten were Giff Booth Sr., Will Price, and Marcellus Murdock—three members of Harry Stanley's committee responsible for publishing *The Five Ships and Cargoes*. The extension of Rotary into a satellite town of Wichita seemed a logical step in 1918 because Augusta lacked any "commercial organization," and so the club sought to do "a considerable amount of commercial and civic work together with boys work."[68] Also, Wichita Rotarians like Murdock and Booth saw it as their duty to bring their nearby business counterparts and community leaders into the fold, no matter how small and provincial the town. Though Jesse Fisher's devotion to RI's vision of a "world fellowship of businessmen and professionals" may have stood out in the Augusta club, there were many in Wichita who were very much in accord with him. For both the Wichita and Tokyo Rotarians, there was often a fine line between boosterism for the sake of their city's and nation's economic expansion, on the one hand, and business and cultural internationalism for the sake of world peace and cooperation, on the other.

EMPIRE AND BOOSTERISM—TOKYO STYLE

A sense of arrival pervades the Tokyo club's activities and speeches throughout the 1920s as the Japanese clubs grew in reputation worldwide—and the Japanese Empire itself continued its expansion. Members of the Chinese Rotary clubs, however, began complaining by the early 1930s that the Japanese Rotarians were using their clubs in Manchuria and their control of the seventieth district as a vehicle for expansion of the Japanese Empire into all of East Asia and the "South Seas."[69] The Chinese Rotarians had good reason for concern.

When Suzuma Suzuki (classification "Linen Goods—Mfg.") spoke on his visit in Mukden and Dairen in August 1929, he recounted the eagerness of fellow Japanese businessmen of those cities to establish their own Rotary clubs because, he explained to his Tokyo club,

> Manchuria is considered by the world as the richest treasure house, and all nations are making investigation concerning it. The key to the hidden treasure is now held by our brother Rotarians in Dairen and Mukden, and they are anxiously waiting to show us the secret, so that we may all come back millionaires. This is the best and probably the only opportunity we shall have for grabbing the treasure which all nations are looking for![70]

For Suzuki, time was of the essence. The future Rotarians of Manchuria could prove an invaluable resource for the expansion of Japanese economic interests in those key cities, so Suzuki formed the "on-to-Dairen-and-Mukden committee" that week as a way to drum up support for a joint business trip to those cities by Tokyo Rotarians. Forming such a committee was standard procedure in Rotary's brand of boosterism. When the Dairen-Mukden Charter Night came to pass in early October 1929, seventy-two Rotarians and spouses from Tokyo arrived in the Dairen harbor and were greeted by "Rotary flags streaming upon the roof of the pier, and many members with ladies waiting to welcome us."[71] At the celebration dinner itself, "the dining room was tastefully decorated with the flags of many nations and that of Rotary International. Vice-president Ohdaira [of the new Dairen Rotary club] . . . spoke of the phenomenal growth Rotary is making throughout the world" while the club's other vice president, Furusawa, told of "how the club had been originally conceived and brought into existence through the kindness of Tom Sutton."[72] Since Tom Sutton, RI's international president in 1928–1929, had given active support to the idea of establishing clubs in these cities while presiding over the Second Pacific Rotary Conference hosted by Tokyo in the fall of 1928, the boosterism of Suzuki, Ohdaira, and Furusawa carried the imprimatur of RI's highest officials.

Yet, despite the veneer of Rotarian neutrality, the Dairen-Mukden Charter Night was an all-Japanese affair. The next day the entire group of Tokyo and Dairen Rotarians and spouses went to Port Arthur to be "shown the old battle ground" (where the Japanese destroyers shot the opening salvos of the Russo-Japanese war in 1904 with a surprise attack on the Russian fleet stationed there) while Ohdaira, representing the South Manchuria Railway Co., hosted a dinner "with all sorts of Japanese dishes at different tables," followed by "a Chinese play." Many of the guest Rotarians then continued on to visit Mukden "by way of a visit to the Iron Foundry in Anshan," where the newly hatched Mukden Rotarians "at a signal from the Chairman, stood up and, forming a circle about the hall with flags and pennants in hand, 'ringed' around the seated guests singing Rotary songs in Japanese."[73]

By their arrival in Harbin, "the future commercial centre of the Far East," it was becoming evident how little space there was between these Japanese Rotarians' visions of trade expansion and the growing imperial ambitions of the Japanese Empire in Manchuria.[74] Indeed, Governor General Saito in Seoul invited the visiting Rotarians to tea at his official residence on 10 October 1929: "Through his courtesy we were allowed to see the Korean Palace and hear the old classical Korean court music. Governor General Saito is well informed of the Rotary principles. He made a careful study of it, and wishing to have a club organized in Seoul, he invited the leading businessmen of the city and laid the matter before them for consideration, and soon afterward it was organized."[75] Nor was Saito alone in seeing the usefulness of Rotary as a form of cultural diplomacy on Japan's behalf, as Acting Consul General Kishi in Sydney wrote to Vice-Minister Yoshida of the Department of Foreign Affairs that same week "requesting that steps be taken to have the Rotary club of Tokyo send a very large delegation including many Rotary-Anns [RI's informal term for spouses of Rotarians since 1914] to the Third Pacific Conference [of RI]" to be held in Sydney in March 1930.[76] In other words, the circuits of contact and influence emanating from the Tokyo Rotary club followed and strengthened the sinews of an emerging Asian Pacific power all the way to Australia.

Manchuria, however, was not the only land brimming with economic potential in the eyes of Japanese Rotarians. The following week, Rotarian Masaharu Sakamoto (classification "Stock Raising") took a similar view as he looked southward. He reported on his recent trip to the "South Sea Islands," specifically the plantation in Sumatra of "our fellow member Sohma, and received special attention from the officers of the company." Showing great admiration for European style colonialism, he described how "he was greatly impressed by the business-like management of the Dutch Colony. The agricultural and mining output is said to be nearly two billion guilders a year, out of which nearly 500,000,000 guilders to go to Holland." Sakamoto was convinced that "the South Sea Islands will be one of the richest spots on the face of the earth 10 or 15 years hence."[77] With Tokyo's Mayor Horikiri becoming a full member that same meeting, the private service club continued down the path of blurring lines between the imperial state and the expanding industrial base of Japan at all levels.[78] Mayor Ariyoshi of Yokohama seemed to have it right: the syncretism of Japanese nationalism and Rotary's principles of "business morality" was rather tenable—only the admixture seemed much less neutral in practice than in theory. Apart from RI's gentlemanly request that the Tokyo Rotarians remain apolitical, there were no logical or institutional guarantees that the lofty ideals of RI's civic internationalism could not become handmaidens to Japanese imperialism.

The first real test of the Japanese Rotarians' devotion to empire or to Rotary's civic internationalism came in the aftermath of a small explosion close to a railway line owned by the South Manchuria Railway on 18 September 1931. Later dubbed the Manchurian Incident, the explosion was blamed on Chinese dissidents by the Imperial Japanese Army, already based in Manchuria to defend the growing interests of the Japanese Empire. The explosion became a casus belli for Japan, resulting in a full-scale invasion of Manchuria and, six months later, the creation of the puppet state known as Manchukuo. How would the Japanese and Chinese Rotarians respond to the incident? Would their national allegiance trump their internationalist creed? A clear answer came with the Tokyo club's publication in English of a booklet, "The Manchurian Problem," in December 1931. Put simply, the booklet made the case of the Japanese Empire: Chinese "troops" had attacked the railway in hopes of regaining rights lost in 1915 under the "Twenty-One Demands," the Japanese army was only responding in defense of the railway, Manchuria would only benefit from greater trade with Japan, only Japan was capable of defending Manchuria from the encroachments of Russia, and Japan had no "territorial designs" in the region—only the desire to provide "her civilizing efforts." The booklet also highlighted the many parallels between the presence of the Japanese Empire in Manchuria and the United States in Latin America. Just as the US had its Monroe Doctrine, so did Japan. Might the Rotary clubs in both nations find common cause in restoring regional peace? From Past-Governor Yoneyama's perspective, that seemed unlikely since "the members of the Rotary Clubs in China do not mainly consist of the Chinese themselves." This was a heavy blow not only to the Chinese Rotarians, but to Rotary International itself as a safe harbor for peaceful exchange and cooperation among international businessmen.[79]

When reconfigured by Japanese Rotarians, Rotary's vision of civic uplift and harmony of interests could serve the purposes of Japanese corporations and the Japanese Empire just as it could serve US interests abroad, both public and private. However, despite the Manchurian Incident, the creation of Manchukuo, the Lytton Report's denunciation of Japan as an aggressor state, and Japan's subsequent withdrawal from the League of Nations in March 1933, the Japanese Rotarians' brand of civic internationalism carried on unabated through weekly meetings, regular conferences, worldwide publications, and lecture tours.[80] As the Japanese Empire transitioned from the Taishō Democracy (1912–1925) to an increasingly unstable parliamentary system (1925–1932) to the militarism, protectionism, and fierce nationalism of the Greater East Asia Co-Prosperity Sphere (1932–1945), the "fellow Rotarians" of China and East Asia came to discover that RI's civic internationalism had its limits.

In mid-June 1940, Rotarian Takashi Komatsu took the stage before more than 3,700 Rotarians and their guests as one of the featured speakers in an "international round table" at RI's annual international convention—in Havana, Cuba. Mr. Komatsu, managing director of the Asano

Shipbuilding Company and a member of the Tokyo Rotary club since 1929, was a close friend and protégé of Umekichi Yoneyama. Also, having lived in "an American home" as a high school student and having subsequently graduated from Monmouth College, a Scottish Presbyterian frontier college surrounded by Illinois cornfields, Mr. Komatsu knew both America's heartland and the business world of Tokyo very well.[81] But, with war breaking out in both Europe and East Asia, this was a delicate time for Rotary to hold a roundtable on international peace and understanding. And Komatsu knew it. Though there was a net gain of 99 new clubs for RI in the previous year, more than 75 clubs had been terminated as a result of political change, conflict, and conquest, most of them in Spain or Czechoslovakia that particular year. Clubs in Germany, for example, had already been banished by the German government three years earlier.

The Rotary clubs in Japan, however, were still—somehow—going strong in the summer of 1940, despite the US government's termination of the 1911 commercial treaty between Japan and the United States the year prior. In fact, Mr. Komatsu explained that their old district within RI had grown so much that they had formed three new separate districts, with 19 clubs in northeastern "Japan proper," 19 in southwestern Japan, and 8 clubs in Chōsen (Korea) and Manchukuo (Manchuria). Moreover, the Japanese Rotarians had formed their own "Advisory Committee" for all those clubs—much as the Canadians and Europeans had done years before—and expected soon to have more than 100 clubs organized within those three districts.[82]

Komatsu exuded confidence and good will as he described the "spirit of fellowship" among the 500 Rotarians and families at his club's latest conference in Yokohama a month prior, the 30–40 "overseas Rotarians" who visited his club each week in Tokyo, and the student exchanges run by the club with counterparts in the United States. In a folksy and heartfelt way, Komatsu invited the Rotarians in the Havana audience, about two-thirds from the United States and Canada and about one-third from Cuba and Latin America, to visit the Tokyo club:

> When you reach our meeting place you will be welcomed by the members of our fellowship committee, and you will wonder

> whether you are really so many thousand miles away from home. Perhaps the only sense of strangeness will come to you when you notice that the people about you are talking in an unintelligible tongue. But in this you need have no anxiety, because you will soon be surrounded by many friends who will be able to speak to you in one of the languages familiar to you.[83]

There would not be any demands or expectations that the visitors speak Japanese, he further assured them. Indeed, the Tokyo club's meetings always began with the singing of their national anthem and "a Rotary song," much as in the United States, Canada, and Great Britain. Though the Japanese were not known for their "community singing," he explained that "under the leadership of one of the American members [namely, Ed Berton], we learned to sing some of the simpler songs in English." The club, in fact, had developed many of its own club songs in Japanese since Berton's departure on the day of Jesse Fisher's visit back in July 1928. But the service club stood for something much more than lunchtime sociability and businessmen's camaraderie. Komatsu then reviewed the origins of the Tokyo orphanage and children's home started by his club:

> At the time of the great earthquake of 1923, the Rotarians of the world showered upon us their deepest sympathy in the contributions which they sent. I am sure there must have been generous gifts from many of you present here today. You will be interested to know that a Rotary home was erected with this money, and our members have assumed the responsibility of maintaining and perpetuating it. In this home the young women who are brought up at the orphanage, before they are sent out to take their places in life, are given courses in domestic science, arts and crafts, and in cultural training such as flower arrangement, tea ceremony, music, painting, and so forth.[84]

The orphaned girls of Tokyo had a place to go, a roof over their head, and a way to become proper Japanese women thanks to the Tokyo Rotarians. The Tokyo club had found its own unique way of blending patriotism and philanthropy under RI's umbrella of international fellowship and good will. The club's philanthropic credentials established, Komatsu then announced that the Japanese clubs were expanding into Manchukuo—not Manchuria.

But the global tensions of 1940 could not be erased so easily by the sunny disposition of Komatsu. That took some explaining. Komatsu spoke after Rotarian Gardiner of Ceylon, who described himself as a "full-blooded Tamil" and then proudly explained how his name was a product of Portuguese traders and American missionaries, and just before Rotarian Jorge Fidel Durón of Tegucigalpa, Honduras, who drew much applause for his comments on "American ideals of liberty and democracy" and how America—both North and South—was "the continent of the future."[85] Komatsu therefore knew he was expected to provide his own insights into the meaning and direction of international relations in the near future. "Surely we are living today in a troubled world," he began,

> but let us not be dismayed by the darkness of the hour, nor forget our responsibilities as Rotarians. . . . Let us avoid any action which might be interpreted as casting stones of blame. Let us not lose sight of the fact that the peoples of the world do not possess the same psychological approach to the problems of life. The nations are still far apart in their understanding of human needs and interests in their ideals and aspirations, and even in their conceptions of right and justice.[86]

Komatsu had done his best to assert the same claims to Japanese autonomy within RI that so many other Japanese Rotarians had done before. But, despite the applause, RI's Board of Directors and conventioneers knew some position had to be taken on the outbreak of warfare in both Europe and East Asia. By convention's end, Resolution 40–15, "Rotary and World Conflict," was adopted: "In these catastrophic times, . . . Rotary is based on the ideal of service, and where freedom, justice, truth, sanctity of the pledged word and respect for human rights do not exist, Rotary cannot live nor its ideal prevail."[87] In the face of war, RI began to link the core concept of civic internationalism—"service above self"—

to an incipient language of universal human rights. It was anyone's guess what would happen to RI's service ideology—as an apolitical, private approach to community service—during and after a period of global, industrialized war.

Exactly three months after Takashi Komatsu's artful evasions in Havana, the Tokyo Rotary club voted to disband, along with all other clubs that fell under Japan's "Advisory Committee." The dream of more than one hundred Rotary clubs within the Japanese Empire within a year had quickly passed into memory as President Roosevelt signed the Export Control Act only weeks after Komatsu's speech in Havana, which ended the exporting of military equipment and war matériel to Japan. Meanwhile, the US government began moving to enforce its oil embargo on the Japanese Empire. The last Tokyo club meeting, not coincidentally, opened with Rotarian Nagasaki's distribution of his pamphlet "on the petroleum in the Dutch-Indies, and the Industrial Alliance in Germany." The final order of business then came to the floor: the formal disbanding of the Tokyo club, only months shy of its twentieth anniversary. Confusion and regret hung over the final meeting's conversations and debates, since the exact reason for the elimination of the clubs was not clear. Described as "a desperate situation" and "a painful experience," the club members voted unanimously to vote for disbanding in deference to their officers' advice. Only Umekichi Yoneyama's speech could provide any sense of closure as he

> in distressing mood sadly dragged himself to the speakers' stand and said, "In twenty years of Rotary this is the first time I have had to speak before you with such painful feelings. . . . I simply wish to express my heartfelt humble apology for not being able to save our club from such a fatal condition. However, we did not and could not sit idly looking on with folded arms at the changing current of the time."

He then suggested the reorganization of the Japanese Rotary clubs as "a new association based upon national unit administration" with clubs calling themselves by the day of the week on which they met. Yoneyama stipulated only that "it is absolutely necessary to maintain the international spirit even in the new organization. Without the ideal of service, its application to our business and community lives would be meaningless." To the bitter end, Yoneyama wished to remain true to RI's "Sixth Object" and its creed of civic internationalism. Kitty Kitashima wrote down the final words of the club's end: "It is the earnest hope of all the members of the Tokyo Rotary Club that the time may come soon when we can peacefully join again in world fellowship for the advancement of the Rotary principles." The Tokyo Rotary club thus severed official ties with RI in September 1940, renamed itself the Wednesday Club, and continued meeting faithfully through the war, apparently even through the destruction of large parts of Tokyo in the firebombings of March 1945. Though Yoneyama survived the war, he never lived to see his beloved Japanese Rotary clubs reinstated. He died in April 1946. In the conflagration of 1923, the Tokyo club found its raison d'être; and in that of 1945, its demise.[88]

Or did it? While returning from administrative duties in India in the fall of 1948, George Means stopped off in Japan to inform the de facto proconsul of the United States, General MacArthur, of his plans to reestablish the extensive network of prewar Rotary clubs in Japan. MacArthur told Means, later to become the third general secretary of RI (1953–1972) and a critical figure in RI's postwar national and international expansion, that "Washington" would have to authorize his request. Means did not welcome this kind of intrusion into the doings of a private nongovernmental organization. "Rotary cannot operate if it must be subject to the authority of governments."[89] To RI's officers and approximately 250,000 members worldwide, such oversight would have been especially galling since more than forty Rotary clubs had spread throughout Japan from 1920 until 1940 with virtually no direction or help from the US government. Also, General MacArthur was well aware of Rotary's extensive presence in East Asia since one of his own top aides during the war, Carlos Romulo, had been a high-ranking international officer and very active Rotarian from Manila in the 1930s.[90] Furthermore, MacArthur was already an honorary member of the Rotary clubs of Milwaukee, Melbourne, and Manila.[91]

George Means soon got his "permission" without any formal approval from Washington. He then found the ideal translator for the task at hand—Mr. Takashi Komatsu, who was now speaking in places very different from the Centro Asturiano in Havana and was undoubtedly using terms like "international peace" and "world fellowship" from a different perspective. With help from Komatsu, and because the clubs had continued through the war as "day-of-the-week" clubs, the reorganization of the Rotary clubs throughout Japan went forward with little difficulty. When the Tokyo club was formally reinstated into Rotary International in March 1949, one of the Tokyo club's first honorary members was General MacArthur, who explained that Rotary was "sorely needed in this time of so much world unrest." Eventually, thirty-three other clubs also emerged from the rubble by 1950–1951, including Hiroshima and Nagasaki. As Means explained it, Rotary International was "the first non-religious international organization readmitted to Japan after the war."[92]

Because General MacArthur could grasp the import of RI's success in Japan from personal experience, however, he was able to harness it for his and his government's own ends. While reestablishing the Japanese Rotary clubs, George Means "had an opportunity to tell General MacArthur of the progress being made" but emphasized that he "did not report to him, and neither did [he] ask for his approval."[93] But that was a question of formality. RI's civic internationalism, under postwar US military occupation of Japan, served far different ends than ever imagined by Yoneyama, his fellow Japanese Rotarians, and their American counterparts in cities like Wichita. Like Japan itself, RI's civic internationalism had a definite role to play in a new and ever-deepening cold war. With the outbreak of warfare in Korea in June 1950, the signing of the Treaty of San Francisco in September 1951, and the formal end to US occupation by April 1952, Japan moved quickly from occupied nation to critical ally and key component in the defense perimeter of the US national security state. And with rapid reindustrialization came explosive postwar growth of Japanese Rotary clubs, under the aegis of US political and military direction.

5

UNDER THE SHADOW OF ROTARY

When Main Streets Compete

With much of Europe under Nazi occupation, representatives from the nations and colonies of the Western Hemisphere met at the Havana Conference in July 1940 to agree upon a hemispheric strategy of collective military security. One month earlier, a very different kind of international meeting occurred in Havana when more than 3,700 members and guests of Rotary International (RI) descended for their thirty-first annual international convention. While the majority of the conventioneers were from all over the United States, RI had a particular interest in the non-US Rotarians and guests in attendance—especially the 900 from Latin America and the Caribbean, including about 800 from Cuba alone. Their presence testified to RI's official creed of international cooperation and community service among the businessmen of the world—in short, RI's civic internationalism. Given the limited attendance from outside the Americas as a result of the onset of war in both Europe and East Asia, RI's annual convention in Havana also had the aura of a great meeting of the Americas. Much like the Havana Conference soon to follow, Rotary's 1940 convention was a unique opportunity for the international organization and its members to proclaim their commitment to pan-American unity in the face of impending global war.[1]

Lost in the rhetoric of the conventioneers' fellowship and international comity, however, were any assertions of *Cubanidad.* Cuba's secretary of state opened the ceremonies by reading a speech by Cuba's president, Federico Laredo Brú, meant to capture the spirit of the convention: "How extraordinarily timely is this meeting of thousands of persons from such distant places of this world, all having the same thought in mind and the same purpose of working more and better for the benefit of humanity and of *our* civilization" (emphasis added). The possessive adjective "nuestra" ("our") called for some elaboration:

> Cuba . . . making, as you Rotarians do, friendship the standard of our international relations with other countries . . . in this uncertain time . . . feels itself to be most closely joined to the nations of this continent and tightens its fraternal bonds of friendship and understanding even more and principally with the great nation which, in such a brilliant, effective and disinterested manner, ... put an end . . . to the false legend of expansion and imperialism, thus acting, when we declared our independence and sovereignty, in a manner very different from other nations.[2]

Soon to be replaced by Fulgencio Batista, Cuba's de facto leader since 1934, Laredo Brú envisioned a shared civilization among the Americas premised on friendship as the "standard of our international relations." Rather than reinforce José Martí's enduring call for hemispheric equality over US hegemony through "nuestra América," however, Laredo Brú's use of "nuestra" pointed to common republican values embodied foremost by the one exceptional nation to the north, the United States of America. Mixing notions of progress and pan-Americanism, Laredo Brú linked the highest aspirations of the republic of Cuba with the ideals of the visiting Rotarians and their guests. According to his logic, the "fraternal bonds of friendship and understanding" between Cuba and the United States served as counterevidence to the "false legend of expansion and imperialism" by the United States.

Laredo Brú spoke not just in the comforting language of Rotary's civic internationalism but also in accord with the familiar narrative of the

United States as both progenitor and protector of the Cuban republic since 1898. Though a parade of speakers from Canada, Great Britain, Finland, Palestine, Ceylon, Honduras, Nicaragua, and even Japan underscored the Cuban president's opening call for unity and international friendship, Laredo Brú followed a familiar script for US-Cuban relations first established when President William McKinley, in his war message before US Congress in 1898, lumped together "the cause of humanity," "our duty" to Cuba as a neighbor and struggling republic, protection of US life and property in Cuba, and the prevention of "serious injury to the commerce, trade, and business of our people" as reasons for war with Spain.[3] The "destruction" of the USS *Maine* then capped the list. Just as trade and warfare were twinned in US political discourse at the birth of the Cuban republic, so were US expansion into Cuba and denial of that encroachment: "I speak not of forcible annexation, for that cannot be thought of. That, by our code of morality, would be criminal aggression."[4] Congress enshrined McKinley's renunciation of territorial conquest in the Teller Amendment the following week. With its anticolonial credentials intact, the US government sent its troops into Cuba with the promise "to leave the government and control of the Island to its people."[5] Within a few years, the Platt Amendment made its appearance first as a rider to a US Army appropriations bill, then as a part of the Cuban constitution in 1901, as a condition of US military withdrawal in 1902, and finally within the Permanent Treaty between the United States and Cuba in 1903. In effect, Cuba surrendered its ability to conduct foreign policy on its own so that "the United States may exercise the right to intervene for the preservation of Cuban independence."[6] Over the following decades, the Platt Amendment became the focal point of growing Cuban resentment toward the expanding presence of the United States in Cuba. The amendment's formal abrogation in 1934, however, did not prove to be the long-awaited gateway to Cuban independence and full sovereignty.[7] Even without the amendment, Cuba remained dependent on the United States in multiple, interwoven forms of political, cultural, and economic control in the summer of 1940.

The history of Rotary clubs in Cuba during the interwar period, therefore, provides important insight into how the deep contradic-

FIG 5.1: The first Rotary Club outside the Anglophone world took root in Havana, Cuba, in 1916. At the time of this 1923 photo, Rotary clubs could be found throughout all of Cuba, the Caribbean, Spain, and Latin America, with new clubs forming on a regular basis. *Courtesy of Rotary International.*

tions of US power built into the Teller and Platt Amendments played out among Cuban businessmen and their US counterparts in Cuba as well as throughout the United States. The Havana Rotary club represented Rotary's first uncertain steps outside of the Anglophone business world, thus revealing the exotic peer—the idealized partner and colleague at the core of Rotary's "world fellowship"—in the first stages of its social construction during and after World War I (figure 5.1). Moreover, approaching the Havana club itself as a "microsite of rule" by the United States exposes how the imagined "bonds of friendship" between US and Cuban Rotarians operated more like the "intimacies of empire" rather than a counterfactual to the "false legend of expansion and imperialism."[8] In this capacity, RI's many activities and means of influence in Cuba serve as a case study in US cultural and economic imperialism in one nation over several decades. The real impact of RI's civic internationalism was its power to operate in both directions, blinding businessmen both in Cuba and in the United States to the sometimes subtle yet always pervasive nature of US economic and political control in Cuba. The origins and evolution of the Havana Rotary club during the interwar period, in short, illustrate in detail the nature of US-Cuban business relations under the shadow of the Platt Amendment.

FROM "THE LATIN RACES" TO FELLOW ROTARIANS

That a Rotary club took root in Havana as early as 1916 should not be a complete surprise. As Louis Pérez demonstrates in abundant detail, Cuba came to define itself in total opposition to Spain and all things Spanish by 1898. Instead, Cuba looked north to the United States: "Much in the Cuban sense of future and of place in that future was shaped by or otherwise derived from the encounter with the North."[9] This deepening sense of a modernity gap between the newfound republic of Cuba and the established republic of the United States powered the central dynamic in the two nations' relations for more than half a century:

> The success of U.S. hegemony in Cuba [became] less a function of political control and military domination than a cultural condition in which meaning and purpose were derived from North American normative systems. U.S. influence expanded from within, usually in non-coercive forms, just as often introduced by Cubans themselves as by North Americans. U.S. culture spread rapidly across the island and emerged as one of the most accessible means by which to aspire to well-being and thus was a powerful motivator in the acceptance of new social norms and new cognitive categories. This was the principal way that Cubans entered the postcolonial order, the circumstances under which social institutions were formed and moral hierarchies established, the means by which many citizens arranged the terms of their familiarity with the world at large.[10]

The United States, in other words, permeated Cuba's national identity, economic systems, cultural patterns, and everyday social interactions to an unprecedented degree.

Given the Cubans' unusual openness to developments in US political, consumer, and business cultures, the establishment of a Rotary club in Havana should have been an easy task. By 1915, Havana already had its own chapter of the Woman's Christian Temperance Union (WCTU), the American Society for the Prevention of Cruelty to Animals, the YMCA, the Boy Scouts, and the Loyal Order of Moose Lodge, as well as various fraternal associations and other US-based social organizations.[11] Also, Rotary had already merged its ideology of civic uplift, community service, and progressive business practices to its business internationalism when the National Association of Rotary Clubs became the International Association of Rotary Clubs (IARC) in Duluth, Minnesota, in 1912, in recognition of new clubs in Canada, Ireland, and Great Britain.[12] The Duluth convention went even further by crystallizing its commitment to international expansion in its constitution with a simple, new objective: "To encourage and promote the organization of Rotary clubs *in all commercial centers of the world*."[13]

Despite their sweeping ambitions, however, many remained reluctant to expand "Rotarianism" beyond the Anglo-Saxon world. In particular, Chesley Perry, general secretary of the IARC based in Chicago, had strong reservations about opening a new club in a city like Havana, where he had served as a soldier during the US occupation after 1898:

> I know the city pretty well and also have talked with men who are in business there and we have had visitors who have undertaken to start a club there. It is still a Latin-American city and neither are conditions of thought among the Latin-Americans right for the starting of a Rotary club nor is Rotary itself sufficiently well developed to be translated into Spanish and conducted among the Latin races.[14]

Yet Perry's reticence stood in contrast with the views of regional members who advocated on behalf of expansion into Cuba. Ernest Berger, a

Rotarian from Tampa and executive at the Tampa-Cuba Cigar Company, had a different perspective: "I discussed the matter both with American, Cuban and Spanish business men, and feel convinced that a Club consisting of men from these various races will be a big success. It would never do to confine it to Americans alone." John Shelby, a piano manufacturer from Birmingham, Alabama, and the district governor for all Rotary clubs in the southeastern United States in 1914–1915, concurred: "After discussing this matter with the Tampa and Jacksonville Clubs I am thoroughly convinced that this will mean a great deal for Rotary, and the boys in that part of the country are very anxious to take hold of this matter at once."[15] The growing acceptance of Rotary as an international organization, fueled in particular by regional and international business interests, eventually overrode Perry's initial misgivings. In the organization's internal debates over expansion into Cuba, preexisting, cross-border business networks trumped prevailing racial categories of strict Anglo-Saxonism. The civic whiteness used by US Rotarians to identify potential recruits within the United States widened its circle, as Havana's "Latin races" gained entrance into Rotary's "world fellowship."[16] Though Afro-Cubans never fell within the compass of this civic whiteness, all other Cubans throughout the country did—or at least could—once professional and economic parameters for club membership were met. Reputation in the marketplace merged with imagined capacity for self-governance to define citizenship in a mutually reinforcing manner, blending economic citizenship with political virtue. With "conditions" in Havana deemed ready for "Rotarianism" by regional representatives of Rotary, all of Cuba became an opportunity for growth.

But the story of Rotary's move into Havana was more complex. First, Chesley Perry's ultimate conversion was crucial to expansion first into the Caribbean and then ultimately all of Latin America. As the general secretary, Perry had more input into the planning, direction, and growth of Rotary clubs than anyone else from 1910 until his retirement in 1942. Without his blessing, the push for "this missionary work of establishing Rotary clubs in other cities" would have been all but impossible.[17] As late as August 1914, Rotary's highest leadership was divided between those who expected a natural progression from British Rotary clubs into Paris and Berlin, and those such as Arch Klumph (soon to become president of the IARC in 1916) who were actively pushing for extension into Mexico City, Buenos Aires, Rio de Janeiro, and eventually all of Latin America. Perry and Klumph proved powerful allies in Rotary's eventual expansion southward during and after the Great War.

The turning point for both Perry and Rotary's leadership came at the international convention in San Francisco in 1915, held during San Francisco's Panama-Pacific Exposition. Calling the Expo "a remarkable opportunity for us," Rotary's board of directors spent the week meeting with "the representative men from South America . . . at the exhibits of their respective republics." Within months, Allen D. Albert, president of the IARC in 1914–1915, appointed a special committee on "extension work in non-English speaking countries and particularly in Latin America." Perry himself came fully on board after his meetings both at the Expo and with John Barrett, director general of the Pan-American Union from 1906 to 1920 and chairman of Rotary's Foreign Extension Committee from 1918 to 1920. (See Chapter 2.) Given the war in Europe and a growing chorus of "businessmen familiar with South America" calling for "the cooperation of the natives of the various countries [rather] than letting Americans be the organizers," Rotary's extension into Latin America went forward with the active participation of Latin American businessmen.[18] As in Rotary's internal debates over a potential Havana club, prior transnational business networks obviated some racial hierarchies—but not all. Region by region, nation by nation, city by city, and member by member, Rotary clubs were just as capable of redrawing the "global color line" in the world of international business relations as reinforcing it.[19]

In the case of Havana, Perry built on the work of the Tampa businessmen by seeking the help of Rafael Martinez Ybor, the Cuban consul in Tampa, who had extensive business ties in both Havana and Tampa. Most revealing is how Perry approached Ybor:

> In San Antonio, they say the 'The Rotary Club is the warmest thing that has struck the business world in many years.'. . . . It is a revelation of the meaning and the application of the Golden

> Rule. . . . The existence of a Rotary club benefits the community, improves the business world in general and helps to carry forward the human race in its upward march.[20]

Not only did Perry attempt to deflect criticism of Rotary's embrace of the profitability of social networking among businessmen, but he also explained the "missionary work" of Rotary outside the United States in terms quasi-religious in tone but secular in application. Just as the first Rotary club in Chicago in the early days forged a discourse of professionalism and civic responsibility to prove that Rotary was something more than a mere luncheon club of back-scratchers and boosters, so, too, did the "extension" of Rotary clubs outside the United States require something more than "just business" as an explanation. It was not enough to speak of regional and cross-border business interests between Cuba and the United States as the sole impetus for the transplanting of Rotary clubs into Cuba. Rotary's civic internationalism provided a social and cultural framework of meaning and purpose as Rotary expanded in the 1910s and 1920s (see map pp. xii–xiii).[21] When Rotary's membership of business and professional men applied that framework on an international scale, they envisioned a global network populated with professional and reliable peers in "all commercial centers throughout the world." But what about when those "commercial centers" were very far afield and foreign to the chummy environs of a Chicago businessmen's social club?

In 1915, identifying and incorporating these exotic peers outside the English-speaking world into the fold proved more difficult in practice than in theory. When Chesley Perry wrote Alexander Kent, attorney and representative of the Red Feather Cinematograph Company in Havana, to give him authority to form a new club, Perry made one important stipulation: "You are also advised and directed to make up the Rotary Club of Havana with not more than 25 percent of American and not less than 75 percent of Cubans or Spanish-Cubans. What we want to do is to spread Rotary among the native people of other countries more than among our American brethren who happen to be in other countries."[22]

But as the year wore on, Kent was slow in organizing the club and Perry grew impatient: "We are desirous of having a club started in Havana so that following Havana we may be able to introduce Rotary into all of the Latin American countries and thereby intensify the present cordial international relations between all the Americas."[23] At the headquarters of Rotary in Chicago, the founding of Havana's Rotary club was part of a grander strategy. Kent, however, did not share such hopes:

> I think that you had better address yourself to someone else in Havana to organize the local club. The conditions set forth by you are, to my mind, very difficult if not impossible . . . I have never yet seen oil and water mix properly, and I don't believe that Cubans and Spaniards will ever of their own free will join a fraternal organization with Americans. That has already been attempted in Havana and without any success.[24]

For Alexander Kent, "Latin American cordiality does not exist except on paper."[25] Kent was no believer in the transformative powers of Rotary's civic internationalism.

Undaunted, Perry found his answer in the Rotary club of Tampa, Florida. To John Turner, one of three Tampa Rotarians recruited to organize the Havana club and dubbed the first chairman of the Committee on Extension of Rotary in Latin America, Perry made clear his goals:

> The only instructions which I know of to give you are that it has been agreed that in the establishment of Rotary clubs in other countries, the effort should be made to have such clubs formed of representative citizens of the respective countries rather than of Americans or Britons temporarily resident of those countries.[26]

Perry's secretariat in Chicago was now spearheading the project as he gathered the names and addresses of all Cuban consuls in the United States and sent form letters to all US Rotary clubs that opened, "My dear (club president), owing to the fact that we are now making a direct move upon Havana, Cuba through the courtesy of Turner and the Rotarians of Tampa . . . ," and requested the club presidents to invite the consuls to the clubs' weekly meetings and ask the consuls to assert their influence in Havana on Rotary's behalf. The plan met with some success, particularly when the son of Cuba's secretary of state attended the Baltimore club's meeting and came away impressed.[27] The synopsis of the club president in Baltimore revealed the complex overlap of the commercial, diplomatic, and social dimensions of Rotary's designs on Havana: "I found Mr. Desvernine a very high class gentleman, and further learned that he is the son of the Secretary of State of the Republic of Cuba. This no doubt will give us prestige in Havana and trust that the Tampa Rotary Club who has fathered the establishing of a Club in Havana will be successful." But what did it mean to have "prestige" in Havana and for the Tampa club to "father" the Havana Club?

For Perry and the leadership of the IARC, it soon became clear that preexisting regional business and social networks anchored in both Tampa and Havana were the primary drivers in their "move upon Havana." The Jacksonville and Tampa Rotary clubs finally took the initiative in February 1916. Helping Turner organize the Havana club were A. L. Cuesta of "Cuesta, Rey & Co., Manufacturers of Habana Cigars," and Ernest Berger, "Secretary Treasurer for the Tampa-Cuba Cigar Co."[28] When Turner and Cuesta teamed up for a personal visit to Havana in early February, they met with success. Business trips blurred with "missionary work" proved to be far more effective channels of influence and motivation than all the planning and oversight by Rotary's secretariat in Chicago and diplomatic overtures to Cuba's representatives in the United States. Social networking among businessmen of the region drove the process of growth and adoption—but in well-defined terms of class and race. Turner and Cuesta had decided "to form the Club of the old conservative Spanish and Cuban element" believing that "when formed I feel sure it will be a credit to our association."[29] "Prestige," it turned out, had a specific, transferable currency for men in the business classes of Tampa, Jacksonville, and Havana.

By April 1916, the Havana Rotary club held its first official meeting and signed up its charter members. Turner was especially proud of the club's first president: "Rene Berndes is also secretary of the Country Club, treasurer of the Yacht Club, and is prominent socially as well as commercially, speaks fluently Spanish, English, and German, is a native Cuban."[30] Cuesta and Turner recruited many more "joiners" from the Havana social and business world. The Havana club's first vice president,

L. E. Brownson, was director of Banco Nacional de Cuba and a partner of Purdy and Henderson (the largest contractor in Cuba), as well as director of the American Club and a member of the Country Club. Albert Hoffman, manager of the West Indian Branch of National City Bank of New York, served as the club's first secretary (New York City's Rotary club also helped in some phases of organizing Havana's club, apparently with the help of National City Bank as well) while the position of club treasurer fell to C. W. Ricker, assistant manager of the Havana Electric Co. But Turner also noted Manuel A. Suarez, a senator from the Havana Province and tobacco planter, and Angel del Valle, representative of the "Castañeda interests in leaf tobacco . . . among the largest and best of the islands" as important Cuban charter members. Of the original twenty-two charter members, ten had Spanish surnames and twelve Anglo surnames. Apparently Perry's 25 percent cap on US membership was not hard and fast. Moreover, not one charter member had direct ties with the sugar industry, by far the predominant industry in Cuba, while nearly half the new Havana Rotarians worked for or represented US companies in Cuba. Strong representation from Cuba's own tobacco industry reflected the business ties within that industry and with US sponsors in Tampa and provided some counterbalance to US predominance. For Perry and the IARC, however, the club was close enough.[31] Most important was the elite status of the first Havana Rotarians—a pattern, in fact, later followed in most of the non-Anglophone cities where Rotary clubs formed over the interwar period. RI's civic internationalism thrived on such borrowed status as clubs typically formed around a local nucleus of well-established commercial and social elites and then built out.

Secretary Perry also had his own reasons for rushing to organize the Havana Rotary club before the summer of 1916. Rotary's seventh annual convention in Cincinnati was to serve as a showcase for the expansion of Rotary clubs outside the Anglophone world. Turner's success came just in time. Rotary's dignified reach would now encompass 27,000 members among more than two hundred US Rotary clubs augmented by thirteen Canadian, thirteen British, two Irish, one Scottish, and now one Cuban club. Havana's club president, Rene Berndes, was to attend the convention, flashing his cosmopolitanism in any one of his four native languages. But at the last moment, business obligations prevented Berndes from being able to travel. Albert "Bert" Hoffman made the trip instead. Asked to speak as representative of the Havana club to the convention audience of 3,800, Hoffman was first greeted by the cheer "Viva Habana!" The admittedly shy speaker then announced that the "Club Rotario de la Habana" had grown in only three months from 16 charter members to 53 members; expected to offer Cuba's business-friendly president, Mario García Menocal, honorary membership (evoking applause); and planned "to make Spanish the language of the club," adding that "they want to make it distinctly Cuban." Hoffman then lent his own support for "Cubanizing" the club, apologized for not being an actual Cuban himself, and then closed with what turned out to be the club's most important concern: Would the IARC consider holding its 1920 annual convention in Havana? Boosterism knew no bounds—nor boundaries. Instead of an answer, Hoffman was given the official flag of Rotary to take back to Havana for weekly display in their luncheon meetings.[32] The certification of Havana in the world of Rotary's businessmen and professionals had begun through the Havana club's proxy, Bert Hoffman, an officer for National City Bank in charge of its West Indian Branch.[33] What could possibly be "distinctly Cuban" about such a club?

Though John Turner's expectations for the new club had their limits, the Cuban Rotarians were characteristically determined to outperform their US colleagues in their own dedication to progressive uplift and community service. From the newcomers' perspective, the Havana Rotary club had its value as a "distinctly Cuban" demonstration project as well. Reporting to the Cincinnati convention as head of Rotary's "extension" into Latin America, Turner voiced a common view of the Havana club's potential:

> The work of introducing Rotary in Latin-America is most important, in that the Latins, as a rule, have not imbibed the "get-to-gether" spirit, and the Rotary idealism, while there, has never been appealed to or brought out to any extent. This is caused by the business men being self-satisfied with their own businesses and not reaching out and getting on the broader plane that Rotary expects.[34]

Cuban businessmen lacked the public-spiritedness, civic-mindedness, and professionalism in their private endeavors "that Rotary expects," thus revealing their need for tutelage in the ways of civic cooperation and responsible economic citizenship.

Yet the Cuban Rotarians, well aware of tacitly lowered expectations of civic engagement within their business community, showed a great desire and capacity to counteract these low expectations through the club's activities. Laboring in the shadow of their perceived modernity gap, the Cubans felt they had much to prove and so wasted no time. By late summer 1916, the club had already taken on three projects: (1) a study on how to develop tourism in Cuba, (2) improvement of Havana's "means of communication" through formation of a "commission of engineers and citizens" to study the issue (headed by Mariano Diaz and Dr. Carlos Alzugaray); and (3) improvement of traffic flow through better streets, greater legal enforcement, and education and advertising campaigns on better driving.[35] By the next year, the club's agenda swelled with ambition under the label "Platform for the beautification of the city of Havana," which included the following:

1. Buying land to give to the city "suitable for parks and other public uses . . . as playgrounds, gymnasium, and bathing places"
2. More traffic improvement by laying out "a complete system of boulevards and avenues" as well as paving old roads
3. "To procure the removal of all wires, posts, and obstructions from the streets, sidewalks, and entrances"
4. "To bring about the installation of a more artistic and efficient system of street lamps and electric lights in the matter of public lighting"
5. "To make prominent study of the city's internal development and to recommend to Congress the most advantageous plan for securing it"
6. "To study and improve the system of hygienic houses . . . for laborers and persons of small means"
7. The introduction of one-way traffic on key avenues and the prohibition of traffic on narrow streets for the sake of pedestrian traffic[36]

Most remarkable about the Havana Club's agenda for the city was how unremarkable it was in light of parallel trends in the United States during the same period. The Havana Rotarians strove to prove themselves as legitimate business progressives just as much as their counterparts in North America and Great Britain. The club's eagerness to have concrete results in time for its report to Rotary's upcoming international convention in Atlanta in June 1917, however, was unique. As always, the perception of Cuba as an upstart struggling to catch up with the colossus to the north hung over the Cubans. But the Cubans were seeking to gain ground as fast as possible by engaging in and demonstrating their own particular mastery of Rotary's vision of civic internationalism. As the first non-Anglophone members of Rotary's "world fellowship of business and professional men," the Cubans knew they had much to prove. Through their own Rotary club, however, many Cuban Rotarians saw a dual opportunity: development of business networks throughout the United States and demonstration of local capacities for responsible municipal governance and civic engagement.

Meanwhile, the lessons learned in Havana in 1916 proved to be a crucial opportunity for Rotary as well. The challenge of starting the first Cuban club hinged on bridging preexisting social and business networks of urban elites beyond their regional hinterlands and national boundaries. Organic cultural and business links with deep historical roots in the Hispanophone world proved much more fertile for Rotary's growth than formal diplomatic initiatives. Not surprisingly, when Ely E. Palmer, US consul in Madrid, sought to establish a Rotary club in Madrid in 1918, he did not get very far. But when Angel Cuesta offered to help establish a new club in that city during a "pleasure trip" in 1920, Rotary's Chicago office jumped at the chance. It just so happened that Cuesta was particularly well-suited to duplicate his success in Havana in Madrid as well, given his personal history of business dealings and frequent travels as a tobacconist with family roots and social contacts in Florida, Cuba, and Spain. For Angel Cuesta, as in Havana, so in Madrid. As a result, Havana became a template for successful institutional expansion of Rotary not only in the rest of Cuba and the Caribbean, but also in Spain and consequently Latin America as whole. Once Madrid and Barcelona had their own Rotary clubs by 1921, the doors opened up for "Rotarios" to cross back over the Atlantic into Latin America, thus helping establish new clubs in that continent with support from the Iberian Peninsula as much as from North America.[37]

NEUTRALITY AND THE FLAGGING OF CUBAN NATIONALISM

Despite claiming to be just a private, voluntary association of businessmen, the Rotary club often played a distinct public role, especially in public ceremonies. Rotary clubs the world over have always sponsored an array of public ceremonies in the name of the public interest, which anyone may attend. The Havana Rotary club was no different. As the first Rotary club in Latin America, however, the Havana club saw itself in a special role in all its ceremonies both public and private. The club took its identity as the gateway for Latin America and as Havana's bridge to a transnational network of business and professional peers very seriously—and creatively.

In order to celebrate the fiftieth anniversary of "El Grito de Yara," the beginning of Cuba's war for independence from Spain on October 10, 1868, the club organized a parade in Havana "with the idea of presenting a flag to the National University." The Rotary club of Havana saw it as a natural duty to organize "the largest and greatest parade ever had in this country" in order to "raise the patriotic spirit of the people, which in later years has been greatly demoralized." The club was intensely proud at succeeding "in getting representatives from all the social classes to parade with us."[38] Rotary's civic internationalism thrived on such local pride of place.

The Havana club's public commemoration of El Grito de Yara, however, had many precedents in the United States. One of the most significant public events in Rotary's early history came soon after the entrance of the United States into the Great War. The first major gathering of Rotarians after President Wilson's declaration of war on Germany in April was Rotary's eighth annual international convention in Atlanta, June 17–21, 1917. Attending the conference as representatives of Havana and all of Cuba were Dr. Carlos Alzugaray, Avelino Perez, and L. S. Salmon.

While the IARC saw the convention as a prime opportunity to showcase its patriotic support of the war against "the Hun," the Atlanta Rotary club also wanted to use the convention to publicize its existence and purpose to the rest of Atlanta and the South in general. Both the international and the local found their interests neatly met through a very large public event centered on the national cause of winning the war in Europe. It was also the Havana Rotarians' debut before their North American and British counterparts in business as well as "the first public recognition of Cuba as an ally by the people of the of the British Empire and the United States."[39] The Atlanta convention of 1917 also had its uses for Cuban patriots.

The first day of the convention being a Sunday, the Atlanta Rotarians had the churches throughout the city focus on the general theme of "Service." Indeed, many of the sermons were given by visiting Rotarians of the cloth. But the culmination of the opening ceremonies was not in the pulpits and pews of Atlanta. Instead, the Atlanta club orchestrated a massive patriotic rally and flag-raising ceremony in Piedmont Park attended by an estimated fifteen thousand persons. Amid "patriotic concerts" and "stirring speeches," the open-air event

> was kaleidoscopic: Rotarians mingled with the great crowd, the pink hats of the Chicagoans, the green hats of the Tulsans, the black and white umbrellas of the Kansas Cityans, the dark old rose of the Chattanoogans, the red, white, and blue umbrellas of the Cincinnatians, the white "jack tar" suits of the Savannahans, all vying with the brilliant colors of the summer costumes of the Atlanta ladies.[40]

It was an outpouring of boosterism and conventioneering by Rotarians and rubbernecking by thousands of Atlantans. But the call to patriotic duty and fervent nationalism in unity against the German menace imbued the festivities with palpable urgency. Despite the frivolity, everyone understood that it was a profoundly challenging moment in the nation's history. The massive flag-raising ceremony was staged to capture the solemnity of the times:

> A flag pole had been erected and streamers had been run to its peak setting against the rare blue of the afternoon sky the colors of all the nations—save one—now fighting for the liberty of the world. The one flag missing was that of the United States. Five trumpeters blew "Assembly." The famous Chicago band played "The Star Spangled Banner." Two marines of the United States raised aloft a little square of blue cloth. An American Indian of full blood, Chief Silvertongue, eagle feathers waving from his war bonnet, sang the first few words of the American anthem. The breeze unfolded the little square of blue into the Stars and Stripes. With a roar the thousands caught up the song—and the spirit of the 1917 convention had been fixed.[41]

The event may have been an effective way to meld God and country, but it was also great publicity for the Atlanta Rotary club and their Rotarian guests. Though Chief Silvertongue, "the Indian attorney from Kansas City," began the national anthem with "his mighty tenor voice," it was soon drowned out by the voices of thousands of Atlantans and thousands more visiting businessmen. Not all of those singing the anthem were from the United States.[42]

Atlanta's flag-raising ceremony had particular effect on one important Rotarian from Havana. As Dr. Alzugaray interpreted the ceremony, "at that convention the banner of service became the flag of country and all those Rotary clubs began to offer their most effective services by contributing to recruitment of troops, . . . conservation of food, and fundraising for the Red Cross, the YMCA, the United War Camp Community Service and similar organizations." Alzugaray was also impressed with nationwide efforts by the clubs to construct zones near army camps for the "moral and physical preservation of the recruits" and efforts to obtain industrial experts for the war effort and other services that would help meet the needs of the US government in its mobilization of the American Expeditionary Force.[43] Alzugaray saw his first contact with US Rotarians in Atlanta as much more than an introduction to a luncheon club's annual gathering. The massive flag ceremony galvanized public action in the war effort. More important, he expected to duplicate the feat in Havana and thus unleash a similar flood of voluntarism, solidarity, and organization in service to the public good and Cuban patriotism. The Rotary club of Havana might just be the accelerant for republican virtues, national development, and economic cooperation that Cuba still lacked in its infancy as an independent nation. Amid the patriotic fervor of Atlanta in 1917, Alzugaray hoped that the International Association of Rotary Clubs could mesh well with his own *Cubanidad.*

Grafting themes of Cuban nationalism onto Rotary's civic internationalism soon became a common occurrence in the Havana club and then in all Cuban clubs that followed. In time, many other Cuban Rotarians could see what Alzugaray saw in Atlanta: the chance to inject their own nationalist aspirations into their Rotary clubs' goals and activities. The most public events, therefore, became ideal opportunities to stage publicly their own nationalisms. The Cubans, in fact, were not alone in this trend. On the eighteenth anniversary of Rotary's founding in Chicago, the Barcelona Rotary club presented the Havana club with the Spanish flag in a formal ceremony.[44] The following month, the Rotary club of Mexico City presented the Mexican flag to the Havana club with Mexico's "Encargado de Negocios" in Cuba in attendance. All members were strongly urged to attend as the Havana club planned on formally giving the Cuban flag in return to "a sister republic, so heroic, noble and generous—loved and respected by all" the following week in the name of "Rotarian brotherhood." R. Gomez de Garay, a native Mexican and member of the Havana club, held the Mexican flag with honor for the ceremony's photograph, an event later recounted in local newspapers as well as in RI's own monthly magazine for worldwide consumption.[45]

The practice of exchanging national flags under the aegis of Rotarian "world fellowship" could serve many purposes and many interests. In January 1924, the Rotary club of Paris formally presented the French flag to the Havana club while a French army captain, a representative of the commercial attaché of France in Cuba, the French minister to Cuba, the attaché to the Ministry of France, and several other French and Cuban dignitaries looked on with approval. The Havana club president for that year, Emilio Gomez, warmly accepted the French banner and then put the ceremony in context for all those assembled:

> Some time ago the Rotary Club of New York sent us that beautiful American flag that you are seeing, and it was quite natural that from there came such a good occurrence because it was in the United States of America where Rotary was originated. We, the Cubans, were pleased that it was the American flag first to join our national insignia. With similar pleasure we received the English, the Spanish, the Mexican flags sent by Rotary Clubs of those countries, all of them belonging to nations to which we are united by bonds of friendship and in some cases strong blood relationship.
>
> It was for a long time since we were longing for that beautiful flag of that Universal Country to which we are united by bonds of affect. At last, today, our longing has been accomplished in receiving the heroic emblem . . . and [it] will be united to our flag as it is already united in the bottom of our hearts.[46]

This was a simple speech, but powerful in its symbolism. The order in which the Havana club received its flags reflected a reimagining of the international order in the wake of World War I for the Cubans. Under the terms of the Platt Amendment, Cuba's international trade shifted its focus from Europe to the United States. But its cultural and intellectual compass had made the shift as well.[47] Now, in a public ritual, the two were placed in formal alignment.

But how much of this international order was really new? The Havana club's flag ceremony left no doubt about the centrality of the United States to the Cuban republic's identity, but the ceremony did not in any way challenge what Dipesh Chakrabarty calls "the hyperreal Europe."[48] The Cuban Rotarians' model nation-state—the United States—was still understood within the Enlightenment metanarratives of progress, modernity, and capitalism. Gomez's reference to France as "that Universal Country" highlighted this presumed continuity. However, the Cubans were attempting to shift away from the old template of Eurocentrism to the Americas. Although Gomez was not seeking to overthrow the normative configuration of Western nation-states, he suggested that the interactions between those states should be determined by the "united bonds of friendship" now made manifest by the network of Rotary clubs in each country and city. The gift-giving of national flags among these clubs ostensibly occurred within a broader context of international peace and stability engendered through friendship and "bonds of affect." Friendship, cooperation, and sentiment, however, had their exchange value in the world of international business as well as diplomacy—a currency soon to be negotiable in most "commercial centers of the world."

In this way, Rotary International offered its Havana members a way of forging international ties among nations that both transcended and incorporated each nation. The service club's presumed neutrality, particularly its discourse of civic engagement and international cooperation for their own sake, could serve as a metaphysical glue for Cuban pride and patriotism. As with their parade in 1918 for the National University, Cuban Rotarians were just as likely to organize and sponsor public events celebrating key moments and personages of Cuban history as Latin American, North American, and European ones. For the Havana club members, the Rotarian vision of world peace and cooperation became the unseen, unacknowledged ideological backdrop of so many flag-draped luncheon podiums, hotel ballrooms, and diplomatic and civic ceremonies, thus pervading not only the club members' Cuban identity but also mediating Cuban relations with all other nations. Thus the Cuban Rotarians did more than place the United States at the top of a hierarchy of nations; they allowed the United States to define the terms of Cuba's international relations, albeit because those terms promised local empowerment and needed reform. The Platt Amendment, in short, was not the only way for the United States to permeate, mediate, and constrain Cuba's sovereignty.[49]

The Havana club's 1924 flag ceremony exemplified an expanding cultural practice of acting out Cuba's international identity according to stage directions established elsewhere. Plattism had its cultural dimensions, even in the world of international business. RI's civic internationalism performed, literally, the cultural work of US economic hegemony.

"SERIOUS CONSEQUENCES FOR CUBA"

Within a few short years, the Havana Club's international reputation was sterling: it was an unusually serious and ardent club in its devotion to progressive reform. But the club's progressive agendas were not shared equally among its members. In 1920, Dr. Carlos Alzugaray, then head of the Asociacíon de Comerciantes de La Habana and eventual member of the Supreme Council of the Veterans' and Patriots' Movement in 1923–1924, complained to Chesley Perry about the tendency of the "elemento americano" to leave the initiative for reform and community action to the Cuban members. Alzugaray's explanation of Cuban Rotarians' zeal for reform through their own club, especially when compared with non-Cuban Rotarians in Havana and in the United States, revealed a critical fault line in the Cuban republic. In Alzugaray's view, the Havana club concerned itself with serious matters of reform and had little time for social "distractions" primarily because "we have many serious things going bad and that by necessity we must confront, that demand the attention of men who are concerned for their country."[50] As a result, Alzugaray claimed that the Havana Rotary club was "today the institution, corporation or entity with the most prestige as civic, patriotic, and altruistic."[51] According to Alzugaray, nothing serious, noble or uplifting went on in Havana without the involvement of the "Club Rotario," despite its critics. Even allowing room for exaggeration, Alzugaray's description of the Cuban Rotarians' role in Havana reform movements pointed to both the pressing needs for systemic reform within Cuba and the minimal means of effecting change available through the political process. The service club from the United States, in Alzugaray's view, was and ought to be an outlet for the simmering reformist impulse driving some of Havana's key business and professional leaders.

But not everyone shared Alzugaray's progressive vision for the Havana Rotary club. Cuban Rotarians were initially at odds over the degree of latitude suitable for club debates over politics and political reform. In a letter to Perry, Avelino Perez raised concern over how fellow club members discussed openly their disdain for abuses during the elections in 1918. He felt Rotary's bylaws and constitution did not permit such open political debates in the club, and he requested English copies of the constitution, bylaws, code of ethics, and club statutes in order to support his contention.[52] The problem, Perry wrote back, was hardly new for those at Rotary's headquarters in Chicago: "I might tell you privately that the members of the Board feel that the Havana Rotary Club is fully competent to interpret sanely and wisely Article V of the Constitution of a Rotary Club, and without a personal understanding of the local political conditions it would be better for the rest of us not to undertake to make an interpretation." Perry then admitted in a follow-up letter "that we are finding difficulty in drawing the line between what is real community service or patriotic interest in public affairs and what may be considered politics or partisan or personal politics. . . . It seems that it best can be solved by each club working it out according to local conditions and circumstances."[53] It is quite possible, in fact, that Perry had in mind the active involvement of Chicago Rotarians in the American Protective League during World War I when responding to Perez's request. On the surface, the Cuban Rotarians seemed to have maximum freedom to work out their own terms and limits of debate for social and political reform within their own Rotary club. In the world of Rotary, the Cubans were free to define what was political and act accordingly within their own community and country, since there was plenty of Cuban autonomy in the moral universe of US benevolence.

But the problem resurfaced within a year. Mario MacBeath, the Havana club's young and vibrant club secretary, wrote Perry for advice on the same matter but from a different position from Perez. MacBeath summarized Cuba's struggle for political and social reform in the face of enduring obstacles. He reviewed the "local conditions and circumstances" for Perry:

> It is recognized by everybody in Cuba that the men who have formed our different governments since we became independent have not been of a high moral or mental level. The moneyed in-

> terests, the merchants, the manufacturers, most of them foreigners, have kept away from politics, except in some few cases when they have joined hands with some politicians to defraud the people.
>
> The better class of Cubans keep [sic] away from any contact with the government, even to the extent of not voting. The result of this lack of interest in the government on the part of our financial, commercial, and manufacturing interests on the one hand and the better class of Cubans on the other, has brought about a situation that prophesies serious consequences for Cuba.[54]

MacBeath was describing the profound division between the economic and political classes in Cuba, which resulted in a political system based on patronage and personal connections and a business community largely unconnected and unconcerned with bringing an end to ongoing graft and corruption, let alone advancing real civic, economic, and political reforms. This faultline ran throughout all of Cuba, not just Havana.

The Rotarians of Havana, after the 1918 election, saw themselves caught between these two worlds.[55] As a service club premised on the activities of influential businessmen and professionals united for the purpose of community service and civic reform, the Rotary club's attempts at bridging the gap between the political and economic spheres in Cuba would seem natural. Many Havana Rotarians thus forged ahead, seeking solutions through their own reform agenda. MacBeath was speaking on behalf of Havana Rotarians like Alzugaray who knew what they were up against and saw the inherent risks if no structural reforms were forthcoming. The problems went beyond immediate political housecleaning. To MacBeath, they were part of a broad moral and nationalist project: "Last November our elections were a disgrace to Cuba, and were they to be made along the same lines again, Cuba would see many black days. The Havana Rotary Club, right after the election, passed a resolution condemning it and asking all Cubans, without regard to parties, to get together and insist on a change in the Electoral Law."[56]

Even though all the members agreed that their Rotary club was not the place to take up overt political platforms, the need for real reforms was so compelling that the Rotarians decided to take what action they could. In spite of the reluctance of members such as Avelino Perez, the majority of the club supported the resolution. It seems that for most of the Cuban Rotarians in Havana, the club was finally engaging in the mission for which it was created: pushing for and instigating genuine progressive and structural reforms in the Cuban political economy. Furthermore, this first attempt at promoting reform had a dramatic impact. An association was commissioned to draft a revised Electoral Law, and when its work was submitted to Cuba's legislature, it contained many of the club's recommendations. It seemed logical to capitalize on this success in Havana by extending the effort to the growing number of Rotary clubs in the rest of Cuba: "Today Gonzalez del Valle . . . recommended that the Club adopt a resolution asking the other Rotary clubs of the Island to start a movement of education so as to obtain the producing classes (all those who earn an honest livelihood) to take an interest in politics and in the formation of political parties and their platforms."[57]

Gonzalez del Valle, in line with MacBeath and Alzugaray, envisioned an island-wide "movement of education" that would inculcate the "producing classes" in the ways of responsible economic citizenship and civic engagement through the emerging network of Cuban Rotary clubs. (By 1940, in fact, Cuba had forty Rotary clubs spread throughout the country and were organized as their own administrative "district" within Rotary International.)[58] The Cuban Rotarians seemed to have found their calling, their own voice for enduring political reforms.

Or had they? Debates still persisted on the possibilities of engendering reforms. The Cubans looked to the United States and its clubs for guidance. As MacBeath put it,

> I remember that some time ago one of the Rotary Clubs in the States started a campaign to have all citizens vote on election day; another Club, a campaign to Americanize the people of their city, to have the foreigners become American citizens. So it seems to me that what Gonzalez del Valle wants the Club to do is not outside the province of Rotary Clubs. It all hinges on

> the interpretation of the word politics, as mentioned in Article 5 of the Constitution. Next week the matter will be put to a vote at the regular meeting, but it seems to me that it is a case to be decided by International headquarters.[59]

MacBeath was very careful not to divide the club "on this or any other question" and so turned to Secretary Perry in Chicago for advice in a "personal letter." MacBeath, like his fellow Rotarians, showed great deference in trying to maintain the cordiality of the club's atmosphere. But he also understood the matter would not and could not go away:

> This will not be the last time that the Club will have to express an opinion on matters of this nature, and it is well that we have a definition of the term "politics" as used in the Constitution. Alzugaray, Gonzalez del Valle and myself believe that it is used in the narrower sense, that is politics in a party sense, not in the higher sense, that is as "the branch of civics that treats of the principles of civil government and the conduct of state affairs." What will you say?[60]

The question was how to move beyond the rigid structural limits on reform endemic to the Cuban republic under the shadow of the Platt Amendment and overwhelming US capital interests—how to move into politics "in the higher sense" and, in this case, effect meaningful electoral reform. Yet key Cuban citizens in Havana, economically empowered and driving toward overdue political reforms through their own local Rotary club, ultimately chose to contain their reformist impulse within the limits of personal deference and the bonds of "friendship and understanding" with their US peers. The Cuban Rotarians turned to Rotary's headquarters for direction on how to manage the growing tensions in Havana and Cuba because the Cubans believed themselves to be a part of Rotary's vision of advancing greater "understanding, good will, and international peace." They were seeking to emulate what they saw as a private, nonstate institutional role model for coping with the civil, economic, and political difficulties in their own city and country.

But that emulation came at a price. Playing the Cuban counterpart to the US Rotarian required the adoption of certain sensibilities, codes of behavior, and ways of seeing. Secretary Perry cabled back: "Party or partisan politics is politics forbidden and not unselfish betterment of public welfare."[61] The distinction, for all its loftiness, could not have been more debilitating. Given the conditions of Havana and of Cuba, reform in such terms was no reform at all. In tune with the "elemento americano" in the Havana club, Perry's advice would have placed too many limitations on the actions of Cuban Rotarians like MacBeath, Alzugaray, and Gonzalez del Valle.[62] After serving as the Havana club's president and then the first district governor for all the Cuban clubs in 1921–1922, Dr. Carlos Alzugaray eventually resigned from the Havana Club's Board of Directors in 1922 in order to devote all his time and energy to the "purification and moral regeneration of the public agencies."[63] For Alzugaray, the "fraternal bonds of friendship" among Rotarians were indeed tight—to the point of constraint.

As so often happened in Cuba, shadowed as it was by the United States, an opportune moment for substantive reform by Cubans for Cubans dissipated—in this case, in the genteel civilities of service club decorum. Initially, Rotary's civic internationalism seemed a way to advance the interests of Cubans through the agency and empowering of homegrown leaders through joint civic action. However, when the Cuban Rotarians deferred to the interests of the US leadership and conceived of "politics" and "reform" in terms approved and defined by the US Rotarians, the Cubans had to abandon their push for much-needed electoral reforms. The marketplace, in theory, was prior to and indifferent toward politics. The precise reason for the Havana Rotarians' acceptance into the international world of Rotary—their status as businessmen and professionals in the business world—prevented their having any voice outside of that world. In this way, the microcosm of friendly relations among US and Cuban members of a "world fellowship of business and professional men united in the ideal of service" recapitulated the rhetoric of Cuban political autonomy amid the harsh realities and asymmetries of de facto imperial relations.

TARIFF MINDING

In the waning days of World War I, all Havana Rotarians were in agreement about one goal: finding ways to increase the economic strength and diversity of the Cuban economy. To that end, the Havana club published in 1918 a small pamphlet touting Cuba's economic potential in a burgeoning international marketplace. Its blend of boosterism and nationalism demonstrated just how well the Havana Rotarians had learned to speak the salesmen's language of their counterparts in the United States. Opening with a glowing description of Cuba's location in the "channels of trade and the great markets of the world," the pamphlet emphasized Cuba's proximity to "the great American markets and centers of distribution" to the north; the "sister republics" of Argentina, Brazil, and Chile to the south; and Mexico and Central America to the west. But the vision of Cuba's role in international markets swept airily past any pan-American limits because "with the opening of the Panama Canal we have Japan, China, Siberia, and India; and to the east, across the Atlantic lies Europe." In short, there were no imagined limits to Cuba's economic growth in the minds of the Havana Rotarians of 1918.[64]

Blessed with "more fine deep water harbors than any other country in the Western Hemisphere" and a population becoming more and more white European through immigration each year, Cuba also had a modern public education system thanks to "the American Intervention" in 1900 and a good transportation system of railroads and paved roads. Havana was the pinnacle of trade, since "more merchandise enters and leaves [Havana] . . . than any other port in the Western Hemisphere, with the exception of New York." Given the relative youth of Cuba as an independent republic, the pamphlet then summarized economic statistics from the prior two years to demonstrate the country's potential for rapid expansion. The sudden increase in demand for so much of Cuba's products as a result of the war in Europe—especially sugar—escaped mention as the obvious cause for its increase in "foreign commerce" of more than 500 percent since 1902. Still, with their US audience of fellow Rotarians clearly in mind, the pamphlet reduced it all to terms simple enough for any denizen of Main Street America: "All but 15% of Cuba's exports go to the United States," while "90% of Cuba's imports come from the United States." In effect, through informal cultural diplomacy, Havana Rotarians were seeking to find their own voice in the "cultural politics of sugar" and to enhance Cuba's leverage within the evolving tariff competitions and parallel developments of "the U.S. Sugar Empire" in the wake of World War I.[65]

There was one problem with the Havana Rotarians' vision of international trade. With well over three-quarters of Cuba's agriculture devoted to sugar production, the Havana Rotarians highlighted Cuba's capacity "to furnish the world with all the sugar it needs," and this "in spite of the fact that labor is much higher in Cuba than in other cane sugar producing countries."[66] The quality of Cuba's sugar would always speak for itself. The pamphlet then closed with a review of all industries other than sugar. The next sizable industry was tobacco, at about one-tenth the volume of the sugar industry. After tobacco, the industries diminished rapidly in scale and importance from fruits and hardwoods to cattle ranching and mining. Though Cuba's overall economic structure was heavily tilted toward the mass production, refining, and exportation of sugar to the United States, that was clearly a temporary state of affairs, a function of Cuba's youthfulness as an independent republic and the unusual needs of wartime supply and demand. The Havana Rotarians looked to a future of economic diversification and growth:

> A marvelous soil, a climate unexcelled, a location directly in the pathway of Western and Southern commerce, an ambition to excel in those things which make for good government, and a most liberal encouragement to outside capital, together with friendly international relations, presage for this Republic most exceptional industrial development . . . and [with] but 25% of the available soil adapted to the production of sugar under cultivation, the possibilities of future growth along other lines than that now producing the greatest revenue are apparently marvelous. These opportunities are open to and challenge the capital and enterprise of the world.[67]

Their message having been well honed and published in a glossy, colorful, and readable pamphlet for mass mailings and public consumption, the Havana Rotarians had only one task left: getting the word out to their intended audience—the more than forty thousand Rotarians of the world, most of whom in 1918 were in their principal market of the United States (figure 5.2).

The task, in the end, was not a difficult one. Mario MacBeath knew that Chesley Perry was the one man at Chicago's headquarters who could make it happen for the Havana Rotarians. Their confidence in him paid off. Given MacBeath's regular correspondence with Perry, he and his fellow Cubans were already a very well-known quantity in the halls of Rotary's administrative offices on Lake Michigan. Perry also drew from his own experiences in Cuba during the first US military occupation and could attest that "many of the pictures in the pamphlet are not overdrawn." Perry then put his administrative machinery to work on behalf of Havana: "Without doubt there is a great deal of valuable information in this pamphlet which would be of interest to Rotarians in the United States and this fact, coupled with the fact that the Rotary Club of Havana is taking such a keen interest in the affairs of Cuba, leads me to conclude that it would be well to send a copy of the pamphlet with one of the issues of the Weekly Letter." Perry's efforts translated into Rotary's headquarters sending out more than 3,200 copies of the pamphlet to all Rotary clubs throughout North America, Canada, and Great Britain. Indeed, Perry had originally typed "2,500 copies" and then crossed that out with "3,200" in pen.[68] After all, Rotary clubs were popping up all over North America by 1918.

The Havana Rotarians had hit the jackpot. Thousands of Rotary clubs in the United States were about to receive a beautiful pamphlet placing Cuba in the best possible light imaginable. The Havana Rotarians' close association with the International Association of Rotary Clubs was about to reap handsome benefits, as Perry's introduction for the pamphlet was "calling attention to . . . the activities of the Rotary Club of Havana in exploiting the natural resources of Cuba."[69] Representative of an entrepreneurial bourgeoisie newly emerging during and because of World War I, the Havana Rotary club—along with the new clubs the Habaneros established in Matanzas, Cienfuegos, and Santiago de Cuba—would appear as the vanguard of Cuba's economic and political development to scores of thousands of US Rotarians. Moreover, with only Montevideo,

FIG 5.2: Seeking to establish itself in primary export markets, the Havana Rotary club was an early adapter in publishing promotional materials throughout the Rotary clubs of the United States. *Courtesy of Rotary International.*

San Juan, and Panama City slated for the establishment of Rotary clubs in the coming months, Havana could still lay claim to being the main gateway for US, British, and Canadian Rotarians into all of Latin America. The 1918 pamphlet encapsulated well the high hopes and expectations of businessmen and professionals in the principal cities of Cuba and especially in its capital city. Meanwhile, Rotary's "world fellowship" was proving itself a booster's dream and a Cuban patriot's best friend as the promises of Rotary's civic internationalism—cooperation, support, and respect in the name of civic development among business and professional peers across and despite borders—seemed to be paying off where and when it mattered most.

The club had occasion again to communicate with all the Rotary clubs in the United States in 1921. Boosterism had given way to tariff issues and protectionism in the face of recession in the United States and depression in Cuba, after the "dance of the millions" in early 1920. The end of war meant the end of prosperity in the Americas as Europe recovered and demand in general fell off. While the severe drop in agricultural prices in the United States came to preoccupy the Republican Congress after 1920, the price of sugar in Cuba dropped precipitously from 22.5 cents per pound in May 1920, to 8 cents in September, to 3.8 cents in December.[70]

For a country relying on sugar for more than 90 percent of total export value by 1920, this price drop was calamitous. The old political class of Cuba, so accustomed to running the government without serious electoral challenge, found itself by 1921 confronted with a growing and self-aware economic class of Cubans no longer tolerant of government corruption and public malfeasance and much more committed to *la patria* than the preceding generation. The Havana Rotary club—or at least certain of its members—already saw the club as part of this broader trend by 1918. As the wild speculation and easy credit of 1919 and early 1920 slipped into bankruptcy and stagnation, Cuba seemed to have lost its bearings economically. Meanwhile, given the messy and contested 1920 national elections and continuing revelations in the newspapers of rampant corruption by those in public office, the republic of Cuba looked more and more like a prodigal son in the eyes of many Cubans and Americans. The young nation was faltering both economically and politically, in serious danger of surrendering its birthright as a "sister republic" of the Americas. It was not long before enforcement of the Platt Amendment commenced. By the end of 1920, General Enoch Crowder arrived in Cuba as the "special representative of the president," staying in total for two years. The US government sent Crowder to do some "housecleaning" in the new government of Alfredo Zayas. Once an "honest cabinet" had been created under Zayas as an inoculation against persistent government corruption, Cuba received a $50 million loan from

J.P. Morgan and Company in order to rectify the country's debt problems.[71] Amid this economic and political turmoil, the Havana Rotary Club sought the help of its fellow club members in the United States.

But the United States was dealing with its own economic turmoil. By January 1921, Joseph W. Fordney, representative of Saginaw, Michigan, and the Republican chairman of the House Ways and Means Committee, began work on an Emergency Tariff bill. The hiatus of protectionism since 1913 under the Democrats' Underwood-Simmons tariff system had come to an abrupt end amid declining losses among so many farmers and growing Republican control of Congress. With Fordney blaming the postwar recession in the United States on low tariffs, he sought to construct a protective barrier especially for farm imports to the United States. Sugar tariffs were one of several prime targets for Fordney's rate hikes. Not a single Cuban could fail to appreciate the threat represented by Fordney's bill in the US Congress. But alas, unlike the interests in the sugar-producing states of Louisiana, Michigan, California, and Colorado, no Cubans had any voice or way to lobby the US Congress directly. By May 1921, the Emergency Tariff Act had replaced the Underwood Tariff, thus setting the stage for the Fordney-McCumber Tariff Act of 1922 and, disastrously, the Smoot-Hawley Tariff of 1930.[72]

Only three days later, the president of the Havana Rotary Club, Alberto Crusellas, wrote both Chesley Perry, Rotary's general secretary, and its international president for that year, Pete Snedecor of Portland, Oregon, asking for permission to send a form letter to all the Rotary clubs of the United States asking their support in reclaiming some $40 million in wartime profits on Cuban sugar sold in the United States. With a letterhead listing all the club's officers, quoting Rotary's motto "He profits most who serves best" in Spanish translation, and reading at the bottom "La Habana Es El Segundo Puerto Comercial de America," club president Crusellas politely requested "permission to place in hands of the presidents of Rotary Clubs of the United States of America the enclosed letter" and invited Secretary Perry in particular to offer his "criticisms" and "impressions."[73]

The urgency of the matter, however, was clear. The Cuban economy was swimming in debt, and Crusellas was acting at the formal behest of the Havana Rotary club, which had voted on a resolution to proceed with such a project the week before.[74] And why not? The precedent was already there. Just as Rotary's headquarters had enabled Havana to spread its message of Cuba's openness to "the capital and enterprise of the world" with its pamphlet in 1918, the headquarters would help in getting Cuba's views and concerns about its massive debt crisis out to tens of thousands of fellow Rotarians throughout the United States in 1921. Even before the passage of the Emergency Tariff bill, the Havana Rotarians were seeking desperate measures for desperate times.[75]

The Havana Rotarians had their sympathizers within the world of Rotary. The incoming international president of Rotary, Dr. Crawford McCullough of Ontario, Canada, saw the Cubans as simply wanting to "get the necessary authentic information on this whole subject before the business men of America and for this purpose it was desired to use the medium of Rotary clubs."[76] The Cubans were fortunate to have a Canadian at the head of the IARC at this juncture, as Canada had its own particular problems with Fordney's proposed tariffs and was open to considering US trade policy from a non-US perspective. But outgoing president Snedecor requested only that the claims made in Havana's circular letter, specifically on the $40 million of profits made by the Sugar Equalization Board in the United States from Cuban sugar during World War I, be confirmed by Herbert Hoover's Commerce Department.

Never one to leave any loose ends, Chesley Perry wrote the secretary of commerce on the matter and explained how "the Havana Club has courteously submitted this matter to us before sending it to any club in the United States." Secretary Hoover's ultimate response was quite telling:

> There is no conceivable possibility of this money ever being used for Cuban purposes. The American government on two occasions purchased the crop of Cuban sugar at prices extraordinarily profitable to Cuban producers and in equalizing its distribution and transportation throughout the United States, in conjunction with domestic sugar, the Board earned the profits to which you refer. *These profits are the property of the American consumer and can only be returned to him by mitigation of*

> *his taxes.* I am intensely sympathetic with the difficulties in Cuba and this Department would be glad to exert itself in any direction to mitigate the situation.[77] (emphasis added)

Despite his "sympathetic" understanding of the Cubans' present plight, Hoover could see the Cubans' case only as a done deal—for the "American consumer." The Cubans had played their dutiful part as an ally in the Great War and now had to move on and cope with the new tariffs emerging from Congress like everyone else. But the Havana Rotarians were trying to cash in one last time on the heady days of wartime prosperity in the midst of economic chaos and as a way to forestall foreclosures on a massive scale. Moving on for the Cubans meant a $50 million loan from J.P. Morgan, the reinforcement of the Platt Amendment, and further entrenchment of the US government and capital in Cuba's political economy. The $40 million the Havana Rotarians were seeking to reclaim through their circular letter would have been crucial in undermining the scope and power of Plattism. Instead, their circular letter was becoming as valueless as their bank notes.

Secretary Hoover's response, however, did not end the Havana Rotarians' quest. Secretary Perry cabled Crusellas in Havana on September 3 reporting that Rotary's international board had approved the sending of Havana's circular letter to all US clubs as soon as possible, since Hoover "did not contradict the statements made in the Havana letter."[78] Crusellas cabled back that Perry's message had been read at the club's meeting, and the members had voted unanimously to express the "clubs [sic] deep appreciation of your deference in this matter to Havana Club which we know is unusual."[79] Havana's circular letter was a study in mounting Cuban frustration with its deepening dependence on an international economic system centered around and managed by the United States. Cuba's profound debt crisis of 1921 only exacerbated the political shame that was the Platt Amendment.

It was a time of change and upheaval throughout Cuba, and also a time of new political assertions and national solidarity. In that vein, the Havana club invoked the language and logic of civic internationalism to make its case. In tone, the form letter was polite, but it was time for Rotary to come through on its promises:

> It is the fundamental motto of our organization to be useful to the society in which it lives, to its own town or city, to its State or Province, to its Nation, and to humanity. And since our Nation is at the moment suffering through the effects of an intense economic crisis for the reason that it has not been able to place the sugar produced during the present crop owing to the lack of demand and consumption in our principal market, which is your country, we desire to avail ourselves of the services of our fellows in Rotary to make known to its people, to whom we are bound by ties of friendship and intense self interests, since to them we owe in a great degree the independence of our country, the causes that have given rise to our crisis.[80]

With increased tariffs on and less demand for sugar in the United States, Cuba's entire economy seized up. A recession in the United States was a catastrophic depression in Cuba. The crisis of 1921 was even more galling, according to the circular, because the US government had urged the Cubans to produce sugar in huge abundance in the name of the allied war effort. The Cubans then pointed to the Sugar Equalization Board in the United States as the source of greatest inequity, as the $40 million in profits went to the US government in its spending for the war rather than to the Cubans who had produced the sugar and could have sold it on the world market at much higher prices. Without those war profits, the sugar planters had to "obtain loans of large sums of money from the banks," resulting in the present debt crisis. Contrary to Hoover's argument, the Cubans reasoned that

> if Cuba realized by contract the sale of two entire crops [of 1917 and 1918], the same was not inspired with the remotest idea of profit but on the contrary agreed to and fixed a minimum price on its product as a co-operative measure in the cause of the Allies, waiving the opportunity brought about by the great necessity of the allied nations to grasp a legitimate profit. We believe therefore we have the right at this time to expect the co-operation of the great people of the United States in our economic difficulties, which resolves itself in the elimination of

> measures that descriminate [sic] against the consumption of our sugars.[81]

The lofty sentiments of patriotism and allied solidarity in order to stop the marauding Central Powers of Europe had given way to the economic rationale of Mr. Hoover in 1921. The ornate flag-raising ceremonies of the Atlanta convention were replaced by contracts, urgent Liberty Loan drives by national debt, international cooperation and hemispheric solidarity by market forces and domestic politics.

The circular then closed with a two-pronged strategy. The first centered on the notion of mutual interests given the close economic ties between the two countries. "Since our country imports from the United States nearly all the articles necessary for our subsistence, it is of utmost interest to the commerce of your country . . . that it come out in the defence of our sugar industry, since if our sugar has no value, we cannot purchase from you."[82] In fact, the Cubans' dilemma was prologue for Europe's—and especially Germany's—in the near future: how can war debts denominated in US dollars be paid back unless there was the opportunity to earn US dollars in the first place? If a shared devotion to international friendship and cooperation proved too unpersuasive, then surely the Rotarians of the United States could understand the importance of Cuban markets for their exports. If the Cubans did not have a voice in the US government and its policy-making, at least they might have some influence in the United States because of their aggregate purchasing power of US consumer products. After a review of the rapid increase of US imports to Cuba from 1917 to 1921, showing with "the eloquence of numbers" how much the United States did in fact rely on Cuban export markets, the Cubans concluded their argument: "The campaign, therefore, launched against us in your country by certain refiners, is not only directed against us, but is also an attack against the general interests of the commerce of the United States." But trade reciprocity between the two nations, in the end, did not entail political equality between its citizens. Cuban Rotarians had no pull in US Congress any more than they did in US credit markets.

The second strategy was more of a plea and redolent of the letter's opening: "It would give us great pleasure if you would read this letter at the next meeting of your Rotary club . . . thus cooperating with us and in the spirit of the motto that inspires *our Institution,* and also to transmit to us the impression you may deduce after its reading at that meeting."[83] Here was an opportunity for Rotary to operate as an international network of business and professional peers, to make possible the "commercial square deal" so central to its ideology of civic internationalism, to serve as an impartial platform for international cooperation and understanding among nations and their civic and economic leaders.

But the "parliament of businessmen" had its limits. Though given approval to send the circular letter, no substantial results ever panned out. How could they? Given the scope and scale of the US economy relative to Cuba's, the severity of the economic travails of Cuba did not seem to register in the minds of most US Rotarians. It was one thing for a city's club to put out an international plea for help after a natural disaster, as the Tokyo Rotary club did with great success after the massive earthquake of 1923, but it was quite another to make a plea for compensation from the US government three years after the fact and in the name of wartime solidarity.[84] Systemic economic inequalities and structural limits on Cuban development did not figure in the rhetoric of Rotary's heart-shaped world of international friendship and cooperation. Also, given the discrete and concentrated interests of sugar producers and refiners in the US Congress (where tariffs were debated and set), the Cubans' private, informal approach of businessmen to businessmen had a rather dull edge. Instead, General Crowder oversaw Cuba's debt consolidations to the tune of $50 million from J.P. Morgan thanks to the Platt Amendment, while the US Congress muddled through with the Fordney-McCumber bill the following year.

Rather than back payment on war profits in the midst of a debt crisis, the Cubans got a slap in the face. On 21 September 1922, President Warren G. Harding signed the Fordney-McCumber bill into law, raising the sugar tariff for Cuba nearly twofold, from $1.25 per pound to $2.20 per pound. The move's effects on the Cuban economy were devastating over time, though increasing demand for sugar in Europe mitigated the effect.[85] Meanwhile, Harding, a proud and consummate Rotarian of the Washington, D.C. club, spoke the following June at Rotary's fourteenth annual international convention in St. Louis, Missouri. Introduced by

Rotary's president Raymond Havens of Kansas City, Harding spoke to the nearly seven thousand in attendance: "If I could plant Rotary in every community throughout the world, I would do it, and then I would guarantee the tranquility and the forward march of the world. Statesmen have their problems, and governments have theirs, but if you could plant the spirit of Rotary throughout the world, and turn it to practical application, there would not be so much wrong with the human procession."[86] "Prolonged applause" followed his remarks. America had its moral compass, and Rotary was following it. International peace and progress were a function of managerial skills in "practical application" at the local level through voluntary associations like Rotary.

The next morning, in front of the same convention audience, Havana's own Avelino Perez recounted the many playgrounds, drainage systems, parks, monuments, highways, dispensaries, and summer camps for Boy Scouts the eleven Rotary clubs of Cuba were responsible for in recent years. Speaking as Alzugaray's replacement as district governor for all Cuban Rotary clubs, he explained that "due to the fact that, although Cuba is one of the oldest countries in America, it is one of the youngest in its organization as a republic, the work of the Cuba clubs during the past year has been to try to educate the citizens and inspire in them the real Rotary spirit of Service before Self."[87]

Perez made no mention of the US sugar tariffs or the Cubans' debt crisis—and certainly nothing of the Platt Amendment and its imposition. Contrary to Alzugaray and MacBeath, Perez did not believe a Rotary club was a place for political debate. Rotary's civic internationalism did not allow such questioning of "the fraternal bonds of friendship and understanding"—especially in public. That would have been impolitic.

"ACROSS BOUNDARY LINES"

Business relations between Florida and Cuba, nevertheless, continued to develop over the 1920s. As a result, the Havana Rotary club visited en masse the Miami Rotary club in August 1929 and 173 Miami Rotarians returned the favor in November that same year.[88] RI's monthly magazine, the *Rotarian*, touted these international exchanges as "probably the most significant demonstrations of Rotary internationalism."[89] Over several days, the Cubans treated the visiting Floridians like royalty. Planned activities included a large ceremony at the foot of the monument to Martí in Havana's Central Park—led by Havana's mayor, Miguel Mariano Gomez, a Rotarian—followed by a tour of Havana's new capitol and then topped off by a lush dinner and ball at the Sevilla-Biltmore Hotel, where the entire Miami club was staying. Amid the various luncheons, swimming parties, and sightseeing tours of Cuba's universities, the Columbus Cathedral, and the great Central Highway were grand speeches by Dr. Antonio Sanchez de Bustamente (noted educator and international jurist), by Cuba's secretary of state, and by many other Cuban dignitaries. After an ornate ceremony of flag exchange among clubs, the trip had its culmination: an "audience" with Cuba's president, Gerardo Machado, at the Presidential Palace.

Taking part in this international meeting of Rotarians had its advantages for President Machado.[90] One year into his second term, he was on the brink of entering into the true crisis period of his presidency just as the world was on the verge of the Great Depression. In need of political support wherever he could find it, he introduced himself as a fellow Rotarian (though this was probably an honorary title) and proclaimed his faith in Rotary's "advancement and in its progress, because I knew that it represented the ideals of honesty, of integrity in business, love of fellow men, and above all love of country, and true patriotism, not only in Cuba, but also in the United States and all over the world."[91]

This was a striking introduction, if only because Machado's endorsement of Rotary's ideals stood in stark contrast to the political realities of Cuba and in accordance with his rivals' constant calls for greater honesty and integrity in Cuba's political system. But, as an economic reformer, Machado had sought to move Cuba away from its monoculture of sugar production toward some version of modernization and genuine independence.

Driven by such goals, Machado was happy to foster any US business relations outside of the sugar industry. He chose his words well when characterizing the Floridians' presence in Cuba: "These visits, these gatherings, are very necessary, because they bring a truer understanding and a more sincere esteem between your and our people. As the United

States and Cuba were bound by the ties of blood in 1898, when you came over to fight in our cause for our freedom, so must we continue to be bound forever and forever." Through the alchemy of blood and freedom, Cuba and the United States were bound together in common cause, which then overflowed into the two nations' business and economic ties:

> We must supply goods to the United States and the United States must supply goods to us. As we help your financial institutions, which are practically in many cases Cuban institutions, so you must help in the development and progress of our country, and in the expansion of our economic activities. We must always have a true, sincere, and mutually beneficial economic understanding. We must see in each other as sincere friends and co-operators. Our purposes and our ideals are the same.[92]

With the Platt Amendment challenged more and more by Cubans, the Great Depression only just beginning, and the restrictive Smoot-Hawley Tariff only months away from passage, Machado suggested that the purposes and ideals shared by both Cuban and US Rotarians should be the basis for both mutually beneficial trade relations and for the recognition of Cuban sovereignty and independence. The language of RI's civic internationalism allowed Machado to make these assertions to ringing applause from Miami's top businessmen and professionals.

Machado closed by exhorting his "fellow Rotarians" to return to the United States to serve as "personal witnesses" to Cuba's being "a progressive, peaceful, orderly, and civilized country, a democracy full of civic enthusiasm and deep patriotism" and to counter the recent "publication of biased and untruthful reports about Cuba, which hurt the mutual understanding and good feeling that ought forever to exist between us."[93] Machado's paean to US-Cuban "ties of blood" questioned the inequalities of the Platt Amendment in a language that would reassure rather than offend his audience of Florida businessmen and their spouses. He and the Cuban Rotarians needed their business and investments. Unfortunately, the sunny language of friendship and cooperation could no more derail Cuba's political and economic dependence on the United States than could the promise of "beneficial economic understanding" and trade reciprocity.[94]

The international exchange between the Rotary clubs of Havana and Miami was viewed as such a success that plans were made to turn it into an annual ritual. Tampa's Rotary club, not to be outdone by Miami's, had already invited the Havana club for a visit the following year. A friendly rivalry between Tampa and Miami Rotarians over Havana could only benefit the Cuban Rotarians and their business community. For once, they seemed to have some real leverage in the United States—or at least in the state of Florida. Meanwhile, the *Rotarian* summed up the triumphant moment of internationalism: "Thus Rotary is helping in the great effort toward the supplanting of envy, rivalry, and war with sympathetic international understanding, a force that will eventually put happiness in the place of ill-will and unite the world in the bonds of peace. Good will between countries begins in a friendly handclasp across frontiers."[95]

However, the success was more apparent than real. The rhetoric could paint over the inequities of Plattism for only so long. Within two years, Cuba's sugar exports plummeted as unemployment skyrocketed, leading to "conditions [that] set the stage for political confrontation and social conflict on a scale unprecedented in the republic." Machado's government began to unleash repression that "summoned into existence an extensive police apparatus penetrating every aspect of Cuban social life, not only to arrest, torture, and execute but to maintain surveillance over Cubans not in prison and over the countless thousands who were."[96] By the fall of 1933, Sumner Welles, Roosevelt's assistant secretary of state turned US ambassador to Cuba, had engineered a palace coup to replace Machado and then a second coup to replace the reformist government of Grau San Martín with Fulgencio Batista, a mutinous sergeant turned military strongman.[97] From friendly business visits from Florida to the engineering of palace coups in the name of public safety, the Janus-faced nature of reform and empire, friendship and domination, cooperation and control, permeated US-Cuban relations. The question was—and is—how the two faces have been mutually constitutive.

"NUESTRA ORGANIZACIÓN"

The Cienfuegos Rotary club held a *Concurso Escolar* open to all seventh and eighth graders of the city in 1929 and again in 1930. All students, male and female, from all schools, public and private, participated in the essay competition on "the importance of increasing our industries, and the production of raw products on our soil." Three girls and one boy won medals, diplomas, and books on the competition's topic. The students received their prizes at "a public festivity with the solemnity worthy of an event in behalf of childhood."[98] The twenty-four members of the Cienfuegos Rotary club suggested that Rotary International publish a photo of the event in the *Rotarian.* The previous year, the Matanzas Rotary Club had organized a *Concurso Nacional* for seventh and eighth graders, and now the Cienfuegos club was administering one of its own *Concursos locales.* Cuban Rotary clubs often competed in this manner, copying one another's successful events, activities, and projects while seeking to outdo fellow clubs as well.

The themes for the national writing competition in Cienfuegos, however, were much more telling of Cuban Rotarians' national concerns:

1. Products necessary for the subsistence that can be obtained on our soil—"en nuestro suelo"
2. Application of these products to existing industries
3. Which new industries could establish themselves given the raw materials found in our country?—"nuestra Patria"
4. Why must we augment our commercial and industrial capacity?[99]

Cubans in general shared these concerns, since the Great Depression had already arrived in full force in the country years before becoming a worldwide phenomenon. Cubans' long-held desire to escape the venomous legacies of the sugar monoculture and its dependence on the global market value of sugar dominated these writing competitions for years, as the same desire dominated practically all other aspects of Cuban culture and national discourse.

But the Cienfuegos Rotarians decided to publicize their student essay contest throughout RI's "world fellowship" as well as in Cuba. The club published a pamphlet "in memory of the Contest," which was sent to the twenty-two other Rotary clubs in Cuba and to all other Spanish-speaking Rotary clubs of Latin America and the Caribbean—about 150 in all. Antonio Asensio, the club's secretary and a charter member in 1919, also sent copies of the pamphlet to RI's seventy-six district governors and fifteen board members scattered throughout the Americas, East Asia, and Europe and to RI's top officials headquartered in Chicago.[100] The Rotarians of Cienfuegos wanted to make a splash with their *Concurso Escolar* in the world of Rotary, but especially in the Spanish-speaking portions of it.

To that end, the club drew up a cover letter for the pamphlet in Spanish that trumpeted "the progress of our organization ('nuestra organización') in carrying to the ends of the earth the healthy norms of our Rotarian ethic."[101] The letter explained further how helping the children of the city was the club's principal activity that year and then closed with a request that other clubs share any information with them on similar activities in their own clubs and cities. Presenting the civic projects of the Cienfuegos Rotarians as part of the mainstream of RI's civic internationalism also meant spotlighting Cuba's economic and political troubles before an international audience. The publicity of the *Concurso Escolar* was, in truth, an international plea for help.

That it came from the Cienfuegos Rotarians marked a milestone in the evolution of Rotary clubs in Cuba and of Rotary's civic internationalism. First, the Cienfuegos club was completely homegrown. Key Cuban Rotarians from Havana were instrumental in organizing the club's first meeting on the Fourth of July, 1919. Dr. Adalberto Ruiz, lawyer and charter member in Cienfuegos, celebrated the auspicious date of his club's founding on "this glorious day in honor to the Great American Nation that in this day celebrates the anniversaries of its independence." To mark the occasion, Ruiz reported in broken English to the Chicago headquarters, "Were present, as special invited, the civil, judicial and military authorities, the consuls of United States, France and Spain and representatives of the local press."[102] After apologizing for his English,

Ruiz then touted the club's first president, Sotero Ortega, a "famous and prestigious physician." The Cienfuegos club received a great deal of support in its formation from the president of the Havana Rotary club, Carlos Alzugaray; its club secretary, Mario MacBeath; and Avelino Perez—some of Havana's most devoted Rotarians in 1919. Given particular help from Alzugaray and Perez, Dr. Ortega expected his club to become a full participant in "the great family of Rotary" ("en la gran familia rotaria").[103]

Second, the Cienfuegos club's membership encompassed more of the city's business community than the charter membership of the Havana club. The new club's thirty-nine charter members included a hardware store owner, a civil engineer, a cigar factory owner, a dentist, a sugar exporter, a furniture maker, a corporate lawyer, a distillery owner, a rancher, a real estate agent, a pharmacist, a pediatrician, and so on.[104] The club seemed to embody Rotary's ideal of a "cross-section of representative businessmen and professionals" coming together in mutual cooperation and for the sake of civic improvement. The Cienfuegos club, in microcosm, appeared to be a balanced and diverse local economy.

Third, the club had been started by Cubans and was predominantly composed of Cubans. As part of its founding leadership, joining President Ortega were Vice President Acisclo del Valle, a commercial banker; Club Secretary Adalberto Ruiz, a notary public; Treasurer Florencio R. Velis, a printer; board members of similar backgrounds and reputation; and Luis Hernandez, sergeant-at-arms and broker at the customs house.[105] In other words, the club did not have the "elemento Americano" that Alzugaray and MacBeath contended with in Havana. With no one industry, corporation, or profession predominating, and with nearly 100 percent native Cuban membership, the Cienfuegos Rotary club embodied the promises of Rotary's civic internationalism: local empowerment of business and professional elites for the sake of community service and their incorporation into a transnational network of like-minded peers—completely on their own terms. Only three years after the formation of the Havana club, the IARC had realized its goals in Cienfuegos, while other Rotary clubs soon popped up in much the same manner in Matanzas, Santiago de Cuba, Colon, and dozens of other Cuban cities.

The Cienfuegos Rotary club had a promising start in 1919. The diversity of its charter membership boded well for an emerging, vibrant economic center in Cuba at the end of the Great War. All its weekly meetings, civic activities, and committee business were done in Spanish from its inception and with the improvement of Cienfuegos and Cuba in mind. The club's credentials as a fully Cuban organization firmly rooted in the business and professional communities of the city and country were unassailable. The establishment of Rotary clubs in other Cuban cities over the next decade, therefore, represented an important phase in RI's civic internationalism. Rotary's pervasiveness in Cuba and capacity to attract Cuban members distinguished RI from other US voluntary associations: the Cienfuegos Rotary club was by no means an outpost for Americans abroad. Consequently, the Cienfuegos Rotarians' *Concurso Escolar* and its subsequent publicity in Rotary's transnational network of peers demonstrated both the legitimacy of their own *Cubanidad*—the theme for the competition was, after all, driven by Cuban nationalism—as well as the endemic nature of US imperialism in Cuba, as the competition's theme underscored, without actually naming, the vise-like grip of US economic control on the island nation.

By 1929–1930, however, the looming sense of dependence on the world price of sugar and the political vicissitudes and tariff policies of the United States slowly overshadowed, step by step, year by year, any hope of independent political and economic development for Cuba. As the drive toward a diverse and growing economy tapered off by the late 1920s, the Cienfuegos Rotarians—along with their fellow Cuban Rotarians—put together their national essay competition in an effort to reignite hope, especially in their youth, for a better future. Their fellow Rotarians outside Cuba, however, did not seem to grasp the gravity of the situation. To them, the Cuban Rotarians had a lot of "pep." The borderless world of "nuestra organización" promised by RI's civic internationalism and supported by the Cienfuegos Rotarians did, in fact, have its borders. The "nuestra America" of Jose Martí was not the "nuestra organización" of Rotary—and never could be.

By the time Havana played host to Rotary International's 1940 convention, Cuba seemed to be coming of age. A modicum of trade reciprocity and the Good Neighbor Policy had replaced the hated Platt Amendment since 1934. Economic growth and political stability were emerging. Women's suffrage had passed. And now Cuba was nearing its first real constitution. All the pieces for a vibrant political system and civil society looked to be coming together. So when Geronimo Ramirez Brown, one of RI's top officers worldwide, addressed the convention in a speech entitled "Rotary from an Ibero-American Viewpoint," his triumphalist tones did not seem out of place. Ramirez, from Nicaragua, drew from the now familiar practices, iconography, and discourse of RI's civic internationalism:

> Let us . . . look upon . . . the flags of numerous countries of the world . . . , showing that the idea embodied in Rotary has blossomed out in all parts of the world; men of different races, speaking different languages, from all regions of the earth, have come here . . . to the heart of Rotary which unites them in common human aspiration of improvement.
>
> Many of them did not know each other before today; here, under the shadow of Rotary . . . , they shook hands, they are becoming acquainted and getting together in order to continue working in harmony each in his own sphere, for the good of his city, of his country and of the world.[106]

Echoing the convention's opening address by Cuba's president, Laredo Brú, Ramirez struck all the right chords. The shared mission of civic uplift and global harmony "under the shadow of Rotary" pointed to a universalism that claimed both to transcend and validate local, national, cultural and even some racial differences among certain ranks of business and professional men in the Americas. Rotary's civic internationalism seemed transcendent of any one nation's political and economic interests. Its egalitarianism promised to empower each participant "in his own sphere." For Ramirez, the growing international presence of RI in Latin America was transformative, uplifting, inevitable.

But the cultural power of RI's civic internationalism operated within a larger web of economic, political, and military power relations. It was transformative in ways Rotarian Ramirez would not and could not acknowledge. While thousands of Rotarians were gathering in their convention, US diplomatic representatives were looking to hammer out a series of formal military agreements with Cuba and all other Latin American nations over the summer of 1940 in anticipation of possible Nazi aggression in the Caribbean basin. As the war in Europe progressed, the Caribbean and Latin America looked more and more vulnerable to German incursions. Pan-American unity would require common defense in a time of world war. Military preparations and formal agreements between the United States and Cuba could not be a matter of public debate, however, as the United States was still formally neutral. While Rotarians gathered before massive audiences to give speeches on international peace through understanding, US and Cuban government and military officials were negotiating the details of hemispheric defense against the Axis powers.

The day before Cuban secretary of state Angel Campa's reading of President Laredo Brú's opening address at RI's convention in 1940, the Cuban president and Colonel Pedraza, chief of staff of the Cuban Army, met with George Messersmith, the US ambassador in Cuba, and two US military officers. According to Messersmith, the meeting went well as "full agreement in principle had been reached" and, with Batista's approval in hand as well, the ambassador was happy to report a month later that "the preliminary conversations with Cuba and the other American States so fully conform to the spirit of solidarity existing among the American States."[107] But military cooperation among the United States and Latin American countries was hardly a secret by late July, after the Havana Conference of Foreign Ministers pronounced the Act of Havana, a formal ratification of the political, diplomatic, and military commitments of the "American republics" in defense against any encroachments into the Americas by the Axis powers. By early September 1940, Cuba had granted "full use of Cuban territory" by the United States. Hemispheric cooperation in the shadow of war was not simply a theme for Rotary's convention in Havana in June 1940 but also a military and political priority for all attending Rotarians' countries.

While the president of Cuba had his secretary of state read the president's opening address to Rotary's 3,700 conventioneers, he and the Cuban military negotiated with US military and diplomatic officials. The private meeting of public officials at the president's *finca* reflected one form of US hegemony in Cuba; the public gathering of private businessmen amid the flowers and flags of the Grand Salon in the Centro Asturiano reflected a very different form of hegemony. But the events were mutually reinforcing manifestations of power that formed an interlocking and multifaceted pattern of growing US hegemony in Cuba before, after, and despite the abrogation of the Platt Amendment in 1934. The United States engaged in multiple forms of international engagement during the interwar period, each working to its own effect and in accord with its own means of operation.

Put another way, the cultural practices and social networking at the core of RI's civic internationalism ultimately dovetailed with the military, political, and diplomatic requirements of the United States. The common denominator was acquiescence on the part of Cubans to the demands of the United States and the persistent blindness of many both inside and outside the United States to the imperial nature of those demands. The hierarchy of relations—whether in the name of defending or improving Cuba—still entailed inequality. Likewise, deference to US institutions—whether public or private—only reinforced more overt forms of coercion that pervaded US-Cuban relations after 1898 and through the interwar period. As a result, the tension between the anticolonialism of the Teller Amendment and the imperialism of the Platt Amendment played itself out "under the shadow of Rotary." The denial of empire required immense cultural energy, particularly in Cuba, where US economic and cultural imperialism were so manifest for so long under the shadow of the Platt Amendment.

6

TRAILING ALONG THROUGH ASIA

Main Street Comes Full Circle

The March 1930 edition of the *Rotarian* featured five "Rotary Personalities" of note. Three of the five dignitaries presented were European: Kurt Belfrage, director of the Stockholm Stock Exchange and president of the Stockholm Rotary Club; Alfred Jerger, noted Austrian tenor in the Vienna State Opera and member of the Vienna Rotary Club; and C. Lana Sarrate, metallurgist at the Royal Polytechnic Institute in Barcelona and member of that city's Rotary club. The fourth Rotarian, James L. Ralston, was Canada's Minister of National Defence and representative at the Five-Power Naval Conference in London.[1] The fifth Rotarian, Hamzah bin Abdullah, however, contrasted sharply with the four respectable-looking white men in their suits and ties. Wearing a colorful headdress and a distinctly non-Western shirt, Abdullah is introduced as a "Malayan member" of the Kuala Lumpur Rotary club and "magistrate in the government service" who had recently spoken to his club "on the significance of movements such as Rotary as a factor in bringing together business men with diverse racial and political characteristics."[2] Abdullah's words were not mere rhetoric. At its inaugural meeting in November 1929, the Kuala Lumpur club was already a model of racial diversity for the period. Its charter membership of twenty-six Europeans, seventeen Chinese, nine Ceylonese, four Malays, four Indians, and one Eurasian was headed by Choo Kia Peng, "a well-known rubber estate owner" and the first club president, and L. D. Gammans of the Malayan Civil Service, the first club secretary.[3] But why would Hamzah bin Abdullah speak to his fellow Rotarians of Kuala Lumpur in such sweeping language? Why would Rotary International wish to showcase Rotarian Abdullah and his club before approximately one hundred thousand of the *Rotarian*'s monthly readers? And most obvious of all, how was it that Kuala Lumpur had a thriving Rotary club in 1930, and what did that mean for more than 150,000 Rotarians in the United States and in the rest of the world?

Only a few pages after Mr. Abdullah's image in the *Rotarian,* one finds the second installment of Lillian Dow Davidson's travel series entitled "Trailing along through Asia." The Davidsons had just arrived in the city they knew as "Constantinople" in the fall of 1928 to establish the first of many Rotary clubs throughout Asia, only to find the city renamed "Istamboul" and a "modern Turkey" rapidly replacing the Ottoman Empire in all facets of social, political, and economic life. In her article, Lillian Dow Davidson details "the amazing reforms that are working a magical over-night transformation in Turkey, seen by the wife of Rotary's special commissioner in Asia," James W. Davidson.[4] As the Davidsons continued their journey from the eastern Mediterranean through the Middle East, the Indian subcontinent, Southeast Asia, the Dutch East Indies, southern China, Formosa, northern China, Manchuria, Korea, and finally Japan, from the fall of 1928 to the spring of 1931, Lillian began chronicling their travels in monthly contributions to the *Rotarian* magazine (from February 1930 to January 1933). Lillian's articles soon became so popular that they eventually found their way into more general magazines in reprinted form and were translated into several languages. The Davidsons' travels had become the stuff of romance and lore not just for tens of thousands of Rotarian families in North America, Latin America, and Europe who were following her regular installments, but also for the popular culture in general in several countries. Lillian's particular talent for blending the observational skills of an amateur cultural anthropologist with a kind of homespun journalistic style had an overall comforting, didactic effect for her middlebrow readers, transforming the exotic lands of "Arabian Nights" into more recognizable forms and characters of middle-class North America. Lillian was not just along for the ride. She was a veritable public relations coup for RI's internationalist aspirations.[5]

The common link between Hamzah bin Abdullah's eager embrace of his own, local Rotary club in Kuala Lumpur and Lillian's regular dispatches from Asia was James W. Davidson, "special commissioner" for RI. Davidson's particular task was to fill in the gap between Prague and Shanghai with a "golden chain" of Rotary clubs, thereby allowing RI full circumnavigation of the globe and providing "the Rotary traveler" the chance to "take any of the important steamers plying between London and Tokyo and find a Rotary club at nearly every port."[6] In effect, by the late 1920s, RI's upper echelons—at that point drawn from the United States, Canada, Western Europe, East Asia, and Latin America—had come to view the "gap" between the Eastern European Rotary clubs and the Chinese and Japanese clubs on the opposite end of the Eurasian landmass as an intolerable disconnect. RI mapped out its future international expansion along pre-established lines of international trade and across imperial, political, and geographical frontiers with an astonishing degree of confidence and sense of inevitability. Not unlike the British Empire's "Cape-to-Cairo" geographical imaginings, with the endpoints defined, it was only a question of how and where to connect the dots in between. A native of Minnesota, former US consular agent in several cities in East Asia, experienced world traveler and journalist, and successful Canadian businessman, James Wheeler Davidson was the ideal choice for such a grand project.

The Davidsons' story of "trailing along through Asia," therefore, contrasts with RI's experience in Cuba in revealing ways. The hegemonic presence of the United States in Cuba after 1898 initially promised much in the way of Cuban independence but ultimately allowed little room for accommodation of *Cubanidad* in the most fundamental matters of economic and political interests. Like Cuba itself, the Havana Rotarians began with much promise, as "allies" of the war effort in the 1910s and full partners in RI's civic internationalism, but later found themselves unable to escape from under the shadow of the Platt Amendment and its legacies. Whereas the Cuban Rotarians' transition from cross-border business progressives united in a common destiny to a more marginal status in the early cold war order and finally to the permanent closure of clubs in the wake of the Cuban Revolution all occurred in a fixed space over half a century, the Davidsons' travels took place over a great expanse of space within a period of less than three years (map 3). Examining the

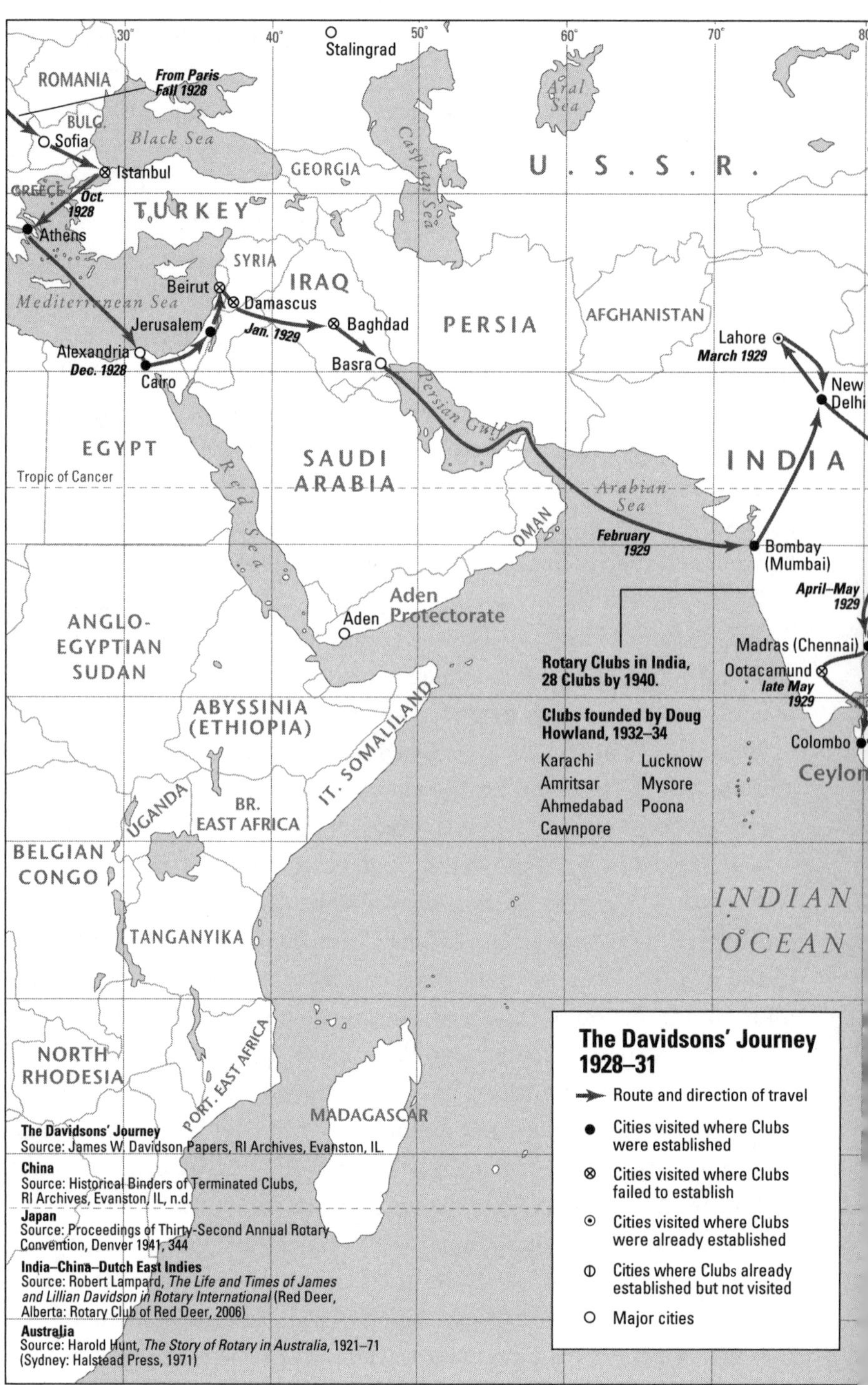

From Paris Fall 1928
ROMANIA
BULG.
Sofia
Black Sea
Istanbul
GREECE
Oct. 1928
Athens
TURKEY
GEORGIA
Stalingrad
Caspian Sea
Aral Sea
U.S.S.R.
SYRIA
IRAQ
Beirut
Damascus
Mediterranean Sea
Jerusalem
Jan. 1929
Baghdad
PERSIA
AFGHANISTAN
Lahore
March 1929
Alexandria
Dec. 1928
Cairo
Basra
Persian Gulf
New Delhi
EGYPT
Tropic of Cancer
SAUDI ARABIA
INDIA
Red Sea
Arabian Sea
OMAN
February 1929
Bombay (Mumbai)
April–May 1929
Aden Protectorate
Aden
ANGLO-EGYPTIAN SUDAN
Madras (Chennai)
Ootacamund
late May 1929
Rotary Clubs in India, 28 Clubs by 1940.
Clubs founded by Doug Howland, 1932–34
Karachi
Lucknow
Amritsar
Mysore
Ahmedabad
Poona
Cawnpore
ABYSSINIA (ETHIOPIA)
IT. SOMALILAND
Colombo
Ceylon
UGANDA
BR. EAST AFRICA
BELGIAN CONGO
TANGANYIKA
INDIAN OCEAN
NORTH RHODESIA
PORT. EAST AFRICA
MADAGASCAR
The Davidsons' Journey 1928–31
Route and direction of travel
Cities visited where Clubs were established
Cities visited where Clubs failed to establish
Cities visited where Clubs were already established
Cities where Clubs already established but not visited
Major cities
The Davidsons' Journey
Source: James W. Davidson Papers, RI Archives, Evanston, IL.
China
Source: Historical Binders of Terminated Clubs, RI Archives, Evanston, IL, n.d.
Japan
Source: Proceedings of Thirty-Second Annual Rotary Convention, Denver 1941, 344
India–China–Dutch East Indies
Source: Robert Lampard, The Life and Times of James and Lillian Davidson in Rotary International (Red Deer, Alberta: Rotary Club of Red Deer, 2006)
Australia
Source: Harold Hunt, The Story of Rotary in Australia, 1921–71 (Sydney: Halstead Press, 1971)

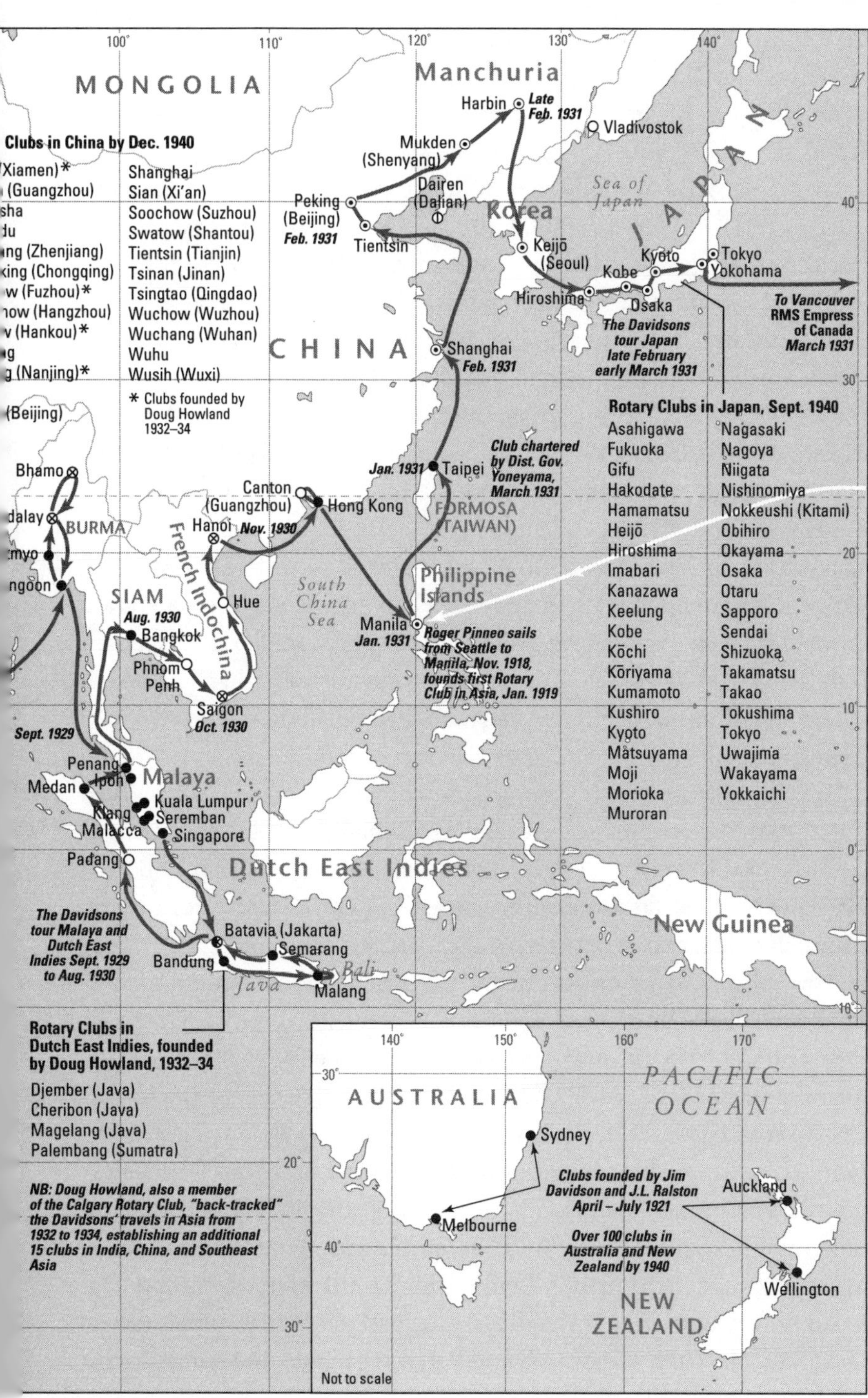
MONGOLIA
Manchuria
Clubs in China by Dec. 1940
Shanghai
Sian (Xi'an)
Soochow (Suzhou)
Swatow (Shantou)
Tientsin (Tianjin)
Tsinan (Jinan)
Tsingtao (Qingdao)
Wuchow (Wuzhou)
Wuchang (Wuhan)
Wuhu
Wusih (Wuxi)
* Clubs founded by Doug Howland 1932–34
Harbin Late Feb. 1931
Vladivostok
Mukden (Shenyang)
Dairen (Dalian)
Peking (Beijing) Feb. 1931
Tientsin
Sea of Japan
Korea
JAPAN
Keijō (Seoul)
Kobe
Kyoto
Tokyo
Yokohama
Hiroshima
Osaka
The Davidsons tour Japan late February early March 1931
To Vancouver RMS Empress of Canada March 1931
CHINA
Shanghai Feb. 1931
Rotary Clubs in Japan, Sept. 1940
Asahigawa
Fukuoka
Gifu
Hakodate
Hamamatsu
Heijō
Hiroshima
Imabari
Kanazawa
Keelung
Kobe
Kōchi
Kōriyama
Kumamoto
Kushiro
Kyoto
Matsuyama
Moji
Morioka
Muroran
Nagasaki
Nagoya
Niigata
Nishinomiya
Nokkeushi (Kitami)
Obihiro
Okayama
Osaka
Otaru
Sapporo
Sendai
Shizuoka
Takamatsu
Takao
Tokushima
Tokyo
Uwajima
Wakayama
Yokkaichi
Club chartered by Dist. Gov. Yoneyama, March 1931
Jan. 1931 Taipei
FORMOSA (TAIWAN)
Bhamo
BURMA
Canton (Guangzhou)
Hong Kong
Hanoi Nov. 1930
French Indochina
South China Sea
Philippine Islands
Manila Jan. 1931
Roger Pinneo sails from Seattle to Manila, Nov. 1918, founds first Rotary Club in Asia, Jan. 1919
SIAM
Hue
Aug. 1930 Bangkok
Phnom Penh
Saigon Oct. 1930
Sept. 1929
Penang
Ipoh
Malaya
Medan
Kuala Lumpur
Klang
Seremban
Malacca
Singapore
Padang
Dutch East Indies
New Guinea
The Davidsons tour Malaya and Dutch East Indies Sept. 1929 to Aug. 1930
Batavia (Jakarta)
Semarang
Bandung
Bali
Java
Malang
Rotary Clubs in Dutch East Indies, founded by Doug Howland, 1932–34
Djember (Java)
Cheribon (Java)
Magelang (Java)
Palembang (Sumatra)
NB: Doug Howland, also a member of the Calgary Rotary Club, "back-tracked" the Davidsons' travels in Asia from 1932 to 1934, establishing an additional 15 clubs in India, China, and Southeast Asia
AUSTRALIA
PACIFIC OCEAN
Sydney
Melbourne
Clubs founded by Jim Davidson and J.L. Ralston April – July 1921
Over 100 clubs in Australia and New Zealand by 1940
Auckland
Wellington
NEW ZEALAND
Not to scale

expansion of Rotary clubs along these distinct spatial and temporal axes of analysis provides us with complementary perspectives on the nature of emerging forms of US cultural and economic influence in very different historical contexts. The Davidsons found themselves operating in a variety of strikingly different political and cultural environments, ranging from Athens, Istanbul, Cairo, and Jerusalem, all in massive political flux, to the oil fields and companies of Iran and Iraq; from the well-established trading centers of the British Empire such as Bombay, Singapore, and Hong Kong, to key cities in the Dutch and French imperial possessions such as Jakarta, Batavia, Saigon, and Hanoi. Nor were the Davidsons limited to European imperial trading centers. With an itinerary that also included Manila, Taipei, Shanghai, Bangkok, Mukden, Harbin, Seoul, and many Japanese cities, the Davidsons were hopscotching through independent nations such as China and Siam as well as Japanese, Russian, and US imperial possessions. Unlike the confined space of Havana under the shadow of Plattism, the scope of operation for the Davidsons was spread over very scattered, complex, and overlapping fields of racial, religious, colonial, and gendered "others" as well as across emerging national, transnational, cosmopolitan, and postcolonial class solidarities.[7]

The Davidsons' "trailing along through Asia," it turned out, marked the high-water mark of RI's civic internationalism during the interwar period. On the eve of the Great Depression and the economic nationalisms and militant fascisms of the 1930s, Jim's establishment of twenty-three new Rotary clubs between Prague and Shanghai and Lillian's popularization of the lands and peoples where those clubs were formed linked the domestic space of Rotarians' hearth and home with interwar projections of US cultural and economic influence "abroad," transforming the far-flung cities of Asia into communities peopled with different yet recognizable faces, where one might consider touring with the family in the near future or seeking new business prospects for the next quarter's planning. Following both Laura Wexler and Amy Kaplan on how "manifest domesticity" and "domestic sentimentalism" can serve as "an imperial instrument," I will explore in this chapter how the Davidsons' "trailing along through Asia" helped reify the ideological content and social regulations of US middle-class business and domestic cultures in the "foreign" lands where they journeyed, providing through their travels and travelogues a kind of stagecraft for American corporate capitalism and domestic sensibilities in theaters of European imperial hegemony once seen as well beyond the purview of US imperial reach.[8] Jim's successful negotiations within the corporate and colonial worlds of European and non-European elites in the name of establishing Rotary clubs, in other words, helped lay the foundations for postwar US global hegemony as well as new structural links of global capitalism. Meanwhile, the "domestic sentimentalism" of Lillian's writings became as important to both her male and female readers as she, as wife and mother, made the presence of Rotary clubs and her own family's travels in such far-off lands seem natural and attainable, fascinating yet comforting. In their own way, both Lillian and Jim were engaging in a form of domestication—Jim with his more than 2,200 sit-down interviews with potential Rotarian recruits among Asia's business and professional elites and Lillian with her family-friendly writings for those back "home."[9]

The appearance of Hamzah bin Abdullah in his headdress and Eastern garb among four white Rotarians in familiar suits and ties had a heuristic quality for the many thousands of readers of the *Rotarian*. Though one of countless everyday moments in which RI inculcated its membership in the expanding world of Rotary's "world fellowship of business and professional men united in the ideal of service," Abdullah's appearance was also an important rupture in the middle-class fabric of Main Street in 1930. While Rotarian Abdullah and his fellow Kuala Lumpur club members learned directly from Jim Davidson about the many social, political, and economic obligations incumbent upon all Rotarians worldwide, the Malaysian Rotarians, it turned out, forced Jim and eventually all of Rotary International to reconfigure some of those same "obligations," particularly in adaptation to the complexities of race and class in Malaysia (and much to the chagrin of RI's own leaders and members). The complex story behind Abdullah's presence in the *Rotarian* in the spring of 1930 constituted not only a poignant historical moment in the development of Rotary's civic internationalism, but also a revealing turning point in the evolution of cultural, racial, and capitalist relations in Asia during the interwar period. Understanding international trade, colonial and postcolonial structures, competing imperial interests, and racial and cultural differences was essential to Jim's recruitment efforts on behalf of Rotary International. The same was true for Lillian's attempts at explaining Jim's efforts and recounting their long journey through Asia for Rotary's readership "back home"—wherever that was. These were extraordinary challenges, and no one was better suited to rise to the occasion than Jim and Lillian Davidson.

AMONG STATES AND MARKETS

Just after the Duchess of Atholl set sail from Montreal on her way to Liverpool in late summer 1928, an announcement was made to all aboard: "Rotarians will please report their names to the purser's office." Jim and Lillian Davidson were behind the announcement. Among others answering the call was E. J. Ottaway, publisher, head of the University of Michigan's alumni association, and former president of the Port Huron Rotary club. For Ottaway and his wife, the voyage was the first leg of their annual European tour. For the Davidsons, however, it was a very different kind of trip. As E. J. Ottaway put it: "For a year [the Davidsons] will be going the rounds of our little universe, in an endeavor to spread the gospel of Rotary in Cairo, in Athens, in Constantinople."[10] What drove the Davidsons to take on such an enormous commitment? How were they any different from their traveling companions, the Ottaways, or from the thousands of missionaries sent out before and since in the name of a different gospel?

Jim, Lillian, and their teenage daughter Marjory were commencing on a trip that would last—as it turned out—well over two years, cost more than $32,000 for RI and about $250,000 for the Davidsons, result in more than 2,200 personal interviews of top business and professional recruits in Asia, give rise to a popular serialization of their travels, and lead to twenty-three new Rotary clubs across the Asian continent.[11] This section sketches a biographical picture of Jim Davidson and then explores his methods of preparation for recruiting the "representative men" of each city he planned to visit in Asia. Quite familiar with the nature of diplomatic protocols as well as the language and practices of corporate cultures, Jim Davidson knew how to use the established social and economic networks of European imperial powers to his and RI's advantage. Indeed, he seemed to admire Europe's imperial powers and their administrative practices. In his own mind, Jim was not so much supplanting European colonial structures as simply improving and modernizing them in terms more amenable to "modern" forms of business practices and civic cooperation—as defined by Rotary International. His was hardly a postcolonial or anti-imperialist agenda. Rather, Jim Davidson blurred his own personal experience within US consular agencies and western Canadian businesses in whichever way would seem most persuasive at the time. In other words, Jim Davidson was just as nimble in diplomatic circles as he was in business meetings, just as comfortable working with European colonial administrators as he was with those colonized by Europeans. This agility proved crucial not only for Jim's success at every point in his long journey but also for the development of RI's internationalist designs in general. The building up of RI's "world fellowship of business and professional men" demanded an artful dodger among state agents, marketplace actors, and nonprofit managers in a variety of cultural, political, and economic circumstances; someone versatile enough to move with ease from corporate office to consular office, from boardroom to tearoom, from hotel lobby to front porch. The project was tantamount to choosing from and credentialing the basic elements of an emerging transnational class formation according to RI's nominal standards of character and understanding of the public good.

Given his personal and professional background, Jim was RI's man for the job. Officially, Davidson was not seeking to establish Rotary clubs in the name of the Canadian or US government. Nor was he explicitly serving the interests of any one industry or corporation. On the contrary, Rotarians saw Davidson as both a missionary and a salesman for RI's civic internationalism. There was a distinct blend of religious aura and salesmanship behind his mission to Asia. When agreeing upon eight principles for international expansion in 1925, for example, RI's Extension Committee proclaimed: "In extending Rotary, Rotarians may be likened to salesmen selling an idea or missionaries preaching a gospel; and a good salesman does not give up because at first his prospective customer will not buy his merchandise; nor does a good missionary quit because the heathen are slow to accept his gospel."[12] That Rotary originally positioned itself somewhere between the evangelical calling of missionary societies and the sales departments of modern corporations was quite consistent with the evolution of its civic internationalism.

No one contributed more to such administrative policy formulations over the course of the 1920s than Jim Davidson. After joining the Calgary Rotary club in 1914 and rapidly moving up the ranks of leadership in Canada, Davidson first became actively involved with the development and expansion of Rotary just after World War I. His first stint on the "publications" committee in 1920 soon led to a position on the Extension Committee (1921–1923, 1924–1926, 1927–1928, 1930–1932), which was renamed the International Service Committee in 1928 and first chaired by him. In short, the merger of good salesmanship and spreading the gospel into one "principle" had its own seamless logic for a mission-minded businessman like Jim Davidson, whose views aligned quite well with the pro-business religiosity of the 1920s most famously captured by Bruce Barton in his best seller, *The Man Nobody Knows* (1925), which portrayed Jesus as a manly, energetic business executive with a "strong magnetic" appeal.[13] In fact, during this period, the *Rotarian* regularly featured articles on subjects such as "Super-Salesmanship as a Civilizer" and advertisements such as "They jeered at me, but I made them applaud me three weeks later."[14]

But Jim Davidson had learned the fine arts of salesmanship, showmanship, and diplomacy long before his service on RI's most important committees in the 1920s. Born in Austin, Minnesota, in 1872, Jim's first job was organizing tours for the Austin Opera House, leading to a job in New York City with the famous impresario and lecture tour manager Major J. B. Pond, who had managed, among other notables, Mark Twain on the North American leg of his world tour in 1895.[15] Thanks to his position with Pond, Davidson met many famous lecturers and performers of the period, among them Lieutenant Robert Peary, whose second North Pole expedition Jim eagerly joined in 1893. He also learned the fine art of "humbug." While returning from the failed expedition after nearly losing a foot to frostbite, he met a Brooklyn newspaper editor en route who refused to hire him as a foreign correspondent in East Asia. Undaunted, Jim left for Formosa in 1894 anyway and soon had the *New York*

Herald and many other newspapers in the United States, Japan, and Hong Kong receiving his dispatches in syndication. When war broke out between Chinese and Japanese troops on the island in May 1895, Jim was ready, thanks to an insider's tip. But his plan to cover the war from the Chinese perspective soon reversed itself as he found himself providing vital intelligence to the Japanese side, which helped lead to an easy Japanese takeover of Taipei. As a result, Jim Davidson received the 5th Class of the Order of the Rising Sun from the Meiji Emperor later that year—one of only a few non-Japanese citizens so honored. (That honor would provide him with unprecedented deference among Japanese Rotary clubs many years later during the final leg of his journey through Asia.)

Jim's syndicated dispatches soon caught the eye of the US government and led to his appointment as a US consular agent in Formosa from 1897 until 1903.[16] During his time in Formosa, Davidson also managed to research and write one of the earliest and most authoritative histories of the island of Formosa (Taiwan). Entitled *Formosa: Past and Present,* the book was so comprehensive that he was awarded a fellowship by the Royal Geographical Society in 1903.[17] Ever after, he would be known as James Davidson, FRGS. That same year, he was transferred to Manchuria, where he served on loan in the Russian Communications Department, chronicling the final phases of the completion of the Trans-Siberian Railroad for US newspapers, and then as commercial attaché and then acting consul general in Shanghai in 1904–1905. Between his consular duties in Shanghai—one of the largest diplomatic delegations at that time—and his work and travels in Formosa and Manchuria, Jim Davidson had garnered a wealth of experience in East Asia, with particular expertise in working within international networks of communication, negotiating amid imperial rivalries, and thinking in terms of historical geography. At the age of thirty-three, Jim Davidson had already traveled, written, and experienced more than most would in a lifetime.

But a bout with typhoid forced a return to the United States in 1906 and Jim's departure from a formal diplomatic career with the US government. On his journey across the Pacific, however, Jim redeemed the time by meeting Lillian Dow. After his own recuperation at home in

Minnesota and the destruction of Lillian's family's business in the San Francisco earthquake of 1906, the two married and moved to Canada, settling down in Calgary in 1907. What lured them was the Calgary Colonization Company, whose investors included Jim's brother Charles. In short order, Jim found himself involved with a very different kind of business and political environment from his consular days. The US investors' purchase of a massive tract of land from the Canadian Pacific Railroad northeast of Calgary translated into massive profits as the company divided up and sold off the parcels of land to farmers immigrating from the United States. The Calgary Colonization Company then repeated the process with twice the acreage, resulting in other large business ventures, including the massive Crown Lumber Company, managed by Jim from 1908 to 1917. But it was not until the Turner Valley oil discovery of 1913 that the Davidsons became truly wealthy through the Royalite Oil Company. With money to spare, Jim returned to his roots—entertainment and promotions—through his investment in Trans-Canada Theatres. As a US citizen and Calgary businessman, Jim Davidson had done quite well for himself by the time Canada entered World War I. Business operations that straddled international borders were already a very profitable game for the Davidsons, as the movement of capital, immigrants, culture, and commodities into and out of Canada formed the core of the Davidsons' wealth. At the behest of his friend, theater manager R. J. Lydiatt, Jim signed up with the Calgary Rotary club on the eve of the war.[18] Within a decade, Jim had become one of RI's most influential advocates for the international expansion of Rotary clubs outside of the Americas and Europe. Once RI voted approval of a $1 charge on each of RI's more than 120,000 members to raise funds for international expansion at the 1926 annual convention in Denver, Jim Davidson and his many allies on the Extension Committee had in place all the institutional, ideological, and financial machinery necessary for "extension" into Asia—a trip that would dwarf his earlier work in Australia and New Zealand on behalf of Rotary.[19]

Jim and Lillian soon began to plan out their trip to Asia as RI's missionaries seeking "to link up into the Rotary chain those great stretches through Asia which were without clubs" so that "one may take any of the great steamers which carry passengers between Great Britain and

Japan and, with the exception of the pause at the Suez Canal, find a Rotary club at every stop."[20] While collecting letters of introduction for the trip, Jim Davidson made sure that, no matter who the endorser was, Davidson was identified first and foremost as a businessman from Calgary. Of the one hundred or so letters written on behalf of Davidson by Canadian, US, Australian, British, French, and Dutch officials as well as by corporate officers, personal friends, religious leaders, and fellow Rotarians, only one referred to him as a (new) Canadian citizen, and in only a few letters does one find any explicit reference to him as a former US citizen or consular agent. According to Davidson's endorsers, his mission to Asia was not under the direction of the United States government nor of any other US interests, corporate or otherwise. Rather, the Calgary businessman represented Rotary International, which was "merely a fellowship of professional men and businessmen who are leaders in their respective . . . occupations."[21] Jim understood how being Canadian had its advantages. But being an agent for an international, nongovernmental organization had even more. Davidson's strategy centered on presenting himself as a private businessman traveling in the name of Rotary and its higher calling of greater international cooperation and progress through civic uplift. Jim knew how to present himself in the most neutral light possible, revealing his keen grasp of both salesmanship and diplomatic protocol. Given his personal devotion to RI's vision of civic internationalism, Jim believed passionately in the gospel he preached, a businessman's gospel that amounted to a claim of neutral status in a world of nation-states by positing a market-based identity transnational in scope and apolitical in nature. On paper, Davidson the businessman and Rotarian trumped Davidson the Canadian or US citizen. His passport was a gray flannel suit; his business card a mission statement; his mission a business proposition.

Of course, given the Davidsons' itinerary through much of the British Empire, being British also had its advantages. In those same letters of introduction, Jim recommended that RI insert the title "Fellow of the Royal Geographical Society" (F.R.G.S.) after his name because "while this means nothing on this side, it gives me a little standing with the British."[22] Davidson understood all too well that he would be in competition with the established British trading networks of Asia. He spent several weeks in London because "it will be necessary for considerable work to be done with the oriental concerns which have their head offices in London. There is a 'hard boiled' English trading caste at many of the points that we should go into and help from London is therefore very important. . . . I will commence to lay this very foundation."[23] It was one thing to be a native English speaker from the United States; it was something very different to speak the language of "the English trading caste" of the British Empire.

He needed all the help he could get. Some of the fiercest resistance to Davidson and his new clubs came not from Asian businessmen and professionals and their governments but from the "'hard boiled' English trading caste." Any club that opened its doors to non-British businessmen and professionals and treated them as colleagues joined in civic cooperation was an inherent threat—all the more so if the club was seen as the vanguard of US cultural and economic influence encroaching on British colonial territory. The shifting grounds of imperial influence even at this mundane level of fraternal business clubs did not go unrecognized and without resistance. F.R.G.S. or not, Calgary businessman or not, Davidson was advancing the cultural, economic, and political reach of Rotary International, a service club based out of Chicago. And many British businessmen and their social clubs in Asia understood what that entailed.[24]

Finally, along with establishing clubs in Asian cities, Davidson understood himself as a mediator for his middlebrow readers of the practical business implications of his experiences. A world of international business was emerging, and it was Davidson's job to drive home the import of that world for the majority of his audience at work on Main Street. Sounding like any other booster from North America, he often turned the tables on his North American and British readers in the midst of his travels in Southeast Asia:

> If Boston or New Orleans or Liverpool were without Rotary Clubs, one can imagine the continuous efforts over many years . . . to get Rotary introduced. . . . Yet these cities occupy in their areas no more important a place than does Singapore in Asia. . . .

> A glance at the map will show the importance of this great Asiatic center. It is the Asian half-way house between Europe and America, the gateway to the very extensive Dutch East Indies, the turning point for steamers to Australasia, site of the important British Naval Base and from here boats sail to all the sea coast trading countries of the world.
>
> I mean this literally. Eighty-eight different lines call at Singapore. . . . Entrances and clearances together [in 1928] totaled 97, 660 vessels. Stupendous, isn't it? Those of you who believe that all the big things are in the West, please get down your almanacs and compare this with London, Liverpool, Hamburg or New York.[25]

The lesson was clear. The numbers did not lie. Like it or not, the new world of business forged ahead, with or without his fellow Rotarians' approval back "home" in North America and Western Europe. To ignore vibrant cities like Singapore and regions like Southeast Asia was to risk falling behind progress defined by the constant thickening of global trade. For Wall Street as well as Main Street, for London as well as Boston, the emerging global markets were a two-edged sword of opportunity and competition. Though the role of cultural mediator for the Davidsons' travels ultimately fell on Lillian, Jim saw himself instilling a more internationalist vision for his readers as much as his new recruits in Asia.

When Jim mapped out his long itinerary before his departure, in fact, he took his own advice. He pulled out a map of the world and planned out his family's travels (figure 6.1). Several details from his own markings on the map, however, reveal the worldview of Jim Davidson and bear some consideration. First, using black ink, he traced out a travel route from Calgary, Chicago, and New York City straight to Athens, Istanbul, and Cairo. Jim had at first imagined traveling directly from North America to the eastern Mediterranean as a function of efficient transportation. But subsequent political considerations required him to travel through London and Paris to collect the necessary letters of introduction for travel and recruiting in the world of European empires in Asia. Second, though using an up-to-date political map of the world,

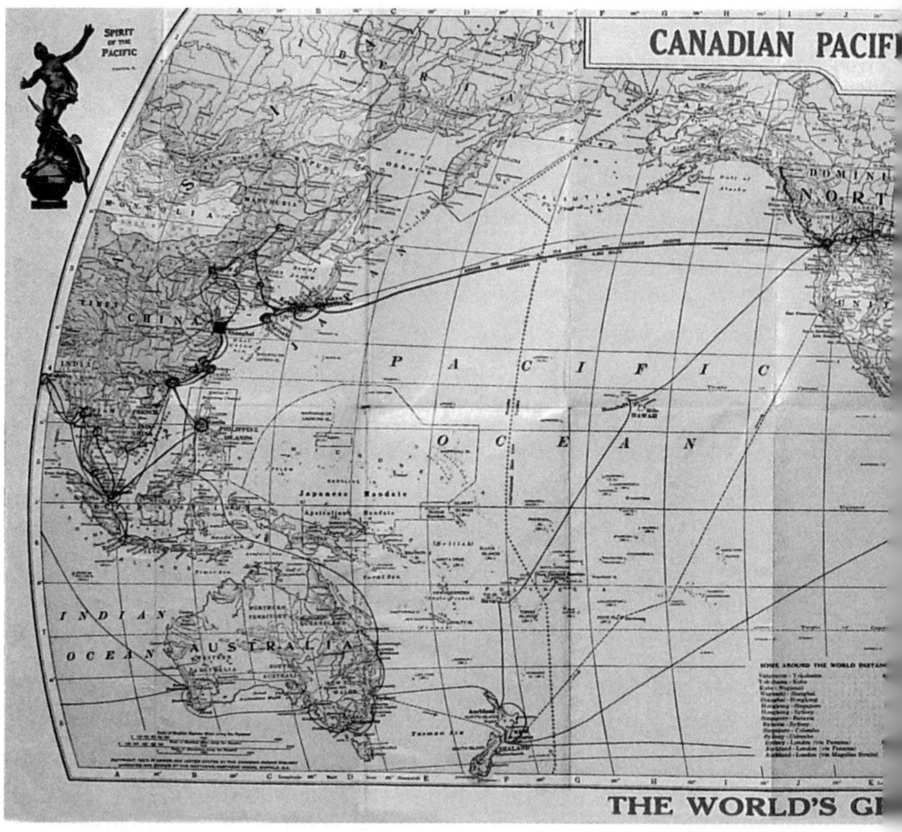

FIG 6.1: While mapping out his trip around the world on behalf of RI from 1928 to 1931, Jim Davidson developed his itinerary according to the map of the Canadian Pacific Railway and Steamships Company, "the world's greatest travel system," provided to international travelers. *Courtesy of Rotary International.* (Photo credit Bob Vuxinic)

Jim circled his points of destination—specific cities—in bold, black circles. Jim thought in terms of connections between cities as nodal points of trade, communication, and transportation. Since the first days in Chicago in 1905, Rotary clubs were formed in and served their own cities first and foremost. Rotary was, after all, a social movement among urban businessmen and professionals before anything else. Third, Jim's map was a generic political map placed underneath a corporate template entitled, "The Canadian Pacific Railway and Steamships Span the World." Given the wealth gleaned through his own dealings with the Canadian Pacific Railway (CPR), Jim's personal map was more than coincidence.

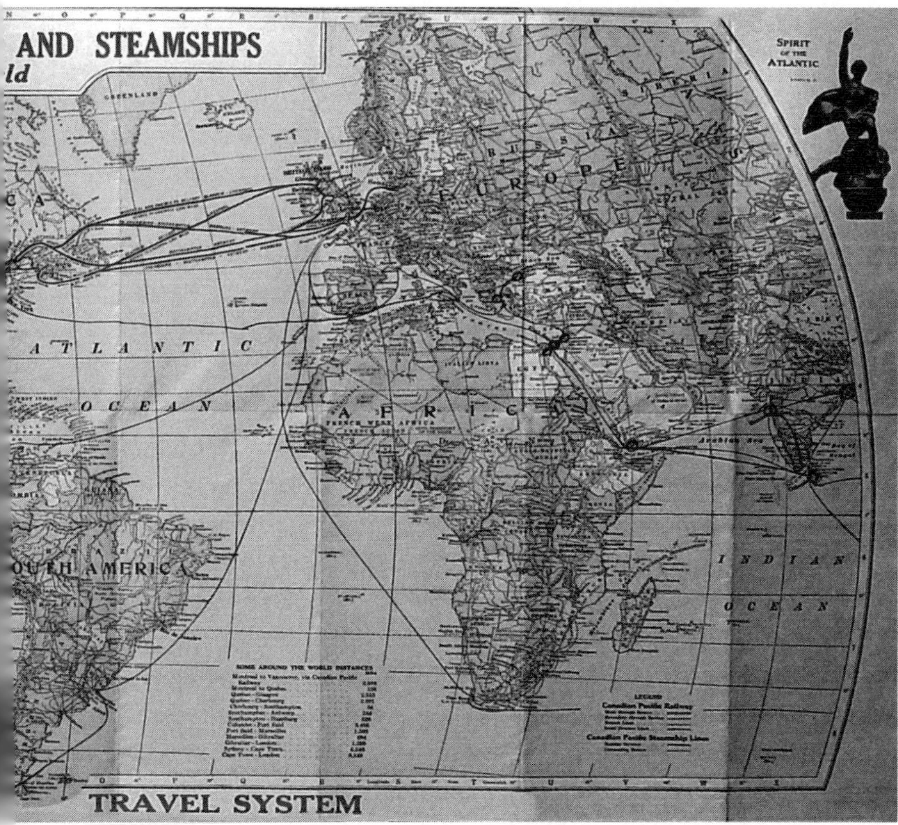

Like Jim's own career in business, the CPR framed the entire project and provided the connective tissues between the "Spirit of the Atlantic" and the "Spirit of the Pacific." Again, like Jim Davidson, the CPR had intercontinental imaginings and profited from the movement of peoples and commodities among circuits of trade and across oceans and borders thanks to "the world's greatest travel system."[26] From its very inception, Jim's itinerary was a complex negotiation of interurban circuits of commerce, distinct European colonial regimes, transnational corporations, and a wide array of systems of transportation and communication. RI's ambitions of filling in the gaps between Prague and Shanghai were premised on such complex negotiations—on working through the emerging machinery and infrastructure of a globalizing economy.

ISTANBUL AND ATHENS—"WE MUST REMEDY THAT"

Jim Davidson was already a member of Rotary's Foreign Extension Committee when it developed its guidelines for future membership of the Mexico City Rotary club in 1921. With US and British citizens so predominant among the club's charter members, the concern was to avoid the creation of an enclave of non-Mexican businessmen and professionals in Mexico City—a situation anathema to RI's civic internationalism. To review, the three basic pillars of that agreement were (1) preference for "the native Mexican" over all other future club prospects, (2) encouragement of the use of Spanish in all club activities whenever possible, and (3) guarantee of Mexican interests and control of the club "for the benefit of the community and nation of Mexico" rather than the creation of "an American or British Colony Club."[27] The agreement on the future of the Mexico City Rotary club became a road map for clubs formed outside the Anglophone world of Rotary's origins. Of all members of the Extension Committee contributing to this institutional policy during the period, Davidson understood best that any hope of legitimacy for such a project hinged upon the inclusion of local "representative men." In his mind, the question was how to determine who those men were and how to bring them under one roof with the many European expatriates he typically assumed to be "representative men" as well. Davidson, in other words, had the challenge of applying the Mexico City agreement to an unknown number of future Asian Rotary clubs. But how would the European and non-European recruits interpret and reconfigure RI's tidy version of civic internationalism?

It did not take long for Jim to experience some disillusion in Istanbul, his first port of call after collecting his formal credentials from the cities of London and Paris and traveling by rail across Europe through Vienna and Sofia to reach "Istamboul":

> I had a happy vision of a Rotary Club, largely Turkish but containing a few outstanding Armenians and Greeks and a smattering of pure Europeans, English and Americans, to support it and insure its success. What a great club it would have been . . . with the opportunity of developing a better understanding

> among these groups. At the same time it would have given the Turks the opportunity of a friendly world contact which they do not possess at present. But I had not been at work an hour before I learned how impossible that was.[28]

RI's "happy vision," crystallized in the Mexico City agreement, was in jeopardy within an hour of Jim's arrival. At the same time, Jim was warned by both the British Ambassador and the Secretary of the US Embassy that the new Turkish government under Kemal Ataturk would be suspicious of any club without Turkish members. He knew he had some work ahead of him. After time spent ascertaining the nature and depth of Turkey's economic, cultural, and racial fault lines, Jim began looking at the massive political changes in Turkey through the lens of his own experiences with the Japanese Empire after the Meiji Restoration:

> Now Rotary in Constantinople . . . can render such a great service . . . in teaching the Westerner that the Turks are making a determined effort to reform and that they must work out their problems in their own way; and also that they have the right to handle their own trade without the intervention of foreign middlemen unless they find such services helpful . . . to become a modern, enlightened, humane nation. The Japanese went through the same transition all within my lifetime. The Turks need and are entitled to the world contact that Rotary can best give them.[29]

Premised on "world contact" yet free from the "intervention of foreign middlemen," Turkey's path to modernity had its model in East Asia and its possible mediator in RI. After all, Jim knew intimately just how well it had all worked for the Japanese Rotarians (see Chapter 4).

But to convince the Turkish government of this view, Jim had to travel to the new capital in Ankara, where he finally coaxed a meeting with the new minister of interior, His Excellency Shukri Kaya Bey. Armed with a "scrapbook" filled with numerous letters of introduction from all variety of dignitaries and officials, Jim gathered some of RI's publications that he had translated into Turkish only days before and laid them out before the minister: "His eyes carefully searched the maps of districts in the Rotary Directory. 'Turkey is not shown!' he remarked . . . 'We must remedy that.'" Jim knew how to harness Turkish national pride. The minister then went over Jim's prepared list of top Turkish prospects pieced together through various interviews and visits in Istanbul beforehand, "marking the names of those from personal knowledge he could assure me were good men."[30] With the minister's approval of his intentions and prospects, Jim returned to Istanbul to convene the first of many "organizing committees," which included the prefect of police, the supervisor of education, the superintendent of higher education, a college professor, a newspaper editor educated at Columbia University, a "prominent attorney," a physician, and an importer. All were Turks strategically placed in both government and business, and all were polyglots. Once persuaded by Jim's oratory on the blessings of membership in RI, the group "then went to work in their own language in earnest, with me as a happy onlooker. They wrote out a list of men they wished in, all Turks, discussed each man fully that the selection might be confined to only high class, ethical men. They discussed methods of approaching their friends." With consensus on whom to approach, the group then divided up the list and agreed to meet again the following week. Jim was concerned that "the committee wanted to start the club as a purely Turkish institution," but "after noting their enthusiasm and considering several of them have been educated abroad, I am inclined to think that they can be quite successful without foreigners as members, though it is their intention, they say, to take in a few later which I trust they will do." Jim took reassurance as well because "these gentlemen were all white men."[31] All looked very promising for Jim's first foray into Asia on behalf of RI. In terms of politics, class, race, and gender, the organizing committee for the Istanbul Rotary Club had passed muster. Once assembled according to Jim's membership and institutional parameters, the Turks were free to assert any agenda and invite anyone into membership they chose.

Confident of success in Istanbul, Jim left for Athens to perform the same task. Knowing the ropes, Jim stopped by the US and British legations and extracted a short list of potential recruits. "First call to Theodore Petracopoulos . . . a wealthy man here, controlling the two leading hotels, knows the rating, financially and otherwise, of everyone, and has kept out of politics, the favorite sport of the Greeks. He was everything I could wish for." Given his wealth, business acumen, and apolitical stance, Petracopolous was exactly Jim's man in Athens. For his confidential readers within RI, Jim then broke down into "three distinct classes here [those] constituting possible club material." His analysis became a template for his organizing activities throughout southern Asia and was easy for his readers to grasp:

1. "Americanized Greeks." Jim believed some "could be useful members of a club because of their American training," but his overall disdain for them was palpable: "It is this type of well dressed, pleasant and efficient men one sees about the hotel restaurants, and who would be glad to join a Rotary Club. They are the men who would perhaps write to International asking to start a club, and yet, they are men who would make no impression on the country, would cheapen our organization and must be guarded against." Like the earliest clubs of the National Association of Rotary Clubs before World War I, Jim was looking to distance himself and RI as much as possible from the appearance of crass salesmanship and the hustling, fast-talking type. The Athens Rotary Club could not afford to be too "American" in its lack of social proprieties and cultural capital, no matter how genuinely Greek the members might be.
2. "Royalists . . . [who] compose many very charming, capable aristocrats of real influence and constitute some of the most famous names in Greece." But this concerned Jim because "a club comprised along this element would not be representative and would, at present, be at least passively anti-government." In short, the Royalists were the opposite of the Americanized Greeks, but with the added political burden of smoldering resentment toward the republican government under Eleftherios Venizelos.
3. "Venizelists or Republicans." This group also worried Davidson, even though he believed them to be "a majority of the business and professional men and the student class," because their predominance in the club "would evidence and rightly so, that Rotary, as far as Greece is concerned, is a political machine."[32]

Jim found fault with all three classes and wondered how to carve out a Rotary club from such elements. After a detailed review of recent Greek history, politics, and culture for his RI colleagues, Jim nevertheless held out hope in organizing his club "among moderates" made up of "twenty-one names that have passed inspection by well informed men on both sides."

But the political rivalry between the Royalists and Republicans put Jim in a particular bind. Rotary International was supposed to transcend the political and yet simultaneously affirm whichever political regime was in place in a given city or nation. The problem had already arisen in Istanbul, leaving that club in limbo after weeks of effort. Confused by the word "International" in RI's name, the Turkish government demanded a formal statement against the Soviet Union for fear RI was merely a vehicle for Soviet influence in the young nation. Amused by the rarity of such a concern, Jim pointed out to Emin Ali Bey, the head of the Government Association, a passage from a pamphlet distributed by the International Service Committee of RI: "Rotary's aim is to develop in each of its members the highest form of citizenship. A Rotarian must be a loyal citizen. Rotary has no room for the man who does not love his country. But Rotary does not feel that there is anything in loyalty to one's country that is incompatible with developing friendship with men of other lands." Little did Emin Ali Bey know that Jim himself had penned those words. For Emin Ali Bey, it was an important clarification for the Istanbul Rotary club's application to the Turkish government. For Jim, it was the only way to do business internationally and basic tenet of RI's civic internationalism. As Jim's world map was sponsored by the Canadian Pacific Railway, so political borders were the backdrop to global trade links, and "the highest form of citizenship" a simple matter of personal loyalty.[33]

Jim's solution in Athens was elegant and instructive. He overcame the "Royalist-Venizelist obstacle" by first befriending "D. Petrocochino, capitalist and a very wealthy man," who was "most favorably known throughout the country" and a "Venizelist." He then persuaded Philip Dragoumis, Royalist and son and grandson of Greek prime ministers, who had lost a brother to the Venizelists, to meet with Petrocochino to form the Athens Rotary club. Though potential enemies who had not spoken in years, when Dragoumis arrived, "Petrocochino arose, stepped forward and the two men smiled and shook hands and were talking in a friendly way when I left the room." The following day, Dragoumis nominated Petrocochino for club president. Other attendees at the meeting included a director for a French insurance company, the head of the newly formed Greek Tourist bureau, an electrical engineer, the director of the Department of Communications, and a top physician. The parallels with the Istanbul club were by design—Jim's design. Within a few weeks, the Athens Rotary club counted more than thirty-five "Royalists" and "Venizelists." Though Jim worried that the whole project would collapse when they saw "each other's names on the paper," the club eventually took root.[34]

The Rotary club of Istanbul, however, did not take root so easily. The nationalist politics and bureaucratic hierarchy being so new, state approval of the Istanbul club dragged on. Also, in Jim's absence, the once eager members of the organizing committee hedged their bets by avoiding signing their names on the club application to the state. Fear of getting themselves into something politically dangerous was very real. But two factors ended the impasse. First, Jim's success in Athens made news in Istanbul. It was one thing for RI to point to hundreds of Rotary clubs outside of North America to demonstrate RI's international credentials; it was quite another for Athens to have its own functioning Rotary club and Istanbul to go without. If a successful Rotary club served as a marker of political stability and modernity, so be it. It would not be the last time local and regional rivalries proved a useful dynamic to Jim and RI. Second, Jim's face-to-face contacts had their effect. After hearing of the delays by mail, Jim wrote back a letter to each member of the organizing committee: "I knew it would be difficult; but I found myself taking such a great interest in the splendid work you are doing in creating a modern and efficient Turkey, that I wanted very much to bring you into the family of Rotary International. The world should know more about your really heroic efforts. . . . I hope you will always consider me as a staunch friend of Turkey."[35] Both sentimental and affirming, the letter had a particularly strong effect on H. E. Sherif Bey, the prefect of police, with whom Jim had spent much personal time. Not strong in English, the prefect had Jim's personal translator read his letter for him.

The translator, Bekir Nuzhet Bey, also spent much time at Jim's side and was responsible for putting all of RI's literature that Jim carried into "modern" Turkish—no small feat in 1928. Bekir Nuzhet Bey felt obliged to write back to Jim in detail on Sherif Bey's reaction to his letter of regret, and Jim, in turn, relayed the letter in all its imperfections back to RI for heuristic effect:

> I sware, Mr. Davidson, he got so sorry and nearly pale on the face and told me 'this man must have left us very sorry.' Then he gave his aide for to hurry the registration of the regulations of the club which was just passing through his office. . . . As soon as you finish there [in Athens] you can start here and be sure until then I will have over thirty members signed and get the meetin to attend the first lunchun.[36]

The personal sense of honor and shame that both the prefect of police and the translator felt toward the whole affair, though hardly quantifiable, was revealing. Nor did the leadership at RI's headquarters miss Jim's point. For his personal efforts, the prefect eventually received special honor in the *Rotarian,* appearing in Lillian's version of events in Istanbul more than two years later.[37] By the time the Davidsons were moving on to Cairo in January 1929, both Athens and Istanbul seemed to be under "the banner of Rotary International." More to the point, Jim had worked out the basic "method of approach" he was to repeat and hone over the coming months and years with more than 2,200 other RI recruits.[38]

BRIDGING HOME AND ABROAD

Though Jim's mission unleashed much commentary and fanfare within the ranks of RI, one of the most revealing insights into the value of his travels came from Leroy Vernon, head of the Washington Bureau for the *Chicago Daily News.* Having read all of Jim's internal reports, Vernon pushed for Jim to publish them in RI's monthly, "for it is just the kind of information our people as a whole need. I can't imagine a better man for your purpose than he is, yet the handicaps and obstacles he has encountered are information worth its weight in gold to the average American business man who wants world contacts. We know they exist but Jim tells us about it in a form which anybody could understand."[39] Vernon knew the Davidsons for more than thirty years and knew that both were gifted writers. Vernon also appreciated the market value of publishing the Davidsons' experiences as a travelogue in the popular press.

But Vernon recognized something else in Jim's reports. Initially meant to inform RI's board of directors and a small circle of friends and colleagues, his reports soon took on a life of their own. Vernon understood, as a newspaperman, that the real value of Jim's reports lay in the unmet demand for such information from US, Canadian, European, and Latin American businessmen seeking "world contacts." As noted in previous chapters, RI was experiencing a crescendo of growth outside North America after World War I, but especially in Latin America and East Asia. With the institution developing into a clearinghouse for many urban elites outside North America eager to establish stable business and political relations with their regional counterparts and with the United States, Great Britain, Japan, Germany, and other powerful nations and economic systems, RI's leaders understood the opportunities before them. Echoing the organization's policy on the Mexico City club in 1921, RI's Extension Committee in 1927 stated the challenge clearly enough:

> If Rotary expects to advance internationally in the true sense of the word, more consideration must be given to obtaining members from the nationals in these countries in which Rotary hopes to advance. To do this we must ourselves cultivate a Mental Hospitality and a consideration and respect for the beliefs and traditions of these people. We are cognizant of the vast differences in the habits of the different people of the earth and the great difficulty that presents itself when we attempt to synchronize these people with their different attitudes towards life together under the banner of Rotary International.[40]

Within the year, Jim's initial experiences in and highly detailed reports on Turkey and Greece had already provided "information worth its weight in gold" for many in RI's leadership and convinced any last holdouts on the educational value of his travels, even if he failed in the actual establishment of new clubs in such foreign environs. To be sure, since the first clubs in Canada and Great Britain, it was obvious to all that the establishment of Rotary clubs outside the United States went hand in hand with the development of new international markets. In tune with trends in the advertising and marketing professions after World War I, however, RI's leadership began to view greater awareness and toleration of cultural differences as the first step in honing more sophisticated messages for multiple audiences in different media markets and national cultures. Of course, the ultimate and unquestioned goal of such tolerance was "to synchronize these people with their different attitudes . . . under the banner of Rotary International." The question was how to harness Jim's travels for the rank and file. In many ways, the modern field of business anthropology was already beginning to develop in Jim's writings.

By the late 1920s, these internal developments began seeping into the pages of the *Rotarian* as more and more non-US and non-Anglo authors received significant attention through feature articles. For example, immediately after the first installment of Lillian's series "Trailing along through Asia" was a contribution by Carlo Bos, commissioner in the Chinese Maritime Customs and president of the Shanghai Rotary Club, on "the myth of western supremacy."[41] Lillian's and Bos's articles underscored a critical departure in RI's editorial policy as well as a new dimension in RI's vision of international engagement. Together, Jim and Lillian were becoming the eyes and ears of RI's readers as well as its leadership. Lillian could weave into Jim's laconic, war-correspondent style of writing her own detailed observations of the style of women's dress, the way children played their games, the manner of negotiating in the marketplace as a woman, the intricacies of dance and customs, the nuances of certain non-English words, the history and architecture of towns and cities, and so on, with each new culture the Davidsons encountered.[42]

The mixture of styles had its effect. Lillian's eye for the anthropological and Jim's crisp, no-nonsense descriptions of interactions with the "local businessmen" appealed to Rotarians *and* their wives. Much more than an evolving brand of internationalism was unfolding within RI and its monthly during the period. As with popular culture in general, more and more advertisements targeting the female reader and consumer began appearing by the mid-1920s. It was soon apparent that RI's restriction of club membership to men only did not extend to its magazine's readership.[43] Though most readers still lived in North America, the *Rotarian*'s audience was not easily defined by gender or even age, since each club member typically had a home subscription, and many clubs provided free copies to local schools and public libraries. With a readership greater than its membership, the *Rotarian* was emerging as a mainstream magazine. As a result, Alex Potter, head of the European Secretariat in Zurich 1925–1930 and manager of RI's Extension Division in the Chicago headquarters after 1930, made sure the Davidsons appreciated just how their exploits were being received on the whole in North America and Europe:

> Really, Jim you can't imagine the romance Rotarians find in the work you are doing. I find that in contacting with different clubs and in writing them inspirational letters, it stirs up their enthusiasm and develops their imagination when I tell them about the work you have done and are doing, and about the clubs you have organized and of the manner in which you have enabled peoples of those Eastern countries to cooperate—to serve for the welfare of their professions, their communities and the world at large.[44]

On a more personal and concrete level, Chesley Perry informed the Davidsons about

> Isaiah Hale, Safety Superintendent of the Santa Fe Railroad at Topeka, Kansas, [who] joined the Rotary club and his first task was to read "The Rotarian." He sent me his criticism of the magazine, said he was very glad to join the organization because of its fellowship, but when he read the Davidson articles he saw the importance of the organization from the standpoint of world

> wide relationships and then he became proud of his membership and realized there was more to it than a social luncheon each week. He went back through the files of the magazine which he obtained from a friend and read the entire Davidson series.[45]

Though we cannot quantify the effect of Lillian's articles during their three-year run, the editors of the magazine frequently received similar comments from Rotarians like Isaiah Hale, not just from Kansas or North America but from around the world. The editors knew that Lillian's coverage of Jim's "mission" was developing quite a following—and helping to attract and keep female readers and national advertisers.[46] And so her regular installments continued with full support from RI.

TURKEY AND EGYPT—"THE RIGHT TYPE"

Lillian's first two installments covered the emergence of Turkey out of the ruins of the Ottoman Empire. Like Jim, she interpreted the transition in light of Japanese history, but in her own distinct and compelling style:

> Never have I seen anything more entrancingly beautiful than the skyline of Constantinople as we approached. . . . The dying rays of a lovely, rosy sunset had given place to a deep purplish blue, which like a color wash, covered both city and sky. In my gallery of memory-pictures this, my first great Near Eastern city, will ever reveal itself as I saw it then—a symphony in blue, with innumerable ethereal minarets soaring skyward above the rounding massive domes of mosques; and fairy-tale-like white palaces lining the shore; an indelible "memory gift" as the Japanese say.[47]

From the start, Lillian's writing style was hardly that of a no-nonsense businessman in search of new market opportunities. The Davidsons' was a bold adventure into Asia, and her articles an invitation to come along.

Though laced with obvious Orientalist tones throughout, Lillian's treatment of Istanbul and Turkish society also offered maps, photos, political history, and geographical information, as well as amusing and detailed descriptions of the street vendors and school children "enjoy[ing] the unusual treat of their first snowfall."

Lillian continued to blur gendered forms of knowledge—"practical" information on business conditions with romantic asides on cultural differences—into an entertaining whole in her second installment. In reviewing the "many important and desirable reforms" unleashed by Mustapha Kemal Ataturk, she focused on the removal of the traditional fez in public and replacement of the Arabic script with the Roman alphabet. But her regard for Kemal, "impulsive, youthful, democratic, not born in the purple," radiated when considering the social changes experienced by Turkish women: "The new Turkish woman is intelligent, keenly progressive and knows how to dress smartly. Hats are not often seen but as a substitute the veil with which they formerly covered their faces, is now wrapped, in the cleverest way, snugly about the head, forming a pretty turban."[48]

Rapid changes in dress and public codes of behavior for Turkish women were the real markers of modernity for Lillian. Unlike Turkish men, however, "there was this difference: the men were forced by law to change, but the women acted on their own initiative."[49] According to Lillian, Turkish women were important agents for Turkish reform and modernity. To drive the point home, an image of a "modern" Turkish woman appeared opposite the respectable portrait of the prefect of the police with the caption: "Gone are the veils and muffling garments of the days of the Seraglio. Chic and stylish, the modern Turkish girl dresses as smartly as her sisters in Paris." For Lillian, the temporal ruptures of Turkish modernity found their deepest expression in the replacement of "ancient costumes" with women's new clothing and codes of behavior. Turkish women also demonstrated their nation's newfound continuities with the West: "They parade the streets, go to the movies, dance at the cabarets, and do generally as girls do in Western countries anywhere. . . . In the bookstores one finds them interested in the fashion magazines. Many of them design and make their own gowns and they dress in exceptionally good taste and look much as our girls do at home."[50] Though Lillian herself mixed up gender barriers in her reportage, the modern women of Turkey followed gendered patterns of consumerism right up to the latest skirt lengths. According to Lillian, the future looked good for Turkey because the women of Turkey now looked good. For "our girls . . . at home," daily living out the same message in a blizzard of advertising, Lillian's point would have made complete sense.

But new dress codes did not translate into new gender relations within the intimate social space of the Rotary club. Word of mouth had spread so well in Istanbul thanks to "the Turkish press" that Turkish women, Jim reported, "have spoken to Mrs. Davidson as though it were an assured thing." Though Jim was looking for all the help he could get, he got more than he bargained for. Turkish women had approached Lillian personally and "spoken enthusiastically about [Rotary] and in each case wanted to know why ladies [were] not included."[51] A graduate of the University of California and a very well-traveled woman herself, Lillian embodied the promises of modernity to the wives of Jim's many recruits in Istanbul in more than just her style of clothing. But RI's civic internationalism did not entail gender equality any more in Istanbul than in Chicago or London. In fact, for all its international growth over the course of the twentieth century, RI managed to enforce the gender barrier well into the 1980s.[52]

Women in Egypt represented something very different for Lillian. Setting the stage for her next two installments on Egypt, she opened her description of the Davidsons' stay in Cairo in a sardonic tone: "If the heroine goes abroad, it is quite the thing in all up-to-date novels, to include Shepheard's Hotel in her travels; invariably, at some stage in the plot, she is on its famous terrace where one can sit in comfort and gaze down upon the changing, captivating street life of Cairo."[53]

Despite her own Orientalist approach to Egypt, Lillian showed some awareness of Europeans' ancient use of "the East" as a backdrop for their own imaginings. As if to undermine her own irony, however, she explained how Egyptian women bore their families' wealth in the form of jewelry carried on their bodies and then offered as evidence an image of a young woman wearing "the *yashmak* that partly conceal[s] the beauty of Egyptian women."[54] As a counterpoint to Lillian's presentation of "modern" Turkish women, the intent was clear: Egypt was no Turkey.

No irony was meant when Lillian revealed the Shepheard Hotel's other use as a backdrop for Western audiences: it was now the official site for the weekly meeting of the new Rotary Club of Cairo. But the men of Cairo had not embraced modern ways of doing business any more than the women had modern ways of dress. Quoting directly from Jim's confidential reports, Lillian laid out for her readers a challenge seen as even greater than Athens and Istanbul:

> The Egyptians have had little experience with organizations such as Rotary—the whole idea is naturally quite new to them. It was doubtful if an all-Egyptian club would function with any degree of success even if it were possible to interest Egyptians into giving it a trial. The logical, in fact, only solution was to organize if possible a club among leading Europeans in Cairo and then to bring in outstanding Egyptians with the hope that later the latter would use their influence in spreading Rotary to the more purely Egyptian communities. The Cairo club, therefore, had to be largely British or international in its membership.[55]

What happened to the principles worked out in Mexico City? Lillian explained, in Jim's voice, how "throughout the East" the business and professional communities of each city remained divided up into "exclusive nationalistic groups" that had "their own social clubs, their own trade associations and their own schools."[56] Given the chaos and fragmentation in the social and business environment of Cairo, Jim focused on British expatriates first and hoped they would act as a core for later inclusion of Egyptians and others.

How and why Jim chose to work through the British in Cairo revealed much about the practical inner-workings of RI's civic internationalism and its close reliance on preexisting European imperial structures and practices for its own expansion. A year before the Davidsons' arrival in Cairo, British Rotarians had already been vectoring in on Cairo's business community through their own networks and independent of RI's

Chicago offices. While visiting London on business, W. R. Todd, manager of the Cairo office for Thomas Cook and Son, met top London Rotarians through a fellow manager in Cook's London office. Todd returned to Cairo tasked with making "a survey" of Cairo in anticipation of starting a club there. Later effort came from another active London Rotarian of great wealth, Sam Gluckstein, managing director of J. Lyons & Co., who traveled on his own to Cairo for the express purpose of establishing a new club. After addressing the British chamber of commerce and interviewing various potential recruits throughout the city, Gluckstein met with no success apart from one devoted convert: R. Clare Martin, "manager for the Shell Oil Company's large interests in Egypt and adjoining countries." Put in contact with each other through London Rotarians, Martin and Todd began holding weekly luncheons in hopes that a club might take off on its own, but to no avail. When the Davidsons joined Martin and Todd later that fall, they had sixteen men "representing eight different nationalities" gathered for the formal organizing meeting, and sights set on six more "most desirable members . . . , including Sir Abdel Hamid Soliman Pasah, a prominent Egyptian official" and minister of communications for the Egyptian government. With Martin as the Cairo club's first president and Todd its first secretary, the Cairo "membership was of the highest type and the success of Rotary in Egypt became thus assured." The club soon had more than thirty-five members from fourteen different "nationalities." To be sure, London had much more to do with the establishment of the Cairo Rotary club than Chicago.[57]

But more important was the dovetailing of British corporate and imperial networks in the creation of the club as a regional epicenter for RI's expansion. As crucial links in the transportation and communication networks of the British Empire, Cairo and the Suez Canal were natural centers of operation for both Thomas Cook, the premiere international travel agency of the period, and transnational corporations like Shell Oil, which was already exploiting the vast oil reserves of the Middle East. Martin and Todd, Cairo's top Rotarians in 1929, were not just local businessmen. They were key actors in an emerging global economy as well as loyal British subjects. Their careers hinged on intimate knowledge of British trade routes and imperial policies. For RI, they were ideal for converting Cairo into a hub for Rotary, with plans for spokes extending into Egypt at Alexandria, Suez, Port Said, Mansura, Assuit, Aswan, and Luxor; into British Palestine at Jerusalem and Baghdad; and into Syria at Damascus and Beirut. Moreover, Lillian artfully edited out of Jim's report his concerns over British disdain for the encroachments of US corporate interests: "Just at present owing to the rapid development of the United States in its export business, there is a tendency on the part of other foreigners to unite in a campaign against Americans and American goods. In my day Great Britain was a favorite foe on which to concentrate." With Todd and Martin at the Cairo club's helm, anti-American sentiment was diminished. Yet Jim quietly went one step further: "The political situation is such that of all nationalities the British should have control [of Rotary clubs in Egypt]. Their hold on the government, however, is slight, and as they are exceeded in numbers by several other nationalities, it would seem not only right but desirable that the Egyptian Clubs be international." RI's civic internationalism softened anti-American attitudes, especially among British businessmen, without whom Rotary had no hope of success in the entire region. The approach was pure strategy. From one perspective, it was rather fortuitous for RI that the London Rotarians were on the vanguard of expansion into Cairo. From another, it was exactly as it should be. RI's co-opting of preexisting British imperial networks required only that RI avoid any direct challenge of British hegemony in the region and instead trumpet RI's internationalist (that is, not necessarily American and certainly pro-British) agenda in all its publications and pronouncements.

Both Jim and Lillian rose to the occasion. Not only did they avoid any questioning of British hegemony, they actively supported it. Lillian left no doubt in her readers' minds of the benevolence of British rule. Citing Jim's notes, she reviewed recent political history of Egypt as it moved toward independence after 1914, summarized the basic elements of the British Protectorate, and then offered up a spirited defense of the British Empire:

> The part played in the past by Britain in the administration of Egyptian affairs has been of incalculable benefit to the country. The British took over Egypt, a bankrupt nation. They placed it

> on its feet and in 1922 turned the government over to the Egyptians financially sound and with a surplus. They added tens of thousands of acres of arable land by the building of dams and extension of irrigation. They gave Egypt a degree of prosperity that had not been known before. They introduced sanitation, established modern hospitals, extended education and brought law and order to all parts of the land. They placed Egypt among the most advanced of Eastern nations and all these services they rendered without material advantage to themselves.[58]

Though she attributed the lines to Jim, they never appeared in that exact form in his reports. Lillian's writing certainly reflected Jim's own views. But Jim's version drew parallels between the British Protectorate in Egypt and the US control of Cuba: "[Britain] is now merely a looker-on, playing much the same role as does the United States in Cuba." For Jim, the apologetics of British imperialism transferred with ease to US-Cuban relations. Did they apply to US foreign relations in general? Was the United States an imperial power akin to Great Britain after all? Lillian did not seem to think so. Shorn of any direct reference to US imperialism, Jim's apologetics for British imperialism became a more palatable discourse on civilizational uplift in far-off lands, the noble work of European powers in Asian lands, rather than the site of US cultural and economic encroachments in cooperation with those European imperial powers.

In the end, the establishment of the Cairo Rotary club "under British control" shadowed the racial logic of British imperialism in Egypt. The syllogism applied in both because the premises were identical: (A) the Egyptians as a race or "nationality" still lacked the capacity for self-government; (B) they could learn the skills of self-government only through the tutelage of a more developed, modern, civilized political and economic power; (C) therefore, the Egyptians were in need of a continuation of the British Protectorate, just as the Cairo Rotary club (and all other Rotary clubs established in Egypt) required a guiding hand from its "international" members for the indefinite future. Like club membership, citizenship had its criteria in terms of class, race, and gender. Jim was clear on this point:

> I am convinced that it would be dangerous to start any club in Egypt without a strong foundation of foreign members unless we were willing to gamble on a failure. An International Club can be conducted here in an efficient and interesting way which would appeal far more to a native than an exclusively Egyptian organization. So constituted, Egyptians even could be found who would serve well as officers and on the board of directors with the exception of the position of Secretary which should always be held by a foreigner. Such a club might eventually have a majority of Egyptian members and render a real service. . . . The officers of that club are alive to their responsibilities in regard to taking in Egyptian members as rapidly as they can interest the right type.[59]

But, as always, what Jim meant by "the right type" was crucial. The club door was open for Egyptian members, so long as they met RI's formal standards on classifications for membership and could grasp the higher purposes of civic cooperation and uplift—as defined by the consent of *all* the "international" members of the Cairo club. As in Athens and Istanbul, Jim worked out new components of his "method of approach." After his time in Cairo, he would as a rule work through preestablished structures and practices of the British Empire by seeking out the most elite British businessmen and professionals first as the nucleus of new clubs and then drawing in "native" recruits as they managed to fulfill the membership criteria of the British as well as RI.

The Cairo Rotary club was a very complex outpost of US cultural and economic influence embedded within preexisting British imperial networks. In this dual capacity, the club also served as an institutional gatekeeper for rising Egyptian elites. The rules of entry and social interaction, however, were defined ultimately by a private, nonstate actor based out of Chicago rather than British colonial policies. Yet, with so many charming anecdotes to tell from their trip to the *Muski,* "Cairo's world-famous native bazaar," and a "side-trip" to see the pyramids, Lillian managed to keep such deliberations out of the pages of the *Rotarian.* Tales of romance and adventure served as euphemisms for imperial power—both US and British.

THE "MARCO POLO" OF ROTARY

Over the spring and summer of 1929, Lillian continued with her coverage of the Davidsons' travels from Cairo to Jerusalem, then to Damascus and Baghdad by "motor-bus," finally arriving in Bombay, India, for work in the Indian subcontinent (figure 6.2). In all three cities, Jim ran into significant problems. The Jerusalem Rotary club eventually came to fruition, but only by following the "method of approach" used in Cairo and Egypt and gathering "a strong British foundation in order to be influential and efficient." The greater concern lay in RI's "10 percent rule" on club membership: no club could draw more than 10 percent of its membership from any "major classification" such as "medicine," "government service," "advertising," and so on. Devised in the United States before World War I in order to prevent domination of clubs by any particular industry or profession, the 10 percent rule had become a significant obstacle for Jim in Jerusalem, because most of the "representative men" of the community were "government officials" within the British

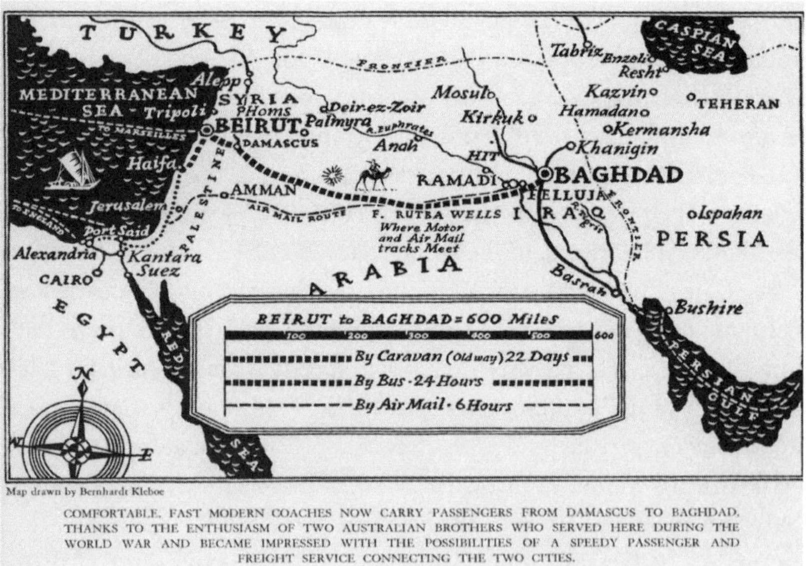

FIG 6.2: The Davidsons' crossing from the eastern Mediterranean through southern central Asia to India and Southeast Asia helped solidify Jim as Rotary's "Marco Polo." *Rotarian*, September 1930, 37. *Courtesy of Rotary International.*

colonial administration. Jim began questioning the rigidity of RI's rules on classification by asking "perhaps we should ask ourselves which is of the greater importance, that Rotary spread the spirit of service into every country or that we conform strictly with a rule which came into existence without consideration of some of the problems that I have encountered."[60] Davidson had not anticipated experimenting with RI's membership criteria in such a fundamental way any more than the directors of RI had. They all considered "the classification principle" to be as basic to their organization's raison d'être as their civic activities, as a kind of stable measuring rod for business and professional identities no matter the political and cultural circumstances. But, given Jim's full embrace of "this very excellent and liberal arrangement" provided by the British Mandate, which had "brought justice and security," the rules had to be stretched, or "the strong British foundation" would not be possible.[61] The white Europeans had to be included despite the rules or else Jerusalem go without a club altogether. Jim ultimately fudged the rules, and the British government officials exceeded the 10 percent cap. The change in Jerusalem was only the beginning of Jim's adaptations of RI's membership criteria.[62]

After visiting both Damascus and Baghdad, however, Jim believed those cities were beyond any possibility of sustaining a club. "With the British as masters in Iraq and with Baghdad, a city of 250,000 people and the most important point over that large part of Asia extending from Palestine to India, it seemed to me important to take at least a look in."[63] Geography and the British Empire drew Jim to Baghdad, where he found that, unlike Istanbul or Athens, there was a minimum of political resistance or rivalry. Instead, the problem, Jim explained, was "the lack of permanency in the British occupation and the difficulties of transportation."[64] In other words, the reasons Jim went to Baghdad were the same reasons he chose not to organize a Rotary club. With the British Mandate due to end in 1932 and with transportation routes to and from Baghdad so erratic, Jim could not imagine any future success for a Baghdad club. Such was Jim's dependence on the political and economic infrastructure of the British Empire in Asia. Further trips to "the Persian cities of Mohammerah and Abadan, headquarters of the Anglo-Persian Oil Company" also failed to produce results for Jim. Unless he were to detail for the public the bloody French suppression of Syrian resistance in Damascus, long bus rides with officials of the Anglo-Persian Oil company, or conversations with German scientists prospecting for oil, there was not a whole lot to write home about in this leg of their journey.[65]

Fortunately, Lillian managed to fill in the gaps for her readers back home. Redacting Jim's encyclopedic knowledge of Iraq's recent emergence from the Ottoman Empire and reiterating the benevolence of British rule could only go so far. Lillian turned to familiar tropes to spice up her narrative: "Baghdad! You who have even a drop of adventurer's blood in your veins will thrill to that name. Get out your atlas, and put your finger on the spot. Baghdad today is almost as isolated as when inspired by Scheherazade, with the 'Thousand and One Tales' as her dice, gambled there with death."[66]

But the romanticizing had its limits as well. Lillian's second installment on their time in Baghdad stepped back from its Orientalism and instead presented a tense, strained political environment ready to erupt during their tours of Baghdad's ancient sites. She and her daughter Marjory hired "an Arab girl" educated at the American University in Beirut and "dressed smartly in European clothes" as their tour guide. Their visit to "Kadhimain . . . one of the three holy cities in Iraq, venerated by Mohammedans of the Shiah sect" revealed a deeper form of resistance than anything experienced beforehand:

> At the close of day, the open square before the great Mosque was filled with Moslems. It was our intention to go just a bit nearer to see the golden domes surmounting gaudy green, blue and yellow tiled walls, but after a half dozen steps the grim crowd of devotees began closing in upon us step by step. One fleeting glance into those fanatical faces and prudence whispered, 'Go back.'[67]

Lillian did not offer any counsel or explanation on the moment for her readers, only that she, her daughter, and her guide in Western dress were dangerously out of place. After touring several other cities in Iraq, the Davidsons caught a British coastal steamer from Basra to Bombay. In the end, Jim had no success between Jerusalem and Bombay. Given his reliance on the British Empire in the region and its relative weakness in Iraq, there was little hope of any other outcome. Lillian, for her part, fared much better with her three dispatches home on the history, cultures, and peoples of the Middle East. Rotary International would not arrive in Beirut until 1932, Damascus in 1938, and both Baghdad and Tehran in 1956.[68]

INDIA—"AT LEAST ONE CLUB OF THIS TYPE"

While passing through on a business trip in the United States in 1918, R. J. Coombes, an Englishman, visited the Rotary club of Grand Rapids, Michigan. So impressed with what he had seen, he returned to Calcutta and within the year had started his own version of the Calcutta Rotary club. Much stricter in its application of the classification principle, somewhat closer to a Freemason lodge than any other Rotary club, and entirely comprising British subjects, the Calcutta Rotary club nevertheless began meeting at Peliti's Restaurant in the fall of 1919, becoming only the third club in all of Asia, following Shanghai and Manila.[69] By 1921, however, the club began to include Indian members and, over the course of the 1920s, slowly came more into alignment with formal institutional policies and practices of RI. Despite almost complete isolation from the rest of RI, the club even managed to start another club in Lahore by 1927.[70] But it was not until Jim's visit to the Indian subcontinent that the Calcutta and Lahore clubs were truly incorporated into RI. Jim had even more changes in mind.

The Calcutta club presented Jim with one significant problem that he sought to rectify the moment he stepped off the steamer in Bombay. Though the Calcutta club's close relations with British colonialism were certainly no issue, the club was "made up almost entirely of the middle class." For Jim, the future success of RI in India hinged on a specific kind of relationship with British and Indian elites: "The type of men I have interested are such that extension in other cities in India will be made easy. Many of the members are heads of firms having branches in practically every city that we would be entering." The middle-class status of the Calcutta club, as such, undermined Jim's top-down recruiting strategies throughout Asia, let alone India. Though he reported that "it is a good and useful club even at that," the club's middling reputation obstructed his "method of approach" in Bombay: "There are a number of knights holding the highest positions in Calcutta but none of them are in the club."[71] Jim saw his challenge in plain terms:

> I had two alternatives. I could organize a club among men of the second strata with retailers and small wholesalers as members. . . . The summer problem would not be such a difficult one with them. . . . Such a club would be very little help to us in extension work. The other alternative . . . was to go after the outstanding men whose names would mean much through India and would therefore be of much assistance in spreading Rotary.[72]

In the end, Jim managed to sign up in Bombay, among others, "four English knights, all of them most important men" since "future extension in India . . . demands at least one club of this type."[73] Jim never considered the first alternative.

Compounding the issue of class status, however, was "the summer problem" when "most of the successful men go either home to England or to the hill stations for the hot season," leaving their firms "in the hands of juniors." Given RI's requirement that *all* clubs hold weekly meetings year round with a minimum percentage of members in attendance, Jim was in a quandary. If the true commercial elites of Bombay, Madras, Delhi, Lahore, and other key Indian cities were to constitute those cities' Rotary clubs, what would come of RI's own institutional demands and time commitments? Without any chance to consult RI's international service committee members scattered throughout the Americas and Europe, Jim reasoned on his own that class status trumped attendance rules because "a great deal can be done with men after they have become interested in Rotary that cannot be done when they are just coming in. I am speaking now of clubs in India, Ceylon, Hong Kong, etc. where the membership will be British." Since the new clubs, in the long term, would be managed by local elites who "submit to the heat more willingly and would not demand a vacation," the "summer problem" would eventually fade.[74] RI's model for growth turned on the high status of its membership much more than on adherence to RI's set practices and conceptions of time. Thanks to Jim, RI drew freely not only from preexisting British imperial infrastructure in Asia but also from its class structures. As in Cairo, the hub-and-spoke model of expansion into India depended on borrowed status from Bombay's elites, rather than Calcutta's "smaller merchant and less important man."[75]

But the "summer problem" and class issues were not the end of Jim's challenges. The charter members of the Madras Rotary club, for example, included three "of the aristocratic type of Eastern merchant which ordinarily maintains a caste distinction which excludes the retailer from their homes and clubs."[76] Yet retailers and the advertising professions were part and parcel of RI's success in North America and Great Britain. Jim understood that their influence in RI could be mitigated only so much by distance. As a result, Jim orchestrated the merger of older class and caste structures of Madras with the consumerist ethos of corporate capitalism in the United States through inclusion of "four leading retail establishments," since "most of the retail trade [was] in the hands of merchants of little responsibility and standing." Retailers, those from the highest corporate levels at least, could sit down for weekly luncheons with the "aristocratic type of Eastern merchant"—under the banner of Rotary International, of course. Among the twenty-five others dining together under RI's banner at the Connemara Hotel in 1929 were G. G. Armstrong, chairman of the Madras Port Trust; F. E. James, representative of the United Planters Association of South India; W. H. Luker, director of Addison & Co.; Morton Chance, hotel chain manager; J. W. Macfarlane, Manager of the South India Export Co.; K. Kay, managing director of Binney & Co., "a key shipping concern"; and M.A. Candeth, listed as "an Indian" and one of the club's directors.[77] Upon the Davidsons' departure for Ceylon, Jim designated F. E. James his "special commissioner" for India's five clubs in Calcutta, Bombay, Lahore, Madras, and Delhi. In the wake of Jim's organizing, F. E. James and then many Indian district governors went to work. By 1947, the year of

India's formal independence from Great Britain, there were seventy-one Rotary clubs encompassing more than 3,100 members throughout all of India. After some "sluggish" postwar growth in the 1950s and 1960s, the Indian clubs began growing rapidly in the 1970s after separation between India and Pakistan and particularly from the late 1980s to the present.[78] With time, though Jim's vision of RI's growth in India largely played out according to design, it was "the second strata" of retailers and wholesalers in Calcutta who got the last laugh, as one of Jim's point men in the Calcutta club, Nitish Laharry, went on to become RI's first international president from Asia in 1962–1963, overseeing 529,000 Rotarians in 11,300 clubs in 128 countries.[79] Not bad for India's "middle-class" club.

But the greatest hurdle for success in India was the emerging politics of Indian nationalism. For an international service club defining itself as an apolitical force for civic cooperation among business and professional elites yet building its own membership on the basis of British imperial networks, demands for "home rule" were the greatest of threats. In his survey of Indian politics, Jim rightly perceived growing Indian resentment toward the British Empire and surging Indian nationalism. Couched within an apologetics for British imperialism, Jim's dismissive review of the activities of Mohandas Gandhi's calls for "Indianization" was redolent of US views on Cuba's "debt of gratitude" toward the United States (see Chapter 5). Jim painted a bleak picture in his report:

> Have not the British the obligations to maintain the blessings of good government even in the face of the opposition of the Indian politicians and the masses whom the so-called patriarch has misled? I think we all recognize that a people have a right to govern themselves even though they do it somewhat badly. In this case, however, it does not mean merely inefficient administration, but does mean the introduction of internecine warfare between the various religious groups, oppression and extortion with the minorities as the principal sufferers and a return of many of the evils that the British did away with when they came in to India.[80]

Jim buttressed his argument with a learned summary of India's religious, linguistic, racial, and ethnic diversity, but the fundamental logic of imperialism finally revealed itself in his conclusion:

> Of course, with their large vested interests and for other obvious reasons, the British have no intention of withdrawing from India. Doubtless they will compromise and endeavor in this way to avoid conflict with the Indian people. Perhaps sufficient wise heads among the Indians will finally appreciate how well off they are and convince their fellow-men that they need the British both for security and for business reasons. Meanwhile, however, a storm is in the offing.[81]

In this case, Empire was shorthand for massive investments and the right of return on those investments. That the Indians were so at loggerheads in so many ways not only proved their lack of self-governing capacities but also justified their continuing need for British tutelage.[82] Poor citizenship skills mapped onto racial categories drove Jim's imperial apologetics in general as well as his "method of approach" in organizing Rotary clubs in India. Though RI's civic internationalism made no reference to such racial categories in its formal policies on club membership, and though the Mexico City agreement committed RI to the affirmation of local and national interests of each host city in RI, race emerged in response to political assertions of Indian nationalism:

> I have interviewed all of the British members on the subject of taking in Indian members and with one exception, they were all in favor of it. They were fearful, however, that men might be selected who were disloyal to the government in thought and might later declare themselves publicly, and thus prove to be most undesirable. If they endeavored to remove the objectionable party on the basis of disloyality[sic], politics might be made of it by the Indian politician. In fact conditions are so strained at present that the attitude of all is one of great precaution. Consequently, although I had a list of outstanding Indians, well

> educated and exceptionally successful in business, in fact leaders in their line, I have hesitated to approach them, even though they had been passed by my committee. I am inclined to think that at present, the clubs will have to be at first largely British and then select slowly and carefully their Indian members.[83]

The formation of Rotary clubs in India in 1929 involved the "politics of recognition" as much as British imperial politics itself.[84] The promise of inclusion came with a tacit set of rules, prime among them being a kind of loyalty test passed only by economic elites who remained above and beyond any push of Indian nationalism. While the politics of decolonization and RI's civic internationalism were not exactly easy allies in India during the interwar years, there proved to be much more room for accommodation in the postwar years than Jim Davidson could imagine in 1929.[85]

BRITISH MALAYSIA—"THE WORLD DO SURELY MOVE!"

From India, the Davidsons set sail for Colombo, Ceylon, and then Rangoon, Burma, establishing in each city a Rotary club in much the same manner as in India. The Davidsons then chose to travel by riverboat up the Irrawaddy River to Thayetmyo, then on to Mandalay, and finally all the way to Bhamo—just 27 miles from the Chinese border. Their efforts resulted in a new Rotary club in Thayetmyo before the Davidsons' departure for the Federated Malay States as well as some consternation for Alex Potter in the Chicago headquarters on how to address their new fellow Rotarians of Burma: "We note names such as U Ba Thein, b.A., U Mg Gyi, M.M. Banerji, and U. Shwe Ni. . . . Is the U similar to Mr. In this country or to Esq. in Great Britain? . . . We are ignorant in this matter and do not want to make a mistake that might show that ignorance or hurt the sensibilities of any of the men in the newly elected clubs."[86] The incorporation of exotic peers into RI's fellowship sometimes brought on such confusion. But Jim's visit to the Kuala Lumpur Rotary club triggered a series of debates within RI of much greater import, over the possibility of "racial classifications" within RI.

Started in the summer of 1928 by L. D. Gammans, an Englishman in the "Co-operative Societies Department" of the Federated Malay States Service, the Kuala Lumpur "Rotary" club was not officially part of RI. Operating without an official charter, the club members anxiously awaited the arrival of the Davidsons from Burma in order to demonstrate their legitimacy as a club within RI and be granted an official charter. Gammans first came into contact with Rotary in 1918 when his wife's cousin invited Gammans, a captain in the British Army at the time, to the Detroit Rotary club. As Jim explained in his report to RI, "Gammans found in Malaya a most happy situation, in fact, a unique one. He found Chinese, Malays, Indians, and Europeans living in harmony to a degree that exists nowhere else that I know of."[87] The racial diversity of the Federated Malay States seemed so complex yet harmonious to Jim that, in effect, he began to recalibrate his methods and positions worked out in India, "with its communal hatreds, its frequent riots between Hindu and Mohammedan, its caste conflicts and the destructive antagonism between Indian and European to appreciate how different it is here."[88] For fear that the harmony might not last, Gammans decided to work through his position in the Co-operative Societies Department, which "brought him in more intimate contact with the different racial groups than would perhaps any other Government office," to establish "a club with a membership comprising different racial groups." Since his own father had been a Rotarian in Portsmouth, England, Gammans chose to write to RI's European Secretariat for pamphlets and publications and then contact Rotarians in Calcutta and Shanghai for more advice rather than start his own club.[89]

When the Kuala Lumpur club filled out the necessary paperwork for securing a club charter in 1928, however, Gammans made an argument for the "widening of the classification rule" in order to accommodate the membership of a Chinese, an Indian, and a European "barrister." Gammans understood that RI's rules on classification permitted only one kind of "barrister" at a time in a given club in order to avoid competition among and inordinate concentration of any particular business or profession in each club—a basic feature of Rotary's club life since its earliest days in Chicago (see Chapter 1). The classification principle was the linchpin to RI's claim that every Rotary club in the world was a "representative cross-section" of its community. But Gammans also understood Kuala Lumpur and Malaysia, arguing that "representatives of the same profession here but of different nationalities normally have less social intercourse with each other than if they were of different professions but the same nationality."[90] In short order, Jim grasped what Gammans was trying to do in stretching the rules on classification: in Kuala Lumpur one could not presume one community comprising distinct business and professional identities, since "community" in Kuala Lumpur was undeniably complicated by various distinct racial, cultural, and religious groups. RI's civic internationalism, as originally conceived in Chicago and increasingly standardized over two subsequent decades of international growth, could not possibly function in Kuala Lumpur—nor in any other Malaysian city—without a genuine grappling with racial differences and identities. With an itinerary that included Ipoh, Penang, Seremban, Klang, and Singapore, Jim knew the problem was not unique to Kuala Lumpur.

The unquestioned solidarity of "whiteness" forged across the Atlantic and only rarely challenged by visiting Japanese and Latin American Rotarians had finally come under scrutiny within the ranks of RI. Or, rather, RI's "extension" into Southeast Asia had finally foregrounded the issue of race as it was impossible to erase nonwhite, marginal businessmen and professionals. It was one thing to pocket-veto proposed Rotary clubs in Port-au-Prince and Kingston, to avoid the recruitment of Afro-Cubans and nonwhite Puerto Ricans, to hope visiting Latin American Rotarians were not too dark-skinned for hotel managers in the United States, and to allow a handful of Asian members of extraordinarily high-class status into clubs "over time," but quite another to reject the Kuala Lumpur club, which was already a known presence in the Federated Malay States, merely awaiting formal approval of its charter and membership by Jim. The club was seen as a fait accompli in the city and its press.[91]

Jim had to think and act fast. There was no time for him to seek and get formal approval from RI's International Service Committee scattered throughout Europe and North America. Not that the committee had much of a chance of coming to a consensus on the issue anyway. Davidson reasoned, "If you will admit that there is a far wider gulf between these men of different racial groups in the same vocation than between any two Europeans in different classifications, are we not then complying with the spirit and following the ultimate aim of the classification rule?"[92] With the expectation of encountering such ambiguous conditions through international growth so far afield, the Extension Committee had chosen Jim Davidson and designated him honorary general commissioner so that he could make such a decision on the ground and in real time.

In effect, Davidson, Gammans, and the Kuala Lumpur Rotarians were also arguing for a broader conception of membership in RI than one's business reputation and activities within the marketplace. RI's positing of transnational market identities in deracinated form was fraying, and Jim knew it. Membership cognizant of racial identity became a feature of the Kuala Lumpur Rotary club and, by extension, in all of the clubs ultimately formed by Jim in the Malaysian peninsula: Singapore, Klang, Ipoh, Penang, Malacca, and Seremban. The racial identities of RI's exotic peers were no longer limited to euphemistic references to "cultural" and "international" differences.

As a result, the new Malaysian clubs took RI's civic internationalism to a new and more complicated level of inclusion. Held at the "roomy Masonic Hall beautifully decorated for the occasion," the club's inaugural ball featured an "international menu" with "Chinese, Malay, Indian and European dishes and with Canadian maple syrup thrown in in honour of my home." The event also attracted His Highness the Sultan of Selangor; Sir William Peel, government chief secretary; and more than one hundred other notables of various racial and cultural origins.[93] Similar to Kuala Lumpur, the charter members in Klang's new club included twenty Europeans, eight Malaysians, seven Indians, four Eurasians, four Ceylonese, and two Chinese members.[94] While in Singapore, Jim had a serious bout of dengue fever but survived to make about "200 calls on men in their offices," resulting in seventy-one charter members who represented "the pick of the officials, of business and professional men, including eleven of the leading Chinese." The charter members did, in fact, represent the top government and business leaders from Singapore's Chinese, European, and Malaysian communities, and within a year the Singapore Rotary club had 144 members, "representing eighteen different nationalities, which constitutes . . . a record for all Rotary, I am sure."[95] Like Cairo and the Suez Canal, Singapore was one of the key chokepoints for international trade in general and for the British Empire in particular. Yet, unlike Cairo, the Singapore club encompassed a broad collection of members from around the world as a reflection of the social, political, and economic realities of the city and its extensive trade networks.

Davidson celebrated the comparatively rich racial diversity of the Malaysian clubs in his reports just as RI began touting his exploits in its publications, especially in the pages of the *Rotarian*. In one instance, F. F. Cooray, a Ceylonese member of the Kuala Lumpur club, announced with confidence that "when the commercial era precipitated new racial and social problems in Malaya, European and Asiatic alike turned to Rotary for the solvent of good-will." By coincidence, Cooray's article, entitled "Malaya—Turnstile of East and West," preceded Lillian's installment on the Davidsons' travels in Jerusalem two years earlier. Cooray was only the sign of things to come for RI. Just one of many contributors to the magazine from Rotarians and non-Rotarians outside of North America and Europe, Cooray—along with Rotarian Hamzeah bin Abdullah of the Kuala Lumpur club—served as ocular proof of RI's gentle expansion into very foreign environments.[96] But no one symbolized better RI's powers of racial and cultural inclusion than the "Malay Chief" of the Ipoh Rotary club. After a very detailed explanation of the history and complexities of British rule in the various Malay States and Straits Settlements and the growing centrality of Singapore, the Malaysian peninsula, and Southeast Asia to the global economy, Jim explained that the Malay Chief's father

> sort of upset things for a while by being responsible for the killing of the British Resident, but the son in the picturesque trappings of his father now haunts the jungle no longer. He plays bridge, drinks scotch and soda, has "Ole Man River" on his phonograph after a ten course dinner and predicts that Ramsay Macdonald's visit to the United States, he hopes will serve as a cement for Anglo Saxon relations. The son-in-law of His High-

> ness, the Sultan of Selangor, another pure Malay, is a member of the Kuala Lumpur club and a delightful fellow he is, with an English education that few Anglo Saxons possess. The world do surely move![97]

As the embodiment of the forces of modernity unfolding in the Malay peninsula, the Malay Chief evidenced RI's vision of progress, its "gospel" of civic internationalism to be "spread . . . among the native peoples of other countries," while Davidson's new clubs in such far-off lands bore a certain demonstration effect in the imagination of RI's readers on Main Street. That his "classification" as "Malay Chief" made no sense beyond the Malay peninsula no longer mattered to RI. Rather than a cause for concern, in fact, it had become an institutional badge of honor. Coupled with Lillian's dispatches, the Davidsons' successes and adaptations in Southeast Asia presented a compelling story of transformation of Asian newcomers from an exotic other to an exotic peer within RI's "world fellowship of business and professional men united in the ideal of service."

THE MANCHURIAN CANDIDATE

While reading through Lillian's dispatches in the *Rotarian* in 1931, Isaiah Hale of Topeka, Kansas (and tens of thousands other Rotarians like him), would have come across Lillian's map of the Dutch East Indies superimposed over the familiar silhouette of the United States and North America (figure 6.3). The map offers a sense of scale for the average reader of the *Rotarian* in striking form: the island of Sumatra occupies much of the southwest, extending from southern Oregon to central New Mexico; the island of Borneo dominates the Rockies, Java rivals Texas in its length; the island of Celebes connects Chicago with Kansas City; and the island of "Dutch New Guinea" only begins upon arrival in Maryland. Lillian's point was clear: not only was it a big world "out there" filled with a broad range of cultural, national, racial, linguistic, and religious differences; it was also physically a big world out there. The Dutch East Indies, representing only one portion of the Davidsons' travels over

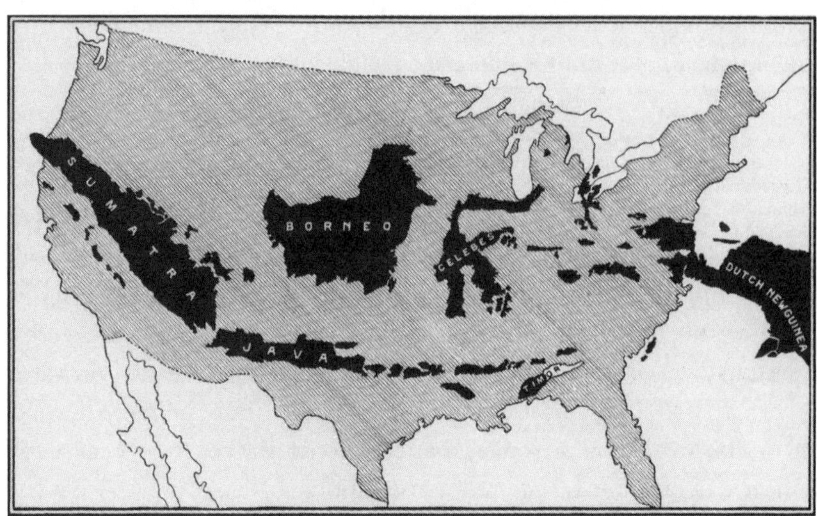

IF ONE WERE TO GET A SIDE VIEW OF THE WHOLE GROUP OF THE DUTCH EAST INDIES, IT WOULD APPEAR AS A GREAT CONTINUOUS LAND SURFACE, EAST AND WEST, EXCEEDING THE DISTANCE BETWEEN NEW YORK AND SAN FRANCISCO.

FIG 6.3: Always in a didactic mode, Jim and Lillian Davidson used their travels to increase Americans' awareness of the world outside the United States. Here Jim and Lillian chose to overlay maps of the Dutch East Indies with the United States in order to convey the comparative scale of each for readers "back home." *Rotarian,* September 1931, 30. *Courtesy of Rotary International.*

two and a half years, required visits to Batavia (Jakarta), Surabaya, Bandung, Malang, and Semarang in Java and Medan in Sumatra (in between trips in Malaysia) and resulted in new clubs in all those cities (map 3).[98] Their time among the islands offered Lillian the chance to dig into the rich variety of cultures of the islands and present them in both narrative and photographic form.[99] The Davidsons also had yet another opportunity to educate their respective audiences on the vast distances and cultural and political complexities of the Dutch East Indies and to explore the region (vicariously) as a potential place to travel, do business, or both.

The Davidsons returned to the Malay peninsula to finish up work started in Malacca (Melaka), Penang, and Klang before heading north to Bangkok, Siam, and then overland through French-controlled portions of Southeast Asia: Cochin China, Annam, and Tonkin. Jim had success with the Bangkok Rotary club largely because it already existed on its own and was awaiting his approval, much like the club in Kuala

Lumpur. But nothing came of his time in Saigon and Hanoi, cities that "at present do not offer Rotary opportunities."[100] After visits to Hong Kong, Canton, and then Manila, Jim was expected to return to the United States, especially since income from membership dues for RI was decreasing thanks to the deepening of the Great Depression, and funding for the Davidsons' trip was drying up. By late summer of 1930, the Davidsons had both become acutely aware of the interest in their travels by so many in RI but also of the economic turmoil on a global scale and its vast consequences. Gone were the heady days of 1926 when RI's annual convention passed a resolution placing a $1 charge on each member for international expansion and even when the Davidsons first set sail on their current journey with the Ottaways in the summer of 1928, replaced by rising tariffs, unpaid debts, plunging stock markets, diminishing investment, and the hardening of trade blocs. The Davidsons' itinerary for their return home in the end might not include any time in Japan and China, where Jim had lived and worked so many years before as a US consular agent and war correspondent, and where Lillian had lived with her family before meeting Jim.

But Jim had his own wealth to draw upon and his own reasons for traveling a few months longer in East Asia: the Japanese Rotary clubs had established branch clubs in the Manchurian cities of Dairen, Harbin, and Mukden. The new clubs, however, spoke Japanese in their meetings and were formed with no attempt at inclusion of the Chinese business communities of those Chinese cities. While in Southeast Asia, Jim assessed the situation fully: "I am astonished . . . that the Japanese have organized a Japanese club in Manchuria at Harbin."[101] Jim understood that, from the Japanese Rotarians' perspective, club growth was occurring within "their" seventieth district as defined by RI: Japan, Korea, and Manchuria. And Jim personally knew its longtime district governor, the ubiquitous and formidable Umekichi Yoneyama of Tokyo, whose "territory is 'South Manchuria.' It would have been perhaps better to have confined him to Japan and Korea, although I believe that the club at Dairen should have been Japanese—it is largely a Japanese city and under their control."[102] But Jim also knew the Chinese Rotarians and especially the city of Shanghai very well. He anticipated the Chinese point of view and the potential diplomatic fallout not just for RI but also for Sino-Japanese relations: "Moukden, as you know, is the Chinese capital of Manchuria. To organize a Japanese club there is as wrong as it would be to have only a Chinese club in Tokyo, and is likely to do all kinds of harm. I fear we will be severely criticized for it."[103] Caught between both sides, Jim offered his services to RI: "Harbin is still further north. I cannot possibly understand his starting a Japanese club there. . . . I wonder if the Board would not authorize me to visit these points. Any readjustment must be handled with the greatest tact, so as not to hurt the feelings of the Japanese."[104] Within a decade of Rotary's introduction to Shanghai in 1919 and Tokyo in 1920, Rotary International was becoming embroiled in regional tensions with a very long and complicated history.

A reflection of the Japanese Empire's expansionist policies into Manchuria, the all-Japanese clubs on Chinese soil were pushing the limits of RI's civic internationalism. The Rotarians (both Chinese and expatriate) in Shanghai, Peking, Tsingtao, and several other key trade centers in the region made clear in RI's internal debates a cascade of reasons for their fears. One telegram from the Shanghai club to RI left no room for doubt:

> Shanghai club learns with great concern Japanese forming Rotary Club in Harbin using Japanese Language *All* Charter Members Japanese Stop Ninetyfive Percent Population Harbin Chinese and Russian with latter universal language Strongly recommend granting charter be suspended pending arrival Davidson.[105]

Like Jim, the Rotarians in China could see the commercial and political repercussions rippling throughout all of East Asia.

Could the "world fellowship" of RI help mitigate the growing presence of the Japanese Empire and its military in China? Of all officers in RI, Jim Davidson was certainly best suited to the challenge. Given his own personal history with the Japanese government, his reputation among Japanese Rotarians, and his own fortuitous presence in the region, he decided to visit both the Chinese and Japanese Rotary clubs before returning to North America. The final leg of the Davidsons' long journey, in other words, ran contrary to all prior efforts. Rather than blazing a trail for new clubs in Southern and Southeastern Asia in happy fulfillment of RI's dreams of forming a "golden chain" of Rotary clubs around the world, Jim was attempting to patch up Sino-Japanese tensions over the expansion of Rotary clubs into Manchuria. RI had become a victim of its own early success in East Asia as "fellow" clubs, repositories for the upper echelons of diplomatic, political, and economic power in both China and Japan, were clashing into one another—with no solution in sight.

The Davidsons arrived in Shanghai in late January 1931 and began work immediately in quelling dissent among the ranks. With a Wilsonian faith in the managerial prowess of all participants, Jim had every confidence that all could be worked out among reasonable, enlightened men from both sides of the issue. In the Shanghai, Tientsin, and Peking Rotary clubs, Jim heard the full list of complaints and concerns regarding Japanese expansionism. His visits to Harbin and Mukden were quite opposite in tone, with an emphasis on fellowship rather than dissension. His job in Manchuria was to make a firsthand survey rather than be pulled into the fray, to represent the seriousness of RI's concerns and willingness to listen to all sides.[106] Before leaving for Japan, the Davidsons dined with Viscount Saitō, governor-general of Korea Keijō (Seoul), former admiral of the Japanese Navy who was directly responsible for the establishment of the Rotary club in the Korean peninsula.[107] (Little did the Davidsons or the Viscount realize that Saitō was very soon to become prime minister of Japan [May 1932–July 1934] in the wake of the assassination of Prime Minister Inukai Tsuyoshi by Japanese naval officers.)

The Davidsons finally wound up their entire tour of Asia where Jim had begun his own diplomatic career decades before: working with the Japanese to resolve tensions with China. This time, however, Jim could not risk taking one side over the other. He visited all the Japanese clubs except Nagoya in a tactful effort to rein in the Japanese Rotarians without offending their sensibilities. It was a significant diplomatic challenge. As detailed in Chapter 4, by 1930, the Japanese Rotarians, and especially the Tokyo Rotary club, had become almost mythic in the world of Rotary as non-Western businessmen and professionals who had grasped the cooperative ethos of RI's civic internationalism and made it all their own. They were not accustomed to anything but praise from RI and Rotarians visiting Japanese clubs from abroad. In the end, Jim's proposal to RI had three parts: (1) expand the "70th district" to include all of northern China as well as Manchuria, Korea, and Japan, thereby undermining the sense of "Japanese control" of the district and forcing the Chinese clubs to deal with the Japanese more directly under the common institutional machinery of RI; (2) revoke the club charter for Harbin, since "the club is just a mistake and a very unfortunate one"; and (3) create two separate Rotary clubs in Mukden, one for the Chinese, Russians, and other internationals and one for the Japanese.[108]

None of Jim's proposals ever came to fruition. Less than six months after the Davidsons' return to Vancouver from Tokyo in late March 1931, the Mukden Incident occurred, marking the start of the Japanese military command's transformation of Japanese foreign policy into an increasingly aggressive posture over the course of the 1930s. Contrary to Jim's suggestion, RI eventually carved out the Eighty-First District for the Chinese Rotarians and supported them in their efforts to build into the interior of China while the clubs in Harbin and Mukden continued unabated as Japanese-dominated clubs. Meanwhile, Jim, Lillian, and their daughter, Marjory, returned to be welcomed as heroes in Vancouver. In early April, Jim arrived at the Chicago headquarters of Rotary International to present his formal report on all his travels. Having spent more than two years and $32,000 of RI's money, Jim had much to account for. But the twenty-three new Rotary clubs formed between "Prague and Shanghai" not only fulfilled RI's particular geographical conceit about circumnavigation but also proved to be significant epicenters of growth for RI after World War II and particularly after the 1960s (see map p. 248–249).

Sydney Pascall, an activist on behalf of the League of Nations, former head of the British Rotary clubs, and the first European president of RI in 1931, echoed the views of many in RI's leadership:

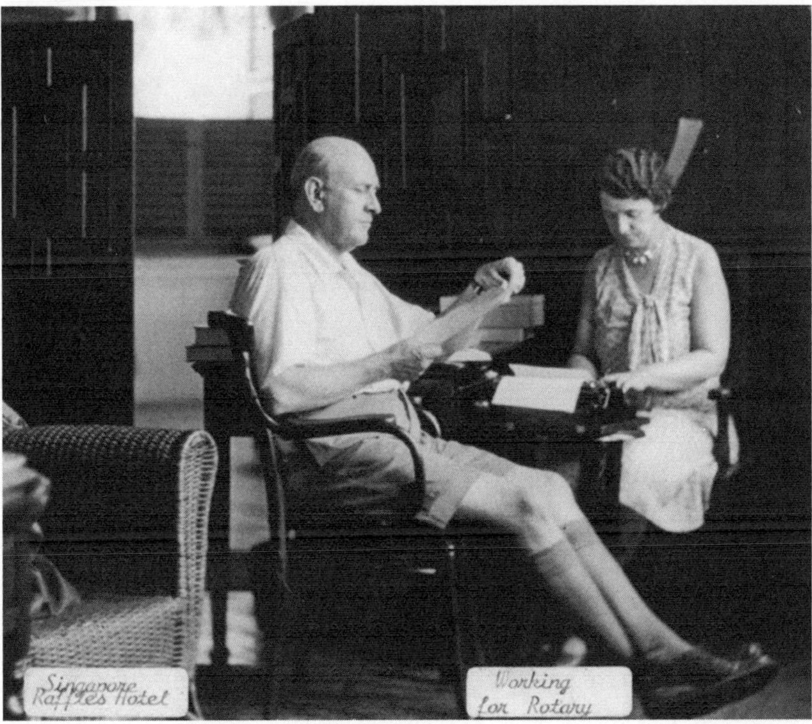

FIG 6.4: Jim and Lillian Dow Davidson working at the Raffles Hotel in Singapore. The couple not only brought the world of Rotary to Asia, they also helped introduce Rotary clubs to the world through Jim's reporting and Lillian's writing. *Courtesy of Rotary International.*

> When Rotary crossed the Atlantic and planted a seed in Great Britain, it set up the first milestone in its international progress. I think the second was the setting up of a club on the Continent of Europe. This ensured the future being really International, rather than almost entirely Anglo-Saxon.
>
> I believe that you have set up another milestone, possibly the greatest of all; you have established Rotary where races meet; you have established Rotary as a common meeting ground for those races; you have made Rotary international, inter-racial.
>
> By far the greatest task now awaiting us is to maintain and develop this pioneer work of yours.[109]

And Pascall was hardly alone in these sentiments. RI's board of directors and all its top officers from around the world eagerly anticipated Davidson's final report in Rotary's headquarters in Chicago, delivered to a standing-room-only crowd. Secretary Perry recounted how Davidson "first used a map of Asia to show us where he had been. Then he presented some of the difficulties which Rotary International must face in its program of extension in the Far East." Along with Davidson's difficulties, Perry and others also heard of "the tremendous opportunities . . . in this densely populated section of the world. Entrancing was the entire picture. . . . The friendships he has made, the mutual understandings he has helped to develop, the closer union of many different races—these are all a part of the intangible reward which is the greatest satisfaction that can come to a man."[110]

Combining a vision of civic uplift, community service, and citizenship development through the local Rotary club with the creation of an international network of business and professional peers defined Rotary's civic internationalism. Its creed promised non-US elites the world over full participation in emerging international markets while masking the growing hegemonic presence of the United States in those same markets. An open invitation was hard to resist. And its acceptance brought legitimacy both for Rotary and for its nation of origin.

But it was Lillian's writings in the *Rotarian* that magnified the effects of Jim's travels significantly in the minds of Main Street's denizens. Providing snapshots of Jim's organizing activities, summarizing his political and historical analyses, and describing the panoply of cultural and national differences encountered in their travels was all in a day's work for Lillian. As mediator and interpreter for RI's readership for more than two years, Lillian developed the linkage between the domestic and the abroad in crucial ways. The construction and expansion of US empire demanded a demystification of the exotic through a normalization of US cultural and economic presence in such distant environs. By the end of Lillian's series of articles in 1933, and in tandem with RI's editorial policies in general during the same period, the appearance of Rotary clubs in cities like Colombo, Jakarta, and Bangkok went from being shocking news to serving as an affirmation of RI's civic internationalism.

In the aftermath of the Davidsons' long travels, it seemed as if there was no part of the world beyond the reach of Rotary International. When it came to business, the world abroad was not so different from the American heartland after all. Or was it? As indomitable as Jim Davidson was in spirit, his body not could keep up. As a result, just as she had done during their three-year odyssey, Lillian spoke in his place at RI's annual convention in June 1932 in Seattle—home to Rotary's fourth club in the world, birthplace of Rotary's Platform on "ethical objectives" in business in 1911, and place of business for Rotarian Roger Pinneo, representative of the Pacific Mail Steamship Company and founder of Rotary clubs in Manila and Shanghai—the first in Asia—in 1919. Thus, in Seattle in 1932, Rotary's circumnavigation of the globe was finally coming together in several distinct ways. But, tasked yet again with providing a narrative summary of their accomplishments in distant lands, Lillian chose to speak instead in her own voice about what mattered most to her: "The women of Asia . . . [who] exert perhaps more influence than is generally believed." While regaling her audience of more than 5,000 Rotarians with her personal experiences and impressions of the women of Greece, Egypt, Syria, India, Ceylon, Burma, Malaya, Siam, China, and Japan, Lillian emphasized not only their distinct customs, cultures, and manner of dress, but also their presence and their agency. But in her description of their travels in Bali she drove home her point: "Bali is a paradise for women. Here the position of the sexes is just reversed. Father stays home, does the house work and feeds the babies on coconut milk while mother handles the money bags." Lillian's skillful narrative went beyond the mode of travelogue and the cultural observation of a privileged white woman in order to confront her massive audience of businessmen with the inversion of gender roles in Bali. Her lesson was clear: the fraternalism at the core of Rotary's civic internationalism was not necessarily the natural order of things. She then concluded her speech not with a celebration of Rotary's coming of age, but rather with a challenge: "No nation and no race has a monopoly of all that is good and desirable. None a monopoly of all the defects." Channeling the cultural anthropology of Margaret Mead and Ruth Benedict, Lillian was pushing Rotary to move beyond the gendered and racial limits of its business-class view of the world. Rotary's circumnavigation of the globe, Lillian implied, would require far more introspection than ever imagined.[111]

But so would the advent of the Great Depression and the rise of fascism. When the Davidsons had left for Europe and Asia in 1928, global trade was still trending upward while faith in the postwar international system remained relatively strong. Meanwhile, what had been only a handful of distant outposts in Asia in the early 1920s was emerging as a center of growth for Rotary thanks not only to the Davidsons but also to the work of many others, including Doug Howland, president of the Calgary Rotary club and long-time friend of Jim Davidson, and Sydney Pascall, the candy maker from London who traveled most of the world during his tenure as RI's president (1931–1932). While Howland "backtracked" Jim's travels in India, China, and Southeast Asia between 1932 and 1934, resulting in the formation of another fifteen Rotary clubs, other Rotarians throughout Asia continued to develop their own clubs and to establish new ones in nearby urban centers through their business and social networks, leading to the expansion of Rotary throughout most of Asia and the Pacific by 1940 (see map 3).[112] Though Jim Davidson is often referred to as the "Marco Polo" of Rotary, a more apropos comparison might be Paul the Apostle, as many of the clubs he founded led to the founding of many others, and many of his earliest converts to Rotarianism on several continents carried forth the gospel to great lengths. Put another way, the genealogies of hundreds if not thousands of Rotary clubs could be traced back to the efforts, resilience, and persuasive powers of Jim Davidson. Perhaps Sydney Pascall, in recounting his own travels through North America, Africa, and Asia at the same convention in Seattle, captured it best:

> Everywhere I went in the Middle East, Jim is known and honored. (Applause.) Indeed, he has almost become a tradition, grown into a cult. . . . The energy of that human dynamo. . . . the way in which he swept all who talked Rotary with him, even those hostile, into his net, answered their arguments, met their objections, removed their doubts, called them to a meeting and, as one of them said, "Before we knew where we were, informed us we were duly installed Rotarians, and with a pat on the back gave us a friendly push off on our Rotary career." . . . Rotary will

> never have a finer pioneer, a more tireless and persuasive missionary. (Applause.)[113]

And if anyone was in a position to know, it was Sydney Pascall, who, like Jim, traveled with his wife and teenage daughter over much of the same terrain. But being British and the first European president of RI, Pascall moved through the British Imperium—from Johannesburg to Nairobi to Bombay to Singapore to Christchurch—with virtual diplomatic status. That Pascall represented a US-based service club was of minimal concern for the many governor generals and other British imperial administrators he met and dined and conversed with during his travels. Instead, their interests centered on, for example, Rotary's facilitation of peaceful relations in India through "more of the friendly Rotary inter-racialism" and Rotary's capacity in the Malay peninsula to serve as "a rallying center of the four races that have to learn to live together."[114] For good reason, Sydney Pascall was chosen to introduce Lillian Dow Davidson in Seattle to the conventioneers. They were two sides of the same story—with Jim in the middle.

And yet the moment was a bittersweet mix of culmination and collapse. While many speeches, assemblies, reports, and publications at the convention celebrated the accomplishments and opportunities of Rotary, many others focused on the ravages of a deepening global depression and the threat it posed to Rotarians' understanding of capitalism as a moral way of life, let alone to their livelihoods and membership rolls. While Lillian and Sydney enthralled their audience with promising tales of far-off lands and peoples joining the world of Rotary in Asia and Africa, Rotary clubs in Europe were under increasing pressure from the rising tide of fascism—a different kind of capitalism. On 18 July 1933, six months after Adolf Hitler was named Chancellor of Germany, five months after Yosuke Matsuoka stormed out of the League of Nations, and two weeks after President Roosevelt torpedoed the World Economic Conference in London with his "bombshell message," Jim Wheeler Davidson, the "tireless and persuasive missionary" of Rotary, passed away in Vancouver at the age of 61. Would the civic internationalism he embodied and had devoted so much of his life to advance survive such great peril? It was certainly not clear to anyone in 1933. Nor would it be for many years to come.

CONCLUSION

From Here On!

Though tempered by the Great Depression, militarism, fascism, economic nationalism, and two world wars, RI's civic internationalism represented a constant movement toward greater international engagement between the American heartland and the lands abroad, between the world(s) of Main Street and emerging markets worldwide. In the name of inculcating civic cooperation in familiar, small-town terms while developing a transnational network of US and non-US business and professional classes, RI sought to position itself as a neutral mediator across national boundaries, racial divides, distinct cultures, and imperial systems, as an institutional bridge among "fellow" businessmen and professionals located in all the "commercial centers" of the world.

RI's civic internationalism stood apart from American missionary internationalism, because RI's approach was ultimately secular in purpose. RI also distinguished itself from large philanthropic foundations, because RI was much more middle-class in nature and collaborative in structure; from both transnational corporations and the US diplomatic corps, because RI was nonprofit in status; and from most INGOs, because of RI's global scale of operations among businessmen well before World War II. Sometimes patriotic in rhetoric, often quasi-religious in tone, and always managerial in approach, RI's civic internationalism operated as a form of Wilsonianism without the state long after the demise of Wilson's own postwar visions of international peace and security. Though plagued by the same racial fault lines, classist contradictions, and gendered inequalities as Wilson's worldview, Rotary International may perhaps be best understood as an important contributor to the "humanitarian awakening" of the early twentieth century as well as to postwar initiatives focused on human rights, modernization theories, state-driven cultural diplomacy, and global humanitarianism.[1]

By imagining and promoting transnational business and professional solidarities, RI opened up a social space for what I call the exotic peer: the economic citizen of today's global capitalism. First in its literature and then in practice, RI's headquarters in Chicago consistently strove to recruit as many prestigious recruits from the ranks of other nations' business and professional elites as possible. RI's civic internationalism also tacitly promised to streamline access to US markets for many of its members drawn from outside the United States and to provide similar access to non-US markets for US Rotarians and clubs seeking the same. For civic boosters worldwide, this was a compelling vision of reciprocity on all levels.

Through countless weekly meetings, constant waves of correspondence, and regular conferences and publications devoted to "international service" throughout even the smallest Rotary clubs in the American heartland, Rotary's civic internationalism defied the presumed "isolationism" of the interwar period—revealing a surprising and misleading inaccuracy to that historical term.[2] In aggregate, all these activities represented a growing awareness of world affairs and an openness to international engagement on the part of Rotarians and their local communities *both* inside and outside the United States even before World War I. Though Rotarians were boosters through and through, it would also be inaccurate to dismiss these initiatives and activities as merely the salesmanship of "promotionalists."[3] To be sure, Rotary International was just one tributary feeding into the rising tide of global community in the twentieth century, but RI's brand of civic internationalism managed to become part of the culture of thousands of small towns and urban centers throughout the United States, and in many other parts of the world as well, long before the outbreak of World War II.[4] At its core, there was—and still remains—an unusual degree of localism in Rotary's globalism.

THE WORLD AT WORK

But once the United States entered World War II, RI began to expand rapidly its commitment to a postwar international system anchored by the United Nations that seemed more in tune with its own longstanding vision of civic internationalism. To that end, Rotary unleashed a series of official publications on international matters with new pamphlets, booklets, radio scripts, and club activities centered on educating its quarter million membership in more than five thousand clubs on the possibilities of a peaceful postwar world (figure C.1). Much like Wendell Willkie's "One Worldism," these publications envisioned a postwar international system led by managerial elites drawn from international businessmen and undergirded by capitalist-friendly international institutions. To that end, wartime initiatives that later led to the formation of the United Nations, the United Nations Educational, Scientific and Cultural Organization (UNESCO), the Food and Agriculture Organization (FAO), the International Monetary Fund (IMF), the World Bank, the UN Relief and Rehabilitation Administration (UNRRA), the World Health Organization (WHO), and related international institutions regularly appeared in a favorable light in all of RI's publications starting in 1942 and continuing well into the 1950s. Moreover, these publications were often presented in coordination with ongoing local celebrations such as "United Nations Week" in clubs throughout the world and complemented with RI's monthly publication of *Report on the UN* (which ran from 1947 to 1952).

Given RI's long commitment to civic internationalism before the war, however, this effort came as no surprise to anyone familiar with the world of Rotary. In 1942, for example, the London Rotary Club—and its affiliated clubs in District 13—became a wartime sanctuary for thousands of European Rotarians living in exile during the war, including

FIG C.1: Rotary International eagerly embraced the postwar international system centered on the United Nations and the Bretton Woods system. RI published a series of booklets on the United Nations and related organizations while encouraging clubs to host "United Nations" events. *From Here On!* was the most successful of these publications, with at least 250,000 copies printed over four editions between 1945 and 1952. © *Rotary International. All Rights Reserved.*

many ministers, military officers, and diplomats. In anticipation of the war's end, the London Rotary club hosted a conference that same year on a peaceful postwar international system—a conference attended by officials, diplomats, and ministers from twenty-one separate governments-in-exile. In official literature sent out regularly to RI's thousands of clubs, RI was more than happy to feature these initiatives by the London Rotarians and to claim at least partial responsibility for what later developed into UNESCO after the war.[5]

In a similar vein, RI's formal presence at the UN Charter Conference in San Francisco in 1945 as an observer organization was understandably promoted as the culmination of RI's prewar vision of civic internationalism. As many as forty-nine individual Rotarians from twenty-nine different nations were present when RI became one of the original signatories to the UN Charter as a consultant organization.[6] RI still had active clubs in 32 of the 50 nations that signed the UN Charter. In the US delegation to the conference there were eleven active Rotarians, including Senator Warren Austin of Vermont, head of the US delegation and the first president of the Rotary club of Burlington, Vermont. Other national delegation leaders included Paul-Henri Spaak, member of the Brussels Rotary club, and first president of the General Assembly; Faris El-Khouri, founder of the Rotary club of Damascus and Syria's prime minister; Ricardo Alfaro, former president of Panama and that country's ambassador to the United States; and Carlos Romulo, former president of the Manila Rotary club (1935–1936) and third vice-president for RI (1937–1938).[7] In other words, along with the formal goals, initiatives, publications, and overall mass media push by RI in support of the UN and its related agencies in 1945, we also find hundreds of well-connected, internationally known representatives and statesmen who helped establish their international careers through their involvement in key positions at Rotary International and their "local" Rotary club in cities like Manila, Damascus, Madrid, Warsaw, Panama City, and London. In this regard, Rotary International was consistent in working to align itself (along with many of RI's key international members) with a postwar world centered on the formation and success of the United Nations and its many specialized agencies—so long as that postwar "machinery" remained friendly to the demands and expectations of RI's business-class membership and their commitment to global capitalism.

Consistently encouraging the "international service" activities of so many clubs, Rotary's headquarters in Chicago sought to inculcate a sense of ownership among its members in a postwar international system superior in design to the League of Nations and its affiliated institutions. Rotary's first real step in this direction was publication of *A World to Live In!*, a compilation of thirty articles by noted authors, intellectuals, and experts, including John Dewey, writing on "human nature"; Gandhi, with "Points for a New World Order"; Justice William Douglas, "The Dynamics of Democracy"; E. W. Kemmerer, "A Scientific Monetary System"; Cordell Hull, "Restore Trade, Promote Peace!"; and Henry Wallace, "Neighbors Working Together." Selected from RI's flagship monthly magazine, the *Rotarian*, which went out to the majority of RI's more than 200,000 members worldwide by 1940, this compilation's simple yet urgent purpose was stated in its foreword: "It is now becoming clear that the world-wide struggle is one to determine who shall shape the destiny of mankind. On the one side are the totalitarian powers, seeking to put the world under the social, political, military, and economic domination of so-called master races." And on the other side? "The national policies" set forth in the Atlantic Charter in August 1941, which is quoted in full. The foreword baldly states the challenge at hand: "The task of planning a post-war world may seem completely baffling, but one factor is definitely favorable: in spite of war's wide desolation, there is in this world a will-to-peace—a will to work, sacrifice, and fight for a just and durable peace."[8] Though not exactly programmatic in nature, the booklet was certainly urgent in its demand for a postwar system that could guarantee international peace and security through mutual collaboration—the very ideals of RI's civic internationalism. In a similar vein, RI published a second anthology, *Peace Is a Process*, before the war's end.

These two booklets became the springboard for three key postwar RI publications: *From Here On!* (1945), *In the Minds of Men* (1946), and *The World at Work* (1949). All three publications proved to be highly successful in advancing RI's central goal of educating its worldwide membership on the pivotal role of the United Nations in any peaceful postwar world. But by far the most popular and transformative was *From Here On!* There were many reasons for the booklet's enduring impact. First, the focus is on the UN Charter itself: "Here is the proclaimed basis of the Peace and Security for which we have striven and fought." The UN Charter, although much heralded in this booklet, "is only an instrument . . . it is the grave responsibility of the free peoples themselves to put the instrument into effective use, in so far as they believe in it." In contrast to the lofty rhetoric of Wilsonianism and the great expectations of the League of Nations, *From Here On!* conditions an enduring peace on the active support of an informed public. Second, instead of drawing from the pages of RI's monthly magazine and featuring the writings of noted writers and experts on how they imagine a postwar world, *From Here On!* offers the reader a simple, structured layout designed to allow both individuals and entire Rotary clubs to engage with each article and paragraph of the UN Charter. It was meant to be a living document, to be the focal point for weekly club meetings, guest speakers, and conferences. To that end, all even-numbered pages on the left present the exact text of the UN Charter, from its preamble to its "ratification and signature," while all odd-numbered pages on the right provide two columns "in order to explain some of the official wording" and "to formulate thought and discussion about the articles" on the opposite page. Third, in the back of the booklet, RI provides detailed advice in a section titled "How to Use This Booklet," a suggested bibliography for further reading, and a glossary of key terms. Much like the UN Declaration of Human Rights of 1948, it would be hard to find a better blend of hard-won idealism and pragmatism.

While it is impossible to gauge just how much impact this booklet had at the local level, there were at least four reprinted editions between 1945 and 1952, totaling approximately 250,000 copies in all during that seven-year run. Within weeks of its first run, the booklet was already receiving high praise from all directions, including from many US senators and members of Congress, the US government, and various officers and administrators at the United Nations, including Warren Austin of Vermont, a senator and subsequently the US ambassador to the UN, and Secretary of State James Byrnes. In fact, the Division of Public Liaison at the US Department of State sent a list of organizations to RI that "have shown particular interest in international affairs," suggesting that RI send copies of *From Here On!* to all those organizations, as well as to the other forty-one consultant organizations that signed the UN Charter along with RI.[9] Based on decades of experience developing its vision of civic internationalism, RI managed to publish a booklet that seemed to outpace even the best efforts of the US government to sell the United Nations to its own citizenry.

Nor was this praise limited to the US government and the United Nations. For example, John Slawson, executive vice president of the American Jewish Committee, wrote to Philip Lovejoy, general secretary of Rotary International, in early 1946, "I have looked through [*From Here On!*] carefully and I consider it one of the finest things of its kind that I have seen. I am particularly impressed by the intelligent support that you give to those sections of the Charter that look to the effective international guarantee of the fundamental human rights throughout the world."[10] Similar high marks came in unsolicited from the American Federation of Teachers, which sent copies to all members of its National Executive Council; the National Council of Negro Women, which recommended the booklet "to our affiliated organizations to be used as a study guide"; the National Council of Women of the United States, which also sent copies to all of the organization's national officers; and many other voluntary organizations.[11] *From Here On!* had more than fulfilled its primary purpose: the demystification and popularization of the UN Charter through local club activities throughout the United States and, indeed, much of the world.[12]

But what happened to Rotary's sweeping internationalist aspirations for a peaceful postwar order? How did RI's stream of publications, programs, and activities translate into the language of Main Street in the cold war era? Put another way, how was the civic internationalism of places like Granite City, Illinois, faring two decades after that club's popular exhibit on world trade and harmony? Even as the cold war deepened in the wake of the Truman Doctrine, the Berlin Blockade, the "loss" of China, the advent of a nuclear-armed Soviet Union, and the outbreak of hostilities in Korea, many Rotary clubs both inside and outside the US were still celebrating "UN Weeks" and still requesting pro-UN copies of RI publications well into the 1950s. There was no sudden turn against the UN in the world of Rotary, in other words, during the early cold war period. Instead, despite the growing anxieties of the early cold war, RI's international growth accelerated over the postwar era while the Rotary

Foundation—RI's philanthropic arm—began to rapidly increase its size and scale of operations after 1947.[13] In the postwar environment, Rotary's global mission became more complicated, but also more wide-ranging and sophisticated. Always resonant with mainstream, middlebrow culture in North America, US Rotary clubs had little trouble recruiting from and communicating with the growing ranks of organization men in their grey flannel suits during the 1950s.[14]

THE SOFT SELL OF A SUPERPOWER

Alongside RI's commitment to the success of the United Nations ran an even deeper commitment to its ideology of service. True to the vibrant print culture of Rotary's past, the July 1954 edition of the *Rotarian* reveals the overlapping and evolving complexities of RI's civic internationalism in the early cold war era. On the growing tensions between national chain stores with local retail merchants, J. C. Penney, "noted merchandising executive and Rotarian," argues against "the delusion that competition is a dog-eat-dog fight for a limited amount of business, essentially an attitude of the 19th Century" and in favor of "the competitor who profits most because he serves best." Turn the page and one finds Henry Cabot Lodge Jr., US Representative to the UN in 1954, providing his own insights on the central role of the United Nations as "the greatest sounding board in the world" and "a place where the free world gets consolidated," followed by a long debate between Kermit Eby, sociologist at the University of Chicago, and DeWitt Emery, founder and president of the National Small Business Men's Association and syndicated columnist in over 3,000 small-town newspapers, on whether there should be a "guaranteed annual wage." Finally, a few pages further, one encounters excerpts from Secretary of State John Foster Dulles's speech at RI's annual international convention held in Seattle in early June, wherein he claims that "the founders of this nation breathed into it a sense of mission. They called on our people to show others, by conduct and example, that a free society could produce good fruits." The juxtaposition of articles and authors is instructive, for it is in this context that the *Rotarian* introduces Herbert J. Taylor, the incoming international president for 1954–1955, Rotary's fiftieth anniversary.[15]

Herbert Taylor was a judicious but also revealing choice. Although the annual election of Rotary's international president from its upper echelons was always a strategic matter, RI was seeking someone who embodied particularly well both the small-town mores of Rotary's brand of Main Street as well as the modern world of international business—much like Paul Harris, Rotary's founder, had done until his passing in 1947. Taylor filled the bill quite well. Born in 1893 in Pickford, Michigan, a small town in the Upper Peninsula of Michigan, Taylor came from a family of successful farmers and businessmen with pioneering roots in both the US and Canada. Neither too rich nor too poor, "Herb's upbringing . . . was pretty typical of Middlewestern, turn-of-the-century, small-town America."[16] But Herb's family had long experience not only with early homesteading and the transformation of an outer settlement into a small commercial center, but also with frontier evangelicalism. As local merchants, the Taylors founded the electric and telephone companies, managed a local bank, and owned and operated multiple retail outlets, ranging from dry-goods to shoes to the grocery store. But as lay leaders in the Pickford Methodist church, the Taylors also had a significant community presence. Little wonder that, after his own personal conversion experience as a teenager, Herb Taylor saw his family's business activities and religious identities as a seamless whole. For the Taylors, there was simply no daylight between capitalism and Christianity.[17]

After working his way through Northwestern University, Taylor served as a relief worker for the YMCA in France just before the United States entered the war in 1917—an international experience with life-long impact. During the war, Taylor left the "Y" to serve as Lieutenant in the US Navy Supply Corps, providing him with crucial experience in the logistical management of military resources and personnel. In the war's aftermath, Taylor returned to the YMCA to serve in a similar capacity. Taylor's managerial success in France "secured his future in the business world," as one historian put it, because it led to a major life decision for the young man and devoted Christian: either commit to a career in the YMCA—a natural choice, given his religious fervor—or enter the world of business. Taylor chose to take a position offered up through his business contacts with the Sinclair Oil Company of Oklahoma, where an oil boom was occurring. For Herb Taylor, however, this was not a stark choice between a religious and secular calling. In fact, returning to the United States, getting married, moving to a small town in rural Oklahoma, and setting down roots in a commercial outpost amidst a booming new industry had its own familiar logic for Taylor, who now defined his entire business career as a function of Christian outreach and community uplift. In short order, Taylor helped establish the Wynnewood Rotary club of Oklahoma, a natural extension of both his business and religious endeavors. A few years later, taking advantage of other business contacts made during his time in France, the Taylors returned to the Chicago area, where Taylor became vice-president for the Jewel Tea Co. and joined the Chicago Rotary Club. While Taylor moved up the "corporate ladder" of Rotary by becoming club president (1939), district governor (1941), international director (1944), vice-president (1945), and eventually international president by 1954, he made a very different and risky decision in 1932 to leave his comfortable job at Jewel Tea Co. to become an investor in and head of the Club Aluminum Company, a debt-ridden producer and seller of aluminum cookware based in Chicago. Soon after taking the reins of Club Aluminum, Taylor had an epiphany that he came to identify over time as the reason for his company's turnaround: "The Four-Way Test."

1) Is it the truth?
2) Is it fair to all concerned?
3) Will it build goodwill and better friendships?
4) Will it be beneficial to all concerned?

Distilled into four basic questions, Herb Taylor had devised a kind of litmus test for best business practices in sales, advertising, client relations, labor-management relations, and production value that was secular, ecumenical, and pragmatic in approach but, in Herb Taylor's mind, also thoroughly Christian in principle. Redolent of the plain speech traditions of the nineteenth century and in line with the truth-in-advertising campaigns of the twentieth, the "Four-Way Test" expressed Taylor's belief in the unity of evangelicalism and commercialism forged in the rugged terrain of Michigan's Upper Peninsula; developed in wartime France through the YMCA and the US Navy, sharpened in the oil fields and civic clubs of rural Oklahoma, and now put into practice in the cut-throat business world of Depression-era Chicago. During the most severe testing of capitalism as a way of life in modern history, Herb Taylor believed he had come across a formula for success that was faithful to his small-town Christian beliefs as well as profitable for his company and its 250 employees. As a moral compass, Taylor's Four-Way Test guided the survival and growth of the company, proving its universal validity and durability not only for his company but also for American capitalism. For Taylor, neither FDR's New Deal nor World War II saved capitalism. Rather, it saved America.[18]

It would be hard to overstate the importance of the Four-Way Test to Rotary International. Formally adopted in 1943, the test became the preferred articulation of Rotary's Progressive-era code of ethics in the postwar era. When Taylor donated the copyright to RI in 1954, the Four-Way Test was already becoming a familiar trope in public schools, religious gatherings, poster / essay contests, and local media throughout the United States due in large part to the boosterism of thousands of local Rotary clubs. But it also took root in many other nations, particularly Japan, during the period. Translated into over one hundred different languages, reproduced constantly in thousands of publications and plaques, and still recited at weekly Rotary meetings worldwide, Herb Taylor's Four-Way Test has effectively evolved into a transnational creed for business: pragmatic in scope, managerial in approach, ecumenical in tone, universal in application. Coupled with Rotary's "Four Avenues of Service"—Club, Vocational, Community, and International, Taylor's Four-Way Test became the postwar distillation of RI's service ideology worldwide and an essential component of its postwar iteration of civil religion.[19]

For Taylor's business evangelicalism, however, creating and maintaining the civic soul of America was not only a sacred calling, but also a cold war priority. Likening himself to John Wanamaker, "America's greatest merchant," Taylor ultimately understood his success in business as a form of Christian witness in modern times as well as a means to many ends. From his devotion to teaching Sunday school in suburban Chicago to his constant donation of money and expertise to the National Association of Evangelicals, Christian Workers' Foundation, Fuller Theological Seminary, the Chicago Evangelism Institute, the InterVarsity Christian Fellowship, and the Billy Graham Crusades, Taylor embodied both the modernist and internationalist impulse of business evangelicalism long before its supposed re-emergence in the 1970s as part of the New Right and in the 1980s of the Reagan Revolution. Taylor's life-long involvement in Rotary was simply one aspect of that greater calling. But so was his devotion to patriotic support of his native land, especially in a time of war. Working as a "dollar-a-year" man during World War II, Taylor also served as Vice-Chairman of the Price Adjustment Board of the US War Department. Little wonder that, speaking only moments after Secretary of State Dulles at the Seattle convention in 1954, he proclaimed his belief in prayer as "the answer to all of the world's problems" and that "if our free nations are to resist successfully the growth of godless Communism, we must become morally and spiritually strong." To that end, Taylor proposed in his address an additional test to his famous Four-Way Test: the citizenship test. Built on ten premises rather than four questions, Taylor's definition of citizenship sounded like a Sunday-school lesson on Christian virtues as well as a handbook on civics and civility. Though Taylor's citizenship test never caught on like his other test (it was much longer and harder to remember and translate), it did capture well the official culture of cold war America: the embrace of religious pluralism, the assertion of hardline anti-communism, and the celebration of manly virtue rising to the occasion. For both Rotary International and the "free world" that comprised its field of operations, Taylor merged the evangelical, corporate, and civic cultures of America under the shadow of cold war exigency.[20]

By the 1970s, however, just as Rotary International's membership outside the United States began to exceed its membership within the United States, Paul Harris's old formula for successful club life began to feel increasingly outdated and out-of-step with the new rhythms of social and political change in America. Consequently, the postwar era meant both opportunity and closure for Rotary International. In the face of rising consumerist values at the expense of civic culture; looming doubts about any national mission amid oil crises, Watergate, and post-Vietnam malaise; and increasing alternatives to the sociability of club life and the wholesome, breadwinner masculinity at its core, Rotary's appeal began to wane in the United States. With consistent international growth masking declining membership in the United States, the challenge was clear: "[RI] must give attention to the developing character of the organization in a wide variety of countries spread around the world."[21] While RI opened up a new Secretariat in New Delhi, India, in 1982 as a part of this initiative, the deeper issue of racial limits on club membership—present at the creation of Rotary—still remained formally unresolved. As RI's incoming president in 1982, Hiroji Mukasa of Nakatsu, Japan, put the annual convention—held in Dallas that year—in historical light by recounting the story of Kisoji Fukushima's introduction of Umekichi Yoneyama to the world of Rotary in 1918 and the pivotal role of the Dallas Rotary club, "the mother of Japan's Rotary," in helping establish the first club in Tokyo in 1920. Just as in Dallas in 1929, it seemed as if RI had come to a triumphant, full circle. But had it come full circle? Since the Rotary club of Birmingham, Alabama had been formed before 1922, its club constitution still contained "a racially restrictive provision." In contrast, "the vast majority of the 19,600 Rotary clubs of 157 nations of the world contained no racially restrictive provisions, as is evident by the many colors, races, and creeds represented at this convention." Sixty years after the adoption of a standard, race-blind club constitution, the legacies of Jim Crow and racial capitalism persisted in the fine print of some early Rotary clubs—if not in more covert, systemic forms as well. But in June 1982 in Dallas, RI chose to deal with at least the fine print: that many "on our Board of Directors" as well as president-elect Mukasa, "could not qualify as members of any club in the Rotary world" was an intolerable contradiction in need of immediate remedy. The more than 13,000 conventioneers were then asked to vote on Enactment 82-2, thus "assuring Rotary and the world that there is no place in Rotary for any vestige or form of racial discrimination." Concern of RI's public image, it turned out, was a driving force in this long-overdue and formally unanimous amendment to its Constitution and By-laws.[22]

But another challenge—a very old and crucial one—also erupted during consideration of Enactment 82-2 in Dallas. During the floor debate, one Rotarian proposed the insertion of the word "sex" as well, "so that we might take this to a natural conclusion, that we are no longer a discriminatory organization." After the "chorus of protest" had died down, it was argued as a point of order that, since the word "male" was embedded in RI's constitution, it would have to be dealt with at the next Council on Legislation in 1983. As noted already, there was a long and complicated history behind that brief floor proposal.[23] But, contrary to the voices of protest, change was imminent. In 1977, in response to dwindling membership, the tiny Duarte Rotary club of California took a bold step: it formally accepted three women as new members. Since 1921, Rotary's standard club constitution and by-laws had precluded any women as club members. Since Rotary International had consistently shut down many prior attempts at incorporating women into its ranks (by clubs much larger and more powerful than that of Duarte), it came as no surprise that RI rejected their memberships as well. But RI revoked the club's charter in 1978. Undaunted, the Duarte club renamed itself "the Ex-Rotary Club of Duarte" and filed suit with the California Superior Court against RI's Board of Directors. After the court sided with RI in 1983, the Duarte club then appealed to the California State Court of Appeals, which reversed the lower court's decision. Now it was RI's turn to appeal to the California Supreme Court, which refused to hear the case. By 1986, the case finally made it to the US Supreme Court. By this time, other Rotary clubs were joining Duarte—"the mouse that roared"—in its challenge to RI's deep-seated tradition of gender discrimination. On 4 May 1987, in *Board of Directors, Rotary International v. Rotary Club of Duarte,* 481 U.S. 537 (1987), the US Supreme Court ruled that California's Unruh Act, which precluded discrimination according to sex, did not violate the First Amendment rights of Rotarians by requiring that California Rotary clubs admit women as members. Since club meetings typically allowed non-members to attend and female members would in no way block the functioning of the organization, Justice Powell argued for the unanimous court that the state's "compelling interest" in ending sexual discrimination trumped Rotarians' right to limit membership to men only. The decision opened the doors for US Rotary clubs to admit women and for many more outside the US as well. But the court had no jurisdiction outside the United States, the result being that there are still countries where women cannot join their local Rotary club.[24]

Put simply, ending gendered discrimination has transformed Rotary International not only by adding new lifeblood to US membership rolls, but also by reinvigorating and expanding RI's civic internationalism into, arguably, a twenty-first century form of global humanitarianism. In the end, the Chicago Rotary club's first awkward forays into civic reforms in 1907 sent the men's private social club down a long and winding road of civic engagement and public outreach, with a plethora of unintended consequences. While limitations on membership based on race were often muted, especially after 1921, discrimination according to gender was celebrated and stoutly defended by RI for most of the twentieth century. Fraternalism, it seemed, was as crucial to Rotary as the professional status and business reputations of its members—until the US Supreme Court said otherwise. What had been unimaginable for so many in 1921—the inclusion of women as equal partners in both club life and professional circles—has become a priority for RI a century later. Indeed, Rotary without women in its ranks would now be unimaginable. But with women still composing only 23 percent of a worldwide membership of 1.2 million and only recently breaking into the highest echelons of RI's governance (including Jennifer E. Jones, RI's president-elect for 2022), it is clear that some legacies of RI's gender discrimination remain.[25]

Meanwhile, even though RI experienced an extended second wave of overall international growth in the postwar era, Rotary's civic internationalism increasingly fell under the shadow of a national security umbrella and a permanent war economy with global reach.[26] The flow of ideas, norms, and practices within the world of Rotary thus began moving away from a middle ground for international engagement toward the gravitational pull of rising US global hegemony—even as the proportion of non-US membership continued to grow. The fates of Japanese, German, Chinese, and Cuban Rotary clubs in the postwar era demonstrate well the opposite ends of this fundamental change in international relations: key postwar US allies once again reemerged as major growth centers for Rotary clubs (Germany and Japan), while new communist states permanently shut down long-established Rotary clubs soon after communist parties came to power (China and Cuba). While Rotary clubs had precarious and ultimately adversarial relations with fascist states in the 1930s, communism was always anathema to Rotary. In fact, given Rotarians' commitment to market-based economic systems and institutional links with global capitalism, Rotary clubs became reliable markers of Western cultural, political, and economic influence, as evidenced by the rapid growth of Rotary clubs in Eastern Europe and Russia after 1991. Though still a nonstate actor formally independent of the US government and its agencies, Rotary International had become a de facto ally in America's cold war. Given Rotary's devotion to capitalism as a way of life, no other outcome was possible.

At the same time, while decolonization continued to unfold throughout the world, many business and professional elites in commercial centers of former European colonies found in Rotary International a willing partner and a useful entrée into transnational networks peopled with business and social counterparts. Social networking can pay off just as much in Jakarta in 1955 or in Mumbai today as it did in Chicago in 1905. For example, though relatively small in numbers before World War II, RI's presence in the Asian subcontinent served as a transitional medium from British imperial administration to postwar independence. As a result, Indian Rotary clubs began to grow in numbers after 1947, eventually becoming one of the densest concentrations of clubs outside the United States—almost 3,900 clubs in 2020—as well as important financial contributors to RI's many philanthropic projects. For Jim and Lillian Dow Davidson—and for all those who supported and followed their travels through Asia—this would be a fantastic dream come true. As of 2020, Rotary clubs number more than 36,000 and are found in almost every country in the world.[27] When joined by some 200,000 members of Rotaract clubs, the world of Rotary encompasses about 1.4 million members in total. With an institutional footprint in so many cities and nations throughout the world, Rotary International has demonstrated that one of the most effective means of soft power during "the American century" has been the soft sell of a service club.

NOTES

ACKNOWLEDGMENTS

INDEX

NOTES

INTRODUCTION

1. *Rotarian,* September 1929, 40. For details on the club's entire history, see "Granite City, Illinois Rotary Club," Club historical files, Rotary International Archives, Evanston, Illinois (hereafter "RI Archives").

2. For the most recent examination of RI in an international context, see Victoria de Grazia, *Irresistible Empire: America's Advance through Twentieth-Century Europe* (Cambridge, MA: Harvard University Press, 2005), chap. 1, which contrasts the Duluth and Dresden Rotary clubs as a way to demonstrate the slow takeover of European bourgeois culture by US consumer culture. For the only complete treatment of service clubs in academic literature, see Jeffrey A. Charles, *Service Clubs in American Society: Rotary, Kiwanis, and Lions* (Urbana: University of Illinois Press, 1993). Though Charles devotes only one chapter to the international dimensions of these organizations, he focuses on service clubs in general within the domestic narrative of twentieth-century US history. My emphasis on the internationalism of Rotary clubs in their own right and as a means to investigating closely how they were representative (or not) of broader trends in US cultural and economic expansion distinguishes the scope and character of Charles's work from this work in significant ways. See also Emily Rosenberg, *Spreading the American Dream: American Economic and Cultural Expansion* (New York: Hill and Wang, 1982), 108–112, and Thomas A. Wikle, "International Expansion of the American-Style Service Club," *Journal of American Culture* 22, no. 2 (1999): 45–52. Two fundamental studies of Rotary International in its first thirty years are Charles F. Marden, *Rotary and Its Brothers: An Analysis and Interpretation of the Men's Service Clubs* (Princeton,

NJ: Princeton University Press, 1935) and the University of Chicago Social Science Survey Committee, *Rotary? A University Group Looks at the Rotary Club of Chicago* (Chicago: University of Chicago Press, 1934). The latter provides much detail about the first decades of the Chicago club, especially its rapid transition from an initial emphasis on business profit through networking with potential business clients to a civic-minded service club of businessmen and professionals bent on serving the community. See also Harold Bahlke, "Rotary and American Culture—A Historical Study of Ideology" (PhD diss., University of Minnesota, 1956), for a close analysis of RI's convention proceedings during its first fifty years from the perspective of the emergence of the middle classes in the United States. Two good, comprehensive histories of RI are David C. Forward, *A Century of Service: The Story of Rotary International* (Evanston, IL: Rotary International, 2003), and David Shelley Nicholl, *The Golden Wheel: The Story of Rotary, 1905 to the Present* (Plymouth, UK: MacDonald and Evans, 1984).

3. There is a growing literature on the history of the phrase "American exceptionalism." One of the most useful examinations of the phrase can be found in Michael Adas, "From Settler Colony to Global Hegemon: Integrating the Exceptionalist Narrative of the American Experience into World History," *American Historical Review* 106, no. 5 (December 2001), 1692–1720, along with Daniel T. Rodgers, "Exceptionalism," in *Imagined Histories: American Historians Interpret the Past,* ed. Anthony Molho and Gordon S. Wood (Princeton, NJ: Princeton University Press, 1998), 21–40.

4. "The Growth of Rotary," in *Convention Proceedings, Twentieth Annual International Convention,* Dallas, Texas, 27–31 May 1929, 6.

5. This long-term periodization of the Progressive Era up to 1940 rather than 1920 follows Daniel T. Rodgers's approach in *Atlantic Crossings* and allows for a continuity between that era and postwar discourses on and institutions for human rights. For a similar approach to periodization of international relations of the United States, see Charles Bright and Michael Geyer, "Where in the World Is America?: The History of the United States in the Global Age," in *Rethinking American History in a Global Age,* ed. Thomas Bender (Berkeley: University of California Press, 2002), 63–99. Within the historical literature on Rotary International, Jeffrey Charles used the term "Ideal of Service" in *Service Clubs in American Society,* while de Grazia preferred "Service Ethos" in *Irresistible Empire.* Meanwhile, Roland Marchand identified the same social and ideological formation as "the Service Ideal" in *Creating the Corporate Soul: The Rise of Public Relations and Corporate Imagery in American Big Business* (Berkeley: University of California Press, 1998), chap. 5, 164–201.

6. The term "middle ground" is meant to reference the interpretive model used in Richard White, *The Middle Ground: Indians, Empires, and Republics in the Great Lakes Region, 1650–1815* (New York: Cambridge University Press, 1991).

7. See Frank Costigliola, *Awkward Dominion: American Political, Economic, and Cultural Relations with Europe, 1919–1933* (Ithaca, NY: Cornell University Press, 1984); Rosenberg, *Spreading the American Dream*, and Emily S. Rosenberg, *Financial Missionaries to the World: The Politics and Culture of Dollar Diplomacy, 1900–1930* (Cambridge, MA: Harvard University Press, 1999).

8. On the central role of NGOs in this context, see Akira Iriye, *Cultural Internationalism and World Order* (Baltimore: Johns Hopkins University Press, 1997), and *Global Community: The Role of International Organizations in the Making of the Contemporary World* (Berkeley, CA: University of California Press, 2002).

9. A charter member of the Washington, D.C., Rotary club in 1912, John Poole, Rotary's president for 1919–1920, also established and ran his own bank, Federal National Bank of Washington D.C., from 1913 to 1933, when he founded the American Company, "a financial and business firm." Poole also served as an officer on many other professional and civic organizations: the National Red Cross, the Young Men's Christian Association (YMCA), the Columbia Institution for the Deaf, and the Advertising Club of Washington, D.C. (for which he served as president). He was chairman of five Liberty Loan campaigns and a trustee of the American University. Altogether, Poole embodied the ideal Rotarian. *Paul Harris and His Successors: Profiles in Leadership* (Evanston, IL: Rotary International, 1997), 37–38. As the incoming president for Rotary in 1919, he spoke to the international convention with a Wilsonian faith in a new, postwar order: "Our boundaries have stretched far out. France has felt the enlivening touch of Rotary; Cuba has been peacefully invaded; Uruguay is the pioneer in South America; China has led off in the Orient; and the far-off Fiji Islands now acclaim a new star of social and business promise. The International Association of Rotary Clubs has fairly won its title, for the sun never sets on Rotarians." *Convention Proceedings of the Ninth Annual International Convention of the I.A.R.C.*, Salt Lake City, Utah, August 1919, 23.

10. For a comprehensive examination of the evolution and centrality of the professional classes within the context of Great Britain during this period, see Harold Perkin, *The Rise of Professional Society, England since 1880*, 2nd ed. (London: Routledge, 2002) and on the emergence of the League of Nations, see Margaret MacMillan, *Paris 1919: Six Months That Changed the World* (New York: Random House, 2003).

11. There is now a vibrant and growing body of scholarship on the political, economic, and cultural complexities of internationalist institutions, movements, and trends during the interwar period and their postwar legacies, including Robert D. Johnson, *The Peace Progressives and American Foreign Relations* (Cambridge, MA: Harvard University Press, 1995); Alan Dawley, *Changing the World: American Progressives in War and Revolution* (Princeton, NJ: Princeton University Press, 2003); Brooke Blower, *Becoming Americans in Paris: Transatlantic Politics and Culture between the World Wars* (Oxford: Oxford University Press, 2011); Julia Irwin, *Making the World Safe: The American Red Cross and a Nation's Humanitarian Awakening* (Oxford: Oxford University Press, 2013); Marian Moser Jones, *The American Red Cross: From Clara Barton to the New Deal* (Baltimore: Johns Hopkins University Press, 2012); Michael G. Thompson, *For God and Globe: Christian Internationalism in the United States between the Great War and the Cold War* (Ithaca, NY: Cornell University Press, 2015); Tony Smith, *Why Wilson Matters: The Origin of Liberal Internationalism and Its Crisis Today* (Princeton, NJ: Princeton University Press, 2017); Mischa Honeck, *Our Frontier is the World: The Boy Scouts in the Age of American Ascendancy* (Ithaca, NY: Cornell University Press, 2018); Benjamin Allen Coates, *Legalist Empire: International Law and American Foreign Relations in the Early Twentieth Century* (Oxford: Oxford University Press, 2016), and most recently Stephen Wertheim, *Tomorrow, the World: The Birth of U.S. Global Supremacy* (Cambridge, MA: Harvard University Press, 2020).

12. Thomas Bender, *A Nation Among Nations: America's Place in World History* (New York: Hill and Wang, 2007), 7. For a helpful overview of the topic, see *Internationalisms: A Twentieth-Century History*, ed. Glenda Sluga and Patricia Clavin (Cambridge: Cambridge University Press, 2017), and Glenda Sluga, *Internationalism in the Age of Nationalism* (Philadelphia: University of Pennsylvania Press, 2013).

13. For a good review of the origins and history of the term "heartland," see Frank Tobias Higbie, "Heartland: The Politics of a Regional Signifier," *Middle West Review* 1, no. 1 (Fall 2014), 81–90. Kristin Hoganson notably explores this aspect of the emergence of US ascendance in *The Heartland: An American History* (New York: Penguin Press, 2019).

14. As we shall see in later chapters, the communications and transportation infrastructure built on a global scale between the American Civil War and World War I—transoceanic cable lines, railroad networks, shipping lines, ports and harbors—greatly enhanced the possibilities for planning out international travel and for administering Rotary clubs and the social networks they embodied on a global scale. On the emergence of these global circuits of commerce and communications, see Emily S. Rosenberg, Akira Iriye, and Jürgen

Osterhammel, eds., *A World Connecting: 1870–1945* (Cambridge, MA: Belknap Press, 2012), and Dwayne R. Winseck and Robert M. Pike, eds., *Communication and Empire: Media, Markets, and Globalization, 1860–1930* (Durham, NC: Duke University Press, 2007).

15. First formulated at the sixth annual convention of Rotary clubs in San Francisco in 1915 and then, after two decades of evolution, named the "Fourth Object" of Rotary International in Mexico City in 1935, this "ideal of service" has been the pillar of RI's international mission and has essentially been worded in this manner ever since, with the gender-neutral language "persons" added only after membership opened up for women as a result of a US Supreme Court decision in 1987: *Board of Directors, Rotary International v. Rotary Club of Duarte,* 481 U.S. 537 (1987).

16. "A Rotary Review of Events," *Rotarian,* September 1929, 6–7, and Helena Weatherly, "The Women of Rotary: What Are Women Doing to Promote World Peace?" *Rotarian,* November 1929, 52–55.

17. For an important analysis from this perspective, see Erez Manela, *The Wilsonian Moment: Self-Determination and the International Origins of Anticolonial Nationalism* (Oxford: Oxford University Press, 2007).

18. Important monographs using this approach include James T. Kloppenberg, *Uncertain Victory: Social Democracy and Progressivism in European and American Thought, 1870–1920* (New York: Oxford University Press, 1986); Paul Gilroy, *The Black Atlantic: Modernity and Double Consciousness* (Cambridge, MA: Harvard University Press, 1993); Ian Tyrrell, *Woman's World / Woman's Empire: The Woman's Christian Temperance Union in International Perspective, 1800–1930* (Chapel Hill: University of North Carolina Press, 1991); Rosenberg, *Spreading the American Dream* and *Financial Missionaries to the World;* Matthew Jacobson, *Barbarian Virtues: The United States Encounters Foreign Peoples at Home and Abroad, 1876–1917* (New York: Hill and Wang, 2000); Dawley, *Changing the World;* Daniel T. Rodgers, *Atlantic Crossings: Social Politics in a Progressive Age* (Cambridge, MA: Belknap, 1998); Iriye, *Cultural Internationalism and World Order* and *Global Community;* Jessica C. E. Gienow-Hecht and Frank Schumacher, eds., *Culture and International History* (New York: Berghahn Books, 2003); Robert Rydell and Rob Kroes, *Buffalo Bill in Bologna: the Americanization of the World, 1869–1922* (Chicago: University of Chicago Press, 2005); Amy Kaplan, *The Anarchy of Empire in the Making of U.S. Culture* (Cambridge, MA: Harvard University Press, 2002); Penny Von Eschen, *Race Against Empire: Black Americans and Anticolonialism, 1937–1957* (Ithaca, NY: Cornell University Press, 1997); de Grazia, *Irresistible Empire;* Kristin Hoganson, *Consumers' Imperium: The Global*

Production of American Domesticity, 1865–1920 (Chapel Hill: University of North Carolina Press, 2007); Aims McGuinness, *Path of Empire: Panama and the California Gold Rush* (Ithaca, NY: Cornell University Press, 2008); and Matthew Connelly, *Fatal Misconception: The Struggle to Control World Population* (Cambridge, MA: Belknap, 2008).

19. Ian Tyrrell, *Transnational Nation: United States History in Global Perspective since 1789* (New York: Palgrave Macmillan, 2007). For a useful examination from several perspectives of the value and meaning of the term "transnational" and its methodological applications, see C. A. Bayly, Sven Beckert, Matthew Connelly, et al., "*AHR* Conversation: On Transnational History," *American Historical Review* 111, no. 5 (December 2006), 1441–1446, and Akira Iriye, "The Transnational Turn," *Diplomatic History* 31, no. 3 (June 2007), 373–376. For an examination of the corporate culture of tobacco firms from this perspective, see Nan Enstad, *Cigarettes, Inc.: An Intimate History of Corporate Imperialism* (Chicago: University of Chicago Press, 2018), and on the impact of transnational reformist movements on the United States, see Marilyn Lake, *Progressive New World: How Settler Colonialism and Transpacific Exchange Shaped American Reform* (Cambridge, MA: Harvard University Press, 2019).

20. Iriye, "The Transnational Turn," 373–376. See also Ian Tyrrell, "American Exceptionalism in an Age of International History," *American Historical Review* 96, no. 4 (October 1991), 1031–1055, and Michael J. Hogan, who called for a closer examination of "non-state actors . . . to include ethnic, racial, religious, and women's groups, as well as business and labor organizations . . . the role of international institutions, from multinational corporations, to UN agencies, to the International Red Cross; and the history of the international women's movement, the peace movement, the environmental movement, and the movement for human rights." Michael J. Hogan, *America in the World: The Historiography of American Foreign Relations since 1941* (Cambridge: Cambridge University Press, 1995), 164.

21. See Paul Kramer, "Power and Connection: Imperial Histories of the United States in the World," *American Historical Review* 116, no. 5 (2011), 1348–1391, and "How Not to Write the History of U.S. Empire," *Diplomatic History* 42, no. 5 (2018), 911–931, for thorough historiographical treatment of this issue.

22. In terms of membership growth, the year 1935 marked the height of non-US participation during the interwar years as Nazi Germany and its European allies began shutting down all Rotary clubs at that time (and Japan by 1940). Of the 160,567 individual members in RI for that year, 71 percent (114,557) were in the United States, 11.5 percent (18,350) in Great Britain and Ireland, and 17 percent (27,660) spread throughout all of Latin America, the Caribbean, Eu-

rope, Asia, northern Africa, and Australia and New Zealand. *Proceedings of the Twenty-Sixth Annual Convention,* Mexico City, Mexico, 17–21 June 1935; Report of the Secretary, table III, "Statement of Membership," 433.

23. Membership statistics are drawn from main websites for all three service clubs: rotary.org, kiwanis.org, lionsclubs.org. Statistics for US military personnel are from https://www.governing.com/gov-data/public-workforce-salaries/military-civilian-active-duty-employee-workforce-numbers-by-state.html. Employment data for the US State Department are from https://careers.state.gov/learn/what-we-do/mission, and for Walmart, https://corporate.walmart.com/newsroom/company-facts. (All data accessed 1 December 2020.)

24. The only national unit ever created under this administrative category was the British Association of Rotary Clubs (BARC) in 1914, which later became Rotary in Great Britain and Ireland (RIBI) in 1922 and still exists today.

25. The transnational turn has also spilled over into the fields of urban history, urban studies, and urban sociology. See A. K. Sandoval-Strausz and Nancy H. Kwak, eds., *Making Cities Global: The Transnational Turn in Urban History* (Philadelphia: University of Pennsylvania Press, 2018), and Michael Peter Smith, *Transnational Urbanism: Locating Globalization* (Malden, MA: Blackwell Publishing, 2001). For a direct application to the world of Rotary clubs in specific cities in Southeast Asia, see Su Lin Lewis, *Cities in Motion: Urban Life and Cosmopolitanism in Southeast Asia, 1920–1940* (Cambridge: Cambridge University Press, 2016), especially chap. 3, 95–137. For a powerful combination of transnational urbanism and US empire, see Andrew Friedman, *Covert Capital: Landscapes of Denial and the Making of U.S. Empire in the Suburbs of Northern Virginia* (Berkeley: University of California Press, 2013).

26. Women's organizations have received good treatment on this point. In addition to Tyrrell, *Woman's World/Woman's Empire,* see Linda Schott, *Reconstructing Women's Thoughts: The Women's International League for Peace and Freedom before World War II* (Stanford, CA: Stanford University Press, 1997); Leila Rupp, *Worlds of Women: The Making of an International Women's Movement* (Princeton, NJ: Princeton University Press, 1997); and Rupp, "Constructing Internationalism: The Case of Transnational Women's Organizations, 1888–1945," *American Historical Review* 99, no. 5 (December 1994), 1571–1600. On the secularization and professionalization of the women's foreign missionary movement and of foreign missionary societies in general, see Patricia Hill, *The World Their Household: The American Women's Foreign Mission Movement and Cultural Transformation, 1870–1920* (Ann Arbor: University of Michigan Press, 1985), 150–170. Hill describes the transition from praying to paying members and from enthusiastic amateurs with religious drive to paid

organizers with knowledge of the foreign mission field. RI's move from almost crass business networking and ad hoc establishment of new clubs to its project of civic internationalism followed a similar trajectory, except that Rotary's starting point was formally secular in nature.

27. For a thorough discussion of the concept of "social trusteeship" and the rise of the professions, see Steven Brint, *In an Age of Experts: The Changing Role of Professionals in Politics and Public Life* (Princeton, NJ: Princeton University Press, 1994), and for the history of the original Rotary club of Chicago, Oren Arnold, *The Golden Strand: An Informal History of the Rotary Club of Chicago* (Chicago: Quadrangle Books, 1966). For a close examination of the developmental relationship between men's and women's organizations in the city of Chicago during this period, see Maureen Flanagan, *Seeing with Their Hearts: Chicago Women and the Vision of the Good City, 1871–1933* (Princeton, NJ: Princeton University Press, 2002), and Flanagan, "Gender and Urban Political Reform: The City Club and the Women's City Club of Chicago in the Progressive Era," *American Historical Review* 95, no. 4 (October 1990), 1932–1050.

28. The full literature on fraternalism, voluntary associations, and club life in the United States is vast, encompassing the colonial to the very recent. See W. Hampton Sides, *Stomping Grounds: A Pilgrim's Progress Through Eight American Subcultures* (New York: Morrow, 1992); Jason Kaufman, *For the Common Good?: American Civic Life and the Golden Age of Fraternity* (Oxford: Oxford University Press, 2002), for an excellent review of the role of voluntary associations, club life, and fraternal organizations in the United States before the New Deal and World War II. On the cross-class nature of lodges and the transition to service clubs, see Mary Ann Clawson, *Constructing Brotherhood: Class, Gender, and Fraternalism* (Princeton, NJ: Princeton University Press, 1989), as well as Clifford Putney, "Service over Secrecy: How Lodge-Style Fraternalism Yielded Popularity to Men's Service Clubs," *Journal of Popular Culture* 27, no. 1 (Summer 1993); 179–190; David T. Beito, *From Mutual Aid to the Welfare State: Fraternal Societies and Social Services, 1890–1967* (Chapel Hill: University of North Carolina Press, 2000); and Alvin J. Schmidt, *Fraternal Organizations* (Westport, CT: Greenwood, 1980).

29. I consider this topic in greater detail in the next chapter. That said, the literature on Paul Harris and on the formation of the original Rotary club is rather sprawling and often bordering on hagiography.

30. Coined by historian Robert Wiebe, the term "island communities" still informs many historians' understanding of small-town America before the twentieth century. Robert H. Wiebe, *The Search for Order: 1877–1920* (New York City: Hill and Wang, 1967). For an examination of the fate of Main Street over

the twentieth century, see Alison Isenberg, *Downtown America: A History of the Place and the People Who Made It* (Chicago: University of Chicago Press, 2002).

31. For the classic study of a small, midwestern town and the role of the Rotary club there, see Robert S. and Helen Merrell Lynd, *Middletown: A Study in American Culture* (New York: Harcourt Brace, 1929), 301–309, and *Middletown in Transition: A Study in Cultural Conflicts* (New York: Harcourt Brace, 1937). In literature, Sinclair Lewis's character "Babbitt" became synonymous with the small-town rube: Sinclair Lewis, *Babbitt* (New York: Harcourt, Brace, 1922); see chap. XXI for Lewis's treatment of the Zenith Boosters' Club, "a world-force for optimism," 257–262. Jeffrey Charles devotes a chapter to Lewis, H. L. Mencken, and other critics of RI's boosterism in *Service Clubs in American Society*, chap. 4, 86–103.

32. There are many important studies on this broad phenomenon for this period and its relationship to the rise of the "new middle classes" in the United States. Still an authoritative text is Wiebe, *The Search for Order;* see also Robert H. Wiebe, *Businessmen and Reform: A Study of the Progressive Movement* (Cambridge, MA: Harvard University Press, 1962). Other important contributions include Richard L. McCormick, "The Discovery that Business Corrupts Politics: A Reappraisal of the Origins of Progressivism," *American Historical Review* 86, no. 2 (April 1981), 247–274; Daniel T. Rodgers, "In Search of Progressivism," *Reviews in American History* (December 1982), 113–131; Alan Trachtenberg, *The Incorporation of America: Culture and Society in the Gilded Age* (New York: Hill and Wang, 1982); and Olivier Zunz, *Making America Corporate, 1870–1920* (Chicago: University of Chicago Press, 1990). More recent contributions include Jeffrey M. Hornstein, *A Nation of Realtors: A Cultural History of the Twentieth-Century American Middle Class* (Durham, NC: Duke University Press, 2005), esp. chaps. 1–3; Michael McGerr, *A Fierce Discontent: The Rise and Fall of the Progressive Movement in America, 1870–1920* (New York: Free Press, 2003), which emphasizes "anti-corruption" as a significant common denominator in progressivism; Walter A. Friedman, *Birth of a Salesman: The Transformation of Selling in America* (Cambridge: Harvard University Press, 2004); and Burton J. Bledstein and Robert D. Johnston, eds., *The Middling Sorts: Explorations in the History of the American Middle Class* (New York: Routledge, 2001). See also Dawley, *Changing the World,* and Rosenberg, *Financial Missionaries to the World,* both of which take on an internationalist perspective. From a transnational approach, see A. Ricardo Lopez and Barbara Weinstein, eds., *The Making of the Middle Class: Toward a Transnational History* (Durham, NC: Duke University Press, 2012).

33. Jui-Cheng Huang and Peter Gould, "The Diffusion in an Urban Hierarchy: The Case of Rotary Clubs," *Economic Geography* 50, no. 4 (1974), 333–340.

34. See Charles, *Service Clubs in American Society,* for the complete story on how Lions and Kiwanis clubs followed in the footsteps of the Rotary club a decade after its establishment in Chicago.

35. Many other international nongovernmental organizations existed before Rotary, of course, but not with this particular formulation. See Jessica Harland-Jacobs, *Builders of Empire: Freemasonry and British Imperialism, 1717–1927* (Chapel Hill: University of North Carolina Press, 2007) on Freemasonry, and David Macleod, *Building Character in the American Boy: the Boy Scouts, the YMCA, and their Forerunners, 1870–1920* (Madison: University of Wisconsin Press, 1983), for a detailed account of the YMCA and the Boy Scouts, especially on the importance of professionalization and secularization in their evolution and growth. See also Tyrrell, *Woman's World/Woman's Empire,* on the Women's Christian Temperance Union (WCTU), and Clarence P. Shedd, *History of the World's Alliance of Young Men's Christian Associations* (London: World's Committee of Young Men's Christian Associations, 1955), on the YMCA. For the International Red Cross, see Caroline Moorehead, *Dunant's Dream: War, Switzerland and the History of the Red Cross* (London: Harper Collins, 1998); and for complementary histories of the American Red Cross, Michele Turk, *Blood, Sweat and Tears: An Oral History of the American Red Cross* (Robbinsville, NJ: E Street Press, 2006), Patrick Gilbo, *The American Red Cross: The First Century* (New York: Harper and Row, 1981), and Irwin, *Making the World Safe.*

36. See, for example, Volker R. Berghahn, "Philanthropy and Diplomacy in the 'American Century,' in *The Ambiguous Legacy: U.S. Foreign Relations in the "American Century,"* ed. Michael J. Hogan (Cambridge: Cambridge University Press, 1999), 379–415.

37. For an important analysis of the international consequences of Wilsonian rhetoric, see Manela, *The Wilsonian Moment,* 15–34.

38. In the eyes of the League of Nations, however, RI's status as a nonprofit organization was not a given. For example, in 1926, RI did not appear in the League's *Handbook of International Organisations,* despite fulfilling all requirements for inclusion, apparently because RI was interpreted as having an "aim at commercial gain or pecuniary profit." *Handbook of International Organisations (Associations, Bureaux, Committee, etc.)* (Geneva: League of Nations, 1926), 5–6. By 1929, however, RI had made its case, appearing under the rubric

of "Humanitarianism, Religion, and Morals," along with the YMCA, the International Red Cross, the Salvation Army, and so on, rather than under the category of "Trade and Industry" alongside the International Chamber of Commerce or under "Economics and Finance" alongside, for example, the International Institute of the Middle Classes. *Handbook of International Organisations (Associations, Bureaux, Committee, etc.)* (Geneva: League of Nations, 1929). For a detailed history of the International Chamber of Commerce before World War II, see George L. Ridgeway, *Merchants of Peace: The History of the International Chamber of Commerce* (Boston: Little, Brown, 1959).

39. It is easy to overlook the collective impact of an INGO like RI because of its positioning between states and markets. How much more so when not considered as a fundamental feature of US international activity? For example, RI's civic internationalism showed little of the "zigzag" of "independent internationalism" in US foreign policy in the period. See Joan Hoff Wilson, *American Business & Foreign Policy, 1920–1933* (Lexington: University Press of Kentucky, 1971). See also Michael J. Hogan, *Informal Entente: The Private Structure of Cooperation in Anglo-American Economic Diplomacy, 1918–1928* (Columbia: University of Missouri Press, 1977).

40. In *Irresistible Empire,* de Grazia makes a compelling case by pointing out the five basic features of what she calls the "Market Empire" of the United States: (1) moral justification for the imposition of US control over non-US public spaces; (2) the exportation of a US model of civil society "meaning its voluntary associations, social scientific knowledge, and civic spirit—in tandem with, if not ahead of, the country's exports"; (3) the "power of norms-making" or the "rules of 'best practice' as spelled out by enterprising businessmen, civic leaders, and conscientious bureaucrats"; (4) the supposed egalitarianism of the consumerist ethos, where "sociability defined liberty as freedom of choice, privileged the marketplace and individual acquisitiveness as the means to access it, and tranquilly asserted that a vote in politics was not significantly different from making a choice in the market"; and (5) the "peaceableness" of common prosperity and the good life—defined as consumer abundance. All five features apply in full with respect to RI's civic internationalism. Literature on "Americanization" and the influence of US popular culture, especially after World War II, is extensive. See, for example, Reinhold Wagnleitner and Elaine Tyler May, eds., *Here, There, and Everywhere: The Foreign Politics of American Popular Culture* (Hanover, NH: University Press of New England, 2000), and Rob Kroes, *If You've Seen One, You've Seen the Mall: Europeans and American Mass Culture* (Urbana: University of Illinois Press, 1996).

41. See Rosenberg, *Spreading the American Dream,* for consideration of a limited US foreign policy apparatus during the interwar years using "chosen instruments" (private organizations and individuals) to effect policy goals.

42. The starting point is Rosenberg, *Spreading the American Dream* and *Financial Missionaries to the World.* See also Akira Iriye, *Cultural Internationalism and World Order;* Iriye, *Global Community;* and Iriye, *The Globalizing of America, 1913–1945,* vol. 3, in *The Cambridge History of American Foreign Relations* (Cambridge: Cambridge University Press, 1993). Iriye in *Global Community* argues that the NGOs and INGOs are the main contribution of the United States to the world over the course of the century. Key texts on the history and role of the nonprofit sector in the United States are Lawrence J. Friedman and Mark D. McGarvie, eds., *Charity, Philanthropy, and Civility in American History* (Cambridge: Cambridge University Press, 2003); David C. Hammack, ed., *Making the Nonprofit Sector in the United States: A Reader* (Bloomington, 1998); and Kenneth Prewitt, Mattei Dogan, Steven Heydemann, and Stefan Toepler, eds. *The Legitimacy of Philanthropic Foundations: United States and European Perspectives* (New York: Russell Sage Foundation, 2006). See also Morag Bell, "American Philanthropy as Cultural Power," in David Slater and Peter J. Taylor, eds. *The American Century: Consensus and Coercion in the Projection of American Power* (Oxford: Blackwell, 1999), 284–297; and Helmut K. Anheier and Siobhan Daly, "Philanthropic Foundations: A New Global Force?" *Global Civil Society 2004/5* (London: Sage Publications, 2005), 158–176.

43. Michael Geyer and Charles Bright, "Where in the World is America?": The History of the United States in the Global Age," in *Rethinking American History,* ed. Bender, 72–73.

44. In contrast to many of its international competitors, the US government did not have any semblance of a coordinated and professional Foreign Service until the Rogers Act of 1924. On the formation of the Foreign Service, see J. Robert Moskin, *American Statecraft: The Story of the U.S. Foreign Service* (New York: St. Martin's Press, 2013), 195–454, and *The Making of the Diplomatic Mind: The Training, Outlook, and Style of United States Foreign Service Officers, 1908–1931* (Middletown, CT: Wesleyan University Press, 1975).

45. William I. Robinson and Jerry Harris, "Towards a Global Ruling Class? Globalization and the Transnational Capitalist Class," *Science & Society* 64, no. 1 (Spring 2000), 11–54, provides a seminal discussion of this issue from a post-Fordist perspective. While it is hard to determine to what degree RI contributed to the creation of "the transnational capitalist class," RI's civic internationalism did posit its own understanding of transnational class identities.

46. Still the most insightful statement on this point is William Appleman Williams, *Empire as a Way of Life: An Essay on the Causes and Character of America's Present Predicament Along with a Few Thoughts about an Alternative* (Oxford: Oxford University Press, 1980). In recent years, the field now known as the history of capitalism has begun to explode with possibilities. For a thorough accounting of these new historiographical directions and its pertinence to US international and transnational history and to studies in US empire, see Paul Kramer, "Embedding Capital: Political-Economic History, the United States, and the World," *Journal of the Gilded Age and Progressive Era* 15 (2016), 331–362; Sven Beckert, *Empire of Cotton: A Global History* (New York: Vintage Books, 2014); Edward Baptist, *The Half Has Never Been Told: Slavery and the Making of American Capitalism* (New York: Basic Books, 2014); Sven Beckert and Seth Rockman, eds., *Slavery's Capitalism: A New History of American Economic Development* (Philadelphia: University of Pennsylvania, 2016); Louis Hyman and Edward Baptist, *American Capitalism: A Reader* (New York: Simon and Schuster, 2014); and Sven Beckert and Christine Desan, *American Capitalism: New Histories* (New York: Columbia University Press, 2018).

47. See de Grazia, *Irresistible Empire,* 15–74.

48. Wendy Wall, *Inventing the "American Way": The Politics of Consensus from the New Deal to the Civil Rights Movement* (Oxford: Oxford University Press, 2008).

49. Still a seminal contribution on this point is Arjun Appadurai, "Disjuncture and Difference in the Global Cultural Economy," in *Colonial Discourse and Postcolonial Theory: A Reader,* ed. Patrick Williams and Laura Chrisman (New York: Columbia University Press, 1994). See also chap. 2 in *Modernity At Large: Cultural Dimensions of Globalization* (Minneapolis: University of Minnesota Press, 1996).

50. Extensive debates over the nature of the relationship between the state and civil society continue to rage in the social sciences, with one side led by Theda Skocpol and the other by Robert Putnam on social capital. Some recent texts relevant to this study include Theda Skocpol, *Diminished Democracy: From Membership to Management in American Civic Life* (Norman: University of Oklahoma Press, 2003); Theda Skocpol and Morris Fiorina, eds., *Civic Engagement in American Democracy* (Washington, DC: Brookings Institution, 1999); Theda Skocpol, Marshall Ganz, and Ziad Munson, "A Nation of Organizers: The Institutional Origins of Civic Voluntarism in the United States," *American Political Science Review* 94, no. 3 (September 2000), 527–546; and Jocelyn Elise Crowley and Theda Skocpol, "The Rush to Organize: Explaining Associational Formation in the United States, 1860s–1920s," *American Journal of Political*

Science 45, no. 4 (October 2001), 813–829. Publications in support of the social capital thesis are legion. Still the paramount texts are Robert D. Putnam, *Making Democracy Work: Civic Traditions in Modern Italy* (Princeton, NJ: Princeton University Press 1993), and Putnam, *Bowling Alone: The Collapse and Revival of American Community* (New York: Simon & Schuster, 2000). See also Pamela Laird, *Pull: Networking and Success since Benjamin Franklin* (Cambridge, MA: Harvard University Press, 2006) for a more comprehensive approach to US history from this perspective. With respect to Rotary clubs, see also Gerald Gamm and Robert D. Putnam, "The Growth of Voluntary Associations in America, 1840–1940," *Journal of Interdisciplinary History* 29, no. 4 (Spring 1999), 511–557.

51. "Social capital," as defined by Robert Putnam, "refers to connections among individuals—social networks and the norms of reciprocity and trustworthiness that arise from them." Putnam, *Bowling Alone,* 19.

52. For a thorough analysis of the cultural dimensions of the marketplace over several centuries, see Thomas L. Haskell and Richard F. Teichgraeber, eds., *The Culture of the Market: Historical Essays* (New York: Cambridge University Press, 1993).

53. T. H. Marshall and Tom Bottomore, *Citizenship and Social Class* (Concord, MA: Pluto Press, 1992), 39. For an interesting analysis of service clubs, gender, and citizenship at the local level, see Emily J. Heard, "Gendered Notions of Citizenship and Service in Interwar Halifax" (PhD diss., Dalhousie University, Halifax, Nova Scotia, 2001).

54. For a thorough analysis of the theoretical weaknesses of social capital on this point, see Margaret R. Somers, "Beware Trojan Horses Bearing Social Capital: How Privatization Turned Solidarity into a Bowling Team," in *The Politics of Method in the Human Sciences,* ed. George Steinmetz (Durham, NC: Duke University Press, 2005), 233–274, and Somers, "Narrating and Naturalizing Civil Society and Citizenship Theory: The Place of Political Culture and the Public Sphere," *Sociological Theory* 13, no. 3 (1995), 229–274.

55. Within the literature on US empire, see Paul Kramer, *The Blood of Government: Race, Empire, the United States, and the Philippines* (Chapel Hill: University of North Carolina Press, 2006), 18. In addition to Kramer and the monographs on US empire listed earlier, see also Laura Wexler, *Tender Violence: Domestic Visions in an Age of U.S. Imperialism* (Chapel Hill: University of North Carolina Press, 2000); Laura Briggs, *Reproducing Empire: Race, Sex, Science, and U.S. Imperialism in Puerto Rico* (Berkeley: University of California Press, 2002); and Penny Von Eschen, *Satchmo Blows Up the World: Jazz Ambassadors Play the Cold War* (Cambridge, MA: Harvard University Press, 2004) as well as four important anthologies on US empire, including Amy

Kaplan and Donald Pease, eds., *Cultures of United States Imperialism* (Durham, NC: Duke University Press, 1993); Lisa Lowe and David Lloyd, eds., *The Politics of Culture in the Shadow of Capital* (Durham, NC: Duke University Press, 1997); Gilbert M. Joseph, Catherine C. LeGrand, and Ricardo D. Salvatore, eds., *Close Encounters of Empire: Writing the Cultural History of U.S.–Latin American Relations* (Durham, NC: Duke University Press, 1998); and Ann Laura Stoler, ed., *Haunted by Empire: Geographies of Intimacy in North American History* (Durham, NC: Duke University Press, 2006).

56. Kramer distinguishes between competing forms of exceptionalism in debates over the future of the United States as a potential empire after 1898: "national-exceptionalism" versus "racial-exceptionalism." Paul Kramer, "Empires, Exceptions, and Anglo-Saxons: Race and Rule between the British and United States Empires, 1880–1910," *Journal of American History* 88, no. 4 (March 2002), 1315–1353.

57. On the definition of the term "geo-body," see Thongchai Winichakul, *Siam Mapped: A History of the Geo-Body of a Nation* (Honolulu: University of Hawaii Press, 1994). More recently on this subject, see Daniel Immerwahr, *How to Hide an Empire: A History of the Greater United States* (London: Farrar, Straus and Giroux, 2019).

58. Neil Smith, *American Empire: Roosevelt's Geographer and the Prelude to Globalization* (Berkeley: University of California Press, 2003), 3.

59. For David Harvey, Henry Luce's famous phrase "the American century" was key to US denial of empire because "the power conferred was global and universal rather than territorially specific, so Luce preferred to talk of an American century rather than an empire." David Harvey, *The New Imperialism* (New York: Oxford University Press, 2003), 50.

60. Quoted in Henry R. Luce, "The American Century," in Hogan, ed., *Ambiguous Legacy,* 20.

61. In *Service Clubs in American Society,* Jeffrey Charles details well the transition from the fraternal orders in the nineteenth century to the service clubs of the new middle classes in the twentieth century (see chaps. 1–3 in particular). That transition, however, is presented primarily within the confines of political, social, and economic change within the United States.

62. On the use of this phrase, see Wertheim, *Tomorrow, the World,* 1–14.

1. COOPERATION AMONG GENTLEMEN

1. Arch C. Klumph, *Rotary Throughout the World* (pamphlet), 1918 Convention of National Association of Rotary Clubs, Kansas City, Missouri,

Archives of Rotary International, Evanston, Illinois (hereafter, "RI Archives"). Klumph's speech is also found in *Proceedings of the 1918 Rotary Convention* (Evanston: Rotary International, 1918), 217–222.

2. Klumph, *Rotary Throughout the World.*

3. Klumph, *Rotary Throughout the World.*

4. See *Proceedings of the 1918 Rotary Convention,* 12–15.

5. The literature on Woodrow Wilson and "Wilsonianism" is extensive. For a compelling case for the continuities of Wilsonianism over the course of the twentieth century, see Frank Ninkovich, *The Wilsonian Century: U.S. Foreign Policy since 1900* (Chicago: University of Chicago Press, 1999). For the consequences of Wilsonian rhetoric in the international arena, Erez Manela, "Imagining Woodrow Wilson in Asia: Dreams of East-West Harmony and the Revolt against Empire in 1919," *American Historical Review* 111, no. 5 (2006), 1327–1351, and Manela, *The Wilsonian Moment: Self-Determination and the International Origins of Anticolonial Nationalism* (New York: Oxford University Press, 2007). See also Lloyd C. Gardner, *A Covenant with Power: America and World Order from Wilson to Reagan* (London: Macmillan, 1984); Lloyd E. Ambrosius, *Wilsonian Statecraft: Theory and Practice of Liberal Internationalism during World War I* (Wilmington, DE: Scholarly Resources, 1991); Ambrosius, *Wilsonianism: Woodrow Wilson and His Legacy in American Foreign Relations* (New York: Palgrave Macmillan, 2002); John Milton Cooper, Jr., *Breaking the Heart of the World: Woodrow Wilson and the Fight for the League of Nations* (Cambridge: Cambridge University Press, 2001); David M. Esposito, *The Legacy of Woodrow Wilson: American War Aims in World War I* (Westport, CT: Praeger, 1996); Ross A. Kennedy, "Woodrow Wilson, World War I, and an American Conception of National Security," *Diplomatic History* 25, no. 1 (Winter 2001), 1–31; and Thomas J. Knock, *To End All Wars: Woodrow Wilson and the Quest for a New World Order* (Princeton, NJ: Princeton University Press, 1992).

6. The name "Rotary" refers to this rotation of venue and to the expectation that club membership and leadership were on a rolling basis, subject to constant review and turnover.

7. From a membership promotion circular (1907–1908) reprinted in the University of Chicago Social Science Survey Committee, *Rotary? A University Group Looks at the Rotary Club of Chicago* (Chicago: University of Chicago Press, 1934), 6. As noted in the Introduction, the literature on the life of Paul Harris and on the early history of the original Chicago Rotary club is now extensive and well-documented. For a comprehensive history of the original Rotary club of Chicago, see Oren Arnold, *The Golden Strand: An Informal*

History of the Rotary Club of Chicago (Chicago: Quadrangle Books, 1966). For a clear statement on the purpose of the Rotary club as a social movement that is national in purpose, see Paul P. Harris, "Rational Rotarianism," *National Rotarian,* vol. 1, no. 1 (January 1911), 1–3.

8. University of Chicago, *Rotary? A University Group Looks at the Rotary Club,* 73.

9. Harris, "Rational Rotarianism," *National Rotarian,* January 1911, 3.

10. "Loud Demand for Comfort Booths," *Chicago Daily Tribune,* 25 October 1907, 4.

11. Chesley Perry, "Early Objects of Rotary," 27 October 1920, 2003–3, box 7, VIP Membership Records, Rotary Club of Chicago Archives (hereafter, "Chicago / Rotary One Archives"). At the bottom of the "Early Objects of Rotary," Perry added that he was "unable to locate any earlier statement of objects."

12. "Rotary, a Unique Club," 2004–10, box 4, History of Rotary Committee 1905, Chicago / Rotary One Archives.

13. For an examination of how gender differences, the "idea of separate spheres," and "corporate domesticity" played out in the emerging corporate world of the late nineteenth and early twentieth century in the United States, see Angel Kwolek-Folland, *Engendering Business: Men and Women in the Corporate Office, 1870–1930* (Baltimore: Johns Hopkins University Press, 1994). On the gendered politics of the war period, see Susan R. Grayzel and Tammy M. Proctor, eds., *Gender and the Great War* (Oxford: Oxford University Press, 2017).

14. "Bar Women from Rotary Clubs: Hard to Manage," *Los Angeles Herald,* 18 August 1910, 5.

15. In fact, after the 1914 Rotary Convention in Houston, wives of Rotarians who worked in an auxiliary manner with Rotary clubs became known as "Rotary Anns"—a shorthand that lasted for decades and took root in clubs worldwide. The phrase came from Ann Brunnier and Ann Gundaker, wives of two top Rotary officials during that period.

16. On the tensions between women's organizations and men's organizations in Chicago during this period, see Maureen Flanagan, *Seeing with Their Hearts: Chicago Women and the Vision of the Good City, 1871–1933* (Princeton, NJ: Princeton University Press, 2002).

17. On this phrase in this context, see Steven Brint, *In an Age of Experts: The Changing Role of Professionals in Politics and Public Life* (Princeton, NJ: Princeton University Press, 1994).

18. Still classic texts on the subject are Robert H. Wiebe, *The Search for Order, 1877–1920* (New York: Hill and Wang, 1967), and Wiebe, *Businessmen*

and Reform: A Study of the Progressive Movement (Cambridge, MA: Harvard University Press, 1962). See also Robert D. Johnston, *The Radical Middle Class: Populist Democracy and the Question of Capitalism in Progressive Era Portland, Oregon* (Princeton, NJ: Princeton University Press, 2003); Jeffrey M. Hornstein, *A Nation of Realtors: A Cultural History of the Twentieth-Century American Middle Class* (Durham, NC: Duke University Press, 2005); Burton J. Bledstein and Robert D. Johnston, eds., *The Middling Sorts: Explorations in the History of the American Middle Class* (New York: Routledge, 2001); and esp. Alan Trachtenberg, *The Incorporation of America: Culture and Society in the Gilded Age* (New York: Hill and Wang, 1982), and Olivier Zunz, *Making America Corporate, 1870–1920* (Chicago: University of Chicago Press, 1990).

19. *Chicago Convention Proceedings,* 15–17 August 1910, reprinted in the *National Rotarian,* September 1910, 13–14.

20. Although there is now a great deal of information available online about the earliest phases of women in Rotary, there remains little formal scholarship on the same. For a basic history and timeline, go to "History of Women in Rotary," https://www.rotary.org/en/history-women-rotary; see also "The History of Women in Rotary International," 13 June 2012, https://www.rotarysjee.org/stories/the-history-of-women-in-rotary-international; "Women in Rotary: A Potted History," https://rotarywomen.org.au/about-us/; and "A History of Women in Rotary," revised 4 April 2020, https://newtonrotary.org/stories/a-history-of-women-in-rotary-4-24-20-revised; all accessed 20 November 2020.

21. *Chicago Convention Proceedings,* 15–17 August 1910, 45. Also quoted in Arnold, *The Golden Strand,* 39.

22. *Chicago Convention Proceedings,* 15–17 August 1910, 43–45.

23. This was a very common theme in Rotary publications out of Chicago and London. Arthur F. Sheldon, at the 1911 Portland national convention, first coined the motto "He profits most who serves best." On the origins of the emphasis on "service" from Arthur F. Sheldon, see "Members, Sheldon Arthur F.," box 73, folder 3, Chicago Rotary / One Archives. There are numerous articles in the *Rotarian* from 1912 onward; in particular, see articles under the heading "Salesmanship—Science Plus Art," *Rotarian,* June 1915, 91–96. See also "The Philosophy and Ethics of Successful Business: An Extract from the Buffalo Convention Address," *Rotarian,* September 1913, 113; and "The Ideal of Service as the Basis of All Worthy Enterprise" and "Perpetuating the Ideal of Service to Humanity" in Central Files / Subject Files, Pamphlets, RI Archives. On service as a "profitless ideal," see William Leach, *Land of Desire: Merchants, Power, and the Rise of a New American Culture* (New York, 1993), esp. chap. 5; Roland Marchand, *Creating the Corporate Soul: The Rise of Public Relations and*

Corporate Imagery in American Big Business (Berkeley, CA: University of California Press, 1998), chap. 5 on the "Service Ideal"; and Emily Rosenberg, *Financial Missionaries to the World: The Politics and Culture of Dollar Diplomacy, 1900–1930* (Cambridge, MA; 1999). On the rise of salesmen as respectable professionals, see Walter Friedman, *Birth of a Salesman: The Transformation of Selling in America* (Cambridge, MA: Harvard University Press, 2004), esp. chap. 6. On the cross-class nature of lodges and the transition to service clubs, see Mary Ann Clawson, *Constructing Brotherhood: Class, Gender, and Fraternalism* (Princeton, NJ: Princeton University Press, 1989). One could make a compelling argument that the service ideology forged in the service clubs (Lions and Kiwanis included after World War I) was the middle-class parallel to the philanthropy of magnates like Rockefeller, Mellon, and Carnegie. In 1917, in fact, this became a central argument in favor of creating the Rotary Foundation and then expanding it greatly by the mid-1930s. After World War II, the Rotary Foundation became more and more the centerpiece of Rotary's mission.

24. The fifteen clubs represented, in order of their entrance into the National Association, were Chicago; San Francisco in 1908; Oakland, Seattle, Los Angeles, New York City, and Boston in 1909; and Tacoma, Minneapolis, St. Paul, St. Louis, New Orleans, Kansas City, Lincoln, and Portland in 1910. Though Detroit had just established a new club, it did not send a delegate to the first convention. *Chicago Tribune,* "Rotary Clubs of America Meet in Chicago Tomorrow," 14 August 1910, 7.

25. See Richard L. McCormick, "The Discovery that Business Corrupts Politics: A Reappraisal of the Origins of Progressivism," *American Historical Review* 86, no. 2 (April 1981), 247–274, for a cogent analysis of this point.

26. *Proceedings of the Buffalo Convention,* "Report of President Glenn C. Mead," reprinted in the *Rotarian,* September 1913, 20.

27. *Proceedings of the Buffalo Convention,* "Report of President Glenn C. Mead," 21.

28. *Proceedings of the Buffalo Convention,* "Report of President Glenn C. Mead," 20.

29. For more details, see University of Chicago, *Rotary? A University Group Looks at the Rotary Club of Chicago,* 2–15.

30. Rotary's national expansion throughout the West Coast spread through business ties within the Traveler's Insurance Company, among other business and social networks. Other corporate networks through which Rotary operated in its early expansion included, among others, National Cash Register, the Pacific Mail Steamship Company, National City Bank, the Grace Corporation,

and US Steel. The list of corporations that regularly worked with and through Rotary clubs over the twentieth century would likely encompass hundreds of companies and firms—a veritable Who's Who of transnational corporations. Moreover, if one includes the YMCA, the Boy Scouts, the Red Cross, and similar international organizations and religious groups, the list of organizations cooperating with Rotary clubs worldwide would likely total well over a thousand.

31. "The Rotary Platform: Adopted by Rotary Conventions Portland 1911 and Duluth 1912," from *Pamphlet No. 1: The Rotary Club,* RI Archives.

32. This was also one of the most significant structural differences between Rotary clubs and its imitators, the Lions and Kiwanis clubs, which did not have such restrictions on membership. Each Rotary club had to have committees on membership and classification which examined any potential member's personal as well as professional or business credentials.

33. See standard club constitution, article II, section 1. For details on the formal adoption of the standard club constitution, see *Twelfth Annual Convention of the International Association of Rotary Clubs,* 13–16 June 1921, Edinburgh, Scotland, 64–69, 507, 563.

34. *Rotarian,* September 1912, "President Glenn C. Mead," 14.

35. Ivan Allen, *Rotary in Atlanta: The First Twenty-Five Years* (Atlanta: Darby, 1939), 280.

36. *Proceedings of the Buffalo Convention,* "Report of President Glenn C. Mead," reprinted in the *Rotarian,* September 1913, 21.

37. Allen, *Rotary in Atlanta,* 27 and 38. Allen is referring to the 1913 club constitution, article III, section 1, "Membership Qualifications." On the social politics of businessmen in Detroit, Philadelphia, and Atlanta during this period, see Daniel Amsterdam, *Roaring Metropolis: Businessmen's Campaign for a Civic Welfare State* (Philadelphia: University of Pennsylvania Press, 2016).

38. University of Chicago, *Rotary?*; Daniel Amsterdam, "Toward a Civic Welfare State: Business and City Building in the 1920s," in *Capital Gains: Business and Politics in Twentieth-Century America,* ed. Richard R. John and Kim Phillips-Fein (Philadelphia: University of Pennsylvania Press, 2017), 43–57.

39. Given the explosion of Rotary clubs both inside and outside the United States after World War I and the high degree of autonomy of each club, the term "community service" came to mean a great number of club activities loosely defined as such. Over the course of the 1920s, club documents show an expansion of committees tasked with a variety of goals, with each committee making more and more demands on its membership for financial support. In response, at the fourteenth annual convention in St. Louis in June 1923, Rotary International adopted Resolution 34, which "sought to lay down the broad general lines

on which Rotary clubs should engage in community service." In contrast with the first wave of Rotary's expansion during the 1910s, the goal was to distinguish club activities from those of other community organizations such as the chamber of commerce and to avoid "the launching of a dozen new enterprises a year unless these enterprises were truly community responsibilities with a burden that might eventually be shifted to all the community, where it belonged." Clinton P. Anderson, Chairman, RI's Community Service Committee, "What Is the Right Answer?" *Rotarian,* May 1930, 17–19. In effect, RI was seeking to find a balance between ad hoc charitable endeavors of individuals and long-term philanthropic activities and club planning. *Proceedings of the Fourteenth Annual Rotary Convention,* St. Louis, Missouri, 18–22 June 1923, 204–206. Note that since 1919, Anderson had been an active member of the Rotary club of Albuquerque, New Mexico, and he went on to become a member of the International Board of Directors and then president of Rotary International in 1932. Upon completion of his one year as president of RI, he then got involved with the Democratic Party of New Mexico and made a successful run for US Congress in 1940. He became secretary of agriculture under President Truman in 1945 and then served as senator from New Mexico from 1949 to 1973. In many ways, Anderson's career arc was part of a larger pattern, as thousands of businessmen like Anderson also first got their start in politics based on their experience in their club's parliamentary structure and Rotary's institutional forms of governance.

40. *Rotarian,* August 1928, 33.

41. Publications at all levels of Rotary reinforced this message for decades. For example, see "Frederick E. Baker, "Got Five Minutes for a Boy?" *Rotarian,* February 1934, 34–35, 57. But notions of "fatherhood" and "parenting" were hardly limited to the rearing of boys. For example, see Owen Rutter, "My Daughter and I: Here's a Dad Who Wants His Girl to Grow Up with Eyes Wide Open," *Rotarian,* April 1934, 27–28, 43. In fact, there was such a wide variety of club activities centered on "Boys Work," RI also passed Resolution No. 2 at the St. Louis convention in June 1923, with the goal of clarifying the "working relationship" between Rotary clubs and other community organizations in order to "develop boys into good citizens and efficient and honorable business men." See *Proceedings* of the *Fourteenth Annual International Convention,* St. Louis, Missouri, 18–22 June 1923, 164–168.

42. See University of Chicago, *Rotary? A University Group Looks at the Rotary Club,* 224–225, in particular.

43. *Rotarian,* October 1933, 43.

44. *Rotarian,* July 1928, 40.

45. *Proceedings Thirty-Second Annual Convention of Rotary International,* Denver, Colorado, 15–20 June 1941, 24 and 330–331. For statistics on the number and distribution of Rotary clubs in the world for 1940–1941, see *Proceedings Thirty-Second Annual Convention of Rotary International,* Denver, Colorado, 15–20 June 1941, "Report of the Secretary: Member Clubs of Rotary International by Countries and Geographical Regions," 345.

46. See David Shelley Nicholl, *The Golden Wheel: The Story of Rotary, 1905 to the Present* (Plymouth, England: MacDonald and Evans, 1984), on the earliest club formation in Ireland, Scotland, and Great Britain, and Oren Arnold, *The Golden Strand: An Informal History of the Rotary Club of Chicago* (Chicago: Quadrangle Books, 1966), 88–95, for a general account of the sudden burst of clubs in San Francisco, Oakland, Seattle, and Los Angeles in 1908–1909 and resistance within the original Chicago club to this national expansion, and for the founding of the first Canadian club in Winnipeg in 1911–1912.

47. *Rotarian,* "Post-Convention Number," September 1912.

48. Rotary expected its members to join the local chamber of commerce but not to set their club in competition with the chamber's purposes. Harmony and cooperation were above all the goal.

49. For Pittsburgh, *Rotarian,* June 1912, front cover. For Boston, *Rotarian,* May 1912; Philadelphia, July 1912; New York, November 1912; Cleveland, December 1912.

50. Starting with Spokane, Washington, in January 1913, the *Rotarian* also featured that year San Antonio, Houston, Seattle, Providence, and Oakland; in 1914, Kansas City, all of Texas, Peoria, Syracuse, and Cincinnati; and in 1915 Toledo, Lincoln, Atlanta, and all of California. Along with monthly editions devoted to specific cities, one finds short features and blurbs on the industry and progress taking root in any given city or town with a club.

51. Analysis based on three membership files: "History & Archives_Archives\Ready Reference\Club Histories\First Rotary Clubs in Several Areas (1999–2007)," "First 150 Clubs—Dates," and "List of Clubs Thru 1915," all located in RI Archives. See also Jui-Cheng Huang and Peter Gould, "The Diffusion in an Urban Hierarchy: The Case of Rotary Clubs," *Economic Geography* 50, no. 4 (1974), 333–340.

52. Analysis based on files: "First 150 Clubs—Dates," and "List of Clubs Thru 1915," RI Archives.

53. See Robert Staughton Lynd and Helen Merrell Lynd, *Middletown: A Study in Contemporary American Culture* (New York: Harcourt, Brace and Co., 1929) and *Middletown in Transition: A Study in Cultural Conflicts* (New York: Harcourt, Brace and Co., 1937).

54. John Bodnar, *Remaking America: Public Memory, Commemoration, and Patriotism in the Twentieth Century* (Princeton, NJ: Princeton University Press, 1992), 113–114.

55. For example, all 110 members of the Dallas Rotary club proudly joined some 20,000 others in that city's Preparedness Day parade in May 1916. *The Rotary Club of Dallas, Silver Anniversary, 1911–1936* (1936). See Cecilia O'Leary, *To Die For: The Paradox of American Patriotism* (Princeton: Princeton University Press, 1999), on the origins and depth of this form of US nationalism during World War I.

56. Chesley Perry, "Peoria, a Heritage Left by Sturdy Pioneers," *Rotarian,* special issue on Peoria, Illinois, July 1914, 23.

57. For a compelling history of the "culture of development on the frontier," see Elaine Naylor, *Frontier Boosters: Port Townsend and the Culture of Development in the American West* (Montreal: McGill-Queen's University Press, 2014); for continuities in US empire from westward expansion in the nineteenth century into the twentieth century, see Katharine Bjork, *Prairie Imperialists: The Indian Country Origins of American Empire* (Philadelphia: University of Pennsylvania Press, 2019); and for an authoritative work on how Chicago emerged as the central hub for regional growth, *see* William Cronon, *Nature's Metropolis: Chicago and the Great West* (New York: W.W. Norton, 1991).

58. "Exemplifying the Kansas City Spirit," *Rotarian,* May 1914, 25.

59. Literature on this subject and on the biography and writings of Paul P. Harris is extensive, but useful sources include Paul P. Harris, *My Road to Rotary: The Story of a Boy, a Vermont Community, and Rotary* (Evanston, IL: Rotary International, 1945), and James P. Walsh, *The First Rotarian: The Life and Times of Paul Percy Harris, Founder of Rotary,* edited by Harry Treadwell (Shoreham by Sea, Great Britain: Scan Books, 1979). Victoria de Grazia details this point in de Grazia, *Irresistible Empire,* chap. 1, "The Service Ethic: How Bourgeois Men Made Peace with Babbittry," esp. 26–36.

60. For example, in the *Rotarian* (March 1925), one finds articles titled "What Is Business Honesty? Reminiscences of a Business Man," "The Workers' Share: A Description of a Partnership Plan That Is Solving the Problems of Labor in an Industrial Concern," and "Service: An Old Word in New Guide," and then an advertisement, "For Business Men: A Special Course in Chain Store Technique." *Rotarian,* March 1925, 10–11, 40–44; 15–16, 55–56, 20–21, 53. The advertisement is on page 44.

61. In addition to Harris, *My Road to Rotary,* and Walsh, *The First Rotarian,* see Paul P. Harris, *This Rotarian Age* (Chicago: Rotary International, 1935), on how his childhood in Vermont and his many travels both inside and outside

the United States informed his vision of Chicago's first Rotary club and its international expansion.

62. Paul P. Harris, *The Founder of Rotary* (Chicago: Rotary International, 1928), 3.

63. For a detailed analysis of the centrality of the Panama Canal to the emergence of the United States as an imperial power, see Aims McGuinness, *Path of Empire: Panama and the California Gold Rush* (Ithaca, NY: Cornell University Press, 2008) and Julie Greene, *The Canal Builders: Making America's Empire at the Panama Canal* (London: Penguin Press, 2009). On Rotary clubs lobbying on behalf of San Francisco, "Rotary Club Aids Exposition Work," *San Francisco Call*, 25 May 1910, 3.

64. See, for example, *Rotarian*, March 1913, 3, paid for by "Rotarian G. A. Lenoir of Bare Bros, Furniture, Carpets, and Draperies."

65. On the Committee on Public Information, see George Creel, *How We Advertised America: The First Telling of the Amazing Story of the Committee on Public Information That Carried the Gospel of Americanism to Every Corner of the Globe* (New York: Harper and Brothers, 1920); Creel, *Complete Report of the Chairman of the Committee on Public Information* (Washington, DC: US Government Printing Office, 1920); and Creel, *The War, the World and Wilson* (New York: Harper, 1920); as well as Gregg Wolper, "The Origins of Public Diplomacy: Woodrow Wilson, George Creel, and the Committee on Public Information" (PhD diss., Department of History, University of Chicago, 1991).

66. See Julia Irwin, *Making the World Safe: The American Red Cross and a Nation's Humanitarian Awakening* (Oxford: Oxford University Press, 2013).

67. Since the original Chicago club was officially founded on 23 February 1905, this edition was celebrating the "tenth anniversary" of Rotary.

68. For example: "It is just as much a law of mind as the law of gravitation is a law of matter, that favorable attention, properly sustained, induces interest, and interest, properly augmented, changes to desire, and desire, made strong enough, changes to action. These are not theories; they are nature's laws." Arthur Frederick Sheldon, "The Philosophy and Ethics of Successful Business: An Extract from the Buffalo Convention," in the *Rotarian*, September 1913, 113.

69. See, for example, Friedman, *Birth of a Salesman*, esp. chaps. 3 and 4; Marchand, *Creating the Corporate Soul*; and Jackson Lears, *Fables of Abundance: a Cultural History of Advertising in America* (New York, NY: 1994).

70. Both the Dallas and Atlanta Rotary clubs formed out of the nucleus of active members of the American Association of Advertising Club.

71. For a detailed review of how the Chicago Rotary club began its national expansion first into the Bay Area of California and then spread through business ties within the Traveler's Insurance Company, among other business and

social networks, see William J. Mountin, *History of the Rotary Club of San Francisco* (San Francisco: Rotary Club of San Francisco, 1940); *The History of the Rotary Club of Los Angeles* (Los Angeles: Rotary Club of Los Angeles, 1955); *Rotarily Yours: A History of the Rotary Club of Oakland* (Oakland: Rotary Club of Oakland, 1969); Linda Parker Hamilton, *The Rotary Club of Oakland: A Century of Service and Friendship* (Oakland, CA: Stories to Last, 2018); and the *Seattle Rotary's Golden Years: The History of Rotary Club Number Four* (Seattle: Rotary Club of Seattle, 1960).

72. Paul P. Harris, founder of the first Rotary club in Chicago, "National Rotarianism," *National Rotarian,* January 1911, 1–3; Chesley R. Perry, general secretary, "The Philosophy of Rotary," *Rotarian,* July 1914, 24; and University of Chicago, *Rotary? A University Group Looks at the Rotary Club.*

73. Hon. Ed. F. Harris, "The Holy Doctrine of Service," *Rotarian,* March 1914, 48–50. Harris ends his opinion piece with a detailed agenda of reforms that covers the breadth of Progressive Era politics: "Co-operation in civic developments, . . . means working together for better streets, better pavements, better lighting . . . and a loftier conception of the value of true popular government."

74. Russell Greiner, IARC president, *Rotarian,* August 1914, cover.

75. *Convention Proceedings,* San Francisco, 1915, 117.

76. From the summary of the "Rotary Code of Ethics for All Business Men": "The Motive of the Code" and "The Value of the Code."

77. *Rotarian,* February 1913, "President-Elect Woodrow Wilson of the United States of America Declares for the Acceptance of Principles Distinctly Rotarian," 33.

78. The Springfield, Illinois, Rotary club actually merged boosterism and Lincolnalia with a full-page advertisement in the *Rotarian:* "The Rotary Club of Springfield, Ill invites International Rotary and all its friends to visit this world shrine." *Rotarian,* May 1923, 250. With the annual international convention being held in St. Louis in 1923, the Springfield club pushed the matter further, getting its own feature article in the *Rotarian.* See Nellie Browne Duff, "Rotary Memorial Tribute to Lincoln: Visitors to Convention at Saint Louis Participate in Special Services Conducted by the Rotary Club of Springfield, Ill., at Lincoln's Tomb," *Rotarian,* August 1923, 29–30, 47.

79. See Glenda Sluga and Patricia Clavin, eds., *Internationalisms: A Twentieth-Century History* (Cambridge: Cambridge University Press, 2017), and especially for the many varieties of Christian internationalism see Michael G. Thompson, *For God and Globe: Christian Internationalism in the United States between the Great War and the Cold War* (Ithaca, NY: Cornell University Press, 2015), Heather D. Curtis, *Holy Humanitarians: American Evangelicals and*

Global Aid (Cambridge, MA: Harvard University Press, 2018), and David P. King, *God's Internationalists: World Vision and the Age of Evangelical Humanitarianism* (Philadelphia, PA: University of Pennsylvania Press, 2019).

80. James W. Davidson to all members of the Extension Committee, Rotary International, 28 February 1923, Peking Club Historical Files, vol. 1, Rotary Archives, Evanston, IL.

81. W. Rudolph F. Stier, Tokyo YMCA, Kenda Tokyo, to C. B. Harris, IARC, 12 July 1920, John Barrett Papers LOC, box 51, General Correspondence, 1–16 July 1920.

82. Guy Gundaker was one of the founders of the National Restaurant Association.

83. Guy Gundaker, "President's Address," Toronto, 17 June 1924, Guy Gundaker Papers, RI Archives. See also Guy Gundaker, "Campaign of the International Association of Rotary Clubs for the Writing of Codes of Standards of Correct Practice for Each Business and Profession," *Annals of the American Academy of Political and Social Science* CI, no. 190 (May 1922), 228–237, and Benson Y. Landis, *Professional Codes: A Sociological Analysis to Determine Applications to the Educational Profession* (New York City, 1927), for a contemporary view of how professional codes emerged in various professions.

84. Internal RI documents estimate up to two hundred codes were written between 1915 and 1933 through the efforts of individual Rotarians well placed in their trade associations. For example, Lester Struthers to Guy Gundaker, 13 July 1928, file: [Business Methods Committee 1928–29, Roy Ronald, William R. Ronald, and Lester Struthers], Guy Gundaker Papers, RI Archives. Also, Sydney Pascall, successful British candymaker and first European president of RI (1931–1932), pushed RI's codes of standards of correct practice at the international economic conference held under the auspices of the League of Nations in Geneva in 1927. In response to passage of the National Industrial Recovery Act (NIRA) and its codes of fair competition for all industrial groups in 1933, RI president John Nelson of Montreal convoked the US National Assembly within RI, which appointed an ad hoc committee of US Rotarians that sent a message to all US clubs urging acceptance of Franklin Delano Roosevelt's "blanket" code as a compromise between the chaos of no codes on one hand and industrial codes on the other. The committee was then also tasked by the RI board of directors to study how US Rotary clubs might help with reemployment programs. These developments came in addition to lively debates within the *Rotarian* and the weekly newsletter for all clubs on the NIRA while the ad hoc committee on the NIRA examined the industrial codes and made recommen-

dations to Rotary based on them. The Supreme Court's overturning of the NIRA in 1935 brought an end to this ad hoc committee and the whole process, resulting in Rotary's return to the promotion of ethical business practices as a private, voluntary matter after 1936. *Convention Proceedings, Twenty-Third Annual International Convention,* Boston, 1933.

85. Jacob Mazer, quoted in the Chicago Rotary club's bulletin, the *Weekly Yell,* 5 October 1918, Chicago / Rotary One Archives.

86. *Rotarian,* May 1923, 26.

87. On the Boy Scouts of America's role in the rise of US hegemonic power during the twentieth century, see Mischa Honeck, *Our Frontier is the World: The Boys Scouts in the Age of American Ascendancy* (Ithaca, NY: Cornell University Press, 2018).

88. Chesley Perry to George Treadwell, Club Secretary, Chicago Rotary Club One, 17 September 1921, 2003–03, box 7, VIP Membership Records, Chicago / Rotary One Archives.

89. For complete historical records on this organization, see "Women of Rotary," 2003–13, boxes 1–12, Chicago / Rotary One Archives.

90. For a thorough history of the role of women in British Rotary clubs, see Millicent Gaskell, *Home and Horizon: An Account of the History and Organisation of the Association of Inner Wheel Clubs* (Dartford, Kent: Perry Son & Lack, 1953).

91. The formal end to RI's gender discrimination came only at the end of the twentieth century. In *Board of Directors, Rotary International v. Rotary Club of Duarte,* 481 U.S. 537 (1987), the US Supreme Court ruled that California's Unruh Act, which precluded discrimination according to sex, did not violate the First Amendment rights of Rotarians by requiring that California Rotary clubs admit women as members. We will revisit this revealing turn of events in the Conclusion.

92. See Marchand, *Creating the Corporate Soul,* 1–87.

93. *Proceedings of Eighth Annual Convention of the International Association of Rotary Clubs,* Atlanta, Georgia, 17–21 June 1917, 19.

94. For a recent history of the Rotary Foundation, see David C. Forward, *Doing Good in the World: The Inspiring Story of the Rotary Foundation's First 100 Years* (Evanston, IL: Rotary International, 2015).

95. If we include Rotary's immediate service-club cousins—Lions and Kiwanis—which forged their own brand of civic internationalism since 1917 and 1915 (respectively), then we can appreciate how enduring and extensive have been the contributions of these organizations to the modern world.

2. NO FOREIGNERS ALLOWED

1. *Proceedings, Twenty-Sixth Annual Convention of Rotary International,* Mexico City, Mexico, 17–21 June 1935, 10.

2. Lions International, founded in Chicago in 1917, boasted a membership of about 79,000 in 2,707 clubs almost exclusively in the United States. Rotary International in 1935 comprised about 162,000 members in 3,842 clubs spread throughout much of the world. Great Britain alone had 400 clubs. See Paul Martin, *We Serve: A History of the Lions Club* (Washington, DC: Regnery Gateway, 1991) and *Proceedings, Twenty-Sixth Annual Convention,* Mexico City, Mexico, 17–21 June 1935, "The Growth of Rotary," 6.

3. *Proceedings, Twenty-Sixth Annual Convention,* Mexico City, Mexico, 17–21 June 1935, 9.

4. *Proceedings, Twenty-Sixth Annual Convention,* Mexico City, Mexico, 17–21 June 1935, 75–76. On the biography of Armando de Arruda Pereira, see Eurico Branco Ribeiro, "Meet Armando! Your Personal Introduction to the New President of Rotary," *Rotarian,* July 1940, 33–34, 59.

5. Chesley R. Perry, general secretary of the National Association of Rotary Clubs, to A. P. Bigelow, manager, Initial Towel Company, 19 December 1911, Club historical file, London Rotary Club, RI Archives.

6. Perry to Bigelow, 19 December 1911, London club historical file, RI Archives.

7. In London, for example, Arthur Bigelow learned of Rotary through his business associate, Harvey C. Wheeler, a member of the newly minted Boston Rotary club. See Stanley Leverton, *The Story of the Rotary Club of London, 1911–1961* (London: Frederick Printing, 1961).

8. Paul P. Harris to A. P. Bigelow, 26 January 1912, and A. P. Bigelow to Paul Harris, 4 April 1912, Club historical file, London Rotary club.

9. Leverton, *The Story of the Rotary Club of London,* 1.

10. *Rotarian,* September 1913, 29.

11. Chesley R. Perry to Alexander Kent, 7 July 1915, Havana club historical file, vol. 1, RI Archives.

12. Board of directors of IARC, "Minutes of Meetings, Extension Committee 1912–1929": 1 August 1914, "Extension Europe Africa / Asia Minor;" 18 July 1915, "Extension in South America;" and 4–5 September 1915, "Extension Central and South America," RI Archives.

13. *Convention Proceedings, Seventh International Convention,* Atlanta, Georgia, 17–22 June 1917, 80–82.

14. S. O. Harnecker to John Turner, chairman of Extension Committee in Latin America, 16 May 1917, reported in *Convention Proceedings, Seventh International Convention,* Atlanta, 1917, 80–82.

15. *Convention Proceedings, Seventh International Convention,* Atlanta, 1917, 82.

16. Robert W. Bonynge, "Banking and Currency Reform," *Rotarian,* September 1912, 7–8, 34–35.

17. Bonynge, "Banking and Currency Reform," 35–36.

18. Over the course of the twentieth century, club secretaries were slowly replaced by salaried executive directors, a process reflecting the professionalization of charitable activities and philanthropic organizations over time. For more on this and related topics, see David C. Hammack, ed., *Making the Nonprofit Sector in the United States: A Reader* (Bloomington: Indiana University Press, 2000), and David C. Hammack and Helmut K. Anheier, *A Versatile American Institution: The Changing Ideals and Realities of Philanthropic Foundations* (Washington, DC: Brookings Institution Press, 2013).

19. On Rotary districts in Japan, see Chapter 4. For the history of Rotary clubs in Australia and the evolution of districts within that country, see Harold Hunt, *The Story of Rotary in Australia 1921–1971* (Sydney: Halsted Press, 1971), and Paul Henningham, *The Story of the Regional Rotary Institutes in Australia* (Netley, South Australia: Griffin Press, 1978).

20. In the case of Rotary clubs in Michigan and western Ontario, for example, there was a long history of "international" districts that were emphatically drawn to cross US-Canadian borders. To see how this played out on a daily basis for a district governor, see Harold Dorr Papers, box 1, file "1957, Correspondence concerning Rotary Club Affairs," Bentley Historical Library, Ann Arbor, Michigan. Comparable "international" districts could be found throughout the world both before and after World War II and were often pointed to as compelling evidence of RI's civic internationalism in regular operation.

21. "What Shall United States Rotary Do in War?," *Rotarian,* July 1917, 7–8.

22. *Gyrator of the Rotary Club of Chicago,* 31 March 1928, "Historic Rotary Service," 2, Chicago / Rotary One Archives, Chicago, Illinois.

23. For a detailed account of APL origins and the key role of Briggs's "friends in the business community," see Richard Gid Powers, *Broken: The Troubled Past and Uncertain Future of the FBI* (New York: Free Press, 2004), 86–92, and Emerson Hough, *The Web* (Chicago: Reilly & Lee, 1919), 19–62, 179–189. For an excellent review of the many private, voluntary organizations

working with federal, state, and local governments to block dissent during World War I, see Christopher Cappozzola, "The Only Badge Needed Is Your Patriotic Fervor: Vigilance, Coercion, and the Law in World War I America," *Journal of American History* 88, no. 4 (March 2002), 1354–1382, and Nancy K. Bristow, *Making Men Moral: Social Engineering during the Great War* (New York: New York University Press, 1996).

24. *Gyrator,* 31 March 1928, "Historic Rotary Service," 2. For a recent contextualization of the American Protective League, see Robert E. Hannigan, *The Great War and American Foreign Policy, 1914–24* (Philadelphia: University of Pennsylvania, 2017), 100–102.

25. Powers, *Broken,* 88–100; Cappozzola, "The Only Badge Needed Is Your Patriotic Fervor," 1367–1370, 1377–1382.

26. *Gyrator,* 31 March 1928, "Historic Rotary Service," 2.

27. For example, in fall 1933, the *Rotarian* asked its world readership, "Should the United States Recognize Russia?." See the *Rotarian,* October 1933, 10–13, 50–51.

28. Harry A. Wheeler, "A Period of Readjustment," *Rotarian,* September 1913, 29–30. On the presumed complementary role of the USCC in the "modern administrative state" during this period, see Laura Phillips Sawyer, "Trade Associations, State Building, and the Sherman Act: The U.S. Chamber of Commerce, 1912-25," in *Capital Gains: Business and Politics in Twentieth-Century America*, ed. Richard R. John and Kim Phillips-Fein (Philadelphia: University of Pennsylvania Press, 2017), 25–42.

29. The first Rotary club in South America, the Montevideo Rotary club, received its charter on 1 February 1919. See Enrique Brussoni, *Historia Del Rotary Club de Montevideo, 1918–1983* (Montevideo: Rotary Club of Montevideo, 1984).

30. *Rotarian,* September 1913, 43.

31. Meeting of the Committee on Foreign Extension Work, 29–30 March 1919, in Central Files—Subject Files / [Committee—Extension], "Committee on Foreign Extension Work" [Minutes Book, March 1919–January 1925], RI Archives.

32. "Report of the Extension Committee to the Board of Directors," for 1924 / 25, Exhibit B, in Central Files-Subject Files / [Committee—Extension, (Minutes Book, July 1925–Aug 1929)], RI Archives.

33. At this time, circulation for the *Rotarian* approximated its membership of about 120,000. By the late 1920s, the *Rotarian* was a key business publication of the period, in company with *Printer's Ink, Iron Age, Fortune,* the *Wall Street Journal,* the *Economist,* and *Commercial and Financial Chronicle.*

34. Minutes of the Meeting of Board of Directors of RI, 28–31 March 1927, "Articles in The Rotarian—Item XIII" (d), 25, RI Archives.

35. Frederick G. Johnson, "Gentlemen—Be Seated!," *Rotarian,* October 1923, 16–17, 50–53. Johnson worked in "an editorial and advisory capacity" for the T.S. Denison Company, a Chicago publishing firm that specialized in "dramatic" publications for minstrel shows. Copies of his guidebook on how to organize and promote an amateur minstrel show were available for all Rotary clubs. Johnson, "Gentlemen—Be Seated!," 6.

36. For thorough examination of minstrelsy in US history, see Eric Lott, *Love and Theft: Blackface Minstrelsy and the American Working Class* (New York: Oxford University Press, 1993).

37. An example of Rotary attempting to move in this direction, but not really succeeding, can be seen in J. Frank Davis, "Rotary Color," *Rotarian,* May 1926, 11–13, 63–68.

38. The Rotary club of Adrian, Michigan, was still presenting minstrel shows as community fundraisers in the 1950s. *The First Fifty Years of the Rotary Club of Adrian, Michigan, Golden Anniversary, 1921–1971,* Bentley Historical Library, Ann Arbor, Michigan.

39. Observation is also based on interview with Herb Ellis, who became the second African American member of the Ann Arbor Rotary club in 1960, Ann Arbor, Michigan, 13 March 2001.

40. For a review of how Rotary clubs became so involved in Boys' Work campaigns, see William Lewis Butcher, "Boys' Week and the Boy Problem," *Rotarian,* April 1923, 195–197, 243, 246. The article proudly recounts how the Boys' Week festivities started by the New York City Rotary club had extended all the way to Cuban cities.

41. The first Rotary clubs in Latin American countries were typically in capitals—for example, Havana, Cuba, 1916; Montevideo, Uruguay, 1918; Mexico City, Mexico, 1921; La Paz, Bolivia, 1927; Asuncion, Paraguay, 1927. See the map "The First Rotary Club in Each Country and Region throughout the World, 1905–1958" for more details.

42. See *Weekly Letter,* 9 June 1924, and "Report of Extension Committee by Crawford McCullough, 1924–25, Jamaica," RI Archives.

43. Chesley R. Perry to Edwin H. Rushmore, secretary, Rotary Club of New York City, 31 March 1938, box 19, file: [Clubs—Rotary] General Correspondence, RI Archives. Perry sent two letters to Rushmore on the same day on the same subject.

44. Paul King to Chesley Perry, 5 March 1929, James Wheeler Davidson Papers, vol. II, RI Archives.

45. For a biography of John Barrett, see Salvatore Prisco III, *John Barrett, Progressive Era Diplomat: A Study of a Commercial Expansionist, 1887–1920* (Tuscaloosa: University of Alabama Press, 1973), esp. chapter 4, and John Barrett Papers (1861–1943), Manuscripts Division, Library of Congress, Washington, DC (hereafter, "John Barrett Papers, LOC"). For an analysis from a much broader perspective, see Richard Cándida-Smith, *Improvised Continent: Pan-Americanism and Cultural Exchange* (Philadelphia, PA: University of Pennsylvania Press, 2017).

46. Much has been written on the growing interconnectedness of the global economy during this period; two of the most comprehensive works are Emily S. Rosenberg, ed., *A World Connecting: 1870–1945* (Cambridge: Harvard University Press, 2012), and Dwayne R. Winseck and Robert M. Pike, *Communication and Empire: Media, Markets, and Globalization, 1860–1930* (Durham, NC: Duke University Press, 2007). For greater contextualization of Wilsonian rhetoric within the specific context of communications and transportation revolutions in 1919, see also Erez Manela, *The Wilsonian Moment: Self-Determination and the International Origins of Anticolonial Nationalism* (New York: Oxford University Press, 2007), 15–54.

47. For statistics on simultaneous growth of membership and clubs worldwide for the first half of the twentieth century, see *Rotary, Fifty Years of Service, 1905–1955* (Evanston, IL: Rotary International, 1955).

48. Interoffice memo, D. B. Ledo to Chesley Perry, "Rotary for Barcelona," 30 December 1919, John Barrett Papers, LOC, box 49, December 17–31, 1919. The meeting in Boston was attended by David Harrell, special representative for the US Department of Agriculture; J. Frank Lanning, of J. Frank Lanning Co., Pittsburgh; H. C. Watkins, representative for the Burroughs Adding Machine Co.; C. H. Abbott, director general of "las Escuelas Internacionales"; J. Nelson Wisner, secretary of US Chamber of Commerce in Buenos Aires.; and Noel F. Tribe, manager, First National Bank of Boston, Buenos Aires branch. See Chesley Perry to John Barrett, 2 January 1920, John Barrett Papers, LOC, box 49, General Correspondence, January 1–11, 1920.

49. John Dyer, first vice president, IARC, to Chesley Perry, general secretary of IARC and key member of the Foreign Extension Committee, 3 December 1919, John Barrett Papers, LOC; box 49, General Correspondence, December 1–16, 1919.

50. Richard Meriweather, president, Dallas Rotary club, to Dr. Robert E. Vinson, University of Texas, Austin, 31 October 1919, John Barrett Papers, LOC, box 48, General Correspondence, October 15–31, 1919; and Chesley Perry, general secretary of the IARC, to the Committee on Foreign Extension, 12 Feb-

ruary 1920, John Barrett Papers, LOC, box 49, General Correspondence, February 2–14, 1920.

51. Chesley Perry to C. H. Abbott, director general, Escuelas Internacionales, 2 July 1919, John Barrett Papers, LOC, box 48, General Correspondence, July 1–14, 1919.

52. Chesley Perry to Oliver Brothers, Inc, New York City, 15 November 1919, and Chesley Perry to John Barrett, 15 November 1919, John Barrett Papers, LOC, box 48, General Correspondence, November 15–30, 1919.

53. Chesley Perry to John Barrett, 6 December 1919, with transcript of letter from Mr. W. E. Bleo, vice president, Electric Company, of Port-au-Prince included and list of proposed club officers and charter membership, John Barrett Papers, LOC, box 49, General Correspondence, December 1–16, 1919.

54. Chesley Perry to John Barrett, 8 December 1919, and John Barrett to Chesley Perry, 10 December 1919, John Barrett Papers, LOC, box 49, General Correspondence, December 1–16, 1919.

55. Haiti Legation in Washington, D.C., to John Barrett, 9 December 1919. John Barrett Papers, LOC, box 49, General Correspondence, December 1–16, 1919.

56. L.J. Bourgeois, Secretary, Superintendant of Public Instruction, Republic of Haiti to "Rotary Club of the United States, Committee on International Affiliations," 26 November 1919, John Barrett Papers, LOC, box 48, General Correspondence, November 15–30, 1919.

57. C. Edgar Elliott, President of HASCO, Port-au-Prince, HASCO letterhead, to Chesley Perry, 19 January 1920, John Barrett Papers, LOC, box 49, General Correspondence, January 12–31, 1920.

58. C. Edgar Elliott, President of HASCO, Port-au-Prince, HASCO letterhead, to Chesley Perry, 19 January 1920, John Barrett Papers, LOC, box 49, General Correspondence, January 12–31, 1920.

59. Chesley Perry to Foreign Extension Committee, IARC letterhead, 10 February 1920, John Barrett Papers, LOC, box 49, General Correspondence, February 2–14, 1920.

60. Albert Adams, President of IARC, to Chesley Perry, 17 March 1920, John Barrett Papers, LOC, box 49, General Correspondence, March 15–31, 1920.

61. John Barrett to Chesley Perry, 1 April 1920, John Barrett Papers, LOC, box 49, April 1–14, 1920.

62. Arch Klumph to Chesley Perry, 5 April 1920, John Barrett Papers, LOC, box 49, April 1–14, 1920.

63. John Barrett to Chesley Perry, 1 April 1920, John Barrett Papers, LOC, box 49, April 1–14, 1920.

64. Herbert P. Coates, Special Commissioner for RI, to John Barrett, 21 May 1920, John Barrett Papers, LOC, box 50, General Correspondence, April 15–30, 1920.

65. Report of the meeting of the Foreign Extension Committee held in the Casino of the Steel Pier, 25 June 1920, 1, John Barrett Papers, LOC, box 95, Subject file: 1899–1935, International Association of Rotary Clubs.

66. Principles and Policies for Extension Work for 1925–26, Exhibit No. 13, January 11–13, 1926, Subject: Extension West Indies, Minutes of the Meeting of Board of Directors of RI, Extension Committee, 1912–1929.

67. Report of the 1923–1924 Committee on Extension, July 18–21, 1923, Minutes of the Meeting of board of directors of RI, Extension Committee, 1912–1929.

68. For example, Doug Williams, an African American community leader in Ann Arbor, Michigan, joined the Ann Arbor Rotary Club, in the late 1950s. Interview with Herb Ellis, 13 March 2001. Jeffrey Charles points to the early 1950s as the earliest known membership of an African American in a US Rotary club, in Healdsburg, CA. Jeffrey Charles, *Service Clubs in American Society: Rotary, Kiwanis, and Lions* (Urbana and Chicago: University of Illinois Press, 1993), 155.

69. On this crucial point, see Michel-Rolph Trouillot, *Silencing the Past: Power and the Production of History* (Boston, Beacon Press: 1997).

70. Chesley Perry to Edwin H. Rushmore, Secretary, Rotary Club of New York City, 31 March 1938, box 19, file: [Clubs–Rotary] General Correspondence, RI Archives. Perry actually sent two letters to Rushmore on the same day on the same subject.

71. Perry to Rushmore, 31 March 1938.

72. Perry to Rushmore, 31 March 1938.

73. See Manela, *Wilsonian Moment,* chap. 2. On the mutually constitutive nature of racism and capitalism long before the twentieth century, see Cedric Robinson, *Black Marxism: The Making of the Black Radical Tradition,* 2nd ed. (Chapel Hill: University of North Carolina, 2000); for a compelling application of Robinson's concept of "racial capitalism" to the experience of Haiti in the early twentieth century, see Peter James Hudson, *Bankers and Empire: How Wall Street Colonized the Caribbean* (Chicago: University of Chicago Press, 2017). From a broader perspective, see Justin Leroy and Destin Jenkins, eds., *Histories of Racial Capitalism* (New York: Columbia University Press, 2021), Robert Vitalis, *White World Order, Black Power Politics: The Birth of American International Relations* (Ithaca, NY: Cornell University Press, 2015), Manning Marable and Vanessa Agard-Jones, eds., *Transnational Blackness: Navigating the Global Color Line* (London: Palgrave Macmillan, 2008),

and Marilyn Lake and Henry Reynolds, *Drawing the Global Colour Line: White Men's Countries and the International Challenge of Racial Equality* (Cambridge: Cambridge University Press, 2008). W. E. B. Du Bois famously first recognized that "the problem of the twentieth century is the problem of the color-line," in W. E. B. Du Bois, *The Souls of Black Folk* (New York: Penguin, 1903).

74. On the formation of the first Rotary club in Asia, see Roger D. Pinneo to Chesley Perry, 25 November 1918, John Barrett Papers, LOC, box 45, General Correspondence, 20–30 November 1918. See also the *Rotarian*, March 1919, 122; the *Rotarian*, May 1919, 231; and Arthur Melville, "Over the Great Wall," the *Rotarian*, February 1924, 13–14, 45–46.

75. On the early history of the Manila Rotary club, see "First Decennial Handbook, 1919–1929" and "The History of the Manila Rotary Club," 2004–04, box 5, "Manila. Philippine Islands," Chicago / Rotary One Archive.

76. Dr. Julian Petit to Chesley Perry, general secretary of Rotary International, 2 August 1922. Letter written on the official letterhead of the Shanghai Rotary Club, Shanghai club historical file, vol. II, RI Archives.

77. John Barrett, chairman of Foreign Extension Committee to Chesley Perry, 25 July 1919, on Pan American Union letterhead. Perry forwarded Barrett's letter to Dr. Petit, 23 September 1919. Shanghai club historical file, vol. I, RI Archives.

78. See Eileen P. Scully, *Bargaining with the State from Afar: American Citizenship in Treaty Port China 1844–1942* (New York: Columbia University Press, 2001) for a thorough examination of the complex business and political environment in Shanghai before World War II and how the concept of "citizenship" and its relationship to the state evolved in that environment.

79. A. Giovannini to Chesley R. Perry, 23 June 1936, with list of club committees and members. Shanghai club historical files, vol. IV. See the same for excerpt from "Welfare Work for Needy Children. Shanghai Rotary Club's Widespread Activities" by Robert Fan in *The Far Eastern Rotary Review*, October 1936, which recounts the details of the club's "major charity object" of raising $40,000 to establish a "Rotary War for Crippled Children." The club expected the project to be "much more than local in interest, because the influence of this humanitarian work will be eventually nationwide."

80. Alex Potter, Report on trip to Asia and Europe, 4 April 1939, Shanghai club historical file, vol. VIII.

81. One of many examples of coordination among charities occurred at Christmas with the charity committee's annual toy drive. The "Rotary Anns," or wives of the club members, selected toys that were packaged and distributed through US corporations run by Shanghai Rotarians to more than twenty-

five different charities, "from YMCA, Red Cross, and Salvation Army to local hospitals, missionary organizations, and settlement houses and beggar guilds." Donations also came in from the Women's Christian Temperance Union, the Chinese Welfare Association School, the Little Sisters of the Poor, the Hebrew Relief Society, and the Russian Commercial School. The Shanghai Rotary club, much like its counterparts around the world, was supposed to operate in this fashion in fulfillment of RI's commitment to community service. *Pagoda,* 11 January 1934, "Report of Charity Committee for Christmas 1933," file: "Shanghai 1926–1937," Chicago / Rotary One Archives.

82. Report of Director Richard Currie on visit to Shanghai and Hong Kong, 11 September 1939, at sea between Manila and Saigon, Shanghai club historical file, vol. VIII, RI Archives..

83. C. T. Wang was part of China's delegation in Paris in 1919. He then served in the Senate, as minister of foreign affairs, acting prime minister, minister of finance, and then as member of the Central Political Council of the Central Executive Committee and National Government of China through the 1920s and 1930s, and finally as ambassador to the United States. As president of China University in Peiping (Beijing), chairman of the board of directors of the Kiaochow-Tsinan railroad, and president of the Chinese Red Cross Association as well as a graduate of the University of Michigan and Yale Law School, C. T. Wang was the perfect Chinese "native" to serve as Rotary's first governor of all Rotary clubs in China, Hong Kong, and the Philippines, 1935–1937, and as a member of Rotary's Council on Legislation, one of the highest positions in the organization's international administration. Statement from *Proceedings, 27th Annual Convention of RI,* Atlantic City, 22–26 June 1936, "What Rotary Means in My Country," 79, 99–103.

84. According to "Report of Rotary Meeting, August 6, 1925" by Fong Sec, Club historical files, Shanghai, vol. IV. The club roster from May 1925 lists 88 members, 15 of whom have obvious Chinese surnames and businesses. Sec's estimate was not far from the mark.

85. The Shanghai club had particular success with this goal, becoming the predominant group in the Shanghai Rotary club by 1937. The nationalities of the membership of 127 broke down in the following way that year: 30 percent Chinese, 21.3 percent US, 18.1 percent British, 7.1 percent Japanese, 4.8 percent French, 3.9 percent German, and another eleven nationalities ranging from Swedish to Australian to Italian. Shanghai club historical file, vol. IV, Official Club Membership and "Classification Survey 1936–37." One of the top officers of RI in Chicago commented that "going through the list is a very useful bit of education; if it were not for some such classifications as 'Shintoism' and 'Taoism' under 'Religion,' and some Chinese names under other majors, it would hardly

differ from a list of a European or American business center." Russell Williams, Assistant Secretary of RI, to Mrs. A. Giovannini, Shanghai Rotary club executive secretary, 16 December 1936, Shanghai club historical file, vol. VII. For full account of the year's gains and losses in Rotary clubs, see *Convention Proceedings, Twenty-Eighth Annual Convention,* Nice, France, 6–11 June 1937, 8. The number of Chinese Rotary clubs roughly equaled the 33 clubs in Japan. Meanwhile, the 42 Rotary clubs in Germany were abolished by December 1937, followed by dozens of others in countries allied with the Nazis, Romania, and Czechoslovakia in particular. See also Victoria de Grazia, *Irresistible Empire: America's Advance through Twentieth-Century Europe* (Cambridge, MA: Harvard University Press, 2005), 71.

86. See, for example, club historical files for Chungking (Chongqing) and Hankow, RI Archives. Though founded in 1919, the Shanghai club was still dominated by non-Chinese members in 1936, resulting in resignation on the part of the Chinese members that the club "will undergo little change from the present status" in the future and thus would "never be truly representative of Greater Shanghai." Formation of "a parallel club of Chinese nationals" was given serious consideration. Report by Crawford C. McCullough to President and Board of Directors on visit to District 70 (Japan) and 81 (China, Philippines), April / May 1936.

87. For the sake of simplicity and following the lead of both Japanese and Chinese Rotarians from the period, I have maintained the anglicized names of Japanese and Chinese cities to remain consistent with the historical record.

88. Among the thirty five clubs in Mexico in 1935, for example, RI estimated that 75–80 percent of members were "native Mexican citizens." *Proceedings, Twenty-Sixth Annual Convention,* Mexico City, Mexico, 17–21 June 1935, 150.

89. In East Asia, Shanghai in particular, several clubs survived long after the start of open hostilities between China and Japan in 1937. In Latin America, in fact, World War II accelerated Rotary's expansion even more, resulting in RI's first international president from the region, Fernando Carbajal of Lima, Peru, 1942–1943.

90. "Memo of Agreement between Special Representative Arch C. Klumph and F.W. Teele, President of the Rotary Club of Mexico City," undated, but very likely April / May 1921, Mexico City club files / Ciudad de Mexico, D.F., Mexico, RI Archives.

91. Mexico City Rotary Club Constitution, article III, section 5, on "Membership," and article VII, section 1, on "Avoidance of Politics," Mexico City club files / Ciudad de Mexico, D.F., Mexico, RI Archives.

92. *Proceedings, Thirty-Second Annual Convention of Rotary International,* Denver, Colorado, 15–21 June 1941, "The Rotarian Amid World Conflict,"

Address to the Convention by Armando de Arruda Pereira, President of Rotary International, 21–27 and 327.

3. THE ELIMINATION OF DIFFERENCES

1. *Convention Proceedings, Twentieth Annual Convention,* Dallas, Texas, 27–31 May 1929, 430–431.

2. *Convention Proceedings, Twentieth Annual Convention,* Dallas, Texas, 27–31 May 1929, 423–425.

3. *Convention Proceedings, Twentieth Annual Convention,* Dallas, Texas, 27–31 May 1929, 425.

4. On the emergence of a postwar permanent war economy, see Ann Markusen, *The Rise of the Gunbelt: The Military Remapping of Industrial America* (New York: Oxford University Press, 1991); Bruce Schulman, *From Cotton Belt to Sunbelt: Federal Policy, Economic Development, and the Transformation of the South, 1938–1980* (New York: Oxford University Press, 1991); Robert P. Patterson, *Arming the Nation for War: Mobilization, Supply, and the American War Effort in World War II* (Knoxville: University of Tennessee Press, 2014); A. J. Baime, *The Arsenal of Democracy: FDR, Ford Motor Company, and Their Epic Quest to Arm an America at War* (Boston: Houghton Mifflin Harcourt, 2014); and Mark R. Wilson, *Destructive Creation: American Business and the Winning of World War II* (Philadelphia: University of Pennsylvania Press, 2016). For a social, political, and cultural approach to the same topic, see Michael Sherry, *In the Shadow of War: The United States since the 1930s* (New Haven, CT: Yale University Press, 1995), and for a good analysis of the evolution of the aviation industry in the same context, see Sherry, *The Rise of American Air Power: The Creation of Armageddon* (New Haven, CT: Yale University Press, 1987), John Buckley, *Air Power in the Age of Total War* (Bloomington: Indiana University Press, 1999), and Jeffrey A. Engel, *Cold War at 30,000 Feet: The Anglo-American Fight for Aviation Supremacy* (Cambridge, MA: Harvard University Press, 2007).

5. Sadao Asada, "Between the Old Diplomacy and the New, 1918–1922: The Washington System and the Origins of Japanese-American Rapprochement," *Diplomatic History* 30, no. 2 (April 2006), 211–230. On the period of "Shidehara diplomacy" from 1922 to 1931, see Tomoko Akami, *Internationalizing the Pacific: The United States, Japan, and the Institute of Pacific Relations in War and Peace, 1919–1945* (London: Routledge, 2002); Ian Nish, *Japanese Foreign Policy in the Interwar Period* (Westport, CT: Praeger, 2002); Akira Iriye, *The Cambridge History of American Foreign Relation,* vol. III, *The Globalizing of America* (Cambridge:

Cambridge University Press, 1993), 73–115, for a review of diplomatic relations from outside the perspective of US-Japanese relations; and Masamichi Royama, *Foreign Policy of Japan: 1914–1939*, reprint ed. (Westport, CT: Greenwood Press, 1973), for a Japanese perspective from the period.

6. Christina Klein, *Cold War Orientalism: Asia in the Middlebrow Imagination* (Berkeley: University of California Press, 2003), 1–17, for use of phrases in quotation marks.

7. Klein, *Cold War Orientalism.*

8. The notion of soft versus hard power receives particular treatment in Joseph S. Nye, *Soft Power: The Means to Success in World Politics* (New York: Public Affairs, 2004), and David Held and Mathias Koenig-Archibugi, eds., *American Power in the Twenty-first Century* (Cambridge: Polity, 2004).

9. On Chicago as an imperial city with such influence, see William Cronon, *Nature's Metropolis: Chicago and the Great West* (New York: W.W. Norton, 1991).

10. As quoted in Joyce Suellentrop, *Rotary Club of Wichita, Kansas: The First Seventy-Five Years, 1911–1986* (Wichita, KS: Rotary Club of Wichita, 1986), 1–3.

11. For a significant treatment of the concept of social capital in the world of business and specifically on Rotary International, see Pamela Walker Laird, *Pull: Networking and Success since Benjamin Franklin* (Cambridge, MA: Harvard University Press, 2006), 87–91. While Laird is correct to treat RI as the vanguard of service clubs (Lions, Kiwanis, National Exchange, Optimists, and so on) and as a mainstream movement of middle-class businessmen in the United States before World War II, she overlooks the international aspects of RI. There is no reason the fundamental dynamics of social capital—bridging and bonding—cannot operate across political borders just as business itself does.

12. Suellentrop, *Rotary Club of Wichita,* 4.

13. Individual US club reports in the 1920s and 1930s, for example, often claimed that 70–90 percent of their members also belonged to the town or city's chamber of commerce.

14. This is according to Will Price, president of Wichita Business College, owner of Wichita's first Ford automobile dealership from 1916 to 1952, and the third president of Wichita's Rotary club in 1914–1915. See Suellentrop, *Rotary Club of Wichita,* 4–5.

15. Suellentrop, *Rotary Club of Wichita,* 5–7.

16. Suellentrop, *Rotary Club of Wichita,* 7–8.

17. On the transition from party politics to professional politics during this period, see Michael McGerr, *A Fierce Discontent: The Rise and Fall of the*

Progressive Movement in America, 1870–1920 (New York: Free Press, 2003), and Gabriel Kolko, *The Triumph of Conservatism; A Reinterpretation of American History, 1900–1916* (New York: Free Press, 1963), for a classic view on the function of business interests shaping state structures for conservative rather than genuinely progressive ends.

18. Form letter of the Wichita, Kansas, Rotary Club to the Rotary Clubs of the United States, 14 May 1925, duplicated in the Wichita Rotary Club's publication, *Round and Round,* 16 May 1925, Guy Gundaker Papers; file "Rotary General—Notes on Convention at Pittsburgh," RI Archives. See also "Meeting of the Extension Committee, July 28–30, 1925, Chicago," file "Committee—Extension—1925–29," RI Archives.

19. Form letter of the Wichita, Kansas, Rotary Club to the Rotary Clubs of the United States, 14 May 1925.

20. *Convention Proceedings, Sixteenth Annual Convention,* Cleveland, Ohio, June 1925, Resolution # 19, and Wichita Rotary Club bulletin, *Round and Round,* 16 May 1925, Guy Gundaker Papers, file: ["Rotary General—Notes on Convention at Pittsburgh"], RI Archives.

21. *Rotarian,* August 1925, 37.

22. John G. Swain, President, Whittier Rotary Club, to all US Rotary clubs, 12 May 1926, Guy Gundaker Papers, file: ["Rotary General—Notes on Convention at Pittsburgh"], RI Archives. The real impetus behind the Whittier Club's emphasis on improving international relations was provided by Herbert E. Harris, professor of English at Whittier College and chairman of the "Sixth Object Committee"—soon renamed by RI the "International Service Committee" for all clubs. RI's "Sixth Object," first formally adopted in 1922 and later renamed as the "Fourth Object," reads: "The advancement of understanding, good will, and international peace through a world fellowship of business and professional men united in the Rotary ideal of Service." Herbert Harris eventually ascended to the chair of RI's International Service Committee for the entire organization in 1929–1930. The other four members of the International Service Committee under Harris were Ernesto Aguilar (plate glass distributing) of Mexico City, Mexico; Joseph Caulder (dairy financing) of Toronto, Canada; L. R. Grote (physician) of Frankfurt, Germany; and H. Norton Matthews (public school) of Bristol, England. *Convention Proceedings,* Dallas, Texas, 27–31 May 1929, 549.

23. For similar contemporary views on the Red Cross, see "Address of President Wilson Opening the Campaign in New York for the Second Red Cross Fund," 18 May 1918 (Washington, DC: Government Printing Office, 1918), and "Address of President Hoover on the Occasion of the Celebration of the Fif-

tieth Anniversary of the American National Red Cross," 21 May 1931 (Washington, DC: Government Printing Office, 1931).

24. Jay Price, "Cowboy Boosterism: Old Cowtown Museum and the Image of Wichita, Kansas," *Kansas Historical Quarterly* 24, no. 4 (Winter 2001), 301–317. On the history of the city of Wichita, see Glenn W. Miller and Jimmy M. Skaggs, eds., *Metropolitan Wichita: Past, Present, and Future* (Wichita, KS: Wichita State University, 1978).

25. Quoted in Frank Rowe and Craig Miner, *Borne on the South Wind: A Century of Kansas Aviation* (Newton, KS: Mennonite Press, 1994), 29.

26. Rowe and Miner, *Borne on the South Wind,* 29–41.

27. Rowe and Miner, *Borne on the South Wind,* 54.

28. Developments in broom-corn warehousing and marketing also added to the pool of available capital. Rowe and Miner, *Borne on the South Wind,* 59.

29. Beech and Stearman combined in 1925 to form Travel Air Manufacturing Co., where Cessna was vice president. A year later Stearman left for Venice, California, but he returned in 1927 to create Stearman Aircraft Co., where he was president and general manager. In 1929, Boeing of Seattle bought Stearman Aircraft, forming what became known as Boeing Wichita by 1941.

30. Rowe and Miner, *Borne on the South Wind,* 57–58. Quotation taken from the *Wichita Eagle.*

31. Jean Hays, "Wichita Tooted Aviation's Horn," *Wichita Eagle,* 25 February 1985.

32. In the club's 1924 roster, for example, he is listed as chairing the committee on "Rotary Membership Education." Wichita Rotary Club Membership Roster, 1924, Wichita club historical file, RI Archives.

33. Membership in a Rotary club in this period, however, required attendance at the weekly luncheon meetings. Attendance below 60 percent constituted absenteeism that was usually grounds for removal from the club. Wichita's club seemed to follow this same rule of thumb. As such, all members of Rotary clubs were at least active in the minimal sense of attending well over half of all weekly luncheons. In the case of Murdock, his chairing of the "Rotary Education Committee" in 1924 and his responsibility for establishing various clubs in nearby cities before and after indicate a level membership well above the average. Wichita Rotary Club Membership Roster, 1924.

34. Rowe and Miner, *Borne on the South Wind,* 77.

35. Rowe and Miner, *Borne on the South Wind,* 73–75.

36. The club was also lobbying to move the international headquarters for RI from Chicago to Wichita for several years. Harry Stanley was also in charge of that project, as the club roster of committee chairs (1924–1925) lists him as head of "International Headquarters" as well as "International

Convention." Other club committees included Program and Entertainment, Fellowship, Public Affairs, Rotary Membership Education, Rotary Extension Education, Boys' Work, Big Brother, Civic Clubs, Grievances, Inter-City Rotary Relations, Eats and Hotel, Round & Round (club bulletin), Correspondence, Resolutions, Flowers and Calling, Glad Hand, Attendance, and Business Methods.

37. The sixteen committee members present a typical slice of the 230 members of the whole club, with the exception of members in the oil industry, who composed almost 5 percent of the club in 1924. Following are their names and their business or professional classifications within the club:

Chair, Harry Stanley	Insurance Salesman	Founder of the Wichita Rotary club
Marcellus "Marsh" Murdock	Morning Newspaper	The Wichita Eagle
Billy Ingram, "Billy"	Chain Lunch Stands	
Msgr. William Farrell	Catholic Priest	
Wash Lilleston	Law Partner	Vermillion, Evans, Carey, and Lilleston
Giff Booth, Sr.	Printing	
Pierce Atwater	Wichita	Community Chest
Sylvester Long	Refrigerating Machines	
Orville Boyle	President / Gen. Man.	The Boyle Co. or, simply, "Potatoes"
"Bob" Timmons	Investment Securities	Kansas Gas and Electric
W. M. G. Howse	President	Johnston and Larimer Dry Goods Co.
Bob Zimmerman	Dental Supplies	
Charley M. Jackman	President	Kansas Milling Co.
H.W. Cardwell	unlisted	
Will Price	President	Price Auto Service Co., Auto Retailing
C.Q. Chandler	not given	

Data source: Joyce Suellentrop, *Rotary Club of Wichita (1911–1986):* Club No. 30, 21.

38. As of June 1928, there were 2,932 clubs in forty-four separate countries, with 301 new clubs in the previous year from thirty different countries. Ecuador, Bolivia, Germany and Paraguay were the newest countries to the fold, while Chile and Mexico each saw the establishment of seventeen new clubs. For club and membership statistics, *Nineteenth International Convention Proceedings*, Minneapolis, Minnesota, 18–22 June 1928, 6.

39. *The Five Ships and Cargoes,* Rotary Club of Wichita, 1928, foreword.

40. *Five Ships.*

41. *Five Ships.*

42. "Acquaintanceship," *The Five Ships and Cargoes,* Rotary Club of Wichita, 1928.

43. "Acquaintanceship."

44. "Friendship," *The Five Ships and Cargoes,* Rotary Club of Wichita, 1928.

45. "Kinship," *The Five Ships and Cargoes,* Rotary Club of Wichita, 1928.

46. Conclusion, *The Five Ships and Cargoes,* Rotary Club of Wichita, 1928.

47. *Twentieth International Convention Proceedings,* Dallas, Texas, 27–31 May 1929, 38, 493. There were 100 new clubs in the US and 114 outside the United States in the period from July 1, 1928, to July 1, 1929. (The "fiscal year" for RI was July 1 to June 30, when all administrative turnover occurred from the lowest club official to RI's board of directors and international president.) Overall cumulative totals were 2,345 clubs in the United States out of approximately 3,146 clubs outside the United States (not including another 21 non-US clubs pending approval). In the summer of 1929, in other words, about 25 percent of all Rotary clubs were outside the United States, but the proportion was increasing appreciably. There were several specific areas of rapid growth outside the United States in the previous year:

Country	Clubs as of 1 July 1928	Clubs as of 30 June 1929	Net gain in clubs
Australia	18	24	6
Brazil	5	11	6
Chile	26	34	8
Czechoslovakia	11	21	10
Denmark	4	7	3
France	17	24	7
Germany	3	7	4
Great Britain	282	310	28
Holland	8	12	4
Italy	15	20	5

Data source: *Twentieth International Convention Proceedings,* Dallas, Texas, 27–31 May 1929, 493. The previous year, Mexico nearly doubled its number of clubs from 19 to 37 while Chile exploded, going from 4 clubs to 26 in just one year.

48. *Twentieth International Convention Proceedings,* Dallas, Texas, 27–31 May 1929, 49.

49. Most of this growth was the result of the travels and organizing of Rotary clubs by Jim and Lillian Davidson from 1928 to 1931, the focus of Chapter 6.

50. *Twentieth International Convention Proceedings,* Dallas, Texas, 27–31 May 1929, 69.

51. *Twentieth International Convention Proceedings,* Dallas, Texas, 27–31 May 1929, 431.

52. *Twentieth International Convention Proceedings,* Dallas, Texas, 27–31 May 1929, 505. Yoneyama's translation of Harris's autobiography, *My Road to Rotary,* led to its translation into Spanish by Guillermo Carvallo, RI's special commissioner for the establishment of new clubs in all of Latin America.

53. *Twentieth International Convention Proceedings,* Dallas, Texas, 27–31 May 1929, 57. For an explanation of how Japanese religious syncretism prepared the way for cultural adaptations to international business relations, see Roland Robertson, *Globalization: Social Theory and Global Culture* (London: Sage, 1992). But such syncretism was not unique to Yoneyama and the Japanese. In a speech to a plenary session, for example, Rotarian Keats S. Chu of Beijing, China, provided his own religious interpretation of Rotary: "Two thousand five hundred years ago, Confucius taught the Chinese people the Golden Rule and the doctrine of universal brotherhood and peace. . . . Rotary, therefore, is not alien to China, but Rotary in its concrete manifestation, in its effective organization, and in its practical application . . . as carried on by many men of earnestness and zeal all over the world in their respective trades and professions and general conduct of life, is a new revelation to China. Rotary in China is only in its infancy." *Twentieth International Convention Proceedings,* Dallas, Texas, 27–31 May 1929, 437.

54. *Twentieth International Convention Proceedings,* Dallas, Texas, 27–31 May 1929, 430–431.

55. *Twentieth International Convention Proceedings,* Dallas, Texas, 27–31 May 1929, 41–46.

56. *Twentieth International Convention Proceedings,* Dallas, Texas, 27–31 May 1929, 342.

57. *Twentieth International Convention Proceedings,* Dallas, Texas, 27–31 May 1929, 343.

58. *Twentieth International Convention Proceedings,* Dallas, Texas, 27–31 May 1929, 316, 330.

59. *Twentieth International Convention Proceedings,* Dallas, Texas, 27–31 May 1929, 316–317.

60. A significant exception to this practice was the active involvement of Lillian Dow Davidson in chronicling the activities of her husband in articles in the *Rotarian.* See Chapter 6.

61. *Twentieth International Convention Proceedings,* Dallas, Texas, 27–31 May 1929, 383. The International Service Committee was responsible for updating RI publications on the topic and overseeing the nature and scope of club activities of the same. As more non-US and non-Anglo clubs entered the fraternity, RI's board of directors and administrative committees were expected to reflect the changes. The highest echelons of RI's administration listed in 1928–1929 included, for example, Thomas Stephenson in Edinburgh, Scotland; Eduardo Moore in Santiago, Chile; William C. Achard in Zurich, Switzerland; and Josef Schulz in Prague, Czechoslovakia.

62. *Twentieth International Convention Proceedings,* Dallas, Texas, 27–31 May 1929, 385–386. Arthur Mayhew (lumber retailing), later became a member of RI's board of directors in 1933–1934, alongside Fong Sec, Chinese diplomat from Shanghai; Clinton P. Anderson, later to become US congressman and long-time senator from New Mexico as well as secretary of agriculture under President Truman; and other successful businessmen from Canada, Europe, Asia, and Latin America. Just as RI was trying to incorporate more and more leadership from outside the United States to deflect criticism that the organization was too centered on US interests, so RI was also seeking to include as many as possible representatives from the smallest towns and cities within its fold, such as Uvalde, Texas.

63. *Twentieth International Convention Proceedings,* Dallas, Texas, 27–31 May 1929, 387.

64. *Twentieth International Convention Proceedings,* Dallas, Texas, 27–31 May 1929, 389.

65. *Twentieth International Convention Proceedings,* Dallas, Texas, 27–31 May 1929, 388.

66. *Twentieth International Convention Proceedings,* Dallas, Texas, 27–31 May 1929, 412–415.

67. *Twentieth International Convention Proceedings,* Dallas, Texas, 27–31 May 1929, 415.

68. For a summary of RI's important work with the World Health Organization and the drive to eradicate polio, see David C. Forward, *A Century of Service: The Story of Rotary International* (Evanston, IL: Rotary International), 229–247; for a detailed history of the postwar activities of the Rotary Foundation and its partnership with the World Health Organization, see Sarah Gibbard Cook, "For All the World's Children: Rotary and the Vision of a Polio Free World," 2nd installment, unpublished manuscript, 2000, 288–390, RI Archives. For the history of polio and the story of its near eradication over the twentieth century, see David Oshinsky, *Polio: An American Story* (New York: Oxford University Press, 2005).

69. Suellentrop, *Rotary Club of Wichita, Kansas,* 21–22.

70. Suellentrop, *Rotary Club of Wichita, Kansas,* 22.

71. Rowe and Miner, *Borne on the South Wind,* 95–96.

72. Rowe and Miner, *Borne on the South Wind,* 105–106.

73. Jacob Vander Meulen, *Building the B-29* (Washington, DC: Smithsonian Institution Press, 1995) and Rowe and Miner, *Borne on the South Wind,* 128–156.

74. In addition to scholarship on the rise of the permanent war economy, Wichita's transformation, like Rotary as a whole, raises ongoing questions about the "intimate" relationship between US domestic politics and foreign relations in the field of US international history. See Frederik Logevall, "Politics and Foreign Relations," *Journal of American History* 95 (March 2009): 1074—1078.

75. J. Earl Schaefer, "Facts on Air Power: An Address by J. E. Schaefer," Wichita Rotary club, 7 April 1947, J. Earl Schaefer Papers, box 8, "Speeches and articles, 1945–1955," Dwight D. Eisenhower Presidential Library, Abilene, Kansas. See also "The Immediate Necessity for an Adequate Air Force in Being Remarks by J. E. Schaefer to the El Dorado Kiwanis Club," 11 May 1950, J. Earl Schaefer Papers, box 8, "Speeches and articles, 1945–1955," Dwight D. Eisenhower Presidential Library. Schaefer gave a similar talk, entitled "Our Air Force . . . Its Progress and Its Needs for Continued Progress," to the Kansas City Chamber of Commerce, the San Antonio (Texas) Chamber of Commerce, and the San Antonio Post of the American Legion in 1954. For a helpful review of the history of the concept of "national security," see Andrew Preston, "Monsters Everywhere: A Genealogy of National Security," *Diplomatic History* 38, no. 3 (June 2014), 477–500.

76. Rowe and Miner, *Borne on the South Wind,* 158–191.

77. W. C. Coleman, president of the Coleman Company, mayor of Wichita, and active member of the Wichita Rotary club for many years, was considered such a model employer that he was featured in RI's monthly magazine: "an employer without a labor problem tells the story of how a successful business policy was evolved." Charles St. John, "Chief Factors in the Labor Problem," *Rotarian,* March 1923, 128. The Coleman Company also gained many military contracts during the war.

78. Vander Meulen, *Building the B-29,* 36–55.

79. On the importance of this transition to the United States, see Michael Sherry, *The Rise of American Power: The Creation of Armageddon* (New Haven, CT: Yale University Press, 1987). See also Kenneth P. Werrell, *Blankets of Fire: U.S. Bombers Over Japan during World War II* (Washington, DC: Smithsonian Institution Press, 1996).

80. *Wichita Eagle,* 11 March 1945, 4.

81. *Wichita Eagle,* 12 March 1945, 6.

82. *Wichita Eagle,* 12 March 1945, 6.

83. *Wichita Eagle,* 12 March 1945.

84. For example, Coleman was an early member of the Wichita Rotary Club and was club president in the 1920s; his son was actively involved during that period as well and was also club president. The Coleman Co. also benefited greatly as a national manufacturer of sporting goods from wartime demand.

85. Vander Meulen, *Building the B-29 Bomber,* 38–41.

86. *Wichita Eagle,* 12 March 1945.

87. *Wichita Eagle,* 12 March 1945.

4. THROUGH EARTHQUAKE AND FIRE

1. *History of the Tokyo Rotary Club* (Tokyo: Tokyo Rotary Club, 1940), part I, 1.

2. *Japan* (Tokyo: Tokyo Rotary Club, 1927), 115. Roger Pinneo, former president of the Seattle Rotary Club, established the Rotary Club of Manila the same year and in much the same way as Johnstone. By no coincidence, both Pinneo and Johnstone worked for the Pacific Mail Steamship Company. J. I. Hoffman, assistant to the secretary of the International Association of Rotary Clubs, to John Barrett, chairman, Foreign Extension Committee, Washington, D.C., 21 July 1919, Shanghai club historical file, vol. 1, RI Archives. Roger Pinneo, who became port manager for Seattle upon his return to the United States from his time in East Asia, established the Shanghai club with much help from Dr. Julian Petit, a medical missionary and longtime resident of Shanghai. The International Association of Rotary Clubs had formally delegated Pinneo to act on its behalf. See George Treadwell, original secretary for the Shanghai Rotary club, to Carlo Bos, president of the Shanghai club, 27 November 1935, file "Other Clubs—Shanghai," Chicago / Rotary One Archives; and W. G. M. Buckisch, commissioner of private education, "The History of the Manila Rotary Club," 31 January 1929, file, "Manila Rotary Club," Chicago / Rotary One Archives.

3. *History of the Tokyo Rotary Club* (Tokyo: Tokyo Rotary Club, 1940), part I, 1.

4. The final edition of *History of the Tokyo Rotary Club,* part V, provides a complete list of membership from 1920 to 1940, with exact duration of each member's time in the club.

5. *History of the Tokyo Rotary Club,* part I, 8.

6. For analysis of the transitional period and the diplomatic promise it seemed to hold for both nations, see Sadao Asada, "Between the Old Diplomacy and the New, 1918–1922: The Washington System and the Origins of

Japanese-American Rapprochement," *Diplomatic History* 30, no. 2 (April 2006), 211–230.

7. The historiography on US-Japan relations is of course extensive. For a general view of US-Japan relations, see W. G. Beasley, *The Rise of Modern Japan*, 2nd ed. (London: Weidenfeld and Nicolson, 1995); Herbert P. Bix, *Hirohito and the Making of Modern Japan* (New York: Harper Collins, 2000); John W. Dower, *Embracing Defeat: Japan in the Wake of World War II* (New York: New Press, 1999); Dower, *War without Mercy: Race and Power in the Pacific War* (New York: Pantheon Books, 1986); Richard B. Frank, *Downfall: The End of the Imperial Japanese Empire* (New York: Random House, 1999); Ramon Myers, Mark R. Peattie, and Ching-chi Chen, *The Japanese Colonial Empire, 1895–1945* (Princeton, NJ: Princeton University Press, 1984); Walter LaFeber, *The Clash: U.S.-Japanese Relations throughout History* (New York: W.W. Norton, 1997); Michael R. Auslin, *Pacific Cosmopolitans: A Cultural History of U.S.-Japan Relations* (Cambridge, MA: Harvard University Press, 2011); Sayuri Guthrie-Shimizu, *Transpacific Field of Dreams: How Baseball Linked the United States and Japan in Peace and War* (Chapel Hill: University of North Carolina Press, 2012); Michael Schaller, *Altered States: The United States and Japan since the Occupation* (Oxford: Oxford University Press, 1997); Andrew C. McKevitt, *Consuming Japan: Popular Culture and the Globalizing of 1980s America* (Chapel Hill: University of North Carolina Press, 2017), and Kenneth B. Pyle, *Japan in the American Century* (Cambridge, MA: Harvard University Press, 2018).

8. For a good analysis of the central role of private and philanthropic institutions in making the transition possible, see Tadashi Yamamoto, Akira Iriye, and Makoto Iokibe, eds., *Philanthropy and Reconciliation: Rebuilding Postwar U.S.-Japan Relations* (Tokyo: Japan Center for International Exchange, 2006), esp. Kimura Masato, "U.S.-Japan Business Networks and Prewar Philanthropy: Implications for Postwar U.S.-Japan Relations," chap. 9, 279–312.

9. See Sayuri Guthrie-Shimizu, "For the Love of the Game: Baseball in Early U.S.-Japanese Encounters and the Rise of a Transnational Sporting Fraternity," *Diplomatic History* 28, no. 5 (November 2004), 637–662. Managers of US baseball teams regularly visited the Tokyo Rotary club, often because they were already Rotarians in the United States. See, for example, Rotarian Carl Zamloch, "athletic instructor" for the University of California, Berkeley, "who came with the baseball team" to visit the Tokyo Rotary club and Rotarian Baxter of Los Angeles, coach of the Southern Pacific University baseball team. *History of the Tokyo Rotary Club*, part II, 1 June 1927, 57, and 31 May 1928, 205 (respectively). See also the visit of Ishii, captain of the Tokyo baseball team, introduced to the Tokyo club by Rotarian Hiranuma of Yokohama and presi-

dent of that city's Athletic Association. Ishii told the Tokyo Rotarians that several of his men "have made visits to the United States on a baseball tour, and they were always honoured by being invited to the Rotary luncheon at various places." *History of the Tokyo Rotary Club,* part III, 13 August 1930, 154.

10. For the best historical survey of the Institute of Pacific Relations, see Tomoko Akami, *Internationalizing the Pacific: The United States, Japan, and the Institute of Pacific Relations in War and Peace, 1919–1945* (London: Routledge, 2002).

11. See, for example, Makoto Iokibe, "U.S.-Japan Intellectual Exchange: The Relationship between Government and Private Foundations," in *Philanthropy and Reconciliation,* ed. Yamamoto et al., chap. 3, 61–100.

12. See Manako Ogawa, "The 'White Ribbons League of Nations' Meets Japan: The Trans-Pacific Activism of the Woman's Christian Temperance Union, 1906–1930," *Diplomatic History* 31, no. 1 (January 2007), 21–50.

13. *History of the Tokyo Rotary Club,* part III, 27 June 1928, 223–225.

14. *History of the Tokyo Rotary Club,* part III, 225–226.

15. For a detailed history of Yokohama as an international port city, see Eric C. Han, *Rise of a Japanese Chinatown: Yokohama, 1894–1972* (Cambridge, MA: Harvard University Asia Center, 2014).

16. RI president Everett W. Hill to Tokyo club president Eigo Fukai, 15 October 1924, reprinted in *History of the Tokyo Rotary Club,* part I, 85–86.

17. As noted earlier, for the sake of simplicity and following the lead of both Japanese and Chinese Rotarians from the period, I have maintained the anglicized names of Japanese and Chinese cities to remain consistent with the historical record.

18. This administrative feature contrasted with the "national councils" of the Institute of Pacific Relations and other nonstate organizations like the YMCA that tended to mimic national and state structures in their organizations. This feature also inevitably led to many complications in the 1930s, ultimately requiring the creation of the eighty-first district in 1936, which included twenty-one clubs in China, Hong Kong, and Manila and the Philippines. The Chinese Rotarians eagerly interpreted their own "district" status as affirmation of their own interests and identities within the world of Rotary International. See, for example, "The Rotary Supplement," *Shanghai Evening Post and Mercury,* 19 April 1937, Chicago / Rotary One Archives, "Other Clubs" / Shanghai.

19. For a full detailed account of the preparation for and hosting of the Second Pacific Rotary Conference by the Tokyo club in early October 1928, see *History of the Tokyo Rotary Club,* part II, 217–316. The parallels between the goals and activities of the Institute of Pacific Relations (IPR), established in 1925,

and RI's series of Rotary Pacific Conferences between 1926 and 1935 are remarkable. The Pacific Rotary conferences were held in Honolulu (1926), Tokyo (1928), Sydney (1930), Honolulu (1932), Manila (1935), and Wellington (1937). Unlike the IPR, however, RI also held international conventions and scores of district conferences annually and regional conferences on a regular basis before World War II, including European regional conferences at The Hague (1930), Lausanne (1934), and Venice (1934), as well as a Latin American conference at Valparaiso (1936) and a Caribbean conference in Havana (1937). On RI's evolving custom of regional conferences, see "Report of the Commission on Rotary International Administration," in *Convention Proceedings, Twentieth-Eighth Annual International,* 6–11 June 1937, Nice, France, chap. II, "The Present Organization and Structure of R.I.," 31.

20. *History of the Tokyo Rotary Club,* part II, 227.

21. For a complete examination of the Great Kantō Earthquake of 1923 and its crucial legacies, see Joshua Hammer, *Yokohama Burning: The Deadly 1923 Earthquake and Fire That Helped Forge the Path to World War II* (New York: Free Press, 2006).

22. *History of the Tokyo Rotary Club,* part I, 24–25.

23. *History of the Tokyo Rotary Club,* part I, 32.

24. In fact, four Tokyo Rotarians were put on the Board of Reconstruction by the Japanese government: Isomura, Ito, Wada, and Yoneyama. *History of the Tokyo Rotary Club,* part 1, 40.

25. *History of the Tokyo Rotary Club,* part I, 238–239.

26. *History of the Tokyo Rotary Club,* part I, 16–43. Berton also managed to lighten his first time speaking before the club by having a friend bring a guitar and teaching the fifty Japanese club members to sing "The Man Who Has Plenty of Good Peanuts."

27. *History of the Tokyo Rotary Club,* part III, 69–73.

28. *History of the Tokyo Rotary Club,* part II, 239–244.

29. *Proceedings of the Nineteenth Annual Convention of Rotary International,* Minneapolis, Minnesota, 18–22 June 1928, 8–9.

30. *History of the Tokyo Rotary Club,* part II, 486–487.

31. *History of the Tokyo Rotary Club,* part II, 487.

32. *History of the Tokyo Rotary Club,* part II, 488.

33. As club secretary, Kitashima ran a small office that also sent out an average of fifty letters a month in response to inquiries from Rotary clubs around the world. *History of the Tokyo Rotary Club,* part III, 118.

34. Lester B. Struthers, Assistant Secretary of RI, to Special Commissioner Isaka, 13 October 1926, reprinted in *Japan* (Tokyo Rotary Club: Tokyo, 1927), introduction.

35. In many ways, the cultural diplomacy intended with Tokyo club's publication of *Japan* anticipated the creation of the International Culture Promotion Association by the Japanese government in 1934. Akami, *Internationalizing the Pacific,* 216.

36. *Japan,* chap. 1, 5.

37. *Japan,* 98.

38. *Japan,* 99.

39. *Japan,* 34.

40. *Japan,* 41.

41. Ohtani struck such a chord within RI's ranks that he became a member of RI's board of directors in 1933–1934, a position also held by Yoneyama more than once. Only RI's international president ranked higher, and only RI's long-serving general secretary, Chesley Perry, had more input on all significant administrative issues and policies.

42. The club's first visitor "from abroad" was Rotarian Sidney F. Mashbir, hailing from Syracuse, New York, on 10 May 1922. He was the first of thousands until September 1940. *History of the Tokyo Rotary Club,* part 1, 16.

43. *Japan,* 118.

44. Herbert P. Bix, *Hirohito and the Making of Modern Japan* (New York: HarperCollins, 2000).

45. *Japan,* 118.

46. *Japan,* 118–119.

47. On the international appeal of Wilsonian rhetoric in Asia, see Erez Manela, *The Wilsonian Moment: Self-Determination and the International Origins of Anticolonial Nationalism* (New York: Oxford University Press, 2007).

48. Akami, *Internationalizing the Pacific,* 202.

49. Akami, *Internationalizing the Pacific,* 202.

50. Akami, *Internationalizing the Pacific,* 105.

51. Yusuke Tsurumi, "International Friendship: An Address upon the Occasion of a Dinner to American Guests Given by the Rotary Club of Tokyo," *Rotarian,* November 1926, 21.

52. When Rotarian Palmer from the Honolulu club was visiting the Tokyo club, he spoke on the immigration laws just passed by the US Congress, saying "it was like the shock of the earthquake that we had last year, but sooner or later things will be restored to normal." *History of the Tokyo Rotary Club,* part 1, 1 October 1924.

53. In Tsurumi's case, his attitude changed after election to the Japanese Diet in 1928. As Akami points out: "His criticism of the international order and the League of Nations became stronger after Japan's withdrawal from the League of Nations in 1933. He argued that peace for Britain, the United States,

the USSR and France meant that they would preserve their privilege. 'Real' peace, he continued, would not come until Japan achieved 'justice' by abolishing these countries' racial discrimination and unfair tariffs." Akami, *Internationalizing the Pacific,* 86.

54. The chapter on Japanese theater was the only "cultural" chapter authored by a Japanese member of the club (see Table 4.1).

55. *History of the Tokyo Rotary Club,* part V, appendix.

56. As of 1936, Harry L. Sommerer, managing director of Victor Talking Machine Co. of Japan, was the only non-Japanese Rotarian ever to serve as a club president in any Japanese Rotary club. Report by Crawford C. McCullough, past president of RI, to the president and board of directors on his official visit to the 70th and 81st districts, April–May 1936, file: [China - Japan, Relations between—Data re: CCM's visit to Japan and China Conferences], RI Archives.

57. *History of the Tokyo Rotary Club,* part II, 241–244.

58. *History of the Tokyo Rotary Club,* part II, 241–244.

59. *History of the Tokyo Rotary Club,* vol. II, 241–245; *Augusta Rotary Club since 1918* (Augusta, KS: Augusta Rotary Club, 1968).

60. *History of the Tokyo Rotary Club,* part II, 485–486.

61. *Augusta Rotary Club since 1918,* "Notes on the Beginning." This is not actually true, as a few clubs of that size in Michigan and Illinois were receiving charters as early as 1915–1916. But the Augusta club was one of the smallest clubs in Rotary when established in 1918 and for several years thereafter.

62. District Governor's Report, 30 September 1929, Augusta club historical file, RI Archives.

63. *Augusta Rotary Club since 1918; History of the Tokyo Rotary Club,* part II, 269–310, for detailed coverage of the Tokyo club's hosting of the Second Pacific Rotary Conference, October 1–4, 1928, and the highest attendance of members and visitors ever seen.

64. *History of the Tokyo Rotary Club,* part III, 25–26.

65. Kingston, Jamaica, and Port-au-Prince, Haiti, waited almost forty years to get their own clubs precisely because such "intimate and friendly relations" threatened racial hierarchies and race-based codes of interaction in the United States. See Chapter 2.

66. *Augusta Rotary Club since 1918.*

67. *Augusta Rotary Club since 1918.*

68. *Augusta Rotary Club since 1918.*

69. For example, see Chesley Perry to E. F. Harris, Shanghai Club President, 22 April 1933, Shanghai club historical file, vol. VI; the Shanghai Rotarians had

heard of a Japanese representative who managed "to slip in some resolution condemning boycott" to protest Japanese military aggression in Manchuria after the Mukden Incident of 18 September 1931. The Rotary club of Shanghai had sent a letter to RI's board of directors entitled "Report of efforts of Rotary club of Shanghai, China, in connection with the Sino-Japanese Conflict at Shanghai," wherein the club registered its collective concern about Japanese military expansion. The board and RI's president, Sydney Pascall of England, concluded that the letter reflected "the Rotarian approach to a difficult and delicate problem and it reflects great honor on the members of the Shanghai club who undertook this piece of work." But, in the end, there was no formal discussion or any decision imparted by RI's board. See Chapter 5.

70. *History of the Tokyo Rotary Club,* part II, 28 August 1929, 458.

71. *History of the Tokyo Rotary Club,* part II, 475.

72. *History of the Tokyo Rotary Club,* part II, 476.

73. *History of the Tokyo Rotary Club,* part II, 476–478.

74. *History of the Tokyo Rotary Club,* part II, 478.

75. *History of the Tokyo Rotary Club,* part II, 480.

76. *History of the Tokyo Rotary Club,* part II, 9 October 1929, 479–480.

77. *History of the Tokyo Rotary Club,* part II, 4 September 1929, 459–60.

78. *History of the Tokyo Rotary Club,* part II, 463. Attempts at maintaining an "apolitical" atmosphere in the club became increasingly absurd before the emergence of a military state in 1932. For instance, when the Tokyo club asked Masanori Ito (classification "News Service Bureau") to speak on the Naval Conference going on in London, he was told to do so "without touching on the political side of the problem, for in Rotary we refrain from discussing political questions." Ito wondered if it was possible to do so without exploring the complex political negotiations, so he spoke instead on "a strange type of ship coming into existence within two or three years. . . . They never thought of such a thing . . . until the conference, a cruiser of 9,000 tons, with a deck at the stern, for 15 airplanes." Ito was describing the first aircraft carriers. *History of the Tokyo Rotary Club,* part III, 9 July 1930, 139. After the Mukden Incident in September 1931, Japanese Rotary clubs began to align their weekly songs, speeches, activities, and publications more and more with the expectations of the Japanese military governments.

79. "The Manchurian Problem: Compiled by the Tokyo Rotary Club for 'Advancement of Understanding Goodwill and International Peace,'" Tokyo, December 1931. Former district governor and founder of the Tokyo Rotary Club, Umekichi Yoneyama, reproduced his formal letter to Sydney Pascall,

president of Rotary International, in this booklet. "The Manchurian Problem," Yoneyama to Pascall, 4 November 1931, 6–8.

80. In fact, Paul Harris, Rotary's founder, and his wife, Jean, briefly visited Tokyo, Kobe, and Kyoto in February 1935 while en route to the Pacific Rotary Conference in Manila. Paul and Jean were accompanied by RI President Robert E. Lee Hill of Columbia, Missouri, and his wife. In the world of Rotary, this was effectively a high-level state visit confirming Japanese Rotary's high status.

81. George L. Treadwell, club secretary for Chicago Rotary club, to George Fitch, Chinese YMCA, 17 March 1932, file: ["Other Clubs—Shanghai: 1926–34": 10-5], Chicago / Rotary One Archives, Chicago, Illinois.

82. *Convention Proceedings of the Thirty-First Annual International Convention of Rotary International,* Havana, Cuba, June 1940, 118–122.

83. *Convention Proceedings,* Havana, Cuba, June 1940, 121.

84. *Convention Proceedings,* Havana, Cuba, June 1940, 121.

85. *Convention Proceedings,* Havana, Cuba, June 1940, 117–119 and 122–123, respectively.

86. *Convention Proceedings,* Havana, Cuba, June 1940, 122.

87. *Convention Proceedings,* Havana, Cuba, June 1940, 420–421. Serious environmental issues were also under consideration: Resolution 40–14, proposed by Rotarians of Upper Darby, Pennsylvania, called for the "restoration and conservation of soils, waters, forests, and related resources of the various nations" because "the conservation of these natural resources constitutes a problem of vital importance." *Convention Proceedings,* Havana, Cuba, June 1940, 420.

88. *History of the Tokyo Rotary Club,* part V, 265–273. In stark contrast to the Japanese Rotary clubs, Rotary clubs in Germany and Italy were shut down several years prior. As Prentiss Gilbert, Charge d'Affaires, US Embassy in Berlin, explained to Cordell Hull, US Secretary of State that ". . . while the Nazi party never entirely approved of Rotary it was permitted to exist in Germany because it had expelled all Jews and the members had made use of their international connections to combat the atrocity propaganda of the Jews abroad. The present ostensible objection to Rotary is that it is internationally organized and headed by a president, . . . wherein a foreigner could give instructions to a German organization, contrary to the interests of the German people." See Prentiss Gilbert to Cordell Hull, 27 August 1937, Folder GRC 862.43 "Rotary," Box 6795, RG 59, National Archives and Records Administration II (hereafter NARA II), College Park, MD. Meanwhile, like the Vatican, Mussolini had little tolerance for Italian Rotary clubs but "due to powerful business pressure exerted from Turin, Milan, and Genoa, [Rotary] eventually succeeded in estab-

lishing itself. This success was apparently also due to the untiring efforts of Prince Ginori-Conti of Florence, a friend of the Royal Family who influenced the King in Rotary's favor." But once Germany banished all Rotary, Mussolini followed suit. See Edward L. Reed, Charge d'Affaires ad interim, US Embassy, Rome, to Cordell Hull, Secretary of State, 15 November 1938, 865.43 Rotary / 1, M1423 Roll #15, RG 59, NARA II, College Park, MD. That Rotary International had such disparate relationships with the governments of Germany, Italy, and Japan during the 1930s is quite revealing.

89. "Reintroduction of Rotary into Japan and Korea: Report of Assistant Secretary George R. Means," 9, in box 149, file: [Special Service Support Committee], RI Archives. See also George R. Means, Gen. Sec., Rotary International (1953–72), "Rotary's Return to Japan," 27, in box 144, file: [Extension—General, 1969–75], RI Archives.

90. Carlos Romulo was very involved with the Manila Rotary club throughout the 1930s, playing host to the Pacific Rotary Conference held there in 1935 and becoming RI's third vice president in 1937–1938.

91. David Shelley Nicholl. *The Golden Wheel: The Story of Rotary 1905 to the Present* (Plymouth, UK: MacDonald and Evans, 1984), 377, 426–429; David C. Forward, *A Century of Service: The Story of Rotary International* (Evanston, IL: Rotary International, 2003), 209.

92. Means, "Rotary's Return to Japan," 27–28; Nicholl, *Golden Wheel,* 428.

93. Means, "Rotary's Return to Japan," 28–29.

5. UNDER THE SHADOW OF ROTARY

1. The composition of RI's official Havana Convention Committee—chaired by Fernando Carbajal of Lima, Peru—reflected this point: Richard Wells of Pocatello, Idaho; Ernesto Santos Bastos of Lisbon, Portugal; Charles Reeve Vanneman of Albany, New York; Julio Zetina of Mexico City, Mexico; and Joaquin Serratosa Cibils of Montevideo, Uruguay. Both Carbajal, an engineer who worked in Panama (where he first came in contact with Rotary), and Cibils later became presidents of Rotary International (in 1942–1943 and 1953–1954, respectively). See Ricardo Mariategui Oliva, *Historia del Rotary Club de Lima, 1920–1955* (Lima, Peru: El Rotary Club de Lima, 1956), 10. For a summary of key points of the Havana Conference from the period, see Ellery C. Stowell, "The Habana Conference and Inter-American Cooperation," *American Journal of International Law* 35, no. 1 (January 1941), 123–132.

2. *Convention Proceedings, Thirty-First Annual Rotary Convention,* Havana, Cuba, June 9–13, 1940, 15. Speeches given in languages other than English appear

in English translation immediately afterward in RI's convention proceedings, as was the case here. For a condensed version of the convention's high points, see Leland D. Case and K. K. Krueger, "New Hope at Havana," the *Rotarian*, July 1940, 28–30, 34–36, 59.

3. *Convention Proceedings*, Havana, Cuba, June 1940, 81–159. "President McKinley's War Message," 11 April 1898, in US Department of State, *Papers Relating to Foreign Affairs* (Washington, DC), 1898, 750–760.

4. "President McKinley's War Message," 750–760. The full message sent to Congress was actually very long and detailed.

5. "Resolution for Recognition of the Independence of Cuba, 20 April 1898," in Michael D. Gambone, ed., *Documents of American Diplomacy: From the American Revolution to the Present* (Westport, CT: Greenwood Press, 2002), 121–122.

6. "Platt Amendment," 22 May 1903, in Gambone, ed., *Documents of American Diplomacy*, 130–131.

7. There are many authoritative texts on this period. See, for example, Louis A. Pérez Jr., *Cuba Under the Platt Amendment, 1902–1934* (Pittsburgh: University of Pittsburgh Press, 1986) and Pérez, *Cuba: Between Reform and Revolution* (New York: Oxford University Press, 1995). On the remarkable vibrancy of Cuba's civil society during this period, see Steven Palmer, José Antonio Piqueras, and Amparo Sánchez Cobos, eds., *State of Ambiguity: Civic Life and Culture in Cuba's First Republic* (Durham, NC: Duke University Press, 2014), esp. chap. 8 on Cuban Rotary clubs.

8. Here I take a parallel approach to that of Ann Laura Stoler: "that the power and authority wielded by macropolities are not lodged in abstract institutions but in their management of meanings, their construction of social categories, and their microsites of rule." See Ann Laura Stoler, "Tense and Tender Ties: The Politics of Comparison in North American History and (Post) Colonial Studies," *Journal of American History* 88, no. 3 (December 2001), 52. See also Louis A. Pérez Jr., *Cuba and the United States: Ties of Singular Intimacy* (Athens: University of Georgia Press, 2003).

9. Louis A. Pérez Jr., *On Becoming Cuban: Identity, Nationality, and Culture* (Chapel Hill: University of North Carolina Press, 1999), 6.

10. Pérez, *On Becoming Cuban*, 10–11.

11. Pérez, *On Becoming Cuban*, 396–397. See also Carmen Diana Deere, "Here Come the Yankees! The Rise and Decline of United States Colonies in Cuba, 1898–1930," *Hispanic American Historical Review* 78, no. 4 (November 1998), 729–765, for a helpful review of why US colonists were going to Cuba at this time and their distribution there, connection with the annex-

ationist project, and attempts at Americanization. This chapter, however, does not and should not treat Rotary clubs in Cuba as a type of "US colony." Rather, the service clubs functioned as an institutional meeting ground, distinguishing them from the US colonies investigated by Deere, as the clubs were predominantly Cuban in membership.

12. When the first sixteen clubs in the United States first came together in 1910 in Chicago, they formed the National Association of Rotary Clubs, which lasted only two years before becoming the International Association of Rotary Clubs (IARC) from 1912 to 1922 and then Rotary International (RI) from 1922 until the present.

13. "The History of the 'Object of Rotary,'" index files, RI Archives (emphasis added).

14. Chesley R. Perry to John Shelby, 22 April 1914, Historical club files, Havana, Cuba, vol. 1, RI Archives.

15. Ernest Berger to Chesley R. Perry, 9 May 1914, Havana, vol. 1, RI Archives; John Shelby to Chesley R. Perry, 22 March 1915, Havana, vol. 1, RI Archives.

16. Many historians have used the term "civic whiteness" in various ways, but usually centering on an ambivalent, transitional, honorary, or threshold status somewhere between the white-nonwhite binary. For example, see Matthew Pratt Guterl, *The Color of Race in America, 1900–1940* (Cambridge, MA: Harvard University Press, 2001), 46; Seth Forman, *Blacks in the Jewish Mind: A Crisis of Liberalism* (New York: New York University Press 1998), 150; and Derek Vaillant, *Sounds of Reform: Progressivism and Music in Chicago, 1873–1935* (Chapel Hill: University of North Carolina Press, 2003), 253.

17. Chesley R. Perry to Rafael Martinez Ybor, 15 April 1915, Havana vol. 1, RI Archives.

18. Board of directors of IARC, minutes of meetings, Extension Committee, 1912–1929: 1 August 1914, "Extension Europe Africa / Asia Minor"; 18 July 1915, "Extension in South America"; and 4–5 Sept 1915, "Extension Central and South America." On the biography of John Barrett, see Salvatore Prisco, John Barrett, *Progressive Era Diplomat: A Study of a Commercial Expansionist, 1887–1920* (Tuscaloosa: University of Alabama Press, 1973).

19. See Marilyn Lake and Henry Reynolds, *Drawing the Global Colour Line: White Men's Countries and the International Challenge of Racial Equality* (Cambridge: Cambridge University Press, 2008) for a thorough analysis of "the global colour line" and how it was drawn through legislation, immigration policies, and intellectual debates both borrowed and shared throughout the Pacific Basin and across the Indian Ocean.

20. Perry to Martinez Ybor, 15 April 1915, Havana, vol. 1, RI Archives.

21. As Rotary was entering Cuba and Hawaii in 1915, the organization already had clubs throughout the United States, Canada, Great Britain, Ireland, Northern Ireland, and Scotland. By 1923, there were clubs in Puerto Rico, Wales, the Philippines, Uruguay, Argentina, China, India, Panama, Australia, France, Japan, Mexico, New Zealand, Spain, Newfoundland, Norway, Peru, South Africa, Brazil, Denmark, the Netherlands, and even the Channel Islands. By 1930, there were 3,349 clubs in 66 countries and, by 1940, 5,066 clubs in 85 countries.

22. Chesley R. Perry to Alexander Kent, 7 July 1915, Havana, vol. 1, RI Archives.

23. Chesley R. Perry to Alexander Kent, 20 November 1915, Havana, vol. 1, RI Archives.

24. Alexander Kent to Chesley R. Perry, 25 November 1915, Havana, vol. 1, RI Archives.

25. Kent to Perry, 25 November 1915, Havana, vol. 1, RI Archives.

26. Chesley R. Perry to John Turner, 1 February 1916, Havana, vol. 1, RI Archives.

27. Frank Waterman, vice president of the New York Rotary club, to Chesley Perry, 15 December 1915; in this letter, Waterman first suggested the idea of inviting each Cuban consul in the United States to attend a local Rotary club meeting to see whether any came away willing to help set up the club in Havana. Waterman attached the complete list of Cuban consuls, and Perry sent out form letters to each Rotary club's president explaining Rotary's goal of setting up a new club in Havana (Chesley R. Perry to club presidents, 4 February 1916). Waterman's real goal was to open a Rotary Club in Buenos Aires, where he had specific business interests; he saw a Havana club as a necessary step in that ultimate goal. See also John B. Berger, president of Baltimore Rotary club, to Chesley R. Perry, 20 March 1916; Chesley Perry to John B. Berger, n.d.; E. Casaus, consul de Cuba in Galveston, Texas, to Frank Allen, president of Galveston Rotary club, 14 February 1916. All letters found in Havana, vol. 1, RI Archives.

28. Based on letterheads from John B. Berger to Chesley R. Perry, 10 March 1916, and A. L. Cuesta to Chesley R. Perry, 16 June 1916, Havana vol. 1, RI Archives.

29. John Turner to Chesley R. Perry, 10 February 1916, Havana, vol. 1, RI Archives. For a complete history of Angel Cuesta's extensive business interests and travels, see José Demetrio Diego, *Angel Cuesta LaMadrid: Tabaquero y Rotario* (Santander, Spain: Gráfica Apel, 2000).

30. John Turner to Chesley R. Perry, "Report of club established," April 1916, Havana, vol. 1, RI Archives.

31. Turner to Perry, "Report of the club established." Scholarship on the dominance of the sugar industry in Cuba is extensive, but classic texts include Fernando Ortiz, *Cuban Counterpoint: Tobacco and Sugar* (Durham, NC: Duke University Press, 1995) and Sidney W. Mintz, *Sweetness and Power: The Place of Sugar in Modern History* (New York: Penguin, 1986). See also April Merleaux, *Sugar and Civilization: American Empire and the Cultural Politics of Sweetness* (Chapel Hill, NC: University of North Carolina Press, 2015) for an examination of the Cuba sugar industry within the orbit of the "U.S. Sugar Empire" after 1898.

32. Rotary International, *1916 Convention Proceedings*, Cincinnati, Ohio, 16–20 July 1916, 133–134.

33. The certification could be read on two levels: as Rotary's formal approval of the first of many Cuban Rotary clubs and as part of the creation of an international network of businessmen and professionals closely associated with and working for transnational corporations.

34. Rotary International, *1916 Convention Proceedings,* 89.

35. Albert Hoffman to Chesley R. Perry, August 1916, Havana, vol. 1, RI Archives.

36. Havana Club's flyer, n.d. but very probably June 1917, "Plataforma por el embellicimiento de la Ciudad de la Habana," led by Dr. Carlos Alzugaray, club president, Havana, vol. 1, RI Archives.

37. The First Rotary Club in Each Country or Geographical Region," Rotary International, 5–6 May 1934, Pamphlet, RI Archives. See also Diego, *Angel Cuesta LaMadrid: Tabaquero y Rotario, 2000,* and club historical files for Madrid and Barcelona, Spain, Zurich Secretariat, Rotary International, Zurich, Switzerland (hereafter: RIZ Archives). For details on how Rotary clubs in Latin America were sometimes seen as "an instrument of American propaganda," on how the Santiago Rotary club "materially advanced American interests" in Chile, and on how Rotary clubs brought together top US and Latin American businessmen and diplomats throughout Latin America, see Wm. Miller Collier, US Embassy, Santiago, Chile, to US Secretary of State, Frank B. Kellogg, 8 May 1928 and 9 July 1928, Box 8347, RG 59, NARA-II, College Park, MD. Collier also sent his letter to colleagues in Buenos Aires, Asunción, Montevideo, Rio de Janeiro, Lima, Quito, and Mexico City.

38. Mario MacBeath to Paul Harris, founder and first president of Rotary, 16 October 1918, Havana, vol. 1, RI Archives. In fact, three years later, on 10 October 1921, the Rotary club orchestrated "a monster parade composed of social, civic, commercial, military and naval organizations followed by an open air mass meeting in one of the large parks of the city" that included a speech by Dr. Alfredo Zayas, Cuba's president. The purpose of the massive event, which occurred in the heart of Cuba's debt crisis in the early 1920s, was "to inspire in

the masses that fuller sense of civic pride and patriotism and to propagate and bring out the finer quality of citizenship and public spirit so essential in a people when the need arises to combat, weather, and successfully overcome national ills." Alberto Crusellas, Havana club president, to Chesley R. Perry, 17 October 1921, Havana club file, vol. 1, RI Archives.

39. *Eighth Annual International Convention Proceedings,* Atlanta, 17–21 June 1917, 12.

40. *Eighth Annual International Convention Proceedings,* Atlanta, 17–21 June 1917, 12.

41. *Eighth Annual International Convention Proceedings,* Atlanta, 17–21 June 1917, 12.

42. *Rotarian,* vol. XI, no. 1, July 1917, 12.

43. "Speech by Dr. Carlos Alzugaray, president of the Havana Rotary Club, on the fifteenth anniversary of 'Rotarismo,'" February 1920, Havana club files, vol. 1, RI Archives.

44. Photograph, 23 February 1923, Havana, vol. 1, RI Archives.

45. Gutierrez Lee to all Havana club members, copy sent to Chesley R. Perry, 13 March 1923; Avelino Perez to Chesley R. Perry, 18 March 1923; photo, 15 March 1923, Havana, vol. 1, RI Archives. The original text in Spanish: "una Republica hermana, tan heroica, tan noble y tan generosa; por todos querida y por todos respetada" and "confraternidad rotariana."

46. Report by club president Emilio Gomez to Rotary district governor of Cuba, Juan Jose Hernandez, including press clippings from Havana press and two photos, January 1924, Havana, vol. 1, RI Archives.

47. On Cuba's economy transitioning from Europe to the United States in this period, see Pérez, *Cuba: Between Reform and Revolution*, and on the complexity and scale of Cuba's cultural and intellectual ties to the United States before World War I (as well as after the war), see Pérez, *On Becoming Cuban.*

48. Dipesh Chakrabarty, *Provincializing Europe: Postcolonial Thought and Historical Difference* (Princeton, NJ: Princeton University Press, 2000), 27–30.

49. For a trenchant exploration of how the United States justified the central contradiction of the Platt Amendment (limiting Cuban sovereignty in the name of helping Cuba), see Louis A. Pérez Jr., "Incurring a Debt of Gratitude: 1898 and the Moral Sources of United States Hegemony in Cuba," *American Historical Review* 104, no. 2 (April 1999), esp. 370–371. Just as Pérez identifies the narrative of 1898 and the "debt of gratitude" as the central driver in the justification of extending US hegemony after the end of military occupation, so I am arguing for the ideological role of friendship, neutrality, and reform as further extensions of the theme of "gratitude." After all, the Teller Amendment—which declared the neutrality of the United States as a prerequisite to its going

to war on Cuba's behalf against Spain—paved the way ideologically for the Platt Amendment.

50. Carlos Alzugaray to Chesley R. Perry, 14 April 1920, Havana, vol. 1, RI Archives. Original quotation in Spanish: "tenemos muchas cosas serias que andan mal y que tienen necesariamente que preocuparnos y que exigir la atencion de los hombres que se interesen por su pais." Translation by author.

51. Alzugaray to Perry, 14 April 1920. Original Spanish: "hoy la institucion, corporacion, o entidad que, tiene mas prestigios como civica, patriotica y altruistica." Translation by author.

52. Avelino Perez to Chesley R. Perry, 15 November 1918, Havana, vol. 1, RI Archives.

53. Chesley R. Perry to Avelino Perez, 30 November 1918 and 23 December 1918, Havana, vol. 1, RI Archives.

54. Mario MacBeath, Havana club secretary, to Chesley R. Perry, 14 August 1919, Havana, vol. 1, RI Archives.

55. For a thorough discussion of this period, see Louis A. Pérez Jr., *Cuba: Between Reform & Revolution,* 2nd ed. (New York: Oxford University Press, 1995), and Robert Whitney, *State and Revolution in Cuba: Mass Mobilization and Political Change, 1920–1940* (Chapel Hill: University of North Carolina Press, 2001). See Pérez on armed rebellion in *On Becoming Cuban,* 223–224.

56. MacBeath to Perry, 14 August 1919, Havana, vol. 1, RI Archives.

57. MacBeath to Perry, 14 August 1919, Havana, vol. 1, RI Archives.

58. *Convention Proceedings,* Havana, Cuba, June 1940, "The Growth of Rotary," 353.

59. MacBeath to Perry, 14 August 1919, Havana, vol. 1, RI Archives.

60. MacBeath to Perry, 14 August 1919, Havana, vol. 1, RI Archives.

61. Cablegram, Chesley R. Perry to Mario MacBeath, 20 August 1919, Havana, vol. 1, RI Archives.

62. This result bears out Whitney's characterization of "oligarchic capitalism" from this period. "The political activity of the Cuban elite was oriented more to negotiating the terms of American hegemony than to challenging it head-on." Whitney, *State and Revolution in Cuba,* 21. However, it would not be fair to put MacBeath, Alzugaray, Gonzalez del Valle, and their followers in the Rotary club in the category of oligarchic capitalists, if only because they saw a modern Cuban state as the key to successful reform rather than treated it as anathema. But the common thread was the unwillingness to challenge US hegemony. See also Jorge Domínguez, "Seeking Permission to Build a Nation: Cuban Nationalism and the U.S. Response under the First Machado Presidency," *Cuban Studies/Estudios Cubanos* 16 (1986), 33–48, and Pérez, *Cuba Under the Platt Amendment.*

63. Letter of resignation to Havana club's board of directors, 2 May 1922, reprinted in "La Rueda del Rotary Club de La Habana," 9 May 1922, Havana, vol. 1, RI Archives. Original Spanish: "purificación y moralización de los organismos publicos." Translation by author. A similar pattern played out between Chesley Perry and Antonio Asensio, longtime club secretary at Cienfuegos. Asensio wrote of a "disconcerting indifference" on the part of many firms and potential members of Rotary in the city, and especially of his worries that so many potential classifications were "unfilled" as a result. It never occurred to Asensio or Perry that club vacancies were indicative of an undiversified local economy structured according to US corporate interests. See especially Antonio Asensio to Chesley R. Perry, 24 September 1930, Cienfuegos club file, vol. 1, RI Archives.

64. *Cuba* (pamphlet; Club Rotario de la Habana, Havana, Cuba, 1918). Havana club files, vol. 1, RI Archives.

65. *Cuba*; Merleaux, *Sugar and Civilization,* esp. introduction and chapter 1.

66. *Cuba.*

67. *Cuba.*

68. Chesley R. Perry to Mario MacBeath, 12 October 1918, Havana club files, vol. 1, RI Archives.

69. Perry to MacBeath, 12 October 1918, Havana, vol. 1, RI Archives.

70. Perez, *Cuba,* 225.

71. Perez, *Cuba,* 226–228.

72. See Edward S. Kaplan, *American Trade Policy, 1923–1995* (Westport, CT: Greenwood Press, 1996), and Edward S. Kaplan and Thomas W. Ryley, *Prelude to Trade Wars: American Tariff Policy, 1890–1922* (Westport, CT: Greenwood Press, 1994). See also Abraham Berglund, "The Tariff Act of 1922," *American Economic Review* 13 (1923), 14–32.

73. Alberto Crusellas, Havana Rotary club president, to Estes Snedecor, president, 1 July 1921, and Alberto Crusellas to Chesley R. Perry, 1 July 1921, Havana club files, vol. 1, RI Archives. Translation: "Havana is the second commercial port in America."

74. Circular letter: the Rotary Club of Havana to the presidents of all the US Rotary Clubs, 1 July 1921. Havana club files, vol. 1, RI Archives. Among other demands, the Havana Rotarians were seeking repayment for money made by the Sugar Equalization Board in the United States during World War I; the $40 million would come in handy in wiping away Cuba's massive debts. Without such financial leverage, the United States might lose its political leverage as well.

75. Massive demonstrations organized by the Matanzas Rotary club on 10 December 1921 speak to this desperation, though the event was set up to pro-

test directly the coming the Emergency Tariff Act. Dripping with "sentimiento patrióco," the event also challenged the "corruption that threatened to invade and extend itself into all public spheres." The club had already hand-delivered to the US vice-consul in Matanzas a formal protest against the tariff. For full details, see posters announcing the event: "Club Rotario de Matanzas: Orden e Itinerario de la Manifestacion del Dia 17" and "Rotary Club of Matanzas: Al Hon. Sr. Gobernador Provincial de Matanzas." The latter document also included in Spanish the statement "Matanzas is the primary port for exporting sugar to the world." The club's very source of civic pride and identity was also its reason for dependence on world markets. Matanzas club file, RI Archives.

76. Crawford C. McCullough, international president, to Chesley Perry, 12 August 1921, Havana club files, vol. 1, RI Archives.

77. Estes Snedecor to Chesley Perry, 2 August 1921; Chesley Perry to secretary of commerce, 16 August 1921; Herbert Hoover, secretary of commerce, to Chesley Perry, 23 August 1921. All from Havana club files, vol. 1, RI Archives.

78. Cable from Chesley Perry to Alberto Crusellas, 3 September 1921, and memo, "Havana Sugar Matter," 16 September 1921, Havana club files, vol. 1, RI Archives.

79. Cable from Alberto Crusellas to Chesley Perry, n.d., Havana club files, vol. 1, RI Archives.

80. Circular letter: the Rotary club of Havana to the presidents of all the US Rotary clubs, 1 July 1921, p. 2. Havana club files, vol. 1, RI Archives.

81. Circular letter: the Rotary club of Havana to the presidents of all the US Rotary clubs, 1 July 1921.

82. Circular letter: the Rotary club of Havana to the presidents of all the US Rotary clubs, 1 July 1921.

83. Circular letter: the Rotary club of Havana to the presidents of all the US Rotary clubs, 1 July 1921 (emphasis added).

84. See *The History of Rotary Club of Tokyo*, vol. 1 (Tokyo: Rotary Club of Tokyo, 1926). In fact, Havana's club donated toward the cause.

85. Roberta P. Wakefield, "Some Factors in Cuba's Foreign Trade," *Economic Geography* 13, no. 2 (April 1937), 109–131.

86. *Fourteenth Annual International Convention Proceedings*, St. Louis, Missouri, 18–22 June 1923, 231.

87. *Fourteenth Annual International Convention Proceedings*, St. Louis, Missouri, 18–22 June 1923, 253–257.

88. In January 1930, there were 163 members in the Havana club. Felix Granados, club president, to Luis Machado, district governor for Cuba, "Informe

de la Junta Directiva al Gobernador del Distrito," 15 January 1930, Havana, vol. 1, RI Archives.

89. "Across Boundary Lines: Rotarians of Cuba and Florida Adopt Rotary's Good-Will Formula," *Rotarian,* 30 January 1930, 26–27, 48.

90. One of the most active and respected members of the Havana Rotary club from the 1920s to the 1950s was Luis Machado, who served as a district governor for Cuba and on RI's board of international directors in the 1930s. See letter from Mario Nuñez Mesa, Havana club president, to George Treadwell, secretary of Chicago Rotary Club, 22 April 1927, Havana, vol. 1, RI Archives. Support for President Machado appeared to be waning among Cuban Rotarians after 1930 even as Luis Machado was forging a stellar career in "international law" as well as in Rotary.

91. "Across Boundary Lines," *Rotarian,* 30 January 1930, 48.

92. "Across Boundary Lines," *Rotarian,* 30 January 1930, 48.

93. "Across Boundary Lines," *Rotarian,* 30 January 1930, 48.

94. On this particular point, see Oscar Zanetti, *Los Cautivos de la Reciprocidad* (Havana: Editorial de Ciencias Sociales, 2003).

95. "Across Boundary Lines," *Rotarian,* 30 January 1930, 48.

96. Pérez, *Cuba,* 253–256.

97. For a detailed account of Welles's "engineering," see Philip Dur and Christopher Gilcrease, "U.S. Diplomacy and the Downfall of a Cuban Dictator: Machado in 1933," *Journal of Latin American Studies* 34, no. 2 (May 2002), 255–282.

98. Program, "Rotary Club of Cienfuegos: Concurso Escolar Celebrado Bajo Los Auspicios Del Rotary Club de Cienfuegos, 1929–1930," Cienfuegos club file, vol. I, RI Archives.

99. Program, "Rotary Club of Cienfuegos."

100. Each district governor was responsible for the oversight of about 40 clubs in a given district. In 1930, there were about 3,300 clubs with 153,000 members worldwide.

101. "El progreso de nuestra organización lleve a todos los lugares de la tierra las sanas normas de nuestra etica rotaria."

102. Dr. Adalberto Ruiz to Chesley Perry, 19 July 1919, Cienfuegos club files, vol. 1, RI Archives.

103. Dr. Sotero Ortega to Chesley Perry, 28 August 1919, Cienfuegos club files, vol. 1, RI Archives. The letterhead for the Cienfuegos Rotary club was already in use and was completely in Spanish.

104. Ortega to Perry, 28 August 1919; see attached membership list, "Lista de Socios."

105. Charter application from club for membership in IARC, 7 August 1919, Cienfuegos club files, vol. 1, RI Archives.

106. *Convention Proceedings,* Havana, Cuba, 9–13 June 1940, 98–99.

107. Ambassador George Messersmith to Under Secretary of State Sumner Welles, 10 June 1940, *Foreign Relations of the United States (FRUS): Diplomatic Papers, 1940,* vol. 5, "The American Republics," 95–96, and Ambassador Messersmith to Secretary of State Cordell Hull, 16 July 1940, *FRUS: Diplomatic Papers, 1940,* vol. 5, 97–98.

6. TRAILING ALONG THROUGH ASIA

1. Of the four, Ralston and Belfrage were the most active members of RI. In fact, Ralston traveled to Australia and New Zealand in the spring and summer of 1921 with James W. Davidson to establish as many Rotary clubs in the Antipodes as possible. In the end, Davidson and Ralston managed to form new Rotary clubs in Melbourne and Sydney and in Wellington and Auckland. Those four clubs, over time, developed into a vibrant portion of the world of Rotary with about 150 active Rotary clubs in both Australia and New Zealand by the end of World War II. For the history of Rotary clubs in Australia, see Harold Hunt, *The Story of Rotary in Australia 1921–1971* (Sydney: Halstead Press, 1971) and for both of Australia and New Zealand, see H. Paul Henningham, "'Service above Self' in the Antipodes: Rotary in Australia and New Zealand, 1921–2014," master of arts thesis, Charles Sturt University, 2016. For details on the activities and travels of Davidson and Ralston and the charter memberships of the Sydney and Melbourne clubs in particular, see Hunt, *The Story of Rotary,* 1–20, and for Henningham, "'Service Above Self' in the Antipodes," 5–17. Belfrage was a very active member of Rotary International's European Advisory Committee, one of the most important regional branches of governance for Rotary before World War II.

2. *Rotarian,* March 1930, 21.

3. Box 70: Central Files / Subject Files: [Honorary General Commissioner] (H750c) James W. Davidson, vol. III, October 1929–30 June 1930), "Letter to Presidents No. 8," Rotary International Archives, Evanston, Illinois (hereafter, "JWD Papers"). See also announcement of the formation of the Kuala Lumpur club under Choo Kia Peng's leadership in the *Rotarian,* February 1930, "Malayan Welcomes Rotary," 7, and JWD Papers, vol. VII, "Original Reports," Report 19, "Federated Malay States," 1. On the life of James W. Davidson, see N. T. Joseph, *James Wheeler Davidson: Profile of a Rotarian* (Evanston, IL: Rotary International, 1987). The most comprehensive publication on James W. Davidson

and Lillian Dow Davidson is Robert Lampard, *The Life and Times of James and Lillian Davidson in Rotary International* (Red Deer, Alberta: Rotary Club of Red Deer, 2006).

4. *Rotarian,* March 1930, 29.

5. Paul Harris made this clear in his introduction to the compilation of all her dispatches; Lillian Dow Davidson, *Making New Friends from Near to Far East for Rotary* (Chicago, IL: Rotary International, 1934).

6. Davidson, *Making New Friends,* n.p. A handful of unofficial Rotary clubs had been started by enthusiastic Rotarians who had moved to Asia for professional reasons, in Calcutta and Lahore in India; Thayetmyo, Burma; Kuala Lumpur, Malaysia; and Bangkok, Siam. In those cases, Davidson was expected to ascertain local circumstances and bring them into formal alignment with RI's constitutional rules, bylaws, and membership credentials (or else remove their right to use the "brand name" of RI and its logo and slogans).

7. For a thoughtful analysis of the wide diversity of settings within which the Davidsons were operating during this period and on the many important differences in understanding what Rotary meant in distinct urban contexts of the region, see Su Lin Lewis, *Cities in Motion: Urban Life and Cosmopolitanism in Southeast Asia, 1920–1940* (Cambridge: Cambridge University Press, 2016), and Su Lin Lewis, "Rotary International's 'Acid Test': Multi-ethnic Associational Life in 1930s Southeast Asia," *Journal of Global History* 7, no. 2 (July 2012), 302–324. See also Saskia Sassen, *Global Networks, Linked Cities* (New York: Routledge, 2002), and Carol A. Breckenridge, Sheldon Pollock, Homi K. Babha, and Dipesh Chakrabarty, eds., *Cosmopolitanism* (Durham, NC: Duke University Press, 2002), for helpful examination of this topic.

8. Laura Wexler, *Tender Violence: Domestic Visions in an Age of U.S. Imperialism* (Chapel Hill: University of North Carolina Press, 2000), esp. chap. 1, on the concept of "domestic sentimentalism." Amy Kaplan, *The Anarchy of Empire in the Making of U.S. Culture* (Cambridge, MA: Harvard University Press, 2002), and Christina Klein, *Cold War Orientalism: Asia in the Middlebrow Imagination, 1945–1961* (Berkeley: University of California Press, 2003) also provide helpful interpretive frameworks for this chapter.

9. For a good analysis of this same dynamic, see Catherine A. Lutz and Jane L. Collins, *Reading National Geographic* (Chicago: University of Chicago Press, 1993), especially chaps. 1 and 2. For good reason, scholarship on the history of travelogues and their role in colonization and subjugation is extensive, including Mary Louise Pratt, *Imperial Eyes: Travel Writing and Transculturation,* 2nd ed. (New York: Routledge, 2008); David Spurr, *The Rhetoric of Empire: Colonial Discourse in Journalism, Travel Writing, and Imperial Administration* (Durham, NC: Duke University Press, 1993); Elizabeth Hallam and

Brian V. Street, eds., *Cultural Encounters: Representing "Otherness"* (New York: Routledge, 2000); and Shelley Osmun Baranowski and Ellen Furlough, eds., *Being Elsewhere: Tourism, Consumer Culture, and Identity in Modern Europe and North America* (Ann Arbor: University of Michigan Press, 2001). See also Mari Yoshihara, *Embracing the East: White Women and American Orientalism* (Oxford: Oxford University Press, 2003) and Kristin Hoganson, *Consumers' Imperium: The Global Production of American Domesticity* (Chapel Hill: University of North Carolina Press, 2007). Much of this scholarship builds on the work of Edward Said, *Orientalism* (New York: Random House, 1979), and *Culture and Imperialism* (New York: Random House, 1993).

10. E. J. Ottaway, "We Have Seen: Being an Account of Six Weeks in England and France in 1928," vol. II, 4, Bentley Historical Library, Ann Arbor, Michigan.

11. Robert Lampard, "Making New Friends: James Wheeler Davidson and Rotary International," *Alberta History* 52, no. 3 (22 June 2004), 2–11. See also David C. Forward, *A Century of Service: The Story of Rotary International* (Evanston, IL: Rotary International, 2003), chap. 7, 77–87; "James W. Davidson: The Marco Polo of Rotary," *Rotarian*, October 1979, 38–39; and for a biography of Jim Davidson, see N. T. Joseph, *James Wheeler Davidson, Profile of a Rotarian* (Cochin, India: Cochin Rotary Club, 1987), and A. O. MacRae, *The History of Province of Alberta* (Western Canada History, 1912), 565–567.

12. "Report of the Extension Committee to the Board of Directors," Principles and Policies for Extension Work for 1925–26, Exhibit no. 13, file: [Committee—Extension—(Minutes Book, July 1925–August 1929)], RI Archives. The Board removed this language in 1925.

13. On the central role played by Bruce Barton in advertising, public relations, and consumerism, see Roland Marchand, *Creating the Corporate Soul: The Rise of Public Relations and Corporate Imagery in American Big Business* (Berkeley: University of California Press, 1998), and William Leach, *Land of Desire: Merchants, Power, and the Rise of a New American Culture* (New York: Random House, 1993).

14. Charles Henry Mackintosh, "Super-Salesmanship as a Civilizer," *Rotarian*, July 1928, 31, 45 and *Rotarian*, September 1928, 1. On the fundamental shift from a focus on "character" to "personality" during this period, see Warren Susman, *Culture as History: The Transformation of American Society in the Twentieth Century* (New York: Pantheon Books, 1984), 99–149.

15. Major J. B. Pond, *Eccentricities of Genius* (New York: G.W. Dillingham Co., 1900).

16. Lampard, "Making New Friends," provides a summary of Davidson's biography. See also Lampard, *The Life and Times of James and Lillian Davidson*

in Rotary International, 30–33, and N. T. Joseph, *James Wheeler Davidson: Profile of a Rotarian* (Evanston, IL: Rotary International, 1987).

17. James W. Davidson, *The Island of Formosa, Past and Present* (New York: Macmillan & Co., 1903). In more than six hundred pages, Jim's treatise covered the "history, people, resources, and commercial prospects" of Formosa in unprecedented detail. Oxford University Press reprinted the book in 1988. For recent scholarship on the importance of Davidson's work to the history of Formosa / Taiwan, see David Curtis Wright and Hsin-Yi Lin, *From Province to Republic to Colony: The James Wheeler Davidson Collection on the Origins and Early Development of Japanese Rule in Taiwan, 1895–1905* (Calgary, Alberta: University of Calgary Press, 2017).

18. Lampard, "Making New Friends."

19. *Convention Proceedings, Twenty-First Annual International Convention,* Denver, Colorado, 14–18 June 1926, Resolution No. 3, 625–629.

20. Lillian Dow Davidson, "Japan Faces the Rising Sun: East Linked to West in Rotary Fellowship," *Rotarian*, January 1933, 45.

21. Letter of introduction by I. B. Sutton, RI president 1928–1929, for James Davidson, 8 August 1928, JWD Papers, vol. I, 1927–1928, December 1928, RI Archives.

22. James W. Davidson to Chesley Perry, 2 August 1928, JWD Papers, vol. I, 1927–1928, December 1928. Davidson received the title in honor of his magnum opus on Formosa.

23. James W. Davidson to Chesley Perry, 23 March 1928, JWD Papers, vol. 1, 1927–1928, December 1928.

24. For a compelling analysis of the crucial role played by the Freemasons in the British Empire, see Jessica L. Harland-Jacobs, *Builders of Empire: Freemasons and British Imperialism, 1717–1927* (Chapel Hill: University of North Carolina Press, 2007).

25. Report 23, "Klang and Singapore," 25 August 1930, JWD Papers, vol. VII, "Original Reports."

26. One the few outside RI to receive Jim's confidential reports on his recruiting tour in Asia was J. S. Dennis of the CPR's Department of Colonization in Montreal, Canada. Jim Davidson to Chesley Perry, November 1928, JWD Papers, vol. VII, "Original Reports."

27. "Memo of Agreement between Special Representative Arch C. Klumph and F. W. Teele, President of the Rotary Club of Mexico City," undated, but very likely late April / early May 1921, Mexico City club historical files / Ciudad de Mexico, D.F., Mexico, RI Archives.

28. JWD Papers, vol. VII, "Original Reports," Report 2, "Obstacles to Rotary," 23 October 1928.

29. JWD Papers, vol. VII, "Original Reports," Report 1, 22 October 1928.

30. JWD Papers, vol. VII, "Turkish Report #3, part 3," 6 November 1928.

31. JWD Papers, vol. VII, "Turkish Report #3, part 3," 6 November 1928.

32. JWD Papers, vol. VII, "Original Reports," Report 5, "Greece," 28 November 1928.

33. JWD Papers, vol. VII, "Original Reports," Report 5, "Greece," 28 November 1928.

34. JWD Papers, vol. VII, "Original Reports," Report 5, "Greece," 28 November 1928. Lillian's version of the formation of the Athens Rotary club appeared as "Trailing along through Asia: A firsthand story of the difficulties experienced in implanting a new idea in the soil from whence sprung our first conceptions of ethical philosophy," *Rotarian*, April 1930, 38–40, 53–55.

35. JWD Papers, vol. VII, "Original Reports," Report 7, "Athens," 12 December 1928.

36. JWD Papers, vol. VII, "Original Reports," Report 5, James W. Davidson to organizing committee members in Istanbul, 20 November 1928, and Bekir Nuzhet Bey to Davidson, 9 December 1928.

37. "Trailing along through Asia," *Rotarian*, March 1930, 30.

38. In the end, however, the Rotary club in Istanbul never took root, marking one of Davidson's few failed attempts to establish a new club. Turkey's first Rotary club was established in Ankara in 1955.

39. Leroy Vernon, *Chicago Daily News*, Washington Bureau, to Chesley Perry, RI Secretariat, Chicago, 22 April 1929, in JWD Papers, vol. VI, RI Archives.

40. "Minutes of the Meeting of the Extension Committee of Rotary International," 9–11 January 1927, file: Committee-Extension-[Minutes Book, July 1925–August 1929], RI Archives.

41. Carlo Bos, "The Myth of Western Supremacy: Reaction of Asiatic Races to the Impact of the West," *Rotarian*, February 1930, 16–18, 61–64. Bos also had a feature article the previous month: "Blind Patriotism and National Madness," *Rotarian*, January 1930, 10–12, 60–64.

42. Jim well understood the predicament of the editorial board at the *Rotarian*: "What a problem 'The Rotarian' must be. It has in reality to be the magazine for American Rotarians who give it 90% of its support, and yet, we all want it to serve these overseas Rotarians as well." James Davidson to Chesley Perry, 4 August 1930, "Re Rotarian," JWD Papers, vol. IV; July 1930–March 1931.

43. The editorial board of the *Rotarian*, in fact, embraced female readers as they helped guarantee a circulation greater than one hundred thousand—the minimum necessary to attract national advertisers. "Handbook for the Annual

Meeting of the Council of Rotary International," August 1924, Third Day Session, 52–60, Guy Gundaker Papers, RI Archives.

44. Alex O. Potter to James W. Davidson, 14 March 1930, JWD Papers, vol. III, October 1929–30 June 1930.

45. Chesley Perry to James Davidson, 22 April 1931, JWD Papers, vol. V, 27 March 1931–14 November 1931.

46. A full-page advertisement in the February issue, titled "You and Co.," served up a lesson on the importance of advertising as "organized guidance" and "help of the most practical kind" for daily life. The advertisement argued that "when you turn to the advertisements in this magazine you call on safe and expert buying counsel" since "they make it easy for you to be an expert purchasing agent for your family corporation." The subordination of family life to the benevolent tutelage of advertising highlighted editorial and institutional priorities set by Rotary from its earliest publications in 1912–1913. The rise of advertising as a profession fit hand in glove with the growth and success of RI and modern forms of corporate capitalism. *Rotarian,* February 1930, 52.

47. "Trailing along through Asia," *Rotarian,* February 1930, 14.

48. "Trailing along through Asia," *Rotarian,* March 1930, 31.

49. "Trailing along through Asia," *Rotarian,* March 1930, 31.

50. "Trailing along through Asia," *Rotarian,* March 1930, 52.

51. JWD Papers, vol. II, "Original Reports," Report 4, 18 November 1928.

52. On gender discrimination in Rotary clubs and its formal end in 1987, see Chapter 1 and Conclusion.

53. "Trailing along through Asia," *Rotarian,* May 1930, 34.

54. "Trailing along through Asia," *Rotarian,* May 1930, 64.

55. "Trailing along through Asia," *Rotarian,* May 1930, 36.

56. "Trailing along through Asia," *Rotarian,* May 1930, 36.

57. "Trailing along through Asia," *Rotarian,* June 1930, 62–63, and JWD Papers, vol. VII, "Original Reports," Report 9, 22 January 1929. On the formation of clubs in Cairo, Alexandria, Jerusalem, and Beirut, see club historical files, RIZ Archives.

58. "Trailing along through Asia: Being an account of a side trip into Egypt to establish a common ground in Rotary upon which members of diverse nationalistic groups may meet in fellowship," *Rotarian,* May 1930, 63.

59. JWD Papers, "Original Reports," Report 9, 22 January 1929.

60. JWD Papers, vol. VII, "Original Reports," Report 10, 11 February 1929.

61. JWD Papers, vol. VII, "Original Reports," Report 10, 11 February 1929.

62. JWD Papers, vol. VII, "Original Reports," Report 10, 11 February 1929.

63. Quoted by Lillian in "Baghdad and the Desert Call," *Rotarian,* October 1930, 28.

64. "Baghdad and the Desert Call," 28.

65. JWD Papers, vol. VII, "Original Reports," Report 11, 14 March 1929.

66. "We Motor to Baghdad: Arabian nights are not what they used to be. The 'magic-carpet' is out-moded by airplanes and automobiles crossing the desert with time-table regularity," *Rotarian,* September 1930, 36.

67. "Baghdad and the Desert Call," 28–29.

68. For details on the establishment, duration, and closure of these clubs, see club historical files of Baghdad, Damascus, and Tehran, RIZ Archives.

69. Forward, *Century of Service,* 85–86. The relationship between RI and Freemasonry is very difficult to pin down since most of RI's records usually do not indicate who was and was not a Freemason. RI's founder, Paul Harris, for example, was emphatically not a Freemason, whereas Chesley Perry, RI's longtime general secretary, was a reasonably active Freemason in Chicago. The overlap in membership, to be sure, would have been much more likely in parts of Asia under the British Empire. But the institutions were distinct on their own terms and occupied distinct roles vis-à-vis the British Empire. The most significant differences between the two would have been clear to any potential British recruit in the British Empire: Rotary clubs did not have lodges or significant membership fees; held meetings in public; regularly mounted a variety of civic projects for local causes; had no particular relationship to any military establishment; and engaged in quasi-nationalistic, public spectacles rather than secretive, quasi-mystical rituals. The significant institutional differences were compounded by RI's particular emphasis on inclusion of local elites as soon as possible, no matter how great its initial dependence on British recruits at each club's formation during the interwar years. For a significant treatment of Freemasonry and the British Empire, see Jessica L. Harland-Jacobs, *Builders of Empire: Freemasonry and British Imperialism, 1717–1927* (Chapel Hill: University of North Carolina Press, 2007). On the conflation of Rotary International with Freemasonry by the Catholic Church, especially in Spain, and the challenges that resulted, see de Grazia, *Irresistible Empire*, 62–67.

70. Forward, *A Century of Service,* 86. For a complete club history of the period, see Somendra Chandra Nandy, ed., *The Diamond Jubilee Book* (Calcutta: Rotary Club of Calcutta, 1981).

71. JWD Papers, vol. VII, "Original Reports," Report 11, 14 March 1929.

72. JWD Papers, vol. VII, "Original Reports," Report 12, April 1929.

73. JWD Papers, vol. VII, "Original Reports," Report 11, 14 March 1929.

74. JWD Papers, vol. VII, "Original Reports," Report 11, 14 March 1929.

75. JWD Papers, vol. VII, "Original Reports," Report 11, 14 March 1929.

76. JWD Papers, vol. VII, "Original Reports," Report 14, Ootacamund, India, 30 May 1929. See also JWD Papers, vol. II, January 1929–October 1929, James Davidson to Chesley Perry, 9 March 1929, where Jim lists his "most important problems" in India: "The chief ones are Indian membership, retail members, and summer meetings."

77. Davidson to Perry, 9 March 1929.

78. In 2020, Rotary clubs in India numbered nearly 3,900. For a complete report on the state of Rotary International in India, see *Rotary News*, March 2020.

79. Forward, *A Century of Service*, 310.

80. JWD Papers, vol. VII, "Original Reports," Report 11, 14 March 1929.

81. JWD Papers, vol. VII, "Original Reports," Report 11, 14 March 1929.

82. Lillian's coverage of their travels through the Indian subcontinent reinforced the general point: "India—Land of Opposites: Where industrial, political, and social life is a labyrinth of superstition and discord, only awaiting a new Theseus to release them," *Rotarian*, November 1930, 9–11, 54–55; "India—The New Capital: India presents a difficult problem for Rotary expansion because of the impermanence of the European population, the summer heat, and the widespread caste system," *Rotarian*, January 1931, 16–19, 54–56; and "India's Jig-Saw Puzzle: A strife-weary country of power and wealth and enchantment where Rotary already has made its impress at five strategic points," *Rotarian*, March 1931, 27–29, 50–56. As with all prior installments, Lillian provided multiple photographs of street life and significant cultural icons.

83. JWD Papers, vol. VII, "Original Reports," Report 11, 14 March 1929.

84. On the "politics of recognition" in a colonial context for the United States, see Paul Kramer, *The Blood of Government: Race, Empire, the United States, and the Philippines* (Chapel Hill: University of North Carolina Press, 2006).

85. The postwar relationship between RI and Indian nationalism became smoother with time. For example, Karl Krueger, editor for the *Rotarian* from 1952 to 1974, reported: "In my blur of memories is a garden party in New Delhi . . . [with] 3,000 or so men and women from around the globe [having] come together under the Rotary banner. . . . Suddenly heads turned toward someone arriving at the edge of the party . . . being surrounded and hugged. It was Pandit Nehru himself." Forward, *Century of Service*, 85.

86. JWD Papers, vol. II, January 1929–October 1929, Alex Potter to James Davidson, 3 October 1929.

87. JWD Papers, vol. VII, "Original Reports," Report 18, 3.

88. JWD Papers, vol. VII, "Original Reports," Report 18, 5.

89. JWD Papers, vol. VII, "Original Reports," Report 18, 6. Gammans considered starting an independent club and naming it the "Concord club."

90. JWD Papers, vol. VII, "Original Reports," Report 18, 6.

91. JWD Papers, vol. VII, "Original Reports," Report 18, 6.

92. JWD Papers, vol. VII, "Original Reports," Report 19, 3–4.

93. JWD Papers, vol. VII, "Original Reports," Report 19, 4.

94. JWD Papers, vol. VII, "Original Reports," Reports 18 and 19, "Part II and III, Federated Malay States," 21 November 1929, and Report 23, "Klang and Singapore," 25 August 1930.

95. JWD Papers, vol. VII, "Original Reports," Report 23, 5. On Singapore, see Lillian Dow Davison, "All Ships Stop at Singapore: East and West overlap in Singapore: Here trails of trade converge, and the Babel of races gives Rotary an unusual opportunity for service," *Rotarian,* July 1931, 26–28, 54–55. Lillian reported the Singapore club's nationalities as American, Arabian, Armenian, Chinese, Dutch, English, French, German, Indian, Irish, Italian, Japanese, Malayan, Persian, Romanian, Russian, Scottish, and Swiss.

96. F. F. Cooray, "Malaya—Turnstile of East and West," *Rotarian,* August 1930, 26, 60. Short biographical features on new members like the chief and other Asian dignitaries such as Japanese businessmen, Chinese generals, Filipino diplomats, and Thai aristocrats joining Rotary clubs were regularly highlighted in the *Rotarian* throughout the late 1920s and 1930s in the section "Rotary Personalities."

97. JWD Papers, vol. VII, "Original Reports," Report 17, 5.

98. JWD Papers, vol. VII, "Original Reports," Report 21, "Java," 16 February 1930, and Report 22, "Dutch East Indies," n.d.; and JWD Papers, vol. IV, July 1930–March 1931, "Record of Cities Visited," 12 March 1931.

99. Lillian's contributions during this leg of the journey included "Bali, Jewel of the South Sea: Tourists haven't yet spoiled this quaint island where women run the business and men devote themselves to music and cock fighting," *Rotarian,* August 1931, 20–23, 44–45; "Java—Gem of the Dutch East Indies: Rare glimpses of the most densely populated land on earth where legend and music play a part in the daily life," *Rotarian,* September 1931, 28–30, 48–50; and "Sumatra—Island of Contrasts: A fascinating land of peculiar customs, curious architecture, rich in agriculture and minerals, where remnants of cannibal tribes may still be found," *Rotarian,* October 1931, 33–35, 53–56. The subtitles capture well the emphasis of each article while the photographs emphasized, as in Turkey, Egypt, India, and Burma, the dress and bodies of women as markers of their cultures' resistance to change in the modern world.

100. JWD Papers, vol. VII, "Original Reports," "Final Report," 6 April 1931. Lack of opportunity for Jim did not stop Lillian from her own contributions:

"Siam—Magic Land of the East: Bangkok throbs to the modern tempo, with Rotary holding an honored place. Fourteen nationalities are represented in the club," *Rotarian,* November 1931, 27–31, 52–53, and "Mystery-Laden Cambodia: Here a lofty city with a million souls was built . . . abandoned . . . forgotten . . . until sixty years ago an orchid-seeker stumbled on to it," *Rotarian,* December 1931, 32–33, 46–49.

101. James Davidson to Chesley Perry, from Penang, 5 August 1930, JWD Papers, vol. IV, July 1930–March 1931.

102. Davidson to Perry, 5 August 1930.

103. Davidson to Perry, 5 August 1930.

104. Davidson to Perry, 5 August 1930.

105. Telegram, George Fitch to Rotary Headquarters, Chicago, 20 August 1930, JWD Papers, vol. IV, July 1930–March 1931.

106. "The Manchurian Situation," 18 April 1931, JWD Papers, vol. V, March 1931–November 1931.

107. Lillian described in detail their visit with Viscount Saitō and their time in Korea in "Where Change Meets Change: A fascinating picture of Korea (Chosen), 'land of the morning calm,' rich in timber and minerals and noted for its scenic beauty," *Rotarian,* December 1932, 30–32, 48–50.

108. "The Manchurian Situation," 18 April 1931, JWD Papers, vol. V, March 1931–November 1931.

109. Sydney Pascall to James Davidson, 5 June 1931, JWD Papers, vol. V, 27 March 1931–14 November 1931.

110. Chesley Perry to RI board of directors, 16 April 1931, JWD Papers, vol. V, 27 March 1931–14 November 1931.

111. *Convention Proceedings, Twenty-Third Annual Convention of Rotary International,* Seattle, Washington, 20–24 June 1932, 148–155.

112. Lampard, *The Life and Times of James and Lillian Davidson in Rotary International,* 33.

113. *Proceedings, Twenty-Third Annual Convention,* Seattle, Washington, 1932, 70.

114. *Proceedings, Twenty-Third Annual Convention, Seattle, Washington, 1932, 60.* For an analysis of US "entanglements" within this transimperial context, see Kristin Hoganson and Jay Sexton, eds., *Crossing Empires: Taking U.S. History into Transimperial Terrain* (Durham: Duke University Press, 2020).

CONCLUSION

1. On the origins and evolution of the "international humanitarianism" of the American Red Cross, see Julia F. Irwin, *Making the World Safe: The*

American Red Cross and a Nation's Humanitarian Awakening (Oxford: Oxford University Press, 2013), and for distinct interpretations of the origins, evolution, and purpose of the United Nations, see Elizabeth Borgwardt, *A New Deal for the World: America's Vision for Human Rights* (Cambridge, MA: Harvard University Press, 2005), and Mark Mazower, *No Enchanted Palace: The End of Empire and the Ideological Origins of the United Nations* (Princeton, NJ: Princeton University Press, 2009). See also Laura Belmonte, *Selling the American Way: U.S. Propaganda and the Cold War* (Philadelphia: University of Pennsylvania Press, 2008), Peter Stamatov, *The Origins of Global Humanitarianism: Religion, Empires, and Advocacy* (New York: Cambridge University Press, 2013), and Robert D. DeChaine, *Global Humanitarianism: NGOs and the Crafting of Community* (New York: Lexington Books, 2005). On the evolution and central role played by philanthropy over the course of the twentieth century, see Olivier Zunz, *Philanthropy in America: A History* (Princeton: Princeton University Press, 2012) and Lawrence J. Friedman and Mark D. McGarvie, eds., *Charity, Philanthropy, and Civility in American History* (Cambridge: Cambridge University Press, 2003), esp. chap. 11, Emily Rosenberg, "Missions to the World: Philanthropy Abroad," 241–257, on how the secularization of missions boards and the professionalization of philanthropy before World War II served as models for the US state.

2. On this point, see Brooke Blower, "From Isolationism to Neutrality: A New Framework for Understanding American Political Culture, 1919–1941," *Diplomatic History* 38, no. 2 (April 2014), 345–376.

3. Daniel T. Rodgers uses the term "promotionalists" to describe the kind of business internationalists that composed much of RI's membership in the larger cities. Daniel T. Rodgers, *Atlantic Crossings: Social Politics in a Progressive Age* (Cambridge, MA: Belknap Press, 1998), introduction.

4. Akira Iriye, *Global Community: The Role of International Organizations in the Making of the Contemporary World* (Berkeley: University of California Press, 2002), and Iriye, *Cultural Internationalism and World Order* (Baltimore: Johns Hopkins University Press, 1997).

5. On the history of the London Rotary club during this period, see Vivian Carter, *The Romance of Rotary in London* (London: RIBI, 1947).

6. For greater detail on the contributions of individual Rotarians also serving as representatives of their respective nations at the UN Charter Conference, see David C. Forward, *A Century of Service: The Story of Rotary International* (Evanston, IL: Rotary International, 2003), chap. 17, 192–203.

7. See Chapter 2 for more details on Romulo and the history of the Manila Rotary club. On the personal history of Romulo's family during US occupation of the Philippines and how he ended up as a top aide-de-camp for

General MacArthur, see Col. Carlos P. Romulo, "My Father Fought Americans, but I Fight for the USA," the *Rotarian*, February 1943, 10–12.

8. J. Raymond Tiffany, "Foreword," in *A World to Live In* (Chicago: Rotary International, 1942), 3–4.

9. Chester S. Williams, assistant chief, Division of Public Liaison, Department of State, to Philip Lovejoy, general secretary of RI, 19 November 1945, subject files, box 310, "United Nations—Conferences—San Francisco—Charter Pamphlet Commentary, 1945–1948." RI Archives.

10. John Slawson to Phillip Lovejoy, general secretary of RI, 15 January 1946, subject files, box 310, "United Nations—Conferences—San Francisco—Charter Pamphlet Commentary, 1945–1948." RI Archives.

11. Slawson to Lovejoy, 15 January 1946,

12. Demand for *From Here On!* continued until 1952, reaching a worldwide distribution of a quarter million copies by the end of the Korean conflict. RI also published follow-up booklets with similar, user-friendly, didactic layouts that focused on UNESCO (*In the Minds of Men*, 1946) and on the entire UN system of specialized agencies (*The World at Work*, 1949). While also received positively by Rotary clubs and the public at large, these publications largely drew their interest from the success of *From Here On!*

13. By 1962, the year of the Cuban Missile Crisis and the closure of scores of long established Cuban Rotary clubs, RI reported a worldwide membership of 519,500, with nearly half its membership outside the United States and Canada: 37,000 in Asia; 30,140 in Australia / New Zealand and sub-Saharan Africa; 67,000 in continental Europe, North Africa, and the eastern Mediterranean; 42,000 in Great Britain and Ireland; and 43,300 in Latin America and the Caribbean. *Proceedings of the Fifty-Third Annual Rotary Convention*, Los Angeles, California, 3–7 June 1962, 294–295. Meanwhile, RI's successful partnership with the World Health Organization in the eradication of polio worldwide from the 1980s to 2020 has been exemplary, while RI's student exchange programs have sent tens of thousands of students across the world since 1947. See Sarah Gibbard Cook, "For All the World's Children: Rotary and the Vision of a Polio Free World," 2nd installment, unpublished manuscript, 2000, 288–390, RI Archives. On the history of the WHO, see Marcos Cueto, Theodore M. Brown, and Elizabeth Fee, eds., *The World Health Organization: A History* (Cambridge: Cambridge University Press, 2019).

14. In 1956, white-collar workers outnumbered blue-collar workers for the first time in US history. The trend has only continued to tip in favor of white-collar over blue-collar ever since.

15. Herbert J. Taylor, "Rotary: Maker of Friendships and Builder of Men," the *Rotarian*, July 1954, 6–7; Richard E. Vernor, "Now Meet 'President

Herb'—and His Family," the *Rotarian*, July 1954, 7–9, 57; J. C. Penney, "Give Me a Good Competitor," the *Rotarian*, July 1954, 10–11, 58; Henry Cabot Lodge, Jr., "The U.N. . . . Novel, Hopeful, Primitive, Exasperating but Essential," the *Rotarian*, July 1954, 12–13, 56; Kermit Eby and DeWitt Emery, "Guaranteed Annual Wage?" the *Rotarian*, July 1954, 14–15, 49–51; and John Foster Dulles, "U.S. Assumes No Mandate to Run the World," the *Rotarian*, July 1954, 27. For Dulles's full speech, see *Proceedings of the Forty-Fifth Annual Rotary Convention*, Seattle, Washington, 6–10 June 1954, 198–207. Dulles's speech, given just one week before the CIA-led coup in Guatemala against the Arbenz regime, referred to arms shipments "from behind the Iron Curtain" as an "alien intervention" by "International Communism" while deflecting claims that "the real concern [was] the protection of United States investments" and the United Fruit Company. Dulles received a standing ovation from over 8,000 conferees and guests.

16. Vernor, the *Rotarian*, July 1954, 9.

17. For a helpful analysis of Herb Taylor's life within the context of mid-century business evangelicalism, see Sarah Ruth Hammond, *God's Businessmen: Entrepreneurial Evangelicals in Depression and War* (Chicago, IL: University of Chicago Press, 2017), especially the introduction and chap. 2, "Herbert J. Taylor, Rotarian Fundamentalist." See also Herbert J. Taylor, *The Herbert J. Taylor Story* (Downers Grove, IL: InterVarsity Press, 1983) and Paul H. Heidebrecht, *God's Man in the Marketplace: The Story of Herbert J. Taylor* (Downers Grove, IL: InterVarsity Press, 1990).

18. Hammond, *God's Businessmen*, chap. 2, Kindle edition; Vernor, the *Rotarian*, July 1954, 7–9, 57; and Herbert J. Taylor, "Serving in Your Business and Profession—Now," *Proceedings of the Thirty-Fourth Annual Convention of Rotary International*, St. Louis, Missouri, 17–20 May 1943, 42–47.

19. The history of Taylor's Four-Way Test is basic to Rotarian lore. As a result, there are countless sources on its genesis in RI's literature from the club level to the international. For a basic overview, see Forward, *A Century of Service*, 153–155.

20. Hammond, *God's Businessmen*, chap. 2; Vernor, the *Rotarian*, July 1954, 8–9, 57; Taylor, *Convention Proceedings*, St. Louis, Missouri, 17–20 May 1943; and *Convention Proceedings*, Seattle, Washington, 6–10 June 1954, 255–257. The "good citizen" is defined as "he" throughout the test.

21. By 1975, only 38 percent of all Rotary clubs were in the United States, with more than 83 percent of new clubs admitted that year taking root outside of North America—a clear trend that has continued into the present. See *1975 Proceedings, Sixty-Sixth Annual Convention of Rotary International*, Montreal, Quebec, Canada, 8–12 June 1975, 150. On the emergence of a "civic malaise"

during this period and one theoretical explanation for it, see Robert D. Putnam, *Bowling Alone: The Collapse and Revival of American Community* (New York: Simon & Schuster, 2000).

22. For the floor debate on Enactment 82-2, see *Convention Proceedings*, Seventy-Third Annual Convention of Rotary International, Dallas, Texas, 6–10 June 1982, 57–60. For Hiroji Mukasa's address to the convention, *Convention Proceedings*, Dallas, Texas, 6–10 June 1982, 151–154.

23. On the floor proposal, see *Convention Proceedings*, Dallas, Texas, 6–10 June 1982, 60. In fact, a large panel discussion was devoted to the topic at that same convention. See "Women Service to Rotary," *Convention Proceedings*, Dallas, Texas, 6–10 June 1982, 114–127. Barbara Bush also spoke during the panel, with particular attention on her role as cultural ambassador during George H. W. Bush's international career and her own experiences with charitable organizations.

24. News coverage of the Supreme Court decision and the facts of the case was extensive and international in scope, indicating that the Supreme Court's decision on a California state law was salient for most of the world because of the worldwide presence of Rotary clubs in 1987. For a brief overview of this history, see Forward, *A Century of Service*, 180–189.

25. "History of Women in Rotary," https://www.rotary.org/en/history-women-rotary, accessed 5 December 2020. See also Emily Goodell, "Women Look Back at 30 Years of Inclusion in Rotary International," *YakimaHerald.com*, updated 15 June 2018.

26. On the rise of the national security state in the United States and its global implications, see Michael Hogan, *A Cross of Iron: Harry S. Truman and the Origins of the National Security State, 1945–1954* (Cambridge: Cambridge University Press, 1998), and Melvyn P. Leffler, *A Preponderance of Power: National Security, the Truman Administration, and the Cold War* (Stanford, CA: Stanford University Press, 1992).

27. Countries without Rotary clubs in 2020 include Cuba, North Korea, Libya, Guinea, Ethiopia, Somalia, Syria, Iraq, Iran, Oman, Turkmenistan, Uzbekistan, Vietnam, and Yemen.

ACKNOWLEDGMENTS

I first heard of Rotary International from a friend who had advised me to look into RI's Ambassadorial Scholarship program. I was young, poor, and looking for ways to study abroad. That friend was Bruce Thielemann, noted Presbyterian minister, lifelong Rotarian, and former Ambassadorial Scholar himself. He encouraged me to apply for the scholarship because he believed in me—at a time when I really needed someone to do just that. As a result, I got to do graduate study in philosophy at the University of Glasgow for a year. But the scholarship also allowed me to spread my wings in so many other ways. I will also never forget the grace and hospitality shown to me by my Rotarian sponsor in Scotland, Rev. Douglas Lamb, and by the many Scottish Rotarians I had the pleasure to meet during my time of study. I can never repay my debt of gratitude to Bruce and to Rotary for making possible that entire year of exploration and discovery. This book, however, should be seen as an attempt to give some small tribute to an old friend who changed my life—and to all those Rotarians like Bruce who have dedicated so much to improving the lives of others.

But this book is also an academic endeavor, representing the culmination of years of education and training in the history department at the University of Michigan. The interdisciplinary approach of that department allowed me to formulate questions, approach texts and topics, and challenge my own thinking about the world in ways I could never have imagined before my arrival in Ann Arbor. In particular, I would like to give sincere thanks to Richard Cándida-Smith, Penny von Eschen, Matt Lassiter, and Peggy Somers. Along with so many fellow graduate students now scattered throughout academia, their patient advice and input helped me forge an academic project out of a personal journey. There were many other scholars—too many to name all of them—who also contributed in their own way to the evolution of this project, including Fernando Coronil, Matthew Countryman, David Hammack, Julia Irwin, Matthew Connelly, and Paul Kramer. I also wish to acknowledge those who provided helpful comments and feedback at various conferences in years past, namely Chris Capozzola, Kristin Hoganson, Trygve Throntveit, Julio Moreno, Charles Hayford, Tamson Pietsch, David Tamayo, David Atkinson, Jason Colby, Emily Rosenberg, Andrew Johnstone, Dawn Berry, among many others. Input from the anonymous readers at Harvard University Press also proved invaluable. I only hope that this project is at least in part worthy of their expectations and high caliber of scholarship.

Institutional support came in many forms, but the most crucial support came through a philanthropy and nonprofit sector research fellowship from the Social Science Research Council, which allowed me to spend a year digging through the archives of Rotary in Evanston as well as other archival holdings in the Chicago area. I also owe much to the Eisenberg Institute for Historical Studies at the University of Michigan, which provided me with a one-year postdoctoral fellowship and the opportunity to continue my engagement with such a vibrant intellectual community in Ann Arbor.

Chapter 3 builds on ideas first discussed in, and Chapter 4 includes portions of text first published as, "Philanthropy and the 'Perfect Democracy' of Rotary International," my contribution to *Globalization, Philanthropy, and Civil Society: Projecting Institutional Logics Abroad*, edited by David C. Hammack and Steven Heydemann (Bloomington: Indiana University Press, 2009). Text from that chapter is reprinted here by permission of the publisher.

This kind of research project is impossible without the help of many archivists, club officials, and dedicated Rotarians who were generous with their time. It is rare for any business organization to take the past seriously, to treat history as something other than a source of entertainment or interesting trivia—and even more so for an organization to put a priority on that history the way Rotary International and its thousands of clubs do all around the world. I wish there were a way to do justice to the sprawling history of this organization and its rootedness in so many communities worldwide, but that is simply not possible in one book. I wish to give a special thanks to the current archivists at Rotary International, Susan Hanf and Andrew Steadham, as well as to Marcelo Bottini and Sylvia Kutzer at the Rotary International office in Zurich, Switzerland and to Dr. Robert Lampard for sharing his thoughts and findings on the Davidsons many years ago. But a special note of gratitude must go to Cyndi DeBock, former archivist at Rotary, who worked with me during the earliest stages of this project. Her joviality and willingness to make helpful suggestions made all the difference. She has become a lifelong friend. Without her gracious support and encouragement, this research project would have remained lost in translation.

I need to thank my colleagues and students at New College of Florida who helped foster my ideas and process them through my course offerings, as well as the staff and administration of New College for providing constant support for travel and research over the years. I would like to add a note of gratitude to Kristi Fecteau, Frank Alcock, Justus Doenecke, Uzi Baram, Keith Fitzgerald, Barbara Hicks, Queen Zabriskie, Sarah Hernandez, and Hugo Viera-Vargas for their encouragement and advice. I am also greatly indebted to Malcom Swanston at Axiom Maps Limited, who generated all three maps for this project, as well as to Kathleen McDermott, editor at Harvard University Press. Without Kathleen's endless patience, this project would never have come to fruition.

Finally, at a personal level, I wish to thank all my friends and family for their bottomless patience over the years. There are too many to thank in this short space, but I would be remiss without thanking in particular my father for always pushing me to complete this project; my mother for rewarding my curiosity all my life; my aunt Ann, for always reminding me that I might actually have something worth saying; and my best friend, Nina, who has been a bedrock of support since the day we met.

INDEX

Note: page numbers in *italics* refer to figures or tables. Those followed by n refer to notes, with note number.